FootprintItalia

Tuscany

Rebecca Ford

Listings

Introducing the region

About the region

Florence

Siena & around

Eastern Tuscany

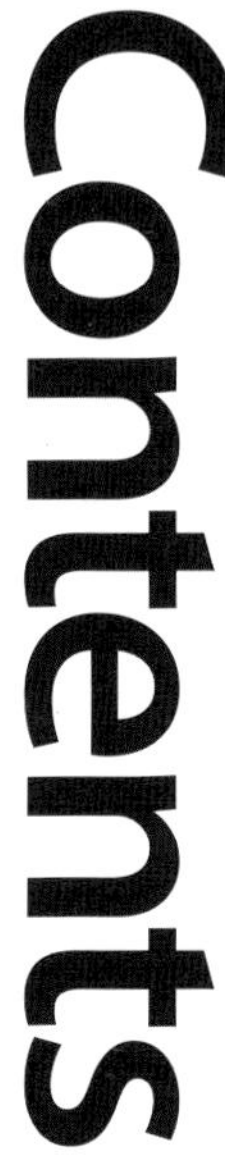

Northern Tuscany

Southern Hill Towns

Southern & Western Tuscany

Practicalities

About the author

Rebecca Ford is an award-winning travel writer. She regularly writes for the Daily and Sunday Express, and has written for many other publications such as the Independent on Sunday, the Evening Standard, the Sunday Herald, Italy magazine and BBC History. She has also written/contributed to more than 30 guidebooks.

She travels widely, writing about everything from city breaks and spas to railway journeys and wildlife watching. She particularly loves Italy and tries to fit in several trips a year. She is the feature writer on Italian Cuisine for the website suite101.com and, while researching this book, set herself the gruelling task of sampling ice-creams across Tuscany in order to come up with her 'top five' list.

Acknowledgements

Rebecca would above all like to thank the following people for all their help: Alessandra Smith and Adriana Vacca at the Italian Tourist Board in London; Lorenza and all the staff at the Hotel Santa Caterina in Siena; Antonella Giusti in Lucca: Marta Pellegrini at Antico Casale di Scansano; Roberta Romoli in Florence, Ilaria Antolini in Pisa, Cecilia Rosa in the Maremma, and Annarita Merlini in Pistoia. Thanks are also due to Maggie Garratt; Elisa at Villa Corte Armonica; Silvia at Toscama; Assunta and Stefano at Casa Palmira; Andrea Cerchiai, Catherine Crone; Giovanni Guidetti; Paolo Pasquali; Francesca Peruzzi, Heather Forty, Sarah Milligan, Michael Birtles, Tiberio Fabbri, Raffaele Pitari, APT Siena and Katherine Ellis. Thanks too to all the Italians who were so generous with their time and offers of reviving plates of pasta, cups of coffee and glasses of wine.

About the book

The guide is divided into 4 sections: Introducing the region; About the region; Around the region and Practicalities.

Introducing the region comprises: At a glance, which explains how the region fits together by giving the reader a snapshot of what to look out for and what makes this region distinct from other parts of the country; Best of Tuscany (top 20 highlights); A year in Tuscany, which is a month-by-month guide to pros and cons of visiting at certain times of year; and Tuscany on screen & page, which is a list of suggested books and films.

About the region comprises: **History**; **Art & architecture; Tuscany** today, which present different aspects of life in the region today; **Nature & environment** (an overview of the landscape and wildlife); **Festivals & events**; **Sleeping** (an overview of accommodation options); **Eating & drinking** (an overview of the region's cuisine, as well as advice on eating out); **Entertainment** (an overview of the region's cultural credentials, explaining what entertainment is on offer); **Shopping** (what are the region's specialities and recommendations for the best buys); and **Activities & tours**.

Around the region is then broken down into six areas, each with its own chapter. Here you'll find all the main sights and at the end of each chapter is a listings section with all the best sleeping, eating & drinking, entertainment, shopping and activities & tours options plus a brief overview of public transport.

Map symbols

Informazioni
Information

Luogo d'interesse
Place of Interest

Museo/Galleria
Museum/Gallery

Teatro
Theatre

Negozi
Shopping

Ufficio postale
Post Office

Chiesa Storica
Historic Church

Giardini
Gardens

Percorsi raccomandati
Recommended walk

Monumento
Monument

Stazione Ferroviaria
Railway Station

Escursioni a piedi
Hiking

Metropolitana
Metro Station

Mercato
Market

Funicolare
Funicular Railway

Aeroporto
Airport

Universita
University

Sleeping price codes

€€€€ over €300 per night for a double room in high season.

€€€ €200-300

€€ €100-200

€ under €100

Eating & drinking price codes

€€€€ more than €40 per person for a 2-course meal with a drink, including service and cover charge

€€€ €30-40

€€ €20-30

€ under €20

Picture credits

headwater.com pages 76, 77

Hemisphere pages 83, 90, 141: Andrea Alborno; page 60: Bertrand Rieger; page 148: Bruno Morandi; page 105: Emilio Suetone; page 124, 143: Laurent Giraudou; page 126: Stéphane Frances.

Julius Honnor pages 81, 133, 174, 214, 218, 224.

italianproperty.eu.com pages 45, 46, 57.

italyweddings.com page 47.

Rebecca Ford pages 3, 9, 15, 16, 61, 83, 90, 94, 100, 103, 110, 115, 116, 120, 125, 127, 151, 157, 169, 173, 179, 183, 186, 190, 191, 193, 195, 205, 206, 207, 208, 210, 212, 223, 228, 229, 230, 231, 233, 235, 236, 241, 242, 245, 277, 282, 283, 284, 285, 287, 288, 289, 292, 294, 299, 306.

Shutterstock page 30: Ackab Photography; pages 72, 252: Albert H Teich; page 11: alysta; page 28: Andrea Danti; page 88: Andrei Nekrassov; pages 103, 104, 106, 187: Bertrand Collet; page 123: bruno pagnanelli; pages 3, 9, 15, 198, 248, 263: Claudio Giovanni Colombo; pages 13, 101: Coia Hubert; page 135: Condor 36; page 63, 171: Darren Baker; page 114: Denis Babenko; page 15: Elena Koulik; page 251: Eline Spek; page 60: Elke Dennis; page 170: Faberfoto; page 191: Fairybloom; page 311: FOTOCROMO; page 167: Heike Pototschnigg; page 255: Hipproductions; page 217: Ho Philip; page 86: Huang Yuetao; page 87: Izoom; page 62: Jasna; pages 50, 254, 262: Javarman; pages 69, 222, 223: Jbor; page 155: jeff gynane; page 219: K Jakubowska; pages 176, 303: Keith Levit; page 38: Ken Durden; page 247: Knud Nielsen; page 170: L F File; pages 17, 290: leonardo_da_gressignano; pages 2, 6: LF File; page 41: Luciano Mortula; page 276: Luri; page 295: M Rohana; pages 1, 2, 26: manuela szymaniak; page 33: Maria Bell; pages 11, 103, 213, 225, 280, 292: Mariëtte Budel; page 13: Marty Metcalf; pages 253, 266: Massimo Merlini; page 195: Mauro Bighin; page 102: Mikhail Nekrasov; page 184: Monkey Business Images; pages 2, 9, 78, 199, 201: Morozova Oksana; page 71: Natalie Adamov; page 82: Nathan Jaskowiak; page 80, 168: Newphotoservice; page 278: NicolasMcComber; page 305: Orientaly; page 14, 98: Paul Merrett; page 113: Pavel K; page 221: Philophoto; page 50: Ruth Black; page 82: Sailorr; page 10, 48: Sherri R Camp; page 49 szarzynski; page 232: Valeria73; page 44: Viktor Pryymachuk;

Marina Spironetti pages 3, 61, 65, 73, 300, 302.

SuperStock pages 2, 3, 9, 51, 54, 56, 59, 71, 83, 91, 95, 107, 123, 112, 131, 139, 145, 149, 164, 180, 188, 200, 260, 265, 274, 273, 286, 291, 296, 304, 312, 313: age footstock; pages 117, 129, 136, 244, 257: Axiom Photographic Ltd; pages 36, 108, 197: De Agostini; page 99: Jean-Pierre Lescourret; pages 83, 74: Mauritius; pages 2, 9, 146: Steve Vidler; pages 111, 196: Superstock.Inc; pages 181, 185, 291: Westend61.

TIPS Images pages 54, 57, 216, 220: Andrea Pistolesi; page 111: Arco Digital Images; page 269: Catalano Piga; pages 18, 132: Chad Ehlers; pages 158, 271, 313: Chuck Pefley; page 68: Clive Evans; page 12: Daniele La Monaca; page 58: Digital Images; page 307: Focus Database; page 150: Gerard Vandystadt; page 52: Giuliano Colliva; page 312: Imagestate; page 309: Juan Manuel Silva; pages 121, 144: Mark Edward Smith; pages 19, 122: Marvin Newman; pages 53, 109: Photononstop; pages 20, 153, 154: Pietro Scozzari; pages 70, 165, 203: Stefano Caporali; pages 92, 93, 118: Tommaso Di Girolamo; page 268: Walter Zerla.

Alamy front cover: Art Kowalsky; back cover: David Noton Photography.

iStock back cover (top): Henk Badenhorst.

Pienza's church and old town hall towers.

Introducing the region

Contents

LEGENDA
A4 Autostrada/Motorway
11 Superstrada/ Dual Carriageway
668 Statale/Regional Road
Ferrovia/Railway
Frontiera Regionale/ Regional Boundary
EMILIA-ROMAGNA
LIGURIA
TOSCANA
UMBRIA
LAZIO
Modena
BOLOGNA
Aeroporto G. Marconi di Bologna
Calestano
Langhirano
S.Polo d'Enza
Vezzano
Crostolo
Scandiano
in Persiceto
S.Giorgio di Piano
Minerbio
Castelfranco Emilia
Mezzolara
Berceto
Tizzano val P.
Casina
Formigine
Maranello
Spilamberto
Budrio
Corniglio
Carpineti
Vignola
Bazzano
Medicina
Palanzano
Castelnovo ne Monti
Zola Pedrosa
S.Lazzaro di Savoia
Pontremoli
Sasso Marconi
Castel S.Pietro
Sesta Godano
Mulazzo
Pavullo nel Frignano
Zocca
Imola
Russi
Bagnone
Ligonchio
Lama Mocogno
Monterenzio
Borghetto di Vara
Vergato
Riolo Terme
Faenza
Fivizzano
Aulla
Montese
Leiano
Casola Valsenio
Brisighella
Piazza al Serchio
Pievepelago
Sestola
Monghidoro
Forlì
Fanano
Castrocaro
Farlimpo
Fosdinovo
Castelnuovo Garfagnana
Porretta Terme
Castiglione dei Pepoli
Modigliana
Aeroporto di Forlì
Bertinoro
Sarzana
Firenzuola
Dovàdola
Mèldola
La Spezia
Lerici
Carrara
Alpi Apuane
Vagli
Palazzuolo sul Senio
Predappio
Portovènere
Barga
Monte Giovo 1991m
Marradi
Trédozio
Isola Palmaria
Golfo di la Spezia
Marina di Carrara
Massa
S.Marcello Pistoiese
Vernio
Barberino di Mugello
Rocca S. Casciano
Soglia al Rubicone
Marina di Massa
Bagni di Lucca
Scarperia
Galeata
Forte dei Marme
Pietrasanta
Borgo a Mozzano
Vaiano
Borgo S.Lorenzo
Mercato Saraceno
Camaiore
Pistoia
S.Sofia
Viareggio
Massarosa
Pescia
Montecatini
Prato
Vaglia
Dicomano
Sarsina
Lucca
Porcari
Sesto F.
Monte Falterona 1658m
Novafeltria
Torre del Lago Puccini
Aeroporto di Firenze
Fièsole
Rufina
Bagno di Romagna
Altopascio
S.Giugliano
Stia
Pennabilli
Bocca d'Arno
Pisa
Vicopisano
Fucecchio
Empoli
Montelupo
FIRENZE
Vallombrosa
Monte Penna 1283m
Cascina
Bientina
Tavarinuzze
Marina di Pisa
Aeroporto Galileo Galilei
Pontedera
Impruneta
Riganano S. A.
Poppi
Bibbiena
Chiusi di Verna
Badia Tedalda
Tirrenia
S.Miniato
Montespectoli
S.Casciano in V. di Pesa
Incisa in Vald.
Pieve S.Stefano
Ponsacco
Rassina
Livorno
Collesalvetti
Castelfiorentino
Greve
Figline Valdarno
S.Giovanni V.
Sansepolcro
Peccioli
Certaldo
Tavarnelle in V. di Presa
Monti del Chianti
Anghia
Antignano
Casciana Terme
Nontaione
Montevarchi
Isola Gorgona
Poggioonsi
Radda in C.
Arezzo
S.Gimignano
Castellina in C.
Castiglioncello
Rosignano M.
Volterra
Colle di V. d'Elsa
Val di Chiana
Castellina Marittima
Rosignano Solvay
Monteriggioni
Castelnuovo Berardenga
Monte S. Savino
Castiglion Fiorentino
Mar Ligure
Marina di Cecina
Cecina
Pomarance
Siena
Rapolano Terme
Umbertide
Cortona
Asciano
Sinalunga
Foiano della Chiana
Tuoro s. Trasimeno
Castelnuovo di V. di Cecina
Monteroni d'Arbia
Donoratio
Castagneto Carducci
Chiusdino
Murlo
Trequanda
Passignano
Lago Trasimeno
Isola di Capraia
Monticiano
Buonconvento
S. Giovanni d'Asso
Capraia
S. Vicenzo
Campiglia Marittima
Castiglione del Lago
Prata
Montalcino
Montepulciano
Venturina
Massa Marittima
S. Quirico d'Orcia
Chianciano Terme
Roccastrada
Chiusi
Bastia, Porto Vecchio
Piombino
Castiglione d'Orcia
Sarteano
Piegaro
Canale di Piombino
Follonica
Monte Amiata 1738m
Montarale 853m
Golfo di Follonica
Gavorrano
Cinigiano
Castel d. Piano
Radicofani
Città delle Pieve
C. della Vita
Marciana Marina
Portoferraio
Rio Marina
Montepescali
Abbadia S. Salvatore
Arcidosso
Marciana
Aeroporto dell'Elba
Punta Ala
Bagno Roselle
Piancastagnaio
Allerona
Ficulle
S. Venanzo
Ólbia, Palermo
Marina di Campo
Porto Azzurro
Castiglione della Pescaia
Grosseto
Roccalbegna
Castell' Azzara
Acquapendente
Castel Viscardo
Monte Peglia 837m
Isola d' Elba
Marina di Grosseto
Scansano
Onano
Orvieto
S. Lorenzo Nuovo
Pianosa
Magliano in Toscana
Pitigliano
Grado
Bolsena
Bagnoregio
Isola Pianosa
Formiche di Grosseto
Talamone
Manciano
Valentano
Lago di Bolsena
Farnese
Montefiascone
Arcipelago Toscano
Campodimonte
Piansano
Capalbio
Canino
Porto S. Stefano
Orbetello
Tuscania
Viterbo
Giglio Castello
Monte Argentario 635m
Isola di Montecristo
Montalto di Castro
Vignanello
Isola del Giglio
Vetralla
Isola di Giannutri
Tarquinia
Monte Romano
Ronciglione
Capranica
A1
A11
A12
A13
A14
A15
E45
E78
E80

Tuscany is quintessential Italy: a land that launched a thousand picture postcards of rolling hills and vineyards, sunflowers and cypress trees, atmospheric alleyways and historic towns. It's home to the nation's most celebrated city: Florence, the birthplace of the Renaissance, where you can see the world's richest concentration of artistic treasures – and taste some of the finest gelati. Then there are exquisite hill towns like Cortona, immortalized in *Under the Tuscan Sun*, and Pienza – one man's vision of Utopia. Here too is medieval Siena, with its shell-shaped piazza, Il Campo, and dazzling humbug-striped cathedral; Lucca, perfectly preserved inside its ancient walls; and Arezzo, where you can see some of Piero della Francesca's finest frescoes.

The list of world-class sights is endless, from Pisa's Leaning Tower to San Gimignano's medieval 'skyscrapers'. And, if you tire of art, you can follow wine trails in Chianti, party all night in Viareggio, go walking in the chestnut-covered hills of the Garfagnana, or ride horses in the wild Maremma. The trouble with Tuscany, in fact, is that there's just too much to see and do. Accept that you can't do it all and allow yourself time to relax as well, for this isn't a place to be hurried.

At a glance

A whistle-stop tour of the region

Tuscany is at the very heart of Italy. It's a region that is both unique and alluring, that gave the world Michelangelo, Leonardo da Vinci and Dante Alighieri. Squeezed between Italy's industrial north and the more agricultural south, it blends characteristics of the two – more laid back than places like Milan, less chaotic than Sicily or Naples. It's a place where lively modern cities thrive and happily rub shoulders with tiny hamlets in which life seems hardly to have changed since medieval times.

Florence, of course, is the tourist honeypot, followed by Siena and the surrounding hill towns such as Montepulciano – a wine lover's dream. But only as you explore more widely can you fully appreciate the glorious variety of the region. Northern Tuscany is the craggiest area, encompassing the mountains of the Apennines and Apuan Alps and the ancient maritime republic of Pisa, while eastern Tuscany is a mix of hills and plains – home to the art city of Arezzo and picturesque Cortona. Most surprising is the area to the south and west, where the Maremma's buttery soft beaches gradually give way to fertile hills and plains, and hot springs spurt sulphurous steam. And this book doesn't even have room to mention the glorious Tuscan islands, such as Elba, easily reached from the southwest coast and well worth a place on your itinerary, or the moonlike landscapes of the Lunigiana, far to the north.

The lowdown

Money matters
Tuscany doesn't come cheap, especially since the advent of the euro. However, prices do vary within the region. Florence is far more expensive than anywhere else. Assuming that you've already paid for your accommodation, you'll need to allow around €60 each per day if you're going into big attractions, less outside the city.

Opening hours
Many museums close on Mondays. Shops often shut on Monday morning too. Attractions, including churches, often close for lunch. You'll also find that places don't adhere to advertised times, so don't be surprised if a museum is shut when it shouldn't be.

Tourist passes
Save money with combined tickets: these allow access to several museums at a reduced price.

Tourist information
For info on Florence, contact the city's APT (tourist information office, T055-290832, firenzeturismo.it). Useful general websites are Tourism in Tuscany (turismo.toscana.it) and In Tuscany (intoscana.it). Or contact the APT in provincial centres and individual towns for more detailed information.

Florence

It may be small but Florence is so full of art treasures, Renaissance palaces and fascinating churches that it takes a long time to explore it properly. Michelangelo's *David*, Donatello's *St George*, Leonardo's *Annunciation*, Ghiberti's Baptistery doors, Fra Angelico's frescoes, Botticelli's *Birth of Venus* – oh, yes, and Brunelleschi's awe-inspiring dome: there's so much to see it can get quite overwhelming. You could spend a weekend in the Uffizi Gallery alone. In high season, the sheer numbers of tour groups – obediently following guides holding umbrellas or sticks aloft like modern-day Pied Pipers – can make it seem as if the city is one big museum. But make time to wander just a short distance from the main sights and you'll be able to see another Florence. Explore the Oltrarno, for example and you'll find craftsmen producing everything from sculptures to handmade shoes; stroll around Sant'Ambrogio Market and you'll find locals buying fruit and vegetables for that night's dinner. In fact, just get lost in the city and you'll enjoy your trip much more.

Siena

Siena, Florence's old enemy, is the most complex, fascinating and unfathomable of cities; a place where the medieval is as much a part of modern-day living as the mobile phone. Most people know it for the Palio, the ancient and brutal horse race held twice a year in the Campo, Siena's famous shell-shaped piazza. But the city also has a deliciously over-the-top cathedral, remarkable 14th-century frescoes depicting secular rather than religious subjects, and a maze of atmospheric streets and alleyways lined with individual shops and characterful bars and restaurants. Between Siena and Florence lies Chianti, the oak-wooded wine country that has long been a second home to the Brits and Germans who 'discovered' it after the 1960s. Also within easy reach of the city is San Gimignano, the many-towered – and much photographed – medieval hill town.

Eastern Tuscany

While it is more industrialized than other parts of the region, eastern Tuscany also contains the wild Casentino with its forests and crags. The area is certainly not short of attractions. In fact it offers art lovers a real treat, for it's here that you'll find the majority of works by Piero della Francesca – from the *Legend of the True Cross* fresco cycle in Arezzo's San Francesco Church, to the depiction of the pregnant Virgin, the *Madonna del Parto*, in the tiny village of Monterchi. Both Monterchi and Sansepolcro, where the artist was born, are on the border with Umbria yet still proudly Tuscan in their outlook. Here you'll also find Cortona, the archetypal Tuscan hill town.

Northern Tuscany

Pisa, as Tuscany's main transport hub, is the gateway to much of the region's northern reaches. It sits at the foot of the Monte Pisano, a small mountain range that sets the scene for more dramatic crags further north. The most famous sight is Pisa's Leaning Tower, but the rest of the area offers a good mix of cultural attractions as well as plenty of opportunities for activities. Lucca, birthplace of the composer Puccini, is not just picturesque but extremely musical, staging a wide range of concerts and performances. And each year the Puccini Opera Festival, on the coast at Torre del Lago, attracts thousands of visitors.

In the northwest corner are the mountains where Michelangelo found the marble from which

he created his compelling sculptures, and where marble is still quarried today. Here too are the thickly wooded slopes of the Garfagnana, perfect country for a food and wine tour or some exhilarating walks. Further east are Pistoia, a small city that barely registers on the tourist radar yet has a beautifully preserved centre, the spa town of Montecatini Terme, and Vinci, birthplace of Leonardo.

Southern Hill Towns

The landscape to the south of Siena is dotted with such a charming mix of medieval hill towns and serene abbeys that it makes perfect touring country. Here are fields of sunflowers and sweetcorn, green hills and rolling waves of smooth clay soil. If you love wine then you won't want to miss visiting Montepulciano, famed for the *Nobile di Montepulciano*, or Montalcino, home of *Brunello*. Between these two is squeezed the less famous, but still delightful, town of San Quirico d'Orcia. Then there's Pienza, Pope Pius II's embodiment of the ideal Renaissance town. More isolated are the beautiful abbeys of Sant' Antimo, Monte Oliveto Maggiore and, further west, San Galgano, where you can see the hilt of a sword sticking out of a stone – buried there, it's said, by the eponymous saint in the 12th century.

Southern & Western Tuscany

This is another Tuscany, one that few people take the trouble to get to know but which is richly rewarding if you make the effort. Volterra, to the west of Siena, comes under the province of Pisa but feels entirely different. It's the place to come if you want to find out about the mysterious Etruscans, whose civilization flourished here before the Romans came. In the southwest you find the Maremma, a world apart from the tourist heartlands of Chianti – less manicured and mannered but with more to offer those with a sense of adventure. The Maremma coast, where the *butteri* (cowboys) still herd their long-horned cattle, provides a habitat for birds, butterflies and wild boar. It also has Tuscany's best beaches. Moving inland you find fields and farms, and wine and olive oil producers. There may be no 'must-see' artworks, but there are quiet churches, expansive landscapes and hill towns where life seems barely touched by the 21st century.

Volterra is the place to come if you want to find out about the mysterious Etruscans, whose civilization flourished here...

Best of Tuscany

Top 20 things to see and do

❶ The Duomo complex

Brunelleschi's famous dome is a triumph of Renaissance engineering, while Ghiberti's golden doors on the Baptistery are considered by some to be the real heralds of the beginning of the Renaissance. Climb the *Campanile* (Bell Tower) for a – literally – breathtaking view of the city, then admire original sacred artworks in the museum. Page 87.

❷ Uffizi Gallery

Italy's top treasure house of paintings takes you from medieval times to the 18th century. Masterpiece follows masterpiece, with works by Giotto, Filippo Lippi, Piero della Francesca, Raphael, Caravaggio and Dürer. Perhaps the most famous works are Leonardo da Vinci's *Annunciation*, Botticelli's *Birth of Venus* and Michelangelo's *Holy Family*. Page 98.

2 Uffizi Gallery.

❸ San Marco

The sense of place envelops you when you enter this Dominican monastery – you almost feel as if the monks have only just left their cells. The rabidly religious Savonarola lived here, as did devout and gentle Fra Angelico – whose frescoes still adorn the walls. Page 104.

❹ Michelangelo's *David*

Of all the works of art associated with Florence, it is this, Michelangelo's mighty *David*, which once stood outside the Palazzo Pubblico. For the sculptor it symbolized the republican city. Carved out of a block of marble that nobody else wanted, it now stands on a plinth in the Galleria dell'Accademia – pure, perfect and alone. Page 105.

❺ Il Campo & the Palazzo Pubblico

The Campo, the shell-shaped piazza at the heart of Siena, is one of the great sights of Italy. It's surrounded by sombre medieval buildings, which include the almost triumphal Palazzo Pubblico, or town hall. Frescoes on its walls include Ambrogio Lorenzetti's vivid reminder of the importance of wielding power wisely – his *Allegories of Good and Bad Government*. Page 151.

❻ Duomo, Siena

Siena's 12th-century *Duomo* (cathedral) is so lavish you hardly know where to look first: striped columns, a marble floor, Nicola Pisano's pulpit and the vivid frescoes of the Piccolomini Library. Behind the Duomo is the 'crypt', where pilgrims once washed before entering the cathedral. Page 157.

❼ San Gimignano

It's one of the most photographed places in Tuscany and no wonder, for San Gimignano's medieval towers make an arresting sight. They were built first for defence and later to show off the wealth of its inhabitants. The town attracts vast numbers of tourists, who come to see the towers, admire the frescoes in the Collegiata – and try the award-winning ice cream. Page 167.

4 *David.*

6 Siena's Duomo.

7 San Gimignano.

8 Montefioralle, Chianti.

❽ Chianti

Squeezed between Siena and Florence, this landscape of wooded hills, isolated farms and pretty villages is prime wine country. Known as Chiantishire since it's become home or second-home to so many British ex-patriots, it is prime touring territory – just follow the SR 222, the Chiantigiana, and stop off at the vineyards and many *enoteche* (wine shops) that line your route. Page 171.

❾ San Francesco Church, Arezzo

Come here to see Piero della Francesca's celebrated fresco cycle depicting the *Legend of the True Cross*. Piero, famously interested in geometry and mathematics, did not just paint biblical scenes but gave them a contemporary twist. Page 193.

12 Lucca.

⑩ Cortona

This town is just irresistibly pretty, with geraniums blooming from terracotta tubs, medieval alleyways and streets so steep your calves will ache. There are wine shops and restaurants, a great gelateria, Etruscan tombs – and a shimmering *Annunciation* by Fra Angelico. Page 199.

⑪ Campo dei Miracoli

A grassy square filled with dazzling white buildings – you can easily see how it earned the name 'Field of Miracles'. Here is the most celebrated architectural muck-up in the world, the Leaning Tower of Pisa. And here too is Pisa's glorious Cathedral and its exquisite Baptistery. Page 215.

⑫ Lucca

This lovely walled town lies to the north of Pisa. Inside its walls you'll feel as if you've entered a different age. There are medieval towers, palaces, artworks such as the 13th-century Volto Santo – a revered wooden crucifix – lovely individual shops and a piazza that preserves the shape of its earlier incarnation as a Roman amphitheatre. Page 224.

⑬ The Garfagnana

Life in the Garfagnana seems even slower than in the rest of Tuscany. This rugged area of thickly wooded slopes has a rich history all its own, with quiet hamlets, isolated churches and some rewarding walking trails. Page 230.

⑭ Montepulciano

Wine buffs flock here to taste its famous *Vino Nobile*, but there's definitely more to Montepulciano than some good glasses of red. It's a well-preserved hill town, perched dramatically on a ridge, with fine churches, lively festivals and good bars and restaurants. Page 252.

⑮ Pienza

Small but perfectly formed, Pienza is the village that was remodelled into a harmonious Renaissance city by Pope Pius II, its most famous son. The embodiment of one man's vision, it symbolizes the ideals and imagination that characterized 15th-century Tuscany. It's also a lovely spot for lunch, with great views over the surrounding countryside. Page 253.

⑯ Monte Oliveto Maggiore

An avenue of cypress trees leads to this isolated Benedictine abbey south of Siena. Come here to see the frescoes on the walls of its Great Cloister: some are by Luca Signorelli; others – the most lively – by Il Sodoma, who cheekily painted himself in one of the holy scenes. Page 260.

⑰ Volterra

Wild, rather windswept and isolated – that's Volterra. It has a unique atmosphere, perhaps because of its location, perhaps because of its Etruscan past. Come and see the gilded ceiling of the *Duomo*, buy a sculpture made of snowy white alabaster, and ponder on the enigmatic figures that adorn the Etruscan burial urns. Page 278.

⑱ Parco Naturale della Maremma

The Uccellina Natural Park, as it's often called, is a glorious protected natural area along the coast of the Maremma. There are pristine beaches, umbrella pine trees and a rich variety of flora and fauna. It's the hidden face of Tuscany, and quite beautiful with it. Page 283.

⑲ Pitigliano

Deep in the southeast corner of the Maremma, close to the border with Lazio, Pitigliano is one of the most individual of Tuscan towns. With a rich legacy of Etruscan and later Jewish settlement, it has a character that is all its own – rising from the tufa like some magical beast. Page 286.

⑳ Massa Marittima

So far only the Germans seem to have discovered this little town, which says much for their taste as it's a real gem. The harmonious central piazza is as picturesque as they come, all focused on its lovely Romanesque Cathedral. Page 287.

19 Pitigliano.

Month by month

A year in Tuscany

January & February

January is a cool, damp month when much of Tuscany seems to hibernate – it gets much colder here than you might expect. New Year's Day is a national holiday, as is Epiphany, 6 January, so shops and attractions will be closed. On the eve of Epiphany, Italian children receive a gift from *la Befana*, a kindly witch. Many restaurants – and some hotels in less touristy areas – take a long break during January, so the streets are quiet.

In February, the weather is still quite cool and damp (particularly noticeable in Florence, which is set in a valley), but the landscape is just beginning to spring back to life. This is usually the month for *carnevale*, held in the run-up to Lent (the dates obviously vary with Easter). The largest event is held in Viareggio on Shrove Tuesday. Some restaurants and attractions will still be closed for the winter, while those that are open should be fairly quiet.

March & April

March can be very pleasant in Tuscany. The weather is warmer and drier, though not reliable, and the fruit trees are in blossom. Attractions and restaurants that closed for the winter should now be open, and accommodation prices will be low. Palm Sunday often falls during March, in which case you will see church processions of people carrying palm branches. On 19 March the *Torciata di San Giuseppe* festival is held in Pitigliano.

By April the weather's getting better and you should have plenty of sunny days (though in recent years the seasons have become less certain). Easter most frequently falls during April and the shops

will be filled with spectacular chocolate eggs. On Easter Sunday the *Scoppio del Carro* festival takes place in Florence. However, Easter is also a very busy tourist time, so attractions will be busy and accommodation prices rise. Easter Monday is a national holiday, as is 25 April, so museums and attractions will generally be closed.

May & June

May is a lovely time to visit Tuscany: the countryside looks glorious, roses are starting to bloom, and while the weather is usually warm and sunny it's not oppressively hot. This is the month for the *Maggio Musicale*, Florence's major music festival, as well as the medieval *Balestro del Girifalco* crossbow festival in Massa Marittima. Museums and attractions will be shut on 1 May, as it's a public holiday. This is mid-season for accommodation prices and Florence is generally not too crowded. It's one of the best times to come on a walking or cycling holiday.

Another lovely month, June, is very warm (it could reach 29°C) and reasonably dry. There is plenty of delicious fresh fruit to eat, and you'll also see dishes made with courgette (zucchini) flowers. The festival season gets into full swing with the start of the *Estate Fiesolana*, Fiesole's summer festival. In Pisa there's the *Gioco del Ponte* contest, in Arezzo the *Giostra del Saracino* and, in Florence, the *Calcio Storico* – the colourful football match played on the feast of St John the Baptist (24 June). It's a pleasant time to visit Florence, which is usually at its best around now, although hotel prices are starting to rise.

July & August

July is extremely busy: arrive at Pisa airport when British schools have broken up and you can hardly move for families queuing to pick up hire cars and set off for a few weeks in their dream Tuscan villa. This is the driest month of the year, as well as the hottest – Florence, which has a less equable climate than other parts of Tuscany, gets extremely humid. In 2008 the temperature exceeded 38°C some days, making sightseeing exhausting and uncomfortable. Accommodation prices are at their peak, sights are likely to be extremely crowded – but everything is open. It is almost impossible to find anywhere to stay in Siena in the first week in July, when the first Palio is held.

Italians take their holidays in August – vast numbers of Tuscans decamp to the coast for the whole month, pushing prices up and making it very difficult to find accommodation by the sea. Florence itself gets so hot and sticky that tourist numbers drop – if you can bear the heat you'll often find museums and attractions surprisingly quiet, while hotel prices fall to around mid-season rates. The big national holiday is *Ferragosto*, on 15 August, when everything shuts: many restaurants close for a week or two around this time. It's not a good time for activity holidays – way too hot. However, in the countryside sunflowers are in full bloom, grapes are swelling on the vines and you have a great excuse to sample lots of delicious gelati. Siena's second Palio is run on 16 August.

September & October

Accommodation prices in Florence rise again in September, as it's generally not so hot and humid, and museums and attractions fill up once again. The beautifully decorated *pavimento* (marble floor) of Siena's cathedral is uncovered for a few weeks, and the city becomes extremely busy. However, once the Italians have decamped, coastal resorts get quieter. It's also a lovely month for outdoor activities. There are a number of festivals to enjoy, including the procession of the *Volto Santo* (Holy Face) in Lucca and medieval competitions in Arezzo and Sansepolcro.

Autumn is the wettest season in Tuscany and you're likely to get quite a few rainy days in October. However, it's usually still warm – great for walkers, and a wonderful time to go on a food and drink trail. Towns and villages around Tuscany start to hold festivals celebrating their local wine – as in Chianti – and autumn produce like chestnuts. This is the time for the grape harvest, so the countryside is very busy. Accommodation prices are back at mid-season levels, while most small museums and attractions remain open.

November & December

November is generally rainy and the temperature drops quite a bit. Florence can get very chilly and misty; in consequence tourist numbers fall, so you're less likely to find long queues for the top museums. Gelaterie often close in November (the Tuscans, not unreasonably, seeing ice cream as a warm weather food) and may not reopen until the end of February. It's a wonderful time for food lovers, as fat fresh porcini mushrooms are in season, truffles start to appear and the olive harvest begins. If you want to see an olive press in operation then this is the time to come. Look out for plump persimmons (rather unromantically named *kaki* in Italy) hanging from the trees – they look like oranges, but are deeper in colour. All Saints' Day on 1 November is a public holiday.

In the run-up to Christmas the food shops burst with festive treats like panettone and panforte di Siena. Christmas decorations in Tuscany are extremely tasteful: there are few gaudy lights here, but instead lots of greenery, small white lights and lovingly arranged *presepe* – cribs depicting the manger scene.

If you visit now you'll be able to buy some lovely presents, whether gifts of food and drink or items from the craft workshops and specialist stores that still flourish here. As you'd expect, public holidays fall on Christmas Day and Boxing Day (St Stephen's Day), but there's also one on the Feast of the Immaculate Conception, 8 December.

It is almost impossible to find anywhere to stay in Siena in the first week in July, when the first Palio is held.

Screen & page

Tuscany in film & literature

Films

Tuscan film locations

A Room with a View
James Ivory, 1985
The Merchant-Ivory version of E.M. Forster's novel featured Helena Bonham Carter as Lucy Honeychurch and Florence as itself.

The English Patient
Anthony Minghella, 1996
Anthony Minghella's Oscar-winning film was shot in various Tuscan locations, including Pienza, Montepulciano and, most memorably, Sant'Anna in Camprena.

The Portrait of a Lady
Jane Campion, 1996
Jane Campion's film, starring Nicole Kidman, featured grand villas in and around Lucca.

Life is Beautiful
Roberto Benigni, 1997
Roberto Benigni's wartime film featured many locations in Arezzo.

Gladiator
Ridley Scott, 2000
Ridley Scott shot a number of scenes in the soft light of the Val d'Orcia.

Quantum of Solace
Marc Foster, 2008
With Daniel Craig as James Bond. Partly shot on location in Siena, the film featured the Palio as well as the city's underground tunnels, the *bottini*.

Books

Tuscany, particularly Florence, was a required stop on the Grand Tour. It made a distinct impression on early visitors and received some evocative mentions in Victorian travel writing.

In the late 20th century, there was a rash of books by people who had fulfilled the middle-class dream, left their noisy cities and gone to live in Tuscany. Here are some of the books worth reading.

Travel writing

Pictures from Italy
Charles Dickens, 1866
An elegant and observant account of a 19th-century Grand Tour.

Italian Hours
Henry James, 1909
A collection of essays covering his travels in Italy at the turn of the 20th century. He turns a keen and enthusiastic eye on art, life and culture.

Etruscan Places
D.H. Lawrence, 1927
Wandering through tombs in Italy's ancient Etruscan cities, including Volterra, Lawrence gives a voice to a vanished people. He visits the Maremma and describes it as "that flat, wide plain of the coast … one of the most abandoned, wildest parts of Italy".

A Traveller in Italy
H.V. Morton, 1964
By the last of the gentlemen travellers, this account of a journey though 1950s Italy has enduring appeal and contains vivid descriptions of places and people.

Fiction & autobiographical accounts

Where Angels Fear to Tread *(1905)*
A Room with a View *(1908)*
E.M. Forster

These are both tragi-comic novels. *A Room with a View* casts light on Edwardian English attitudes to the sights of Florence, while *Where Angels Fear to Tread*, set in San Gimignano, follows the consequences of a middle-class English woman's love affair with an Italian.

War in Val d'Orcia
Iris Origo, 1947

A war diary of 1943-4 by the Anglo-American wife of an Italian marchese.

Summer's Lease
John Mortimer, 1988

Middle-class Brits rent a holiday villa in Tuscany. This was the book that embedded Chiantishire in the imagination.

Where Angels Fear to Tread, set in San Gimignano, follows the consequences of a middle-class English woman's love affair with an Italian.

The English Patient
Michael Ondaatje, 1992
A badly burned man is nursed in an ancient Tuscan monastery in the Second World War.

Under the Tuscan Sun *(1998)*
Bella Tuscany *(2000)*
Frances Mayes
Bestselling memoirs of an American woman who bought and renovated a villa near Cortona. Evoking the gentle rural life, they're a Tuscan version of Peter Mayle's *A Year in Provence*.

Partisan Wedding
Renata Viganò, 1999
Vivid stories based on the real experiences of the author and other female members of the Italian Resistance in the Second World War.

Vanilla Beans and Brodo
Isabella Dusi, 2001
An enjoyable account of how a couple from Australia sell up and make a new life in the wine town of Montalcino.

A Florentine Death
Michele Giuttari, 2007
Former Florence police chief Michele Giuttari's first detective novel, featuring his alter ego – Florence police chief Michele Ferrara.

Non-fiction

The Italians
Luigi Barzini, 1964
An Italian gives an incisive portrait of the morals and manners of his countrymen.

La Terra in Piazza
Alan Dundes and Alessandro Falassi, 1975
Extremely informative account of the Palio and what it means to the Sienese.

The Dark Heart of Italy
Tobias Jones, 2003
Fascinating appraisal of Berlusconi's Italy and the murkier aspects of everyday life in the country.

About the region

Contents

Etruscan necropolis.

History

From a land called Etruria to the Founding of Florence

Walk through the *bottini*, the maze of tunnels that lie beneath Siena, and you can see the remains of tiny sea shells buried in the walls – evidence that, far back in prehistory, much of Tuscany was under water. When the waters receded, early hunter-gatherers began to colonize the region, and Neolithic farmers created early settlements. These Neolithic tribes were more advanced than we usually imagine: they appear to have grown grains such as spelt and emmer in the area around Lucca (they're still grown there today) and to have cultivated vines. Later peoples began utilizing metals to make implements – first copper, then bronze, later iron. At the archaeological museum in Castellina in Chianti, you can see evidence of the sophistication of Bronze Age sheep farmers: there are remains of a kettle and a strainer (showing that they made cheese), tools for carving antlers, and spindles and bobbins showing that they spun wool. Around 1000 BC, evidence appears of the development of an iron-working culture. The Villanovan civilization, as it's known, spread throughout the central area, pretty much covering the area bounded by the Arno to the north and the Tiber to the south.

The Etruscans

But it was the eighth century BC that saw the most dramatic changes in this part of Italy: the Etruscan civilization spread, and Rome was founded in 753 BC. The Greeks called the Etruscans Tyrrhenoi (as in the Tyrrhenian Sea), the Romans called them Etrusci or Tusci. They called themselves Rasenna. Academic opinion is divided over where they came from: some believe, as Herodotus did, that they sailed from Asia Minor; others take the view, propounded by Dionysius of Halicarnassus, that they were native to central Italy; yet others feel that they moved into the region from across the Alps. Wherever they came from, they fairly rapidly absorbed, or subsumed, Villanovan culture and established a distinctive civilization that still fascinates scholars today.

Etruria, as the Etruscan land was known, covered the region we know today as Tuscany and extended into modern Lazio, Umbria and Emilia-Romagna. The northern part of their territory was fairly fertile, with valleys and hills; the south was volcanic and marshy. Experts are still trying to decipher their unique language, so we don't know as much about them as we would like. The Etruscans do, however, appear to have been both industrious and sophisticated, establishing towns and cities across Etruria, building roads, draining the marshes, and mining and trading the metals in which part of their territory was rich. Among the settlements they founded were Siena, Lucca, Fiesole and probably Pisa, while their most important cities included Volterra, Cortona and Arezzo. They established a tradition – which proved lasting in Tuscany – of cities that functioned independently, like mini-states. Though self-governing, they were organized into leagues, notably the *Dodecapoli*, or League of 12 Cities.

Etruscan society both scandalized and fascinated the Romans and Greeks, who felt that their women had far too much freedom. Theopompus of Chios declared: "The women take particular care of their bodies and exercise often ... It is not a disgrace for them to be seen naked. Further, they dine, not with their own husbands but with any men who happen to be present ... They are also expert drinkers and very good looking." Etruscan religion was, unusually for the time, based on a set doctrine thought to have been imparted by the gods. There was a treatise on divination through the examination of animal entrails, and another on reading the significance of lightning. The nearby Romans, who from 616 BC were ruled by the Etruscan Tarquin dynasty, adopted these divination practices, as well as the Etruscan appetite for bloody contests between humans and animals, and that most 'Roman' item of clothing, the toga.

The rise of Rome

But eventually Rome expelled the Tarquins and began its own expansion. In 396 BC the Etruscan town of Veii was destroyed, and Rome began to annex land. Etruria was soon squeezed between the Romans pushing up from the south and the Gauls and Carthaginians invading from the north. In the Second Punic War (218-02 BC), the Carthaginian commander Hannibal tried to enlist the help of the Etruscans, but while he defeated Rome at the Battle of Lake Trasimeno, mighty Rome was soon triumphant. The Romans, very astutely, began to work with the upper echelons of Etruscan society, at the same time establishing their own colonies at places like Lucca, Pisa and Siena. Eventually the Etruscans were made Roman citizens (88-90 BC) and in 59 BC Julius Caesar founded Florence as a settlement for his war veterans.

Roman rule

Under Roman rule the southern part of Etruria was neglected. The marshes that the Etruscans had managed to reclaim gradually returned to their former unproductive state and many settlements declined. Etruscan roads fell into disuse as new Roman roads were built mainly for military needs, running firmly north–south. Settlements in the north, however, prospered. Pisa, for example, became an important port, and Florence grew rapidly. Like other parts of imperial Rome, Etruria, now known as Tuscia, began to experience the spread of Christianity. After AD 313, under Constantine, Christianity became the state religion of Rome, and gradually churches were founded in Pisa, Lucca, Siena, Florence and other cities. But the Roman Empire couldn't last forever. Constantine had united its western and eastern (Byzantine) parts, but at the end of the fourth century it was divided again. There were constant raids from the north and, in 476, Rome and the western empire fell to the Teutonic invader Odovacer.

Julius Caesar.

The Lombards

During the sixth century, Byzantium tried to wrest back control of the former western empire, and its artistic and cultural influence spread into Tuscia. The region's towns and cities became battlegrounds, and a sort of peace was restored only after the invasion of the Lombards, who swept down from the north in 568 and subsequently ruled much of northern and central Italy for approximately 200 years. The Lombards controlled their lands through duchies: the capital of the Duchy of Tuscia was Lucca, which now outstripped Florence in importance. While some of the Lombards were, at least initially, pagan, others were Christian and they built many churches – often over sites of pagan worship. It was a Lombard queen who built an early baptistery in Florence, on top of an existing church, which for a while functioned as the city's cathedral.

Tuscany

In the eighth century the Germanic Franks seized a proportion of Lombard territory – and granted a sizeable proportion of the land to the Pope, thus strengthening papal power. In 774 the Frankish king Charlemagne conquered the Lombards, together with a vast swathe of Italy, and in 800 he had the Pope crown him Holy Roman Emperor, a title that made him the assumed heir to the original western Roman Empire. The Franks secured their territory by establishing administrative regions called margravates – and Tuscany (the name Tuscia lingered until the 13th century) became one, ruled by an imperial margrave based in Lucca, which became known as the Duchy of Lucca. Neighbouring Pisa also grew in wealth and power and was often regarded as the most important city in Tuscia.

More churches and religious centres were built, including the *Badia Fiorentina* in Florence, which was established in 978 by Willa, the widow of Margrave Uberto. (This church, where Dante's Beatrice worshipped, contains the tomb of Willa's son Ugo, carved by Mino da Fiesole.) Religion became increasingly important to the economy of the region, for in 990 Sigeric, Archbishop of Canterbury, travelled to Rome using a route that was to become known as the via Francigena. Lucca and Siena were important stopping places on the way – and the swarms of pilgrims that followed Sigeric brought trade and new ideas into the two cities.

Imperial vs papal power

The margraves had considerable power and some, at least, were not afraid to use it. Enter Matilda, heiress of the vast estates that had belonged to her father, Boniface, Margrave of Tuscany, and no supporter of imperial power. A crisis had long been coming in the rivalry between the Holy Roman Emperor, who now ruled a vast part of Europe including northern and central Italy, and the papacy. In 1076 Emperor Henry IV attracted papal ire by installing an unacceptable figure as an archbishop. The Pope, Gregory VII, excommunicated Henry – a move that weakened his support. Henry walked across the Alps in winter to beg forgiveness from the pope, who happened to be staying at Matilda's family castle in Canossa. She reputedly made the errant emperor wait in the snow barefoot before letting him in.

Matilda's power struggles with Henry continued as he fought campaigns to wrest power from the Pope. She was even reputed to have taken up arms herself. In 1078 she married the Duke of Bavaria, a member of the Germanic Welf (Guelph) dynasty – rather unprepossessingly known as Welf the Fat. However she secretly bequeathed all her lands to the Pope, with the exception of the cities of Florence, Siena and Lucca. When Matilda died in 1115 the scene was set for the rise of the Tuscan city state.

Guelphs & Ghibellines

The development of Tuscany now unravels into a bewildering tangle of historical threads. After Matilda's death, the major cities began to operate as independent, self-governing states, each ruled by a *comune*. This was an association of the great and the good (well, the rich and powerful) and generally included merchants and lawyers. Florence, Pisa, Fiesole, Siena and Lucca all became independent – their existence echoing the politically autonomous cities of the Etruscan era. These city states soon began to jostle for power. And as they became increasingly wealthy (Pisa, for example, grew extremely rich from its involvement in the Crusades, while Siena acquired valuable silver mines and Lucca had a booming silk industry), so each began to cast an acquisitive eye on its neighbour. In 1125 Florence flexed its muscles and seized control of Fiesole.

The situation was already complicated enough, but now a religious element fired the cities' competitive fervour. Relations between the papacy and the empire had been strained for some time when a Swabian leader, Frederick I of the Hohenstaufen dynasty (ancient rivals of the Welfs), marched into Italy and seized as much of the northern and central lands as he could. Frederick, nicknamed Barbarossa ('red beard'), had himself crowned King of Italy and Holy Roman Emperor. He also appointed an imperial official, a podestà, to each *comune* to help wield his power. Many *comuni*, particularly in the north of Italy, resented this display of force and banded together against him. Further conflict ensued when Barbarossa's son and successor Henry VI died, and his child Frederick II was considered too young for the imperial role. Henry's brother, Philip, laid claim to the title of Holy Roman Emperor instead. His claim was heartily disputed by Otto of Brunswick – a Welf – and the Pope determinedly supported the Welf (Guelph) claim. Frederick II eventually became Holy Roman Emperor in 1220, and fought against Otto for control of much of Italy.

Factions & vendettas

By the time Frederick II died in 1250, Tuscany was divided into distinct factions: the Guelphs, who supported the papacy, and the Ghibellines (their name was a corruption of the Hohenstaufen battle cry), who supported the emperors. The various cities became allied with one side or another: Florence was traditionally Guelph, while Siena took the Ghibelline side. The picture was further complicated by internal rivalries. Guelphs tended to come from the up-and-coming merchant classes, who felt that they couldn't really prosper under imperialism, while the Ghibellines tended to be from the old ruling classes who favoured the status quo. Families began to favour one side or another too, often using the Guelph/Ghibelline tags as an excuse for avenging old hurts. In 1215, for instance, on his way to marry a Guelph bride, the Florentine Buondelmonte de' Buondelmonti was stabbed to death on the Ponte Vecchio by members of the Ghibelline Amidei family, who were furious that he had rejected a girl from their clan. The resulting trial tore Florence into rival factions. In 1248 Frederick II helped to force the Guelphs out of the city, but within a couple of years they had regained control.

It goes on like this, with cities and families switching sides with such frequency that one wonders whether they knew themselves what side they were on. The greatest struggles were between the most powerful cities in Tuscany, Florence and Siena. In 1250 Florence established the Chianti League, an association of Chianti towns formed to defend themselves against Siena. In 1260, Siena defeated Florence at the Battle of Montaperti; in 1269 Florence beat Siena at the Battle of Colle di Val d'Elsa. The Guelphs defeated the Ghibellines at the Battle of Campaldino (1289), at which Dante Alighieri fought. The Guelphs then promptly split into opposing factions: the Black Guelphs who favoured absolute loyalty to the Pope, and the White Guelphs (including Dante) who favoured greater independence. Dante was famously exiled from Florence in 1302 and never returned – in 2008 a majority of the city council voted to pardon him.

Florence expanded its power throughout the 14th century, making the most of Pisa's declining fortunes after the loss of its fleet in 1284, and gradually assumed control of Pistoia, Prato, Volterra, Arezzo and – in 1406 – Pisa itself. Although Tuscany was devastated by the Black Death in 1348, which wiped out two-thirds of the population in some places, Florence bounced back better than its rival Siena, making it the pre-eminent city in the region.

The Renaissance & the rise of the Medici

During the 14th century, ruling lords from noble families – *signori* – had assumed control of the cities of northern Italy. Tuscan cities had retained a more equable system of power: the Signoria that ruled Florence, for instance, was a council made up of members of the major guilds (Arti Maggiori), representing figures like bankers, wool merchants, silk weavers and lawyers. Still, the 'lesser' guilds – the Arti Mediane (like shoemakers and iron workers) and the Arti Minori (such as woodworkers, innkeepers and bakers) – could not put members on the council. The labouring classes were not even allowed to form guilds. In 1378 the *Ciompi* (textile labourers) finally revolted. They briefly took over the Palazzo della Signoria (Palazzo Vecchio) and with support from the Arti Minori were given permission to form a guild and achieve representation. This situation wasn't to last, and by the early 15th century the wealthy guilds were back in control.

However, the episode had prepared the ground for the rise of the über-powerful Medici dynasty. The family's fortunes had been laid by financier Giovanni Bicci de' Medici who, in an extremely smart move, had become the papal banker. The family had not been born to riches, and perhaps it was because of this that Giovanni's son Cosimo de' Medici ('Il Vecchio'), had a certain amount of sympathy for the poorer populace and became a popular figurehead. He was also politically astute and forged good relations with the powerful rulers of Milan – handy to have on your side in a quarrel. He so alarmed the members of the Signoria that he was forced to leave Florence for a time. However, in 1434 he was invited to return, and so began an extraordinary period in which the Medici became the unofficial rulers of Florence (and, in consequence, much of Tuscany).

Artistic patronage

Cosimo's influence was pervasive. While it could not be said that he was responsible for the Renaissance – its seeds had already been sown by figures such as Dante, Boccaccio, Petrarch and Giotto – it is hard to imagine the Renaissance without him. In 1439 Cosimo managed to persuade the Pope to hold the Ecumenical Council meeting in Florence. It was an attempt to bring together the western and eastern (Byzantine) sections of the church; earlier, unsuccessful, meetings had been held in Pisa and Siena, but this had some temporary success. It also swept new ideas into the city.

Cosimo continued to run the Medici bank, and was both devout (you can still see his private cell in San Marco, see page 106) and intellectually curious – a generous patron of the arts. He commissioned Donatello to create his bronze David (now in the Bargello) and funded the building and decoration of San Marco – famously frescoed by Fra Angelico. Renaissance ideas were now spreading, and in 1458 Enea Silvius, of the wealthy Piccolomini family in Siena, became Pope Pius II and commissioned the building of his ideal Renaissance city: Pienza.

Cosimo was briefly succeeded by his son Piero, and then his grandson Lorenzo the Magnificent took the helm in 1469, continuing the tradition of funding great works of art. He had the gift of diplomacy and his rule was largely peaceable – unlike that of another ruler afforded the title 'Magnificent': the nobleman Pandolfo Petrucci, who ruthlessly controlled Siena between 1487 and 1512. Lorenzo wasn't so successful at business, however, and nearly bankrupted the Medici bank. When he died in 1492 he was succeeded by his weak son Piero, who in 1494 effectively surrendered the city into the hands of Charles VIII of France. The Medici were expelled by a furious populace and Florence became a republic.

***David* in Bronze.**

Struggles for supremacy

Charles VIII had also passed through Pisa, and the city grabbed the chance to reassert itself on the Tuscan stage, re-declare itself as a republic and liberate itself from rule by Florence (a freedom it achieved only briefly). However, Charles, who wanted to claim Naples for France (it was owned by Spain), was soon forced north and out of Italy again.

Book-burning & corruption

In Florence, the vacuum left by the absence of the Medici was rapidly filled by the Dominican monk Girolamo Savonarola, who exploited the people's fears by effectively preaching that it was the rule of the Medici and their patronage of 'immoral' artworks that had led to the city's problems. He lit his Bonfire of the Vanities (any items deemed to be sinful were banned) in 1497 but was unpopular with the Pope, who excommunicated him. In 1498 he was burned at the stake in Piazza della Signoria, and a less malign republic returned – celebrated by Michelangelo with his magnificent statue of David.

While Cosimo il Vecchio and Lorenzo the Magnificent had, in the main, used their power wisely, their heirs appear to have been corrupted by it; the 16th century saw far less attractive family members assume control of Florence – and effectively much of Tuscany. In 1512 Medici rule returned to the city in the person of Giuliano, Duke of Nemours, one of Lorenzo's sons. His return had been assisted by Pope Julius II – advised by one of his cardinals, Giuliano's brother Giovanni. Giovanni became Pope Leo X in 1513, and his scandalous sale of indulgences to fund the rebuilding of St Peter's in Rome provoked Martin Luther's Reformation. Leo X was succeeded by his cousin, who became Pope Clement VII; he did not choose his enemies wisely and fell out with the enormously powerful Charles V of Spain, the Habsburg heir. Charles sacked Rome in 1527, and the family of the humbled Pope were again expelled from Florence, which once more became a republic.

Clement had to work hard to get back in favour with Charles V, which he did by crowning him Holy Roman Emperor. In 1530, combined papal and imperial forces returned the Medici to power in Florence, while in Siena Charles established a garrison of Spanish troops and introduced the Inquisition. The Pope's illegitimate son Alessandro de' Medici was now installed as the first Duke of Florence and married off to Charles V's daughter, creating a mighty dynastic alliance. Alessandro exploited his position by grabbing absolute power and reportedly torturing his enemies, poisoning his half-brother, seducing women and having an affair with his cousin Lorenzino. He was even accused of killing his mother, thought to be an African slave. In 1537 Lorenzino murdered him and another Medici, Cosimo I, who was descended from Il Vecchio's brother, took control of the duchy and set about enlarging it – Massa Marittima, for instance, was absorbed in 1555.

Grand Duchy of Tuscany

Siena had still not capitulated to Florence, but after the city allied itself with France to drive out the Spanish, it was besieged in 1554 by an overwhelming alliance of Charles V's imperial troops and Florentine forces. Siena was starved into submission and in 1557 was sold to Florence by Philip II, Charles V's son. Cosimo I became the first Grand Duke of Tuscany, with Siena as one of its possessions. Only Lucca now remained independent.

It had been hoped that Cosimo I would be a malleable ruler, but he proved to have strong ideas on how to run things and took every opportunity to settle old scores. He certainly changed the face of Florence, revamping the Palazzo Vecchio with the help of Giorgio Vasari, building an administrative centre – the Uffizi ('offices') – and enlarging the Pitti Palace, into which he eventually moved.

However, the great days of Medici rule were over, and Cosimo's successors saw Tuscany experience economic decline, due partly to bad harvests, plague and a slump in the wool trade. Although one of his heirs, Cosimo II, made an enlightened defence of Galileo when he was accused of heresy, the others tended to be dissolute (Gian Gastone reportedly vomited out of a carriage window, he was so drunk), rabidly religious or a bit strange. In 1737 the last Medici, Anna Maria de' Medici, handed control of the Grand Duchy to Francis Stephen, Duke of Lorraine, who was married to Maria Theresa of the Austrian Habsburg dynasty.

Napoleon, unification & war

The new Austrian rulers of Tuscany ushered in a welcome period of calm. And when Francis' enlightened son Leopold II took control of the Grand Duchy, he instituted a range of benevolent and revolutionary reforms: he ended torture, abolished the death penalty, extended legal freedom to serfs and encouraged free trade and more efficient farming methods. He also attempted to reclaim the marshy Maremma, long left to revert to unproductive malarial swamp, in the hope of making it a grain-producing area.

Invasion & uprisings

However, the French were casting envious eyes at the mighty Habsburg Empire. In the late 18th century Napoleon invaded Italy, capturing first the north and then Tuscany in 1799. The ripples from the French Revolution had been felt throughout Europe, and the French had not been in power long in Tuscany when opposition occurred in the form of the Viva Maria riots. These were peasant uprisings, often led by local clergy, who blamed their hardships on a lack of religious respect shown by foreigners and revolutionaries. In one case a mob took Arezzo, then marched on Siena. It's said that they burned to death a number of Jews and Jacobins in the Campo.

Napoleon renamed the Grand Duchy of Tuscany the Kingdom of Etruria (the region's ancient Etruscan name) and gave it to the Bourbons. In 1805 he turned the north of Italy into the Kingdom of Italy, and in 1807 annexed Tuscany. He made his sister Elisa Duchess of Lucca and then Grand Duchess of Tuscany. But Napoleon's regime didn't last long, and after Waterloo the Habsburg-Lorraine dynasty retook control of the region.

The Risorgimento

It was a benign regime and, as Florence, Siena and other Tuscan towns became 'must-see' stops on the Grand Tour, the region became increasingly open to new ideas. The last Grand Duke, Leopold II, also continued to try and reclaim the Maremma, while new railway lines boosted Tuscan trade. But Napoleon's notion of a united Italy had taken root and there was increasing unrest. Leopold was forced to concede to demands for reform and eventually the clamour for unification, the Risorgimento movement, led to the formation of the Kingdom of Italy, with Savoy monarch Vittorio Emanuele II at its head.

Tuscany joined the kingdom in 1860. Five years later, Florence became the capital and seat of the parliament, and Vittorio Emanuele moved into the Pitti Palace. But the city's period of glory was brief as, once Rome was taken into the kingdom in 1870, the seat of power moved south. However, the face of Florence changed a great deal with the building of avenues and roads, the opening of cafés and the destruction of the old market to make way for the Piazza della Repubblica.

The 20th century

In 1915 Italy entered the First World War on the side of the Allies. After the war there was increasing unrest and support for social change, which was deftly exploited by Benito Mussolini, whose Fascist regime marched on Rome in 1922 and seized power. The dictator did finally complete the reclamation of the Maremman marshes, and constructed the Florence-Bologna railway line – but it was hardly a benign regime. In 1940 Mussolini allied Italy to Nazi Germany, and by 1943 Tuscany was being squeezed between the Nazi forces occupying northern Italy and the Allies advancing from the south. Cities like Pisa had already suffered from bombing, but Florence's great beauty initially protected it.

The Tuscan population was divided and included both Nazi sympathizers and resistance fighters. One of the most outstanding figures was Gerhard Wolf, the German Consul in Florence, who saved many partisan lives and also prevented the removal of art treasures to Germany. Partisans sheltered in rural areas like the Val d'Orcia and Monte Amiata, and fighting was fierce. In 1943 Italy switched to the Allied side, and many villages were destroyed as the Germans retreated. The Nazis fled Florence in 1944, destroying all the bridges bar the Ponte Vecchio as they left.

After the war, Italy became a republic and Tuscany finally experienced some peace. And while it may be under increasing pressure from tourists and traffic in the 21st century, it is still managing to maintain an identity that is Italian, yes, but above all Tuscan.

Etruscan walls in Volterra.

Art & architecture

Etruscan & Roman art

Think of Tuscan art and your mind immediately turns to the famous frescoes of the Renaissance. Yet this was not an innovative art form, for the Etruscans had used frescoes thousands of years earlier to decorate their tombs. Colours such as red ochre (from iron oxide) were applied quickly to a wet lime plaster surface: when it dried, the paint was an integral part of the wall. These tombs provide our main insight into Etruscan art, since few other structures survive. They show that while Etruscan art was certainly influenced by that of the Greeks, it had its own distinctive nature. Many scenes depict everyday activities: hunting, dancing, playing musical instruments and feasting. Oh yes, and sex. Some of the best-preserved Etruscan frescoes have been found in Tarquinia, just across the border with Lazio. They contain unmistakeable images of heterosexual and homosexual sex, as well as naked floggings.

Rather more decorous scenes appear on Etruscan cinerary urns, whose carved sides often bore domestic, classical or battle scenes – although at least one has been found showing severed heads, a reminder that enemy heads were said to have been displayed on Etruscan city gates. On top of the urns, you frequently find representations of the deceased, typically reclining and often bearing a reference to their trade or profession (entrails, for example, for a religious diviner) or with items that they liked, such as a mirror. Some urns even show married couples, such as the *Urna degli Sposi* in the Guarnacci Museum in Volterra (see page 279).

The Etruscans were great sculptors, working in stone, alabaster and bronze. The most immediately recognizable Etruscan figure is the *Ombra della Sera*, or 'Shadow of the Evening' (also in the Guarnacci Museum): a rather enigmatic bronze figure, elongated, naked and somehow ageless. Other famous Etruscan works include the *Wounded Chimera of Bellerophon* (in the Archaeological Museum in Florence), which exhibits a savage pain, and the *Haranguer* (or Orator), a toga-clad speaker of the third century BC. This is interesting as it shows how Etruscan art and culture was starting to be absorbed by that of Rome. Then there's the impressive bronze chandelier in the Museum of the Etruscan Academy (MAEC) in Cortona (see page 199). It could hold 16 oil lamps, is covered with a variety of fantastical figures and was obviously intended for some sacred building.

Although the Etruscans imported large quantities of Greek pottery, they were skilled in making ceramics themselves. They are most associated with *bucchero nero* ware, made from a dense black clay with a polished surface.

In today's Tuscany there is little to be seen of Etruscan architecture. That's partly because not all their buildings were made in durable materials, and also because the Romans either destroyed or built over their towns and cities. Roman remains exist in cities like Lucca, with its piazza Anfiteatro, in the Roman theatres at Volterra and Fiesole, and the amphitheatre in Arezzo. But the Etruscans were skilled architects and engineers (they were the first to drain the Maremman swamps) and much of what we associate with Roman cities was, in fact, borrowed from them. Perhaps the most important structure they gave to Rome was the arch, and you can see one of the earliest examples at the city gate in Volterra. Etruscan cities were carefully planned and surrounded by protective walls (take a look at the massive stones of the Etruscan wall in Fiesole). They constructed sewers (including the *Cloaca Maxima* in Rome), designed villas with a central atrium and sloping roof (to channel rainwater) and even came up with a system of underfloor heating. They also constructed roads, such as the via Cave surrounding Pitigliano and Sovana, where you can see Etruscan tombs.

Five of the best

Etruscan sights

1. Etruscan Arch in Volterra (see page 281)
2. Cinerary urns in the Guarnacci Museum, Volterra (see page 279)
3. Etruscan chandelier in MAEC, Cortona (see page 199)
4. Volterra's Roman theatre (see page 280)
5. Via Cave, near Pitigliano (see page 286)

Art of the Middle Ages

Romanesque architecture

Once Christianity was the official religion of the Roman Empire, ecclesiastical architecture became a distinctive feature of the Tuscan landscape. The earliest churches were much altered over the years, so little of their original fabric can be seen today. However, there are some fascinating remains that date back to the first millennium AD. At the Duomo in Florence, for instance, you can see part of the Church of Santa Reparata, built in the fifth or sixth century, while Sovana's cathedral has an eighth-century crypt and beautifully carved *ciborium*. Barga's cathedral dates from the ninth century, and the Collegiata in San Quirico d'Orcia has some fascinating Lombard carvings above a portal. Other ancient churches include Santi Giovanni e Reparata in Lucca, founded in the fourth century, the Pieve di San Leolino in Chianti and the beautiful San Miniato al Monte in Florence, which was built in the 11th century on the site of a much earlier church.

The term 'Romanesque' is used to describe these post-Roman buildings – an architectural style that effectively lasted until the early 13th century in Tuscany. Although little remains of the very earliest ecclesiastical buildings, those of the later Romanesque period are well represented. Romanesque churches in Tuscany generally have

A fresco in the Siena cathedral library.

thick walls and small windows, round arches and columns with carved capitals and arcades. Sometimes Roman columns were re-used, as on the Pieve Santa Maria in Arezzo.

Two distinct types of Romanesque architecture emerged: Pisan and Tuscan. The Pisan style was influenced by its contacts with the Islamic world, the result of its status as a major maritime state. It is exemplified in Pisa's Duomo, which has black and white stripes inside, tiers of blind arcades, and a façade made from different coloured marbles. The Tuscan style is exemplified by Florence's Baptistery, with its geometric design, use of dark and light marble and classical lines, and by San Miniato al Monte. The glowing mosaics in both these buildings also show that Byzantium was still exerting an influence on the Tuscan artistic world. Pisa's Duomo inspired other cities, and you can see examples of Pisan style in Siena's cathedral, at San Michele in Foro in Lucca and in Pistoia.

Gothic architecture

Eventually the Romanesque style gave way to the Gothic, which came to Italy from France. The Cistercians are generally thought to have introduced it when they built their abbey at San Galgano in the 13th century (see page 265). The Gothic style was sharper, with pointed arches and gables, large open naves and large windows. It was not adopted wholesale in Tuscany but exerted a powerful influence, particularly in Siena. The most striking example of the Italian Gothic is Siena's Duomo (see page 157), which had been built in Romanesque style and consecrated in 1179 but was considered to require a facelift in the 13th century. It was enlarged and given a Gothic façade with lavish ornamentation by Giovanni Pisano. In Florence, the Dominican order built the Gothic Church of Santa Maria Novella, with its huge open nave, and in Pisa the Church of Santa Maria della Spina has characteristic Gothic pointed gables.

While the church was a major commissioner of both art and architecture, it was not the only one, and the rise of the *comuni* meant that there were more funds available for secular buildings. These had to have both practical and symbolic functions. Siena, at the peak of its powers between the 12th and 14th centuries, is the most perfectly preserved medieval city, and you can clearly see the Gothic influence, in the pointed arches of the windows around the Campo, for instance. The tower of the Palazzo Pubblico rises high – asserting the authority of the *comune* above that of the vast ecclesiastical symbol of the Duomo.

The need for defence meant that cities were given sturdy walls, like those of Monteriggioni, while wealthy citizens built themselves fortified houses with towers, like those you can still see in San Gimignano. Florence's Palazzo Davanzati (see page 117), a home built in the 14th century, although altered over the years, still has a decidedly medieval appearance.

Medieval painting & sculpture

Art of the early medieval era in Tuscany was heavily influenced by the traditions of Byzantine art, which was highly stylized and devoted to religious subjects. You see this clearly in the works of early Sienese artists, in which conventions are carefully observed – Madonnas have flattened faces, large eyes and elongated bodies and there is generous use of gilding. But the introduction of the Gothic brought influences from northern Europe. Duccio's *Maestà* (see page 156) ushered in a new, more natural, style of Sienese art, which was taken up to great effect by Simone Martini.

The Sienese School of art is generally considered to be more conventional than that of Florence, yet it was Siena that produced some of the most striking examples of secular art in medieval Tuscany. In 1337 the city's ruling council commissioned Ambrogio Lorenzetti to fresco the walls of the Palazzo Pubblico with the *Allegories of Good and Bad Government*. Here was a political message – rule wisely or else. Good Governance shows a happy, well-ordered city peopled with cheery, industrious citizens, with a fertile landscape outside its walls. Bad Governance is quite the opposite – both town and country a sea of misery and horror. Sienese artists also produced the

Five of the best

Places to see art and architecture of the Middle Ages

❶ San Gimignano for its towers (see page 167)
❷ The eighth-century crypt and ciborium of Sovana Cathedral (see page 291)
❸ Pisan Romanesque architecture in Pisa's Campo dei Miracoli (see page 215)
❹ Siena: glorious Tuscan Gothic buildings around the Campo, the Gothic façade on the Duomo, secular frescoes in the Palazzo Pubblico and Simone Martini's Maestà (see page 150)
❺ Florence: the Romanesque Baptistery and San Miniato al Monte; Gothic Santa Maria Novella Church; Giotto's frescoes in Santa Croce; the Palazzo Davanzati (see page 78)

biccherne, the painted ledgers that were first commissioned in 1257. Again the subject matter is frequently secular and provides an insight into the workaday life of Siena and its people.

These aren't the only early secular works in Tuscany. The extraordinary fresco of the *Fonti dell'Abbondanza* in Massa Marittima, which shows local women grabbing phallic fruit from a tree, has been dated to the 13th century. (It's currently under restoration.)

Sculpture also reacted to the new Gothic influences, as you can see in the works of Nicola Pisano. While his first pulpit, in Pisa's Baptistery, clearly shows some elements of Romanesque restraint, the later one he carved with his son Giovanni for Siena's Duomo (see page 157) has figures in more natural poses, their garments in softer folds.

Tuscan artists were also influenced by Byzantine art, as many painted wooden crosses show. The *Volto Santo* in Lucca (see page 227), probably a 13th-century copy of an earlier work, displays a distinctive Byzantine aspect, as does the Crucifix painted by Cimabue in San Domenico Church in Arezzo. But Cimabue was already breaking away from convention, starting to portray Christ as a real man who was capable of suffering, and his pupil Giotto took this further. Vasari said of Giotto: "He made a decisive break with the ... Byzantine style, and brought to life the great art of painting as we know it today, introducing the technique of drawing accurately from life, which had been neglected for more than two hundred years." In Santa Maria Novella in Florence there is a Crucifix by Giotto in which you can clearly see residual elements of the Byzantine inheritance, the influence of Cimabue and a new naturalism. Other works of his in Florence are the fresh and moving frescoes of St Francis in the Bardi Chapel in Santa Croce (see page 113), in which there is not only emotion but a three-dimensional element; and the *Ognissanti Madonna* in the Uffizi (see page 98).

The Renaissance

It was Giorgio Vasari who coined the term *Rinascimento* (Renaissance) to describe the flowering of fresh art and architecture in the 15th and 16th centuries. It refers, in general terms, to a rediscovery of the art and scholarship of the world of classical Greece and Rome – symmetry, proportion, the use of geometry, the works of Plato, Vitruvius and Aristotle. Although the Renaissance was visually played out in art and architecture, it was also a cultural change that spread throughout Europe. And it had its birth in Florence.

Humanism

The Pisanos and Giotto – and indeed Ambrogio Lorenzetti – were ahead of their time, but their work showed that artists were beginning to shake off the bonds of convention. Writers had also paved the way for Renaissance thinking. The poet and philosopher Petrarch (1304-74), who was born in Arezzo, felt that much had been lost by the neglect of the classical world during the Dark Ages. He espoused a humanist view of the world, with an emphasis on reason and human achievement, which did not have to be at odds with religious worship. He is generally claimed to be the first person since the classical era to have climbed a mountain for the sheer pleasure of it, something that made him focus on his 'inner life'. Dante Alighieri (1265-1321) broke with convention to write his *Divine Comedy* in Tuscan dialect rather than Latin – he's known as the father of the Italian language; and Boccaccio (1313-75) author of the *Decameron*, which was said to have influenced Chaucer, also studied the classics, wrote in 'Italian' and took a humanist approach.

Renaissance thinking allowed a new focus on the individual and encouraged an intellectual curiosity. The plague that swept through Tuscany in 1348 is thought to have played a part in creating a climate amenable to new ways of thinking: either shattering faith and encouraging people to focus on earthly rather than spiritual matters, or inspiring them to new heights of devotion, which they expressed in artistic endeavour, or funding that endeavour. Whether this is the case or not, it can certainly be said that the plague hit Siena so hard that it effectively ended the city's distinctive school of art, leaving Florence, which though devastated had recovered better, to take centre stage. And Florence, most importantly, had the Medici.

Top Renaissance sights in Florence

Michelangelo's *David* – Accademia
Donatello's *David* – Bargello
Masaccio's *Trinity* – Santa Maria Novella – and his frescoes in the Brancacci Chapel
Fra Angelico's *Annunciation* – San Marco
Botticelli's *Primavera* and *Birth of Venus* – Uffizi
Leonardo's *Annunciation* – Uffizi
Brunelleschi's Dome

Detail from inside the dome.

Wealth & patronage

The wealth, intellectual curiosity, piety – and desire to impress – of the Medici banking dynasty meant that there was no shortage of funds to encourage artists to new heights. And flourishing trade meant that there were rich guilds and a clutch of other well-heeled families who were also keen to patronise the best artists of the day: not just for their own glory, but to get one up on rival towns.

Many art historians attribute the 'official' start of the Renaissance to the doors that Ghiberti carved for the Baptistery (see page 89), which seem to provide a bridge between the Gothic and the Renaissance. Others refer to Brunelleschi's dome, a combination of masterly engineering and soaring beauty that he achieved thanks to his study of classical architecture and mathematics. Then there is Donatello's *St George* carved for the Orsanmichele (now in the Bargello, see page 101), a classical statue but imbued with individuality. Another major early Renaissance figure was Masaccio, a pioneer of the use of perspective, as you can see in his extraordinary *trompe l'oeil* fresco of the *Trinity* in Santa Maria Novella, and in his vivid frescoes in the Brancacci Chapel at Santa Maria del Carmine (see page 124).

The Renaissance did not simply revive the art of the classical world, but drew on it to create something new. Cosimo Il Vecchio proved an important artistic patron when he commissioned Donatello to create his bronze *David*, now in the Bargello (see page 101), the first free-standing nude sculpture of the modern era. He also employed Michelozzo to build the restrained Palazzo Medici-Riccardi and the Dominican monastery of

San Marco (see page 166), with its classically proportioned cloister and frescoes by Fra Angelico. Guilds funded new works too, one of the most notable of which is the *Spedale degli Innocenti* (see page 107), Europe's first orphanage, which was designed by Brunelleschi. It exhibits a serene classical harmony.

Perhaps the most ambitious project of the Renaissance was Pope Pius II's remodelling of his home village of Corsignano (see page 225). Perched on a hill to the south of Siena, Corsignano was never going to make it on the world stage until the Pope employed a Florentine architect, Bernardo Rossellino, to turn it into an idealized Renaissance city. Interestingly, in a move that recalls Petrarch's appreciation of the landscape from a mountain, he ensured that buildings in Pienza (as the village was renamed) harmonized with nature and made the most of natural light and views.

The renewed focus on the classical world had led to an interest in geometry, mathematics and perspective. Fra Angelico used perspective in a way that helped bring both spiritual and visual depth to his work. Paolo Uccello, whose work includes the equestrian fresco of Sir John Hawkwood in Florence's Duomo, became obsessed by it and experimented with it almost as a technical exercise. And Piero della Francesca, whose most famous work is the *Legend of the True Cross* fresco cycle at San Francesco in Arezzo (see page 193), even wrote treatises on the subject. Classical mythology also became a subject for Renaissance painters, who imbued it with a distinct sensuality, as exemplified by Sandro Botticelli's *Birth of Venus* and *Primavera* in the Uffizi.

The High Renaissance

This term is used to describe the period around 1500 to the 1520s. In Florence this was a time of turmoil, with the Medici expelled from the city, and Savonarola lighting his Bonfire of the Vanities (in which many Renaissance paintings went up in flames). Three major figures are most associated with the High Renaissance, the first of whom is Leonardo da Vinci. It is impossible to do justice to Leonardo in a few words: his keen mind, his interest in science, his subtle handling of light and shade, and his ability to portray character, drama and emotion made him the ultimate Renaissance man. Younger than Leonardo by some years was Michelangelo, whose *David* was created to celebrate the return of the Florentine Republic. The two apparently loathed one another. In Charles Nicholl's biography of Leonardo, *Flights of the Mind*, he repeats an eyewitness account of a time the artists met in the street. Michelangelo, thinking Leonardo had insulted him, mocked the master: "... you who designed a horse to cast in bronze, and couldn't cast it, and abandoned it out of shame." The third figure of the period was Raphael, who drew on the work of both Leonardo and Michelangelo to create gentle works of his own.

From Mannerism to the Macchiaioli

Florence had been at the heart of the Renaissance, but after 1520 the focus of the art world began to shift away from the city. Leonardo had left it early in the century and died in France, and Michelangelo had moved to Rome where he was working for the Pope.

Mannerism

It was the grandeur and the posed, mannered style of some of Michelangelo's work that ushered in the Mannerist movement, characterized by works that were more calculated and less classically harmonious than Renaissance art. In Mannerist paintings figures tended to be elongated, and there was a use of very bright, clear colours. In Florence, in the Church of Santa Felicità (see page 122), you can see an early example of a Mannerist work – Jacopo Pontormo's *Deposition*, a painting that has an unusual and dramatic composition and uses vivid colour. And in the Uffizi gallery, Parmigiano's *Madonna with the Long Neck* exemplifies the Mannerist tendency to distort and exaggerate figures. One of the most mocked artworks in Florence is Mannerist: Ammannati's bulky *Neptune*

Fountain (see page 92), which Michelangelo thought was a waste of good marble.

It was around this time that Vasari put considerable efforts into glorifying his Medici patrons: on the ceiling of the Salone del Cinquecento in the Palazzo Pubblico, for instance. He also painted over many earlier frescoes in the churches of Santa Croce and Santa Maria Novella, not being a fan of earlier medieval works.

Villas & gardens

The 16th and 17th centuries saw a growth in the building and embellishment of rural villas in Tuscany, notably around Lucca and Florence. The Romans, of course, had established the idea of having a nice place in the country, and the Medici had taken up the idea with enthusiasm, often buying existing buildings and converting them. Cosimo il Vecchio commissioned Michelozzo to build the Renaissance Villa Medici in Fiesole, and Lorenzo the Magnificent employed a vast army of craftsmen to build Poggio a Caiano, a grand rural residence outside Florence. This was altered by successive occupants over the years and shows a real mix of styles. The gardens were also altered according to changing fashions: in the 19th century, they were largely turned into English-style parkland. The Pitti Palace and Boboli Gardens were also subject to changes in contemporary tastes, with new incumbents making sure that they put their stamp on the estate.

Between the 16th and the 19th centuries villas also appeared in the countryside around Lucca, as wealthy residents took the chance to make a statement. The styles ranged from neoclassical to Baroque. A great garden was essential for any self-respecting villa owner, and the Lucchese villas are set off by suitably impressive examples, with citrus trees, fountains and statues.

The 17th century saw the growth of the baroque style, characterized by a lush theatricality in features such as scenes of celestial glories on ceilings. It was a style that spread from Rome and never really flourished in Tuscany. The most striking, and surely tasteless, example of the baroque in Florence is the marble-covered mausoleum of the *Capella dei Principi* (Chapel of the Princes) in San Lorenzo Church (see page 109).

Contemporary art

The Renaissance is a mighty weight of art history to bear, but there are contemporary artists in Tuscany willing to brave the challenge. Names to watch for are Massimo Bartolini, from Cecina near Livorno, who creates experiential artworks that play with space, light and even perfume, and Gianfranco Masi, a video artist. If you enjoy contemporary art you might also like to visit the garden created on the slopes of Monte Amiata by Swiss artist Daniel Spoerri (near Seggiano, 80 km south of Siena, open Easter-Oct, danielspoerri.org), which contains 87 installations by over 40 artists.

The Macchiaioli

The most distinctive Tuscan art of the 19th century was produced by the Macchiaioli artists, who developed a form of Impressionism. They focused on light and shade, and produced works that at the time were thought to look unfinished, but now look deliciously fresh. The best known of the Macchiaioli is Giovanni Fattori (1825-1908), who took inspiration from the landscapes and people of the Maremma. You can see his work in the Galleria d'Arte Moderna in the Pitti Palace.

A young couple gaze over Florence.

Tuscany today

Buying property in Tuscany

There's a small farmhouse with a terracotta tiled roof, shutters at the windows and scarlet geraniums tumbling from pots by the door. There's a garden filled with plump tomatoes, flowers and fragrant basil, and perhaps a field with a few olive trees as well. And there's you and your family enjoying dinner al fresco in your own little corner of Tuscany.

It's easy to get carried away with the thought of buying into the Tuscan dream, of buying a wrecked barn and turning it into a fabulous holiday home, or retiring there to live the good life. Even though the credit crunch has showed us all that property isn't the fail-safe investment we once thought, Tuscany still exerts a pull on the imagination that can make you throw caution to the winds.

The thing to remember is to take your time, think carefully about what you want and, above all, ensure that you get proper advice.

The property

Tuscan property isn't particularly cheap – if you want a bargain, look elsewhere in Italy. The wrecked barns and farms in Chianti that went for a song in the 1960s and 1970s have long gone. If you do want to buy in Tuscany, check out areas such as the Garfagnana, the countryside near Volterra and the inland Maremma, where prices aren't as high as in Chianti or hill towns like Cortona. And while everyone loves the idea of a rural property, perhaps an apartment or small house in a town or village might be a more practical – and cheaper – bet. You might also think of buying in a recently restored *borgo* (hamlet), where everything has already been done.

If you find a property that needs renovation, bear in mind the costs involved – you could pay around €1,000 per square metre. There are strict planning laws, and you'll have to use original materials (or at least good copies) as far as possible. And can you be on site to supervise the work?

If you do want to buy in Tuscany, check out areas such as the Garfagnana, the countryside near Volterra and the inland Maremma, where prices aren't as high as in Chianti or hill towns like Cortona.

Check out the area carefully too, and see what it's like at different times of day. And remember that Tuscany can get very cold in winter.

Useful websites

italianproperty.eu.com
tuscanhomes.com
keyitaly.com
homesinitaly.co.uk
casatravella.com

Getting there

Think about how you're going to use the property. Are you going to live there, or will it be a second home? If it's the latter you must cost in the price of getting there several times a year. And you don't want to be reliant on just one low-cost airline. With fuel prices rising, routes could be cut – so make sure you've got back-up options.

The purchase

Don't rush into things – use a reputable agent (registered with the local chamber of commerce), and ideally both an Italian lawyer and one in your own country. When you see something you like, you'll be asked to sign a reservation contract and pay a 10% deposit. Before the next stage, you should get a survey done by a *geometra* (surveyor/architect), and be sure to check out things like boundaries and rights of way as well. You'll also need to check that the property has been correctly registered, has planning permission, and whether there are any outstanding debts or claims on it.

The next stage is to sign a *compromesso*, or preliminary contract. This binds you into buying the property. You'd be asked to pay a deposit of about a third of the purchase price – which you'll lose if you later pull out of the deal. If you need to arrange an Italian mortgage, remember that it can only be for a maximum of 80% of the property price. The loan period may be 10, 15, 25 or 30 years.

The final stage is the *rogito*, completion of sale – you'll usually need to be present for this and funds will need to be in place. You'll need to pay in euros so your money transfer should be arranged.

Fees & taxes

Don't forget about other costs – agency fees, purchase tax (10% of the value for a second home), notary (lawyer) fees, *geometra* fees, translation costs – and then annual taxes for refuse, TV licence and the property.

Useful websites

ToscAMA toscama.com,

Italy Weddings italyweddings.com

Getting Married in Italy gettingmarriedinitaly.com

Italian Wedding Services italianweddingservices.com

Getting married in Tuscany

More and more people are drawn to the idea of getting married in Tuscany. You get a romantic wedding location, guests get a few days in the sun and your honeymoon is sorted.

Italian weddings are becoming increasingly easy to arrange, with many agencies specializing in organizing everything from the paperwork to the flowers. A lot of hotels, especially those within rural locations with pretty churches nearby, are geared up for weddings too. They can stage the reception, do the catering and also accommodate all the guests. Make sure you plan well ahead to allow time to book the venue, arrange catering, flowers and a photographer, accommodation for you and your guests, and time to ensure all the paperwork goes through correctly and on time.

Of course, bureaucracy makes its presence felt in a Tuscan wedding, just as it does in all aspects of Italian life. So use a reputable agency that will tell you exactly what paperwork you'll need to provide. This varies with your home country, but in general you'll at least need to provide your birth certificate, passport and, if one of you has been married before, either a divorce decree or death certificate of former spouse. All the paperwork must be in place to be checked in Italy about three days before the service.

The ceremony

Think carefully about the type of ceremony you want. If one of you is a Roman Catholic, then you can get married in a Catholic church, but you'll also need to show that you have permission from your local bishop, proof of attendance at marriage preparation classes and proof of baptism, first communion and confirmation. If you're divorced that complicates matters more. If you want a Protestant, Jewish or other faith wedding, there will be different requirements.

A civil ceremony is probably the most straightforward option and is legally recognized worldwide. It must take place in the Town Hall and will be carried out in Italian. An interpreter must be present for non-Italian speakers, as well as witnesses.

Tuscany is the perfect setting for a wedding.

Living with the past

Tuscany is famously conservative, a prosperous but provincial place where the past is not another country but a vital part of everyday life. Surrounded by such a wealth of Renaissance and medieval buildings perhaps that's not surprising. What is remarkable is that the region has – largely – avoided the overt Disneyfication that you might think would be inevitable in such a popular tourist destination. It's not so much that Tuscans resist change, just that they don't see the need for it. Go into a Tuscan home and you'll usually find a surprisingly old-fashioned kitchen and items of furniture that have been passed down through the family. This isn't because they're mean (though Florentines are considered famously stingy), it's just that they think if it works, and it's good quality – why change it? It's this philosophy that explains why ancient crafts – whether sculpting in marble or making gold jewellery – still flourish.

Of course Tuscany has changed a great deal, particularly since the Second World War. With the ending of the *mezzadria* (sharecropping) system, thousands of people left the land, and in the 1960s and 1970s rural areas such as Chianti experienced an influx of foreigners who bought up properties. Tourism has been part of the economy since the days of the medieval pilgrimage, and later the Grand Tour, but it's now reached such levels that sheer weight of numbers threatens to ruin the very things people come to see (literally in the case of Michelangelo's *David*, which experts fear could crack due to the vibrations caused by visitors' feet).

Somehow, however, this region – less industrialized than northern Italy, less laid back than the south – retains its character. This is best summed up by the word *campanilismo* – allegiance to one's own bell tower. The ancient rivalries that saw independent city states such as Florence, Siena and Pisa fight one another ferociously for power have not entirely been forgotten. And within towns and cities, different districts or *contrade* still stage annual contests that can be traced back to medieval times.

Tuscans take pride in their community and its traditions. That's why farmers still harvest olives in the old-fashioned way, why crops are grown organically and people eat locally sourced, produce. All of which is, ironically, very modern.

The golden landscape of an autumn vineyard.

Nature & environment

In our imagination there is just one Tuscan landscape, one where undulating fields roll up to a hilltop town and cypress trees jut from the ground like darkened daggers. There might be sunflowers, a patch of olive trees or heavily laden vines.

But there is much more to Tuscany than this – variety is part of its magic. The region can boast some wonderfully diverse landscapes, ranging from the craggy peaks of the Apennines to the soft clay soils of the Crete Senese. Here you are never far from a sandy beach, a well tended vineyard or a lush green wood.

The mountainous north

The Apennine range is essentially the backbone of Tuscany. The northern reaches, which border Emilia-Romagna, are the highest – people can ski in winter at Abetone, north of Pistoia. In the northwest corner, running roughly parallel with the coast, are the Apuan Alps, the mountains that have for centuries been quarried for their marble. Their heights provide a home for a number of birds of prey: buzzards, peregrine falcons, kites, short-toed eagles and golden eagles have all been sighted. The symbol of the area is another bird, the sea-crow or chough, which may be spotted on a few peaks. The Apennines and Apuan Alps were once the habitat of wolves, and there are still sightings of this much persecuted mammal.

Also in northern Tuscany, squeezed between the Apennines and the Apuan Alps north of Lucca, is the Garfagnana, a rugged river valley characterized by slopes thickly clad with beech and chestnut trees, sparkling streams and isolated hamlets. Wildlife such as wild boar (*cinghiale*), mouflon – a mountain sheep that looks more like a goat – and birds of prey inhabit the area. The chestnut is an integral part of life in the Garfagnana, providing both fuel and food for the local people. Then there is the Casentino, an area of mountain and thick forest north of Arezzo, and the hills of the Mugello northeast of Florence. The ancestral home of the Medici, who used it as their hunting ground, the fertile lower lands of the Mugello are farmed and dotted with olive groves and vineyards – on land that is frequently terraced to make cultivation easier. The higher ground – a mix of oak, chestnut and beech wood – is home to a population of crested porcupines. The animal was introduced from Africa by the Romans and unexpectedly flourishes in many parts of Tuscany.

Chianti & the south

South of the Arno, the river that rises near Arezzo and flows through Florence and Pisa to the sea, the landscape changes quite dramatically. The best-known region is Chianti, where the rough terrain is dotted with world-famous vineyards and slopes that bristle with oak trees, chestnuts and pine trees. This isn't fertile farmland, but the stony soil is ideal for growing grapes, while in autumn the forests provide a rich harvest of delicious mushrooms – particularly porcini.

Perhaps the most characteristic Tuscan landscape lies to the south of Siena. Here there is gently rolling farmland, fields planted with sunflowers and sweetcorn, vineyards, olive groves, cypress trees that pierce the sky and medieval towns perched high on the tops of steep-sided

Nature reserves & parks in Tuscany

If you're keen on watching wildlife or walking, cycling or riding in quiet corners of the countryside, Tuscany's nature reserves and protected areas are well worth exploring. Visitor centres in each park give useful introductions to what you can see and do within them. National parks are:

- Parco Nazionale delle Foreste Casentinesi, Monte Falterona, Campigna to the north of Arezzo, bordering Emilia-Romagna.
- Parco Nazionale dell'Appennino Tosco-Emiliano, in the northwest, shared with Emilia-Romagna.
- Parco Nazionale dell'Arcipelago Toscano, the largest protected marine area in Europe

There are also many regional parks and nature reserves. Go to parks.it for more information.

A Chalkhill Blue butterfly.

Lying between Volterra and Massa Marittima are the Metal Hills. It's an area that looks and feels wild and lonely, a land apart from the rest of Tuscany.

hills. Here too is the strange landscape of the Crete Senese, an almost treeless expanse of thick clay soil gashed by erosion channels known as *calanchi*. Further south is Monte Amiata, an extinct volcano that at 1,738 m is the highest peak in Tuscany. There are thick beech woods and a number of nature reserves here – it's a very popular area for walking, mountain biking, riding and even winter sports. The wildlife of Monte Amiata includes the ubiquitous wild boar, deer, birds of prey, reptiles such as vipers and Hermann tortoises, and even wild cats and skunks.

Mineral resources

To the west, lying between Volterra and Massa Marittima are the Colline Metallifere, or Metal Hills. It's an area that looks and feels wild and lonely, a land apart from the rest of Tuscany. The hills have been mined for their metals since Etruscan times – they are rich in lodes of copper, lead, iron and silver. It was in this area too, at Lake Cerchiaio near Monterotondo, that boric acid was discovered in the 18th century. Monterotondo became the centre of production of this chemical, which was used as an antiseptic, in the making of ceramics, and now in the nuclear industry. In this area, and also around southeastern towns such as Saturnia,

A typical Tuscan view.

On the beach at Grosseto.

are geothermal pools of bubbling mud and searing hot springs that shoot from the earth, hissing and spitting like savage beasts.

Coastal areas

The Tuscan coast is different again. The northern stretch is, in general, heavily developed – especially in areas such as Viareggio and Livorno. Large stretches of beach are private and covered with neat ranks of sun beds and umbrellas. But the southern section is not quite so commercialized, and the protected coastal plain of the Maremma by the Uccellina Mountains is thankfully unspoilt. The Maremma was nicknamed 'La Miseria' in Italy, for the marshes that characterized the area were a prime breeding ground for the malarial mosquito. It was a poor, sparsely populated region, and still has few major centres today, even though the land was successfully reclaimed in Mussolini's time.

Here there are umbrella pine trees, cork oaks and areas of Mediterranean maquis (macchia) – scrubland with dwarf oaks, laurel, myrtle, aromatic rosemary and lavender. It's rich in birdlife (which suffers badly from the Italian passion for hunting in other parts of Tuscany), thanks in particular to the presence of the lagoon at Orbetello. In the Uccellina you can see flamingos, stilts, hoopoes, egrets, herons and maybe even bee-eaters, a kingfisher or an osprey. Maremman wild mammals include porcupines, roe deer and wild boar – an indigenous species that is smaller than those you'll find elsewhere in Tuscany. Off the coast of the Maremma is the Tuscan Archipelago, encompassing Elba and Giglio as well as smaller islands like Montecristo. This is a great area for diving, with rich marine life.

Festivals & events

Festivals play an important role in Tuscany. It's a region in which traditions are part of the rhythm of daily life – they're certainly not there just to entertain the tourists. Many festivals are related to the church calendar: saints' feast days and Easter, for example. There are also art, film and music festivals – mainly held in the cities. The most important, and distinctive, festivals of all are those that celebrate local food and wine. Too numerous to name, they are held in towns and villages throughout Tuscany, and are evidence of the close link that still exists between the people and their land.

Giostra del Saracino, Arezzo.

February

Carnevale
Viareggio, T0584-184 0750, viareggio.ilcarnevale.com.
Lively carnival dating back to the 19th-century.

March

Torciata di San Giuseppe (19th)
Pitigliano
A torchlight procession, followed by a bonfire to herald the start of spring.

April

Scoppio del Carro (Explosion of the Cart)
Florence, Easter Sunday
A cart loaded with fireworks and pulled by oxen is taken in a colourful, costumed procession through the city, from Porto al Prato to the Duomo.

May

Festa del Grillo (Festival of the Cricket)
Florence, Ascension Day

Gioco del Ponte, Pisa.

Brightly coloured crickets (now usually artificial ones) are sold in cages on the Sunday following Ascension Day, then released for good luck. There are other stalls too, and it's an occasion for family picnics.

Maggio Musicale Fiorentino (May Music Festival)
maggiofiorentino.com
Major music festival featuring opera, classical music and ballet.

Giostra dell'Archidado
Medieval crossbow competition, Cortona, late May.

June

Estate Fiesolana (Fiesole Summer Festival)
estatefiesolana.it
This is a general performing arts festival in Fiesole, with jazz, chamber music and theatre. Runs June to early September. Most events are held in the Roman theatre.

Calcio Storico (Football in Costume)
calciostorico.it
Held on 24 June, the feast day of Florence's patron, St John the Baptist, this is a football game thought to have its origins in Roman times. It's played, in costume, in piazza Santa Croce – and has a tendency to turn violent. Each of the four historic quarters of the city fields a team. On the same day there's a procession through the city and a fireworks display on piazzale Michelangelo.

Giostra dell'Orso
Pistoia
The Joust of the Bear on 15 June involves a costumed parade and a jousting contest between the town's four *contrade*.

Gioco del Ponte
Pisa
A sort of 'push of war' – rather than tug of war – on the last Sunday in June, in which rival *contrade* push a heavy cart across the ponte di Mezzo, on the Arno.

Giostra del Saracino
Arezzo, giostradelsaracino.arezzo.it (penultimate Sat of Jun in the evening, and first Sun of Sep in the afternoon)
Jousting contest in which contestants try to hit an effigy of a Saracen to win the Golden Lance.

Festa del Barbarossa (third Sunday)
Medieval festival of flag waving and crossbow competitions. San Quirico d'Orcia.

July

Il Palio (2nd)
This is the first of the Palios and takes place at 1930 in the Campo.

Torre del Lago Puccini Festival
T0584-359322, puccinifestival.it
Major opera festival, staging Puccini's works outdoors.

Siena Jazz
Fortezza Medicea, T0577-271401, sienajazz.it
Major jazz festival, venues in the city centre and surrounding villages. Late July and early August.

Carnival time in Viareggio.

Montalcino Jazz and Wine
T0577-849331, montalcinojazzandwine.com
Popular jazz festival held in the fortezza, with a chance to taste the local wine as well.

Volterra Teatro
T0588-80038, volterrateatro.it
International theatre festival in Volterra, which lasts around 10-15 days in July. Various venues in the city.

Opera Barga
T0583-723250
Opera and classical music concerts at the end of July in this medieval town in the Garfagnana.

August

Fish and Chip Festival
Barga's Scottish connections are celebrated in mid-August with a communal meal of fish and chips, eaten at long tables in the streets.

Il Palio (16th)
This is the second of the Palios. The race takes place at 1900.

Tuscan Sun Festival (Festival del Sole)
Ticket office, open Jul and Aug, T0575-62767 festivaldelsole.com
This is a cultural festival, celebrating music, art, literature and food, held in Cortona in early August.

Cortonantiquaria
cortonantiquaria.it
This is the oldest antique furniture fair in Italy, with large numbers of dealers coming to the little town.

Sagra della Bistecca
This outdoor food festival in Cortona is a celebration of the local Valdichiana beef.

Volterra Jazz
T0588-86099, volterra-jazz.net
Annual jazz festival held in mid Aug.

Volterra AD1398 (third and fourth Sunday)
T0588-87257, volterra1398.it.
Medieval festival with plenty of street stalls, crafts and entertainment.

Bruscello (14-16th)
Montepulciano
Actors re-enact events in the town's history, on the occasion of the Festival of Assumption.

Torneo della Apertura della Caccia (second Sunday)
Montalcino
Celebration of the traditional start of the hunting season, with medieval parades and contests.

Bravio delle Botti (last Sunday)
Montepulciano
The town's *contrade* roll heavy barrels uphill through the centre – the winner receiving a cloth banner (*bravio*).

Folk festival, Pisa.

Palio Marinario (15th)
Porto Santo Stefano, Monte Argentario
A maritime version of the Palio, with teams from local districts competing in a rowing race.

Balestro del Girafalco (second Sunday)
Massa Marittima
Medieval parade, flag waving displays and a crossbow competition.

September

Cacio al Fuso (first Sunday)
Pienza
A celebration of the town's famous pecorino cheese, with plenty of chances to sample it.

Astludio (first Sunday)
comune.volterra.pi.it. Volterra
Medieval flag waving contest.

La Rificolona (Festival of the Lanterns)
Dating back to the times when country people would walk into Florence holding lanterns to celebrate the Virgin's birthday on 7 September, today it's a procession of children, who carry lanterns to piazza Santissima Annunziata.

Settembre Lucchese (13th)
Lucca
The *Volto Santo* (Holy Face) is paraded through the town. The city's most important festival.

Siena Film Festival
sienafilmfestival.it.
The city's very popular film festival.

Palio della Balestra (second Sunday)
Sansepolcro
This costumed medieval festival involves a crossbow competition between teams from Sansepolcro and Gubbio.

Chianti Classico Wine Festival (second Sunday)
Greve in Chianti
Celebration of the region's famous wine.

October

Castiglione d'Orcia Chestnut Festival (last Sunday)
Lots of chances to taste dishes made from the local chestnuts. Particularly focused on the hamlets of Vivo and Campiglia.

Volterra Gusto
volterragusto.com. Volterra
A celebration of local food and wines, starting with cheese and ending with olive oil.

November

Siena International Short Film Festival
ortoitaliacinema.com
This event screens short films, animations and documentaries from around the world.

Florence Marathon (fourth Sunday)
firenzemarathon.it, Florence
Annual race starting at piazzale Michelangelo and finishing at piazza Santa Croce.

Mostra del Tartufo Bianco delle Crete Senesi (second and third weekend)
San Giovanni d'Asso
White truffle festival. The village fills up with stalls selling local white truffles.

December

Festa dell'Olio (first weekend)
San Quirico d'Orcia
Olive oil festival. There are lots of stalls giving you the chance to taste the new season's olive oil (a bit like trying the new Beaujolais), as well as street bands.

Val D'Orcia.

Sleeping

There is no shortage of accommodation in Tuscany, and the range of places to stay is enormous. You can find anything from a five-star hotel to a room on a farm. There are private rooms in historic residences, family-run bed-and-breakfast establishments (B&Bs), self-catering apartments, campsites and villas in the countryside. What you won't find is anything particularly cheap, as Tuscany is such a popular tourist destination. Luckily this does also mean that the general standard of accommodation is pretty high. Many properties are historic, so you will find many that don't have lifts or easy access – do check this on booking if it could be a problem.

Prices

Both prices and standards will vary depending on the part of the region you're staying in: Florence is by far the most expensive place to stay, and Chianti comes in a close second. However, both these areas also have some of the region's most charming hotels and *agriturismi*. There are fewer high quality places to stay in the Maremma, outside the swish coastal resorts, as tourism is less developed in the area, but prices there are lower. All establishments must display their prices, at reception and in the rooms, though these will usually be the top rates they'd quote.

You should expect to pay from €100-150 per double room in most places for accommodation graded three stars or above – but this can rise considerably, to well over €400 for the most luxurious (five-star) hotels in Florence and Chianti. If you want a single room you'll pay a bit more than if you were sharing.

Prices usually include breakfast, but do check this as it's becoming increasingly common – especially in top-of-the-range establishments – to charge separately for breakfast. In high season, especially in agriturismi, you have to book for a minimum of two or three nights even if you are just staying on a bed-and-breakfast basis. Some places, again often agriturismi, insist that you stay on a half-board basis, with an evening meal included in the price.

Self-catering apartments and villas are usually let for a minimum of a week. With these you are likely to be charged for extras like laundry, cleaning services, electricity and so on – check these out when you first book, otherwise you can get an unwelcome surprise at the end of your stay. Serviced apartments, however, should include cleaning costs in their prices.

As you'd expect, prices vary considerably with the season. They're lowest between November to March, highest at times like Easter and July. The coastal resorts are busiest and most expensive in July and August. However, because Florence gets so hot and humid, it tends to be quieter in August and accommodation prices generally drop. Conversely, the fashion shows held in the city in January push up prices in the top hotels. Siena has a limited number of good central hotels, and high season here is around the Palio – 2 July and 16 August – as well as Easter and from late August to early October, when the mosaic floors of the Duomo are uncovered.

Booking

Do book well in advance to secure the accommodation you want in Tuscany. The best *agriturismi* are frequently booked six months in advance, and it's a good idea to try and book this well ahead for hotels or B&Bs too. An increasing number of hotels, particularly the larger ones, don't publish set prices but vary their rates depending on levels of occupancy. More and more bookings are done on the internet, and sometimes you can get better rates that way. It's always worth asking for a special deal if you're going outside peak season. The strength of the euro against the pound and the dollar in the last couple of years has led to a drop in the number of tourists visiting Tuscany, so hoteliers are more amenable to bargaining.

Above: Gritti Hotel. Above right: Down-to-earth comfort.

Always get confirmation of your accommodation in writing – and confirm it again a day or so before you arrive. Also let people know roughly what time you'll be arriving – you don't want your remote B&B to give away your room because they think you're not coming. Remember that most hotels on the coast, and in smaller centres such as Massa Marittima, close down for the winter – generally between November and March.

If you want a room with a view (and who doesn't in Tuscany) you'll need to pay extra and should specify on booking. It's also worth checking whether your room overlooks a noisy road.

You'll be asked for your passport at reception, as accommodation providers have to register you with the police. You should get it back quickly. Some B&Bs, small hotels and rental rooms don't accept credit cards – so do check this when you book.

Hotels

Hotels are graded on a star system, with one star the lowest grade and five stars the highest. A *pensione*, a term no longer officially used, would generally be described as a one- or two-star hotel. You might well have no private bathroom in lower grade hotels – so check when booking.

While the star system is a good guide, you'll find considerable variations – especially in three-star establishments in different provinces, and even in the same location. The television in your room, for example, might be an old one stuck high on a shelf or a sleek plasma screen model tastefully displayed. Furniture can also vary from antique or reproduction pieces to a strange array of stuff that looks as if it's come from a junk store.

One of the many city sightseeing tours.

The bedrooms in Italian hotels have a tendency not to live up to the promise of the reception area. If you're booking your accommodation on the internet, you'll generally be able to see photographs of the *camere* (rooms). If you haven't booked in advance and are just turning up off the street, do ask to see some rooms first. And if you turn up and aren't happy with your room, ask if you can have a different one. But don't be aggressive – that won't get you anywhere here.

Checkout times vary from 1000 to 1200. You might be charged for an extra day if you don't check out in time, but if you ask for a late checkout hotels will often oblige with an extra hour or so if they're not busy.

Agriturismi

In some places, like Chianti, you could be forgiven for thinking that every farm is an *agriturismo*. The true *agriturismo* is a working farm that grows or makes its own food or wine. You either stay in a converted barn or outbuilding (usually self-catering) or on a B&B basis in the main house. However, the market has grown so much that the term *agriturismo* now seems to be applied very loosely to any rural property. The best ones offer things like home-grown food, a swimming pool and a relaxed, welcoming atmosphere.

B&Bs/rooms

Staying at a B&B you can expect a room, usually with private bathroom, in a family home or historic property. Then there are *affiticamere*, or rooms to rent, which may also be in private houses or historic buildings. Some are self-catering (they often have a little kitchen), some offer you the option of breakfast. There will be a reception but there won't necessarily be someone there, or on the premises, all the time.

Useful websites

Villas
renttuscany.com
to-tuscany.com
invitationtotuscany.com
holiday-rentals.co.uk
luxuryexplorer.com
selectresorts.co.uk
timeaway.co.uk
realholidays.co.uk
simplytravel.co.uk
tuscanynow.com
totstoitaly.co.uk

Agriturismi
agriturismo.net
agriturismo.com
agriitalia.it
agriturist.it

B&Bs
uniquehomestays.com
bbitalia.it

Camping and mobile homes
thomsonalfresco.co.uk
ecvacanze.it (Elite Club Vacanze)

Pistachio ice cream.

Eating & drinking

The Italian nickname for Tuscans is *mangiafagioli* ('bean eaters') – a disparaging reference to the region's traditional reliance on beans as a staple foodstuff. There's no doubt this humble ingredient plays a major role in Tuscan cuisine, which is essentially rustic, but don't think this means you won't eat well here. Tuscans take their food as seriously as they take their appearance – more so in fact – and the style of cooking cleverly combines extreme simplicity with great sophistication. Throughout Tuscany you will find dishes based primarily on a few simple, and extremely fresh, ingredients prepared in a way that highlights their respective flavours. Slow cooking is a feature: nothing is rushed and dishes are eaten separately so that you can fully appreciate what you're eating. When you order a plate of beans you get just that, beans; your salad or meat would comprise another course. Seasonal dishes are also a feature – *funghi* (mushrooms) and chestnuts in the autumn, artichokes in early summer, for instance.

A poor man's feast

Traditional Tuscan cuisine is a *cucina povera*, or 'poor man's cuisine' since, until recent years at least, most people survived on whatever they could grow, hunt or gather. That wasn't too difficult given the productiveness of the landscape, with its fertile fields, dense woodlands filled with chestnuts and mushrooms, abundant herbs, and numerous animals like wild boar and rabbits. Nothing ever went to waste, and even today everything, from calves' tongues and brains to tripe and pigs' trotters, is still painstakingly turned into meals. Every Tuscan must know a hundred ways with leftovers. Yet although meat features prominently, Tuscan food is excellent for vegetarians and many dishes are entirely based on vegetables or beans. Look out for delicious *fagioli al fiasco* – beans cooked in a flask (*fiasco*) with olive oil and black pepper – or pasta such as pappardelle with porcini mushrooms. Bear in mind that soups might be made with meat stock, so check when ordering.

While Tuscan cuisine is different to that of other parts of Italy, it also varies throughout the region, and different areas have their own specialities or versions of classic dishes.

Above and below: Fresh natural produce from the region.

Local specialities

While Tuscan cuisine is different from that of other parts of Italy, it also varies throughout the region, and different areas have their own specialities or versions of classic dishes. Viareggio, on the coast, has a special fish soup called *cacciucco*, which is made with several types of fish and seafood (perhaps cuttlefish, red mullet, shrimps, gurnard, octopus or squid) cooked with tomatoes and garlic and served over thick slices of toast. People in the Garfagnana make good use of the sweet chestnuts that grow in the woods, grinding them into flour to make bread or a rich chestnut cake called *castagnaccio*. You'll also find soups made with *farro* (emmer or spelt), an early type of wheat, as it grows well in the fields here. Then there are the various versions of *acquacotta*, a soup whose name literally means 'cooked water'. It's essentially a soup of the Maremma, made with slowly cooked vegetables then served with a freshly poached egg on top. There's not really a set recipe for it, as each town and even each village has its own slightly different version for the dish.

Renaissance dishes

Some of the richer dishes you'll find on menus have their roots in the courts of the Medici and other noble families. There's *cinghiale in dolce e forte*, for instance, which is wild boar in a 'strong and sweet' sauce with chocolate, vinegar, pine nuts, raisins and rosemary – invented by Florentine chefs during the Renaissance, it's the sort of thing you could imagine Henry VIII tucking into. Even some dishes that are usually considered French have Tuscan origins: crêpes, onion soup and béchamel sauce were taken to France by the chefs of Caterina de' Medici when her court moved to France in the 16th century.

Fresh white truffles.

In the morning, a small dish, then some boiled meat, then a roast, after that wafers, marzipan and sugared almonds and pine-seeds, then jars of preserved pine-seeds and sweetmeats. In the evening jelly, a roast, fritters, wafers, almonds, and jars of sweetmeats.

Piero di Marco Parenti, Account of the marriage feast of Lorenzo di Piero di Cosimo, 1469.

Antipasti

A Tuscan meal usually starts with *crostini* (toasted bread topped with something like *fegatini* (liver pâté) and *affettati* (an assortment of cold cuts such as prosciutto and salami). Look out for toppings of *lardo di Colonnata* too: it's seasoned pork fat from the marble-producing area of Colonnata in the Apuan Alps, in northern Tuscany. The fat, taken from the pig's back, is layered with herbs and salt then stored in cool caves for at least six months. However, the favourite starter is simplicity itself: *fettunta*, literally 'greasy slice', consists of toasted bread rubbed with a clove of garlic and topped with olive oil, preferably the freshest available. Local pecorino cheese features on many menus too, as does *bruschetta* – stale bread topped with fresh tomatoes, garlic and oil.

Primi

The first course is *il primo*. Soups are a big deal: hearty, filling and virtually a meal in themselves, such as *zuppa di faro e fagioli* (bean and barley) or a simple bean soup. Many are made with bread. Tuscan bread is unsalted and, as it goes hard after a few days rather than stale or mouldy, poor families used it up in a variety of ways. You'll often see *pappa al pomodoro* (bread in tomato sauce) or *ribollita* (literally 'reboiled') – a bread, bean and vegetable soup. (If you dunk hunks of bread when you're eating it, the locals will think you're mad.)

Five of the best

Gelaterie in Tuscany

1. **Grom** – Florence (page 133)
2. **Gelateria Snoopy** – Cortona (page 207)
3. **Gelateria dei Neri** – Florence (page 134)
4. **Gelateria di Piazza** – San Gimignano (page 180)
5. **Gelateria Monerosa** – Pistoia (page 244)

Colourful market-produce lining a street in Siena.

Bread is also used in *panzanella*, a salad made with soaked stale bread and tomatoes.

Pasta is also served as a first course. In Tuscany this is typically penne, long flat pappardelle, or filled ravioli or tortelli – and it is generally served with fresh porcini mushrooms, a simple tomato sauce or a sauce made from wild boar, rabbit or hare. In Siena you'll often see pici, a sort of thick spaghetti, usually eaten with ragù, a slow-cooked meaty sauce. The Maremma is noted for tortelli Maremmana (pasta filled with spinach and ricotta) and *bottarga* – mullet roe, which is grated over pasta.

Secondi

The second course can be fish but is usually meat, generally served grilled or roasted fairly simply or in a sauce made with a robust red wine. Tuscany's most famous meat dish is *bistecca alla fiorentina*, steak grilled rare or medium and usually served for a minimum of two people (who might be advised to get a new mortgage to pay for it). Favourite meats come from Chianina cattle, raised on the flat lands around Cortona, and from Cinta Senese pigs (black pigs with a distinctive white band – you can see them in the frescoes in the Palazzo Pubblico in Siena). You will also see *lepre* (hare), *piccione* (pigeon), *pollo* (chicken), and the ubiquitous *cinghiale* (wild boar). More hardy types could try *trippa* (tripe) – a traditional Florentine street food. A typical fish is *baccalà* (salt cod), which is often served with tomato sauce.

Vegetables are a strong point, served as *contorni* (side dishes). You'll be able to try everything from spinach to *cavolo nero* (black cabbage). And then there are beans, of course: cannellini, borlotti, the rare *zolfino* (a tiny white bean) and Hannibal Lecter's favourite, *baccelli* (fava beans). They're often served on their own, stewed for hours with tomatoes and fragrant sage leaves.

Dolci

Desserts are usually something simple like fruit, or *cantuccini* (often sold as biscotti overseas) – hard dry biscuits that you dunk into Vin Santo, a sweet wine. You might also see *zuccotto*, a Florentine dessert of cream, almonds and chocolate surrounded by alcohol-soaked sponge fingers. Sienese cakes in particular are distinctive and delicious – make sure you buy them freshly made. *Cavallucci* (the name means 'little horses' as they were originally destined for those who worked in the stables) are dense, aniseed-flavoured buns studded with candied fruits, while *ricciarelli* are deliciously chewy almond biscuits. The traditional Sienese Christmas cake is *panforte*, a stick-to-your-ribs mix of honey, dried fruits and almonds – you'll also find a version made with cinnamon and nutmeg called *panpepato*. Look for *pan coi santi* too: it's a spicy loaf with dried fruit and nuts that's only made around All Saints' Day (1 November). The traditional Tuscan cheese is pecorino, a sheep's milk cheese traditionally from Pienza. It can be eaten young and pale, when the flavour is delicate, or mature, when it's darker and more flavoursome.

The wine of friendship

While you're in Tuscany make sure you try some Vin Santo, a dark, sweet, fortified wine that tastes a bit like sherry. The name means 'holy wine' as it was once used by the priest for Holy Communion – the local joke was that while he was holding it up and making the sign of the cross he was secretly inspecting the quality and hoping the congregation would leave some for him. Today it's generally considered the wine of friendship. Many people still make it at home, and it's often offered to guests. The grapes are dried in a breezy attic room for three months, then pressed and the juice put in a barrel, or *carratello*, which contains the *mama* – the sediment from the last production – to ferment. It's then placed in a loft and left to age with the seasons. It gets no special treatment and is exposed to extremes of temperature – by the time it's ready, a bottle can stay open for months without spoiling.

Olive oil

It would be impossible to imagine Tuscan cuisine without olive oil, which is made everywhere from Lucca to the Maremma. In November, during the olive harvest, families race to get their freshly picked olives to the press as fast as possible. The new oil is hailed with celebratory tastings and festivals – and a gift of good olive oil is always much appreciated. The oil should be kept as airtight as possible, in a dark bottle (to protect it from the light) and out of the heat. The highest quality olive oil is referred to as 'extra virgin' – it comes from the first cold pressing of the olives and must have less than 0.8% acid content.

Wine

Wine accompanies most meals, of course. It's been made in Tuscany since Etruscan times and locals take their wines (which are mainly red) very seriously. Variations in terrain, soil and climate in the Tuscan countryside mean that many different types are produced within a relatively small area. Most are made from varieties of Sangiovese grapes and are now highly rated by wine experts; the days when Chianti was valued mainly for its distinctive – wouldn't-it-make-a-good-lamp – raffia-wrapped bottle are long gone.

The government controls and classifies wines through a system that regulates everything from the types of grapes used to the method of production. Categories start with no-nonsense vino da tavola (table wine), followed by IGT (Indicazione Geografica Tipica). Next up the scale are DOC (Denominazione di Origine Controllata) wines and finally DOCG (Denominazione di Origine Controllata e Garantita) – you can easily recognize these as they'll have a small pink tag on the top.

DOCG wines are determined by the grape varieties used, production methods and geographical area. Look out for the famed, and famously pricey, Brunello di Montalcino, Carmignano, Chianti, Chianti Classico, Vino Nobile di

Wine is an essential part of Tuscan life.

Montepulciano and, the only white in the list, Vernaccia di San Gimignano, which was served at royal weddings in Renaissance times. New kids on the block are the Super-Tuscan wines: made from non-indigenous grape varieties such as Merlot and Cabernet, they've been produced to create a new type of Italian wine with wide international appeal, and are now going at higher prices than traditional DOCG wines.

Chianti Classico bottles are usually distinguished by a black cockerel, but Chianti Rufina and Chianti Colli Fiorentini can be just as good – everything depends on the producer. Don't neglect other parts of Tuscany either. The Maremma is an up-and-coming wine (and oil) producing area. Its best-known wine is the red DOC Morellino di Scansano, but there is also a delicate dry white Bianco di Pitigliano and another DOC red, Montecucco, from the area around Grosseto. Essentially though, don't worry too much about labels, just taste a few and make up your own mind.

Practical information

Tuscan towns and cities, particularly Florence, are well served with places to eat – you'll be able to find restaurants as well as *trattorie* and *osterie*, which are cheaper. Even the smallest village usually has a bar where you can get coffee and a snack. Lunch is generally taken around 1300 and the evening meal not until after 2000. You'll usually pay around €20-30 per person for a couple of courses and a drink – don't forget the dreaded *pane e coperto* (bread and cover charge) and the service charge, which will be added to your bill.

Tuscan towns and cities, particularly Florence, are well served with places to eat – you'll be able to find restaurants as well as *trattorie* and *osterie*, which are cheaper.

Menu reader

General

affumicato smoked
al sangue rare
alla griglia grilled
antipasto starter/appetizer
aperto/chiuso open/closed
arrosto roasted
ben cotto well done
bollito boiled
caldo hot
cameriere/cameriera waiter/waitress
conto the bill
contorni side dishes
coperto cover charge
coppa/cono cone/cup
cotto cooked
cottura media medium
crudo raw
degustazione tasting menu of several dishes
dolce dessert
fatto in casa homemade
forno a legna wood-fired oven
freddo cold
fresco fresh, uncooked
fritto fried
menu turistico tourist menu
piccante spicy
prenotazione reservation
primo first course
ripieno a stuffing or something that is stuffed
secondo second course

Drinks (bevande)

acqua naturale/gassata/frizzante still/sparkling water
aperitivo drinks taken before dinner, often served with free snacks
bicchiere glass
birra beer
birra alla spina draught beer
bottiglia bottle
caffè coffee (ie espresso)
caffè macchiato/ristretto espresso with a dash of foamed milk/strong
spremuta freshly squeezed fruit juice
succo juice
vino bianco/rosato/rosso white/rosé/red wine

Fruit (frutti) & vegetables (legumi)

agrumi citrus fruits
amarena sour cherry
arancia orange
carciofio globe artichoke
castagne chestnuts
cipolle onions
cocomero water melon
contorno side dish, usually grilled vegetables or oven baked potatoes
fichi figs
finocchio fennel
fragole strawberries
friarelli strong flavoured leaves of the broccoli family eaten with sausages
frutta fresca fresh fruit
funghi mushroom
lamponi raspberries
melagrana pomegranate
melanzana eggplant/aubergine
melone light coloured melon
mele apples
noci/nocciole walnuts/hazelnuts
patate potatoes, which can be *arroste* (roast), *fritte* (fried), *novelle* (new), *pure'di* (mashed)
patatine fritte chips
peperoncino chilli pepper
peperone peppers
pesche peaches
piselli peas
pomodoro tomato
rucola rocket
scarola leafy green vegetable used in torta di Scarola pie.
sciurilli or *fiorilli* tempura courgette flowers
spinaci spinach
verdure vegetables
zucca pumpkin

Meat (carne)

affettati misti mixed cured meat
agnello lamb
bistecca beef steak
braciola chop, steak or slice of meat
carpaccio finely sliced raw meat (usually beef)
cinghiale boar
coda alla vaccinara oxtail
coniglio rabbit
involtini thinly sliced meat, rolled and stuffed

manzo beef
pollo chicken
polpette meatballs
polpettone meat loaf
porchetta roasted whole suckling pig
prosciutto ham – *cotto* cooked, *crudo* cured
salsicce pork sausage
salumi cured meats, usually served mixed (*salumi misto*) on a wooden platter
speck a type of cured, smoked ham
spiedini meat pieces grilled on a skewer
stufato meat stew
trippa tripe
vitello veal

Fish (*pesce*) & seafood (*frutti di mare*)
acciughe anchovies
aragosta lobster
baccalà salt cod
bottarga mullet-roe
branzino sea bass
calamari squid
cozze mussels
frittura di mare/frittura di paranza small fish, squid and shellfish lightly covered with flour and fried
frutti di mare seafood
gamberi shrimps/prawns
grigliata mista di pesce mixed grilled fish
orata gilt-head/sea bream
ostriche oysters
pesce spada swordfish
polpo octopus
sarde, sardine sardines
seppia cuttlefish
sogliola sole
spigola bass
stoccafisso stockfish
tonno tuna
triglia red mullet
trota trout
vongole clams

Dessert (*dolce*)
cornetto sweet croissant
crema custard
dolce dessert
gelato ice cream
granita flavoured crushed ice

Useful phrases
can I have the bill please? *posso avere il conto per favore?*
is there a menu? *c'è un menù?*
what do you recommend? *che cosa mi consegna?*
what's this? *cos'è questo?*
where's the toilet? *dov'è il bagno?*

macedonia (di frutta) fruit cocktail dessert with white wine
panettone type of fruit bread eaten at Christmas
semifreddo a partially frozen dessert
sorbetto sorbet
tiramisù rich 'pick-me-up' dessert
torta cake
zabaglione whipped egg yolks flavoured with Marsala wine
zuppa inglese English-style trifle

Other
aceto balsamico balsamic vinegar, usually from Modena
arborio type of rice used to make risotto
burro butter
calzone pizza dough rolled with the chef's choice of filling and then baked
casatiello lard bread
fagioli white beans
formaggi misti mixed cheese plate
formaggio cheese
frittata omelette
insalata salad
insalata Caprese salad of tomatoes, mozzarella and basil
latte milk
lenticchie lentils
mandorla almond
miele honey
olio oil
polenta cornmeal
pane bread
pane-integrale brown bread
pinoli pine nuts
provola cheese, sometimes with a smoky flavour
ragù a meaty sauce or ragout
riso rice
salsa sauce
sugo sauce or gravy
zuppa soup

Street theatre, Pienza

Entertainment

Tradition rules in Tuscany, where the medieval often seems a part of everyday life rather than an earlier age. This is a region that's renowned for its unchanging charm, its history, Renaissance art and timeless landscape. Nightlife is generally laid back and low key. Florence is the liveliest city year round, as you'd expect, followed by Pisa with its large student population. Visitors to Siena always flock to the Campo, but the Sienese still prefer to do their socializing within their own *contrada*, out of sight of visitors. Each *contrada* has its own bar and members regularly dine together. However, from late spring through to early winter, outdoor dinners are held to celebrate past Palio victories. The streets of the *contrada* are decorated, temporary bars are erected and everyone dresses up.

Ask locally to find out if a dinner is taking place while you're there.

Bars

Bars in Tuscany tend to double as cafés, attracting everyone from office workers popping in for a slug of espresso first thing in the morning to 20-something students out for a few drinks in the evening. The biggest change in recent years has been the fashion for having *aperitivi* early in the evening – especially in Florence. Lots of bars now offer a complimentary buffet with their pre-dinnertime drinks: you'll usually pay a set price of perhaps €6-10; then, if you wish, you can often eat as much as you would for a full meal (great if you're travelling on a budget). Aperitifs are generally available from around 1800 to 1930 or 2000, and bars get very lively at these times. In fact, going for aperitivi is bigger in Florence than going clubbing. Afterwards people will maybe head home or go for a leisurely meal in a restaurant.

You'll also find some pubs in the main cities – these generally have an Aussie, English, Irish or Scottish theme and tend to attract young locals and students.

Clubs

The biggest clubs are on the outskirts of the city centres and – as you'd expect – most are around Florence. Some offer a dinner and dance package. In summer the clubbing scene moves outdoors, and venues can change from year to year. The liveliest summer clubbing takes place on the northern Tuscan coast, around Viareggio and Forte dei Marmi.

Gay & lesbian

This area, especially Torre del Lago, also has a thriving gay and lesbian scene. Other than that, the main gay- and lesbian-friendly venues in Tuscany are in Florence. The longest established club is Tabasco Disco Gay (piazza Santa Cecilia 3r, tabascogay.it); Bar 85 (via Guelfa 85r) is a gay bar.

Concerts & festivals

Major international bands tend to miss out Tuscany on their tours. If they do stop, it will be in Florence, where the largest venue is the Mandela Forum, on the outskirts of the city. Contemporary Tuscan acts to look out for include Piero Pelu, formerly with Tuscan band Litfiba; rap artist Jovanotti and experimental outfit Miranda and the Creeping Nobodies. If you want to check out contemporary music/jazz concerts and festivals, the Toscana Music website is worth a look: toscanamusiche.it. There's a wealth of classical music on offer in Tuscany. In Florence, the big event is the Maggio Musicale Fiorentino (see page 53), and there are also plenty of classical concerts in Siena, Lucca and of course Torre del Lago, home of the annual Puccini Festival (see page 53). In Siena, however, the Palio dominates all other events and preparations for it occupy much of local people's time. You'll often find *contrada* members practising their flag waving in a quiet piazza.

Carnival, Viareggio.

Antiques market, Arezzo.

Shopping

You can shop till your credit card squeals in Tuscany. And even if you can't afford to buy anything (this isn't the region to come to for bargains), then you can still have an extremely enjoyable time window-shopping. Staff are generally helpful and courteous – though designer stores can be a tad intimidating, with immaculately dressed assistants sizing you up the instant you step in. Apart from Florence, which obviously has the widest choice of stores, the best shopping is to be had in Lucca (where the main shopping street is via Fillungo) and in Siena, where the busiest streets are via Banchi di Sopra and via di Città.

Clothes & accessories

The Italian obsession with *la bella figura* means that there is no shortage of high quality clothing in Tuscany. Florence has seen an influx of big designer names in recent years, and you'll find everyone here from Dior to Dolce & Gabbana. The department store Rinascente has a good range of designer clothes – as well as a rooftop café with fabulous views of the city. The smartest street in Florence, however, is via Tornabuoni (with some overspill into neighbouring via Strozzi), and you can stroll from Pucci to Prada, Armani to Ferragamo with the Florentine fashionistas. If you want some seriously expensive baubles to set off your new purchases, then just pop in to Tiffany or Cartier, on the same street. Or make for the Ponte Vecchio, which is lined with shops selling both antique and contemporary gold jewellery.

If you like your designer clothes at less eye-watering prices, make for the outlet stores outside the city. These are most easily reached by car, though public transport is an option. You can also book special shopping tours: isango.com, for instance, offer a half-day trip, taking you to the Prada outlet and then on to The Mall, the most famous centre, where you can find a wide range of designer names. These outlets were once a well-kept secret, but word has now widely spread and these days you're very likely to find yourself battling for the bargains with hordes of determined fashion bunnies.

Tuscany also has a good clutch of individual clothes stores, where you can find lesser known designer names as well as handmade – *fatto a mano* – items. Florence, Lucca and Siena are the best places to look. A number of vintage clothes stores have also opened in recent years, mainly in Florence. Then there are accessories: excellent value, particularly leather shoes, belts and handbags. Florence has plenty of accessories shops, and you'll also find a wide selection of leather goods on sale in San Lorenzo market and the Mercato Nuovo.

All kinds of shopping in Tuscany from traditional gifts to designer gear.

Gifts & souvenirs

If you're looking for gifts or souvenirs, you'll be spoilt for choice. Of course there are the usual stalls selling tourist tat in the cities, but you'll also find items like marbled handmade paper, stained glass, linens, beautiful ceramics, and olive wood tableware. Seek out artisan workshops, where you may be able to watch items being made and meet the craftspeople who fashion them, many employing techniques that have been used for centuries. In Florence, the best place to find these workshops is in the Oltrarno, the 'other side' of the Arno. Here you can commission a pair of handmade shoes, watch bookbinders at work and buy a sculpture, lovingly carved in stone, all within a few minutes' walk of the Ponte Vecchio. Florence also boasts some specialist shops that are visitor attractions in themselves. Best known is Profumo-Farmaceutica di Santa Maria Novella, the 13th-century pharmacy that still produces all sorts of delicious-smelling oils and perfumes.

A typical Tuscan souvenir shop.

Artisan workshops are dotted all around Siena, a city that takes enormous pride in its traditions. As well as ceramics, handmade clothes and paper, look out for shops selling items decorated with contrade symbols. You'll see them on everything from flags to plates, although the best buys are probably the scarves: contrade members of both sexes and all ages wear them. In Volterra, the speciality product is alabaster, which is fashioned into lamps, vases and plates, while Colle Val d'Elsa is famed for its sparkling crystal. If you prefer antiques, then the best place has to be the monthly antique fair in Arezzo. Half of Tuscany seems to crowd into the city for a lazy browse around the stalls, which sell large items of furniture as well as more portable pieces such as jewellery and copper kitchenware.

Browsing in food stores and wineries is one of the great pleasures of shopping in Tuscany, and if you want a bottle of Brunello, some organic olive oil, or a piece of *panforte*, you'll find it here. The most enjoyable way to shop for wine and oil is to visit the producers themselves. Some wineries offer tours of the vineyards and tastings, for instance, and if you're in the Tuscan countryside in the autumn you might be able to watch an olive press at work. The Chiantigiana, the road that runs through the Chianti region, is the best-known wine route, and wineries here are well organized, although they do receive large numbers of visitors at peak holiday times. Then there are the vineyards around the hill towns of Montepulciano and Montalcino, famed for production of Vino Nobile and Brunello respectively. If you want to go off the beaten track, visit the lesser-known wine and olive oil producers in the Maremma.

A regional wine shop.

Tip...

When buying olive oil, the glass of the bottle should be dark in colour, as light spoils the flavour of the oil.

Wine and oil suppliers in Tuscany can arrange to ship your goods home for you. This is handy, bearing in mind the restrictions on carrying liquids on board planes these days, as well as national customs' restrictions on food and drink. If you're travelling within the EU you are, at the time of writing, allowed to carry most food products; however, many foods – including soft cheeses such as ricotta – cannot be taken into the US from Europe; bakery items, canned foods and chocolate are generally admissible. It's worth checking on the regulations beforehand (US – **cbp.gov**; UK – **hmrc.gov.uk**). Shoppers resident outside the EU can claim tax refunds on their purchases, if they've bought a certain amount. Shops that are set up for helping you with this will display a 'tax free' sign.

Shopping hours

Tuscan shopping hours are much the same as those in the rest of Italy. In Florence, shops are usually open on Monday afternoon, and from around 0930-1300 and 1500-1900 from Tuesday to Saturday. In Siena, shops often close all day Monday. Food shops tend to open earlier in the morning, then close around lunchtime and do not reopen until about 1630 or 1700 (so buy picnic provisions in the mornings). Some shops in Florence open on Sundays.

During the height of summer, shops often close on Saturday afternoons (especially in smaller towns), while in August shops as well as restaurants may close for a couple of weeks.

Kids racing at Montecatini Terme.

Activities & tours

The gently rolling hills and picturesque hill towns of the Tuscan picture postcard don't exactly conjure up images of all-action adventure. But while the region may not be the place to come for extreme sports, Tuscany's varied landscape offers a surprisingly wide range of activities – you can ski in the winter in the mountains north of Pistoia (abetone.com), dive in the summer off Elba, and walk and cycle all year round.

Cultural

A walking tour with an expert is your best bet if you want an insight into the art, architecture or history of Florence. There are plenty to choose from. Mercurio Tours, (T055-213355, mercurio-italy.org) offer a 2½-hour walking tour covering highlights and 'secrets' of Florence, and a two-hour guided visit to the Uffizi. Then there's Artviva (T055-264 5033, italy.artviva.com) which offers guided walking tours of Florence on specialist themes, such as Michelangelo's *David*. They also do tours of Chianti and Fiesole. For a range of tours in Florence and Tuscany, check out isango.com, which offers everything from wine tours of Chianti to trips to designer shopping outlets.

Cycling

The Italians have a passion for cycling, but their roads aren't exactly cycle friendly. The most demanding cycling would be in the mountains of northern Tuscany – suitable only for experienced riders. Efforts are being made to increase the number of routes. The Siena tourist office has information on a variety of routes, from a gentle ride along an old railway line to long-distance journeys: they're listed on a website, terresienainbici.it. Another useful site is that of the FIAB, the Italian Federation of Cyclists (fiab-onlus.it).

Diving & watersports

The island of Elba, off the Tuscan coast, is the place to go for scuba diving. A number of operators there offer dive courses, such as Diving in Elba (divinginelba.com) in Portoferraio, which also offers diving and snorkelling instruction for children. On the south coast of the island is Talas Diving Centre (T0565-933482, subacquea.com). Ensure that you dive only with PADI-qualified instructors. For watersports, head for Talamone beach in the Maremma. It's great for windsurfing and kitesurfing.

Food & wine

You could spend several weeks just following wine trails in Tuscany. The best-known wine route is the Chiantigiana, the road that runs through the Chianti region. Then there are the wineries around the hill towns south of Siena, between Pisa and Volterra, and in the unexplored Maremma. You can also join tours that take you to meet artisan food producers in the Garfagnana region, run by Sapori e Saperi (sapori-e-saperi.com).

If you want to learn more about fine olive oil, book a stay at Villa Campestri (villacampestri.it) in the Mugello, which runs special olive oil tasting sessions. If you prefer to get hands-on, there's no shortage of cookery courses in Tuscany. Some are residential, others last a few hours. If you want to get the kids involved, check out the multi-activity family holiday near Vinci, run by Activities Abroad (activitiesabroad.com) which includes rock-climbing, cycling and making your own pizza.

Horse riding

The Maremma is the place to ride in Tuscany. It's the home of the famous *butteri*, the Maremman cowboys, with whom you can ride if you're experienced enough (check out alberese.com or cavallomaremmano.it). For hacks and lessons, Antico Casale di Scansano (anticocasalediscansano.it), a resort near Scansano, has a riding centre with options for all abilities.

Walking

Tuscany offers excellent walking. You can go on hikes in the mountains of the north, or strolls along footpaths in the Mugello. You will find that footpaths are not marked on maps with the same accuracy as UK Ordnance Survey, so you may prefer to follow designated paths in one of Tuscany's national or regional parks. For self-guided walking holidays, check out Headwater (headwater.com).

Walking in Tuscany

A personal experience

It's late morning when we stop for a rest. We settle down on a convenient rock and take welcome gulps of water. It's October but the sun is strong and we have to pull down our hats to shade our eyes. Far below us lies a lake, so green it looks as if emeralds have burst and stained the water. Through my binoculars I can see a solitary duck, a dark dot on its otherwise smooth surface. The hills beyond are covered in a fuzzy blanket of trees and scrub, almost aflame with autumn shades of crimson, saffron, russet, green and gold. We sit still, enjoying the thick silence. And then, from behind us, comes the sound of church bells. We turn and discover that it's coming from a medieval monastery, perched high on a hilltop across the valley. It's a sound that seems to stretch across the centuries. We sit and listen for a while, then pick up our packs and walk on.

We're in the Mugello, on a self-guided walking tour organized by **Headwater** (T01606-720199 (UK), headwater.com), who specialize in making walking trips easy. They book the hotels and transport your luggage (so there's no need to lug a heavy rucksack around), provide transport to the start of each walk and detailed notes to help you follow each day's route – handy, as Italian maps don't show the same level of detail as British Ordnance Survey maps. Although we're only around 40 minutes' drive from Florence, this is an area that has hardly been explored by tourists and is wonderfully unspoilt.

Our first day's walk starts from Fiesole, an Etruscan hill town that the Romans found extremely hard to conquer. We take in sights like the Roman theatre and 11th-century cathedral before getting on to the serious business of buying lunch. We purchase fruit and large slices of pizza, then read our instructions: they warn us that this will be "quite a testing day". The road, via Giuseppe Verdi, climbs almost immediately but we're soon rewarded with a panoramic view of Florence. We keep puffing uphill and eventually reach a crag, on top of which a man sits cross-legged, meditating in the morning sun.

We make good progress at first, our route offering us tantalizing glimpses of Florence, but then we manage to get lost among some olive groves and go back and forth for ages. Luckily, Headwater always suggests shortcuts and in the end we retrace our steps to a road, where we pick up the shorter route. Later, once we've rejoined the main walk, we climb a steep hill to a meadow scattered with wild flowers. Butterflies flit around, as large and colourful as tiny birds, and Fiesole lies far beneath us. It's worth the odd blister for this. On Headwater trips each linear walk is followed by a rest day to give you a chance to recover, but you can follow a suggested circular walk if you're feeling energetic.

Our next full day's walk is easier. We follow ancient tracks through thick chestnut woods, and at one point pass a *burraia*, a stone building where farmers made butter – they were used until the 1960s. Later, we come to the ruins of Monte Rotondo, built as a communications tower for the Medici, who came from the Mugello and retained close links with the area. That night we stay at Collefertile, a former hunting lodge, where Andrea Cerchiai, the owner, roasts chestnuts for us on the fire and pours us measures of his family's elisir di China – the recipe is a closely guarded secret but it's a digestive made with cinchona bark, which once served as an anti-malarial.

Our final day's walk leads through chestnut woods and open hills to San Cresci church, founded in the 12th century, and then down to the village of Sagginale, where we picnic by the ponte d'Annibale, a stone bridge built after the Roman conquest of the area. The last stretch takes us through terraced olive groves and fig trees, till we come down to the imposing gates of Villa Campestri, our last hotel. We sit down with a sigh in the elegant garden, unlace our boots and sip cool glasses of fruit juice. Bliss.

Headwater's 'Walking in the Florentine Hills' runs May-Oct, 9 days from £948 pp half board.

Contents

Florence

Introduction

Florence is the jewel in Tuscany's crown. All roads may lead to Rome, but all art lovers head for Florence. It was here that the Renaissance took root, and where the intellectual luminescence it generated, and the new focus it put on humanity, was first felt in both arts and sciences. Wealthy families in Florence, keen to flaunt their riches, commissioned works by exciting new artists and architects. The city became the place to be if you wanted to make your name – and a living – as an artist. Come to Florence today and you'll find works by Michelangelo, Donatello, Leonardo da Vinci, Botticelli and many more. Sights range from the medieval Ponte Vecchio and the magnificent Duomo to the lavish interiors of the Pitti Palace and the quiet simplicity of Santo Spirito.

The trouble is, there's just too much to see, and Florence's small size can tempt you into thinking you can do it all. You can't. The key to an enjoyable trip is to accept that and allow time for non-cultural pleasures too, like lazy lunches and shopping. Planning's important, as you can save hours of queuing by booking tickets in advance. And don't be disappointed if a museum is closed, or a work of art is being restored – there's always something equally amazing nearby.

What to see in...

...one day

Visit the **Duomo**, the **Baptistery** and climb the **Campanile**. See the **Orsanmichele** and have lunch, before a tour of the **Palazzo Vecchio**. Go to the **piazza Santa Croce**, to admire the exterior of **Santa Croce church**, followed by a stroll along the Arno to the **Ponte Vecchio**. There'll be time for window-shopping on via Tornabuoni, a walk through piazza della Repubblica and finally down to the **Mercato Nuovo**, to rub the nose of the **Porcellino** to ensure you return to Florence.

...a weekend or more

Go inside **Santa Croce church**, and visit either the **Uffizi** or the **Accademia**. If you go to the Uffizi, cross the Arno to visit **Santa Maria del Carmine** and picnic in the **Boboli Gardens**. If you choose the Accademia, you can also visit **San Marco**, plus the **Medici-Riccardi Palace**.

Essentials

Getting around

Florence is a compact city, and it is easiest to get around on foot, especially as non-residents have to park in the main car parks, such as that beneath the station, around porta San Frediano or by piazzale Michelangelo (firenzeparcheggi.it). To reach San Miniato al Monte or Fiesole you can hop on a bus at Santa Maria Novella. Taxis are metered, and you will be charged for each piece of luggage. There are plenty of taxis at Santa Maria Novella, and you will also find them by piazza Santa Croce and piazza del Duomo. If you call a taxi, or your hotel calls one for you, you'll be charged an extra €3.

Bus station

International coaches depart from Lazzi Station, piazza Adua (T055-351 061, lazzi.it) next to Santa Maria Novella. **Blue SITA** (T055-294955 or 0800-373760, sitabus.it) coaches arrive and depart from the Sita Bus Station, via Santa Caterina da Siena, near the train station. **Orange ATAF** electric buses lines A, B and C operate in the city centre, and ordinary **ATAF** buses (T800-424500, ataf.net) serve longer routes. Buy tickets at *tabacchi*, bars and newsagents and the **ATAF** booth in **SMN** station: single trip €1.20 (€2 if bought from the driver on the bus) or four tickets for €4.50 – once validated, tickets last 70 mins; 24hr ticket €5, 3-day ticket €12. A tram system is under construction, but there is no date for completion yet.

Train station

The main railway station is Santa Maria Novella (**Firenze SMN**, T055-892021, grandistazioni.it), on piazza della Stazione in the west of the city.

ATMs

Via piazza Santa Maria Novella, others around piazza della Signoria and piazza della Repubblica.

Hospital

Policlinico di Careggi, viale Morgagni 85 (T055-427 7111), outside the city centre. Also Ospedale Santa Maria Nuova, piazza Santa Maria Nuova (T055-27581).

Pharmacy

24-hr pharmacies at Santa Maria Novella station concourse, also **Molteni**, via Calzaiuoli 7r, and **All'Insegna del Moro**, piazza San Giovanni 20r.

Post office

Via Pellicceria 3. Post offices can also be found at the Uffizi and via Pietrapiana 53.

Tourist information offices

Via Cavour 1r, T055-290832/3, firenzeturismo.it, Mon-Sat 0830-1830, Sun 0830-1330; via Manzoni 16, T055-23320, Mon-Fri 0900-1300.

Top sights

The **Duomo** – Brunelleschi's architectural wonder
Uffizi Gallery – masterpieces galore
Baptistery – Ghiberti's gleaming bronze doors
Santa Croce – monumental memorials
San Marco – Fra Angelico's moving *Annunciation*
Palazzo Vecchio – Francesco's secret studio
The **Accademia** – Michelangelo's republican *David*
The **Bargello** – Donatello's daintier *David*
Palazzo Medici-Riccardi – the Chapel of the Magi
The **Brancacci Chapel** – Masaccio's *Expulsion from Eden*

Far left: Florence at sunset. Left: Ponte Vecchio. This page – clockwise from top right: The sunset from Ponte Santa Trinità; *il Porcellino* proudly sits; the Uffizi gallery; a view of the city.

Ten of the best free things to do

1. Have a picnic in the rose garden near San Miniato al Monte.
2. Visit the Antica Farmacia, Santa Maria Novella.
3. Get a cheesy photo taken rubbing the nose of *Il Porcellino*.
4. Admire Ghirlandaio's Last Supper in Ognissanti.
5. Listen to Gregorian chant at San Miniato al Monte.
6. Stand underneath the cupola of the Duomo and marvel at how Brunelleschi did it.
7. Stroll across the Ponte Santa Trinità at sunset.
8. See Pontormo's Mannerist masterpiece at Santa Felicità.
9. Go window-shopping on via dei Tornabuoni.
10. Soak up the atmosphere at Sant'Ambrogio fruit and veg market.

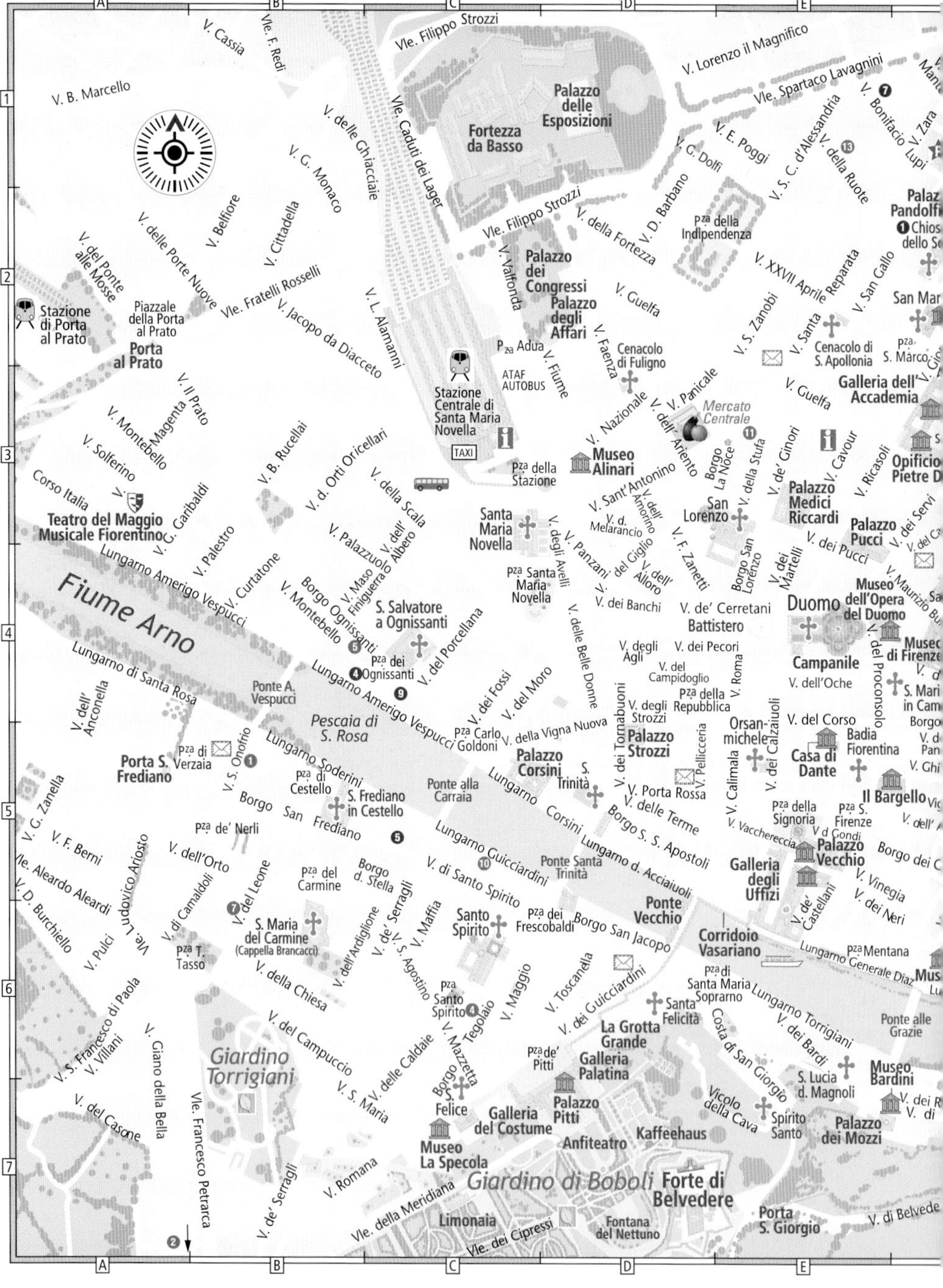

A
B
C
D
E
1
2
3
4
5
6
7
V. Cassia
Vle. F. Redi
Vle. Filippo Strozzi
V. Lorenzo il Magnifico
Vle. Spartaco Lavagnini
V. B. Marcello
Palazzo delle Esposizioni
Fortezza da Basso
V. delle Chiacciaie
Vle. Caduti dei Lager
V. G. Monaco
V. C. Dolfi
V. E. Poggi
V. S. C. d'Alessandria
V. Bonifacio Lupi
V. Zara
V. della Ruote
V. D. Barbano
Pza della Indipendenza
Vle. Filippo Strozzi
V. della Fortezza
V. Belfiore
V. Cittadella
V. delle Porte Nuove
V. del Ponte alle Mosse
Palazzo dei Congressi
Palazzo degli Affari
V. Valfonda
V. XXVII Aprile
V. Reparata
V. San Gallo
Stazione di Porta al Prato
Piazzale della Porta al Prato
Vle. Fratelli Rosselli
V. Jacopo da Diacceto
V. L. Alamanni
V. Guelfa
V. S. Zanobi
V. Santa
Cenacolo di S. Apollonia
Pza S. Marco
Porta al Prato
Pza Adua
V. Fiume
V. Faenza
Cenacolo di Fuligno
Stazione Centrale di Santa Maria Novella
ATAF AUTOBUS
V. Il Prato
V. Magenta
V. Montebello
V. Solferino
V. B. Rucellai
V. d. Orti Oricellari
V. Nazionale
V. Panicale
V. dell'Ariento
Mercato Centrale
V. Guelfa
Galleria dell'Accademia
TAXI
Pza della Stazione
Museo Alinari
V. della Scala
Borgo La Noce
V. della Stufa
V. de' Ginori
V. Cavour
V. Ricasoli
Opificio Pietre D
Corso Italia
Teatro del Maggio Musicale Fiorentino
V. G. Garibaldi
V. Palestro
V. Curtatone
V. Palazzuolo
V. dell' Albero
Santa Maria Novella
V. Sant'Antonino
V. dell' Amorino
V. d. Melarancio
San Lorenzo
Palazzo Medici Riccardi
Palazzo Pucci
V. dei Servi
V. dei Pucci
V. degli Avelli
V. Panzani
V. del Giglio
V. dell' Alloro
V. F. Zanetti
Borgo San Lorenzo
V. dei Martelli
Lungarno Amerigo Vespucci
Fiume Arno
V. Montebello
Borgo Ognissanti
V. Maso Finiguerra
S. Salvatore a Ognissanti
V. del Porcellana
Pza Santa Maria Novella
V. dei Banchi
V. de' Cerretani
Battistero
Duomo
Museo dell'Opera del Duomo
V. Maurizio Bufalini
Lungarno di Santa Rosa
Pza dei Ognissanti
Lungarno Amerigo Vespucci
V. delle Belle Donne
V. degli Agli
V. dei Pecori
V. del Campidoglio
V. Roma
Campanile
V. del Proconsolo
Museo di Firenze
V. dell'Oche
S. Maria in Campo
V. dell' Anconella
Ponte A. Vespucci
Pescaia di S. Rosa
V. dei Fossi
V. del Moro
V. dei Tornabuoni
V. degli Strozzi
Pza della Repubblica
V. Pellicceria
Orsanmichele
V. dei Calzaiuoli
V. Calimala
V. del Corso
Badia Fiorentina
Borgo
Pza Carlo Goldoni
V. della Vigna Nuova
Palazzo Strozzi
Casa di Dante
Porta S. Frediano
Pza di Verzaia
V. S. Onofrio
Lungarno Soderini
Pza di Cestello
Palazzo Corsini
S. Trinità
V. Porta Rossa
V. Ghi
S. Frediano in Cestello
Ponte alla Carraia
Lungarno Corsini
V. delle Terme
Borgo S. S. Apostoli
Il Bargello
V. G. Zanella
Borgo San Frediano
Pza de' Nerli
Pza della Signoria
Pza S. Firenze
V. Vacchereccia
V d Gondi
Palazzo Vecchio
V. F. Berni
V. dell'Orto
Lungarno Guicciardini
Lungarno d. Acciaiuoli
Borgo dei Greci
Vle. Aleardo Aleardi
Vle. Ludovico Ariosto
V. di Camaldoli
V. del Leone
Pza del Carmine
Borgo d. Stella
Ponte Santa Trinità
V. di Santo Spirito
Galleria degli Uffizi
V. Vinegia
V. dei Neri
V. D. Burchiello
S. Maria del Carmine (Cappella Brancacci)
V. de' Serragli
V. Maffia
Santo Spirito
Pza dei Frescobaldi
Borgo San Jacopo
Ponte Vecchio
V. de' Castellani
Corridoio Vasariano
Pza Mentana
Lungarno Generale Diaz
V. Pulci
Pza T. Tasso
V. dell'Ardiglione
V. S. Agostino
V. della Chiesa
Pza di Santa Maria Soprarno
Pza Santo Spirito
V. Maggio
V. Toscanella
V. dei Guicciardini
Santa Felicità
Costa di San Giorgio
Lungarno Torrigiani
V. S. Francesco di Paola
V. Villani
V. Giano della Bella
V. del Campuccio
Tegolaio
V. Mazzetta
La Grotta Grande
V. dei Bardi
Ponte alle Grazie
Giardino Torrigiani
V. delle Caldaie
Pza de' Pitti
Galleria Palatina
S. Lucia d. Magnoli
Museo Bardini
V. del Casone
Vle. Francesco Petrarca
V. S. Maria
Borgo S. Felice
Galleria del Costume
Palazzo Pitti
Vicolo della Cava
Spirito Santo
Palazzo dei Mozzi
Museo La Specola
Anfiteatro
Kaffeehaus
V. de' Serragli
V. Romana
Giardino di Boboli
Forte di Belvedere
Vle. della Meridiana
Limonaia
Fontana del Nettuno
Porta S. Giorgio
V. di Belvedere
Vle. dei Cipressi

Florence listings

❶ Sleeping

1 Antico Dimora Johlea *via San Gallo 80*, F2
2 Camping Michelangelo *viale Michelangelo 80*, G7
3 Four Seasons *borgo Pinti 99*, G3
4 Palazzo Magnani Feroni *borgo San Frediano 5*, C5
5 Regency *piazza Massimo d'Azeglio 3*, H3
6 Residenza Johanna 1 *via Bonifacio Lupi 14*, E1
7 Residenza Johlea *via San Gallo 76*, F1

❶ Eating & drinking

1 All' Antico Ristoro di Cambi *via S. Onofrio 1r*, B5
2 Antica Porta *via Senese 23r*, A7
3 Bistrot Baldoria *borgo Allegri 4r/via S. Giuseppe 18r*, G5
4 Borgo Antico *piazza Santo Spirito 6r*, C6
5 Caffè San Carlo *borgo Ognissanti 32/34r*, B4
6 Cibreo *via Andrea del Verrocchio 8r*, G5
7 Enoteca le Barrique *via del Leone 40r*, B6
8 Filipepe *via San Niccolò 39r*, F7
9 Il Pizzaiuolo *via de' Macci 113r*, G5
10 Nove *Lungarno Guicciardini*, C5
11 Osteria Pepo *via Rosina 6r*, E3
12 Rifrullo *via San Niccolò 55r*, F7
13 Taverna del Bronzino *via delle Ruote 27r*, E1

Around piazza del Duomo

The piazza del Duomo is surely everyone's first stop in Florence – even if you've been several times before it's hard to resist the pull. Many of the city's top sights are crammed into the piazza: the Duomo itself – topped with Brunelleschi's famous dome, the Baptistery, the Bell Tower and the Museo dell'Opera del Duomo. And just a couple of minutes' walk away there's the Orsanmichele, its walls lined with famous statues.

Duomo

Piazza del Duomo, T055-230 2885/215380, duomofirenze.it.
Mon-Wed and Fri 1000-1700, Thu and 1st Sat in month 1000-1530, Sat 1000-1645, Sun 1330-1645, free; crypt (Santa Reparata) €3; cupola Mon-Fri 0830-1900, Sat 0830-1740, €6, entry at porta della Mandorla, north side of cathedral.

There was a church on this site in the fifth or sixth century – you can see the remains of it in the crypt. However, once the Baptistery was completed in the 13th century, the existing cathedral looked "very crude" in contrast and "small in comparison to so great a city", according to a contemporary writer. Even worse, rival cities such as Pisa and Siena already had magnificent cathedrals that outshone Florence's crumbling version. So the foundation stone of a new cathedral, dedicated to Santa Maria del Fiore (Our Lady of the Flower), was laid in 1296, with Arnolfo di Cambio as the architect. The plan was to create the largest church in Christendom. Arnolfo died early in the 14th century, and the work was completed by other architects. By 1418 all that was lacking was the dome, but the design of the building required this to be so large that no one had any idea how to build it.

Brunelleschi's Dome Furious at losing the commission for creating the Baptistery doors to Lorenzo Ghiberti in 1403, Filippo Brunelleschi had decided to abandon his career as a goldsmith and specialize in architecture instead. He studied works by ancient classical masters and travelled to Rome with his friend Donatello to inspect mighty buildings such as the Pantheon. When a competition was launched to find someone capable of building the cathedral dome, Brunelleschi entered and won. He originally had to work with Ghiberti, who was by now very famous, but downed tools when Ghiberti got the credit for his work. Ghiberti proved unequal to the task and Brunelleschi was eventually able to continue alone.

He managed the seemingly impossible. His octagonal dome is a masterpiece of Renaissance engineering – for a start it was built without scaffolding, with innovative hoists carrying both workers and bricks to the top. The bricks were set in self-supporting patterns, and an inner shell was constructed to support the larger outer shell, making a double dome. Around four million bricks were used, and the structure was finished by 1436.

You can go right up into the dome, which is the best way of appreciating Brunelleschi's astonishing achievement and seeing the stained glass windows and frescoes. The views from the top are stunning, but be warned: there are 463 steps.

Cathedral interior The cathedral was not entirely completed until the 19th century, when the lavish façade was added, using white, red and green marble from Carrara, the Maremma and Prato respectively. After the excesses of the façade, the interior is surprisingly restrained and uncluttered. Perhaps the most striking sight as you enter is that of the two equestrian portraits – on the left

Tip...

Most major museums only sell tickets up to 40 minutes before closing time – 1 hour in the case of the Palazzo Vecchio. And watch out for Mondays: many museums in Florence (indeed all over Tuscany) close on Monday. Those in Florence that don't, include the Baptistery, the Brancacci Chapel, the Medici Chapels, the Medici-Riccardi Palace and the Palazzo Vecchio.

Left: The Duomo rising proudly over the city.
Below: Detail from the doors of the Baptistery.

Niccolò da Tolentino and on the right the Englishman Sir John Hawkwood. Hawkwood was a *condottiere*, or mercenary commander, who fought on behalf of Florence and was promised the honour of an equestrian statue after his death. Instead he got this rather cheaper fresco, painted in 1436 by Paolo Uccello, who utilized the newly acquired knowledge of perspective to create something that looked like a statue. The portrait of Tolentino, by Andrea del Castagno, was done later and has far more life and vigour. There is more of Uccello's work above the main entrance – **a liturgical clock** that tells the time starting each day from the previous sunset, just as the church calculates the timing of religious festivals. The inside of the dome is covered in brilliantly coloured frescoes of the *Last Judgement* (1572-9), painted by Giorgio Vasari and Federico Zuccari.

If you go downstairs to the crypt you can see the remains of the ancient basilica of Santa Reparata, which this cathedral replaced. Archaeological excavations here have revealed that four churches lie beneath the Duomo, with remains dating from the early Christian period. Peep through the metal grille beside the gift shop and you can see the inscription on the tomb of Brunelleschi. It translates as "The body of a man of Great Genius".

Campanile

Daily 0830-1930, €6. Evening visits sometimes available Jun-Oct 1900-2300, combined ticket with Battistero €7.

The Bell Tower was started in 1334 by Giotto, but he died before he could finish it. It was completed by Andrea Pisano and later, Francesco Talenti – who had to reinforce the walls to prevent it falling over. The tower stands around 85 m high and offers great views. There are 414 steps to the top.

Below: A stunning view of Florence from the Campanile.

Battistero di San Giovanni

Mon-Sat 1215-1900, Sun and 1st Sat in month 0830-1400, €3. Evening visits sometimes available Jun-Oct 1900-2300, combined ticket with Campanile €7.

For a long time it was supposed that the octagonal Baptistery was originally a Roman temple dedicated to Mars, converted to Christian use. However, most evidence suggests it dates from the sixth century – which still makes it the oldest building in the city. It was here that the poet Dante was baptised. The building was enlarged and reconstructed in the 11th and 12th centuries, and in the 13th century the ceiling was decorated with glorious Byzantine-style mosaics – the main figure is *Christ in Judgment*. The marble floor, also 13th-century, is decorated with signs of the zodiac. A large octagonal font once stood in the centre.

However, it is the **doors of the Baptistery** that are its most famous feature. When one of the city's powerful guilds, the Arte di Calimala, decided that the exterior required embellishment, they engaged Andrea Pisano to create a set of bronze doors (1330-36) containing 28 relief panels depicting scenes in the life of St John the Baptist. These are the **south doors**.

In 1401 the Calimala held a competition to design another set of doors – a competition in which Brunelleschi was famously beaten by Ghiberti (you can see their competition pieces in the Bargello, see page 101). The doors essentially became Ghiberti's life's work. The first set, the **north doors** (1403-24) have 28 relief panels, most depicting scenes from the New Testament. When these were finished, Ghiberti was commissioned to make another set, the now famous **east doors** (1425-50). The doors you see today are copies (the originals are in the Museo dell'Opera del Duomo, see page 89) but they're still an impressive sight. There are ten panels of Old Testament scenes, ranging from Adam and Eve being expelled from the Garden of Eden to Moses receiving the Ten Commandments. Ghiberti employed perspective techniques to great effect, filling the panels with drama and vitality. They were dubbed the **Gates of Paradise**, reputedly by Michelangelo, and are often said to represent the 'official' birth of the Renaissance.

Look at the equally elaborate door frames. Roughly in the middle, on the left-hand door, there's the head of a bald man looking rather pleased with himself; beside him, on the right-hand door, is the head of a younger man. They're Ghiberti and his son Vittorio.

Tip...

There's a Leonardo exhibition (Wed-Mon 1000-1330, 1400-1800, €3) upstairs in the **Loggia del Bigallo**, a beautiful 14th-century building that originally housed a charity that cared for orphans. It contains some precise scale models. The entrance is up the stairs, opposite the Baptistery exit, beside Bar Gallo. The window on the stairs offers a good vantage point for photos of the Duomo. Downstairs is the Museo del Bigallo.

Museo dell'Opera del Duomo

Piazza del Duomo 9, T055-230 2885, operaduomo.firenze.it.
Mon-Sat 0900-1930, Sun 0900-1345, €6.

This museum is devoted to conserving the most precious works, such as statues, associated with the Duomo, the Baptistery and the Campanile. On the ground floor, for example, there are works from the first façade of the cathedral (which was pulled down in the 16th century) including a glassy-eyed Madonna by the first architect, Arnolfo di Cambio. You can also see Ghiberti's original **Gates of Paradise** from the Baptistery.

On the stairs is Michelangelo's *Florentine Pietà*, one of his last works and the sculpture that he wanted on his tomb. He famously became frustrated by it and smashed Christ's arm with a hammer – it was later repaired by an assistant. According to Vasari, the figure of Nicodemus is a self-portrait.

Upstairs you can find many works by Donatello, created for the façade of the campanile. Most famous is the *Prophet Habbakuk*, which the artist

Five of the best

Viewpoints in Florence

1. **Piazzale Michelangelo** (see page 124).
2. The rooftop terrace of **Rinascente**'s café (see page 137).
3. The **Uffizi** café terrace (see page 98).
4. The top of the **Duomo** (see page 87).
5. **Ponte Santa Trinità** – looking towards the Ponte Vecchio (see page 101).

Above: The sunset from Ponte Santa Trinità.
Below right: Detail from the Orsanmichele.

found so realistic that he is said to have grabbed it shouting: "Speak! Speak!" In another room pride of place goes to another work by Donatello, the desperately ravaged figure of *Mary Magdalene* carved in wood. Other treasures in the museum include the death mask of Brunelleschi and the silver altar that was made for the Baptistery.

Orsanmichele

Via dell'Arte della Lana, T055-284944.
Tue-Sun 1000-1700, may open until 1930 on Sat in summer, free.

A short walk from the Duomo, down via dei Calzaiuoli, brings you to the Orsanmichele. If it doesn't look like a church, that's because originally it wasn't one. A ninth-century church once stood here, but it was replaced by a market. However, the place was obviously still imbued with spiritual energy, because a painting of the Madonna on a pillar in the market was soon credited with performing miracles. The first market building burned down and was replaced by the present structure around 1337. It was built specifically to combine commerce and devotion, with the grain market downstairs and the upper floors for religious services. If you look carefully you can still see the grain chutes. The miraculous Madonna was replaced by Bernardo Daddi's painting of the *Madonna delle Grazie* (1346), which was credited with miraculously curing cases of the plague of 1348. The painting is surrounded by an extravagantly decorated marble altar.

However, it's the outside of the Orsanmichele that is most famous. When it was built in its present form, the plan was to celebrate the commercial life of the city. Various guilds, representing trades ranging from bankers to wool merchants, commissioned the finest artists available to make statues of their respective patron saints, which were placed in 14 niches in the walls. Over the years, Ghiberti created a life-size bronze John the Baptist for the *Calimala* (cloth importers), Donatello sculpted St George for the Armourers (it's now in the Bargello) and Giambologna made St Luke for the Judges and Notaries. The statues you see today are copies: the originals are in the Orsanmichele Museum.

Around piazza della Signoria

The piazza della Signoria is one of Florence's finest squares. Linked to piazza del Duomo by via dei Calzaiuoli – the city's main street in the Middle Ages – it has been the heart of civic life since the early 14th century and is rather like an open-air theatre that never closes.

The piazza was created in 1268, after the Guelphs defeated the Ghibellines, and buildings belonging to a prominent Ghibelline family were confiscated and left to fall into ruins as a visible reminder of their dastardly dealings. It grew larger when the Palazzo Vecchio was built to house the Signoria – the republican government. It's perhaps most famous as the site of the **Bonfire of the Vanities** on 7 February 1497, when the zealous monk Savonarola (1452-98) – who had briefly become the city's ruler – ordered that sinful items (anything from mirrors and board games to priceless paintings and books) should be burned. He already operated a sort of religious police, who forced people to dress modestly and observe religious fasts, and even encouraged children to inform on their families. The bonfire was the high point of Savonarola's power. A few months later he was excommunicated, and in 1498 the Florentines turned against him: Savonarola was burned at the stake in this same piazza.

You'll see many statues in the square. There's a copy of Michelangelo's *David* in front of the Palazzo Vecchio, as well as the enormous **Neptune Fountain** (1575), in which a muscular Neptune (who from a certain angle looks, let's say, very pleased to see you) stands surrounded by water nymphs. Michelangelo declared that the sculptor, Bartolomeo Ammannati, had ruined a good piece of marble, and Florentines call Neptune *Il Biancone* – Big Whitey. There's also an equestrian statue of the Medici ruler Cosimo I, by Giambologna. Other statues fill the neighbouring **Loggia dei Lanzi**, including Giambologna's *Rape of the Sabine Women* (1583), sculpted from one enormous piece of marble, and Benvenuto Cellini's bronze *Perseus* (1554) who holds Medusa's head aloft.

The best people-watching spot is outside Rivoire. OK, the coffee's expensive but the seats afford an excellent view of the Palazzo Vecchio and the piazza.

The Palazzo Vecchio entrance.

The Salone dei Cinquecento.

Palazzo Vecchio

Piazza della Signoria, T055-276 8224/276 8325; comune.fi.it.
Fri-Wed 0900-1900, Thu 0900-1400, €6, €4.50 18-25, €2 children 3-17, €14 family of 4, €16 family of 5. €8 combined ticket with Brancacci Chapel, €8 Secret Passages tour.

The building of this forbidding, fortress-like structure – which was designed by Arnolfo di Cambio – began in 1299 and was completed by the early 14th century. It was the centre of power in Florence and is still the city hall. The nine *Priori*, or republican rulers, lived here while in office, as did the Medici when Cosimo I moved here in 1540. It was originally called the Palazzo dei Priori, but when Cosimo later moved to the Pitti Palace on the other side of the Arno, this building became known as the Palazzo Vecchio, the Old Palace.

The interior still largely reflects Cosimo's era. He was keen to put his stamp on the palace and particularly wanted to eradicate anything that celebrated the republic, so employed Vasari, his court architect, to transform it. The lavishness is immediately evident while you queue to have your bags put through airport-style security in the courtyard, which was started by Michelozzo in the 15th century and later embellished by Vasari.

Salone dei Cinquecento Walk upstairs and you come to this vast room, the Hall of the Five Hundred, which was originally the meeting place for the representatives of Florence's republic. The gilded ceiling is covered in richly decorated panels celebrating the wonders of the Medici and the history of Florence – with Cosimo depicted like a Roman emperor. You can also see Michelangelo's statue *The Genius of Victory*.

The room practically echoes with the thunder of horses' hooves, as the walls are covered in Vasari's frescoes illustrating Florentine (and Medici) military triumphs over Pisa and Siena. Originally Michelangelo and Leonardo were commissioned to paint battle scenes here: the former the *Battle of*

Cascina, the latter the Battle of Anghiari. However Michelangelo had completed only the cartoon or preparatory drawing for his fresco when Pope Julius II summoned him to Rome. As conventional frescoes had to be painted very quickly on wet plaster, Leonardo instead tried out an ancient technique known as *encausto* or encaustic painting, in which pigment was mixed with wax, to give himself more time to work. However, he had to use fires to keep the walls warm enough to work – and the wax melted and dripped. Leonardo abandoned the fresco and it was traditionally thought that Vasari simply painted over it, but some now think that he saved it by covering it with a thin wall. The search is on to find the lost Leonardo.

Tip...

The Palazzo Vecchio organizes special tours and events for children, which really help to bring the palace alive (around €8/€4.50). Book by phone or at the desk in the palace: officials will sometimes let you in through the barriers at the side entrance near the Neptune Fountain if you just want to book, which saves queuing for ages. Tours are daily in season, but not all are in English, so check before booking.

Studiolo di Francesco I If you are not on a special tour, you will only be able to peep into this jewel box of a room, in which every surface seems adorned with gilded and painted panels. However, on the Secret Passages tour you can see it properly and get a real insight into the strange world of the Medici. This windowless room was the private studio of Francesco, Cosimo I's son, who was fascinated by alchemy. Designed by Vasari, it was decorated by 30 artists, and each wall is dedicated to one of the four elements – Air, Fire, Water and Earth. The lowest paintings conceal secret cupboards in which Francesco kept his precious objects.

Another room on the Secret Passages tour is Cosimo's study, much smaller than his son's, with a secret door and places where he hid his jewellery, potions and glassware. Also on this floor are the rooms of Leo X, lavishly decorated with frescoes.

Quartiere di Eleonora di Toledo On the next level, if you turn left, you come to the **Quartiere degli Elementi**, a series of rooms decorated by Vasari. You can peep into the **Scrittoio della Calliope** (Calliope Study), dedicated to the Muses – if you look behind the door you can just see a rare stained glass window made by Walter of Antwerp, from a drawing by Vasari. Make sure you go on to the Terrazzo di Giunone and the Terrazzo di Saturno – the views are lovely.

If you turn right, you walk high above the Salone dei Cinquecento and enter the apartments of Eleonora di Toledo, the 18-year-old wife of Cosimo I. The tiny chapel is covered in paintings by Bronzino.

Left: The Neptune Fountain.
Right: The Palazzo Vecchio courtyard.

It's a fact...

Filippo Lippi found it hard to control his lusty nature. At times his patron, Cosimo I, had to lock him up to make sure he got on with his painting instead of chasing women.

Sala dei Gigli You will next come to the **Sala dell'Udienza** (Audience Hall), with its imposing blue and golden ceiling, and then enter the **Sala dei Gigli** (Room of the Lilies), which gets its name from the fleurs-de-lys on the walls and boasts beautiful frescoes by Ghirlandaio. It's here that you'll find Donatello's bronze statue of *Judith and Holofernes* (c1460), which once stood in the piazza della Signoria.

Map room This was originally the *guarderoba*, where a variety of precious items were stored. It is covered with maps, by Egnazio Danti, depicting the known world in the mid-16th century: one shows Nova Spagna, which is possibly California. The maps are on panels, arranged in blocks of four. Look at the top left corner of the bottom right panel in each set, and you will see a little slot for a key – the panels conceal cupboards. Behind 'Armenia' is a secret door: the palace is filled with hidden corridors that allowed the rulers to move around without anyone seeing them.

Before you reach the exit you can visit the oldest part of the palace. These rooms contain the Loeser Bequest paintings, but it's worth just taking a look at the rooms themselves with their brightly painted wooden ceilings. In the last one, behind a thick wooden door, is a stone toilet.

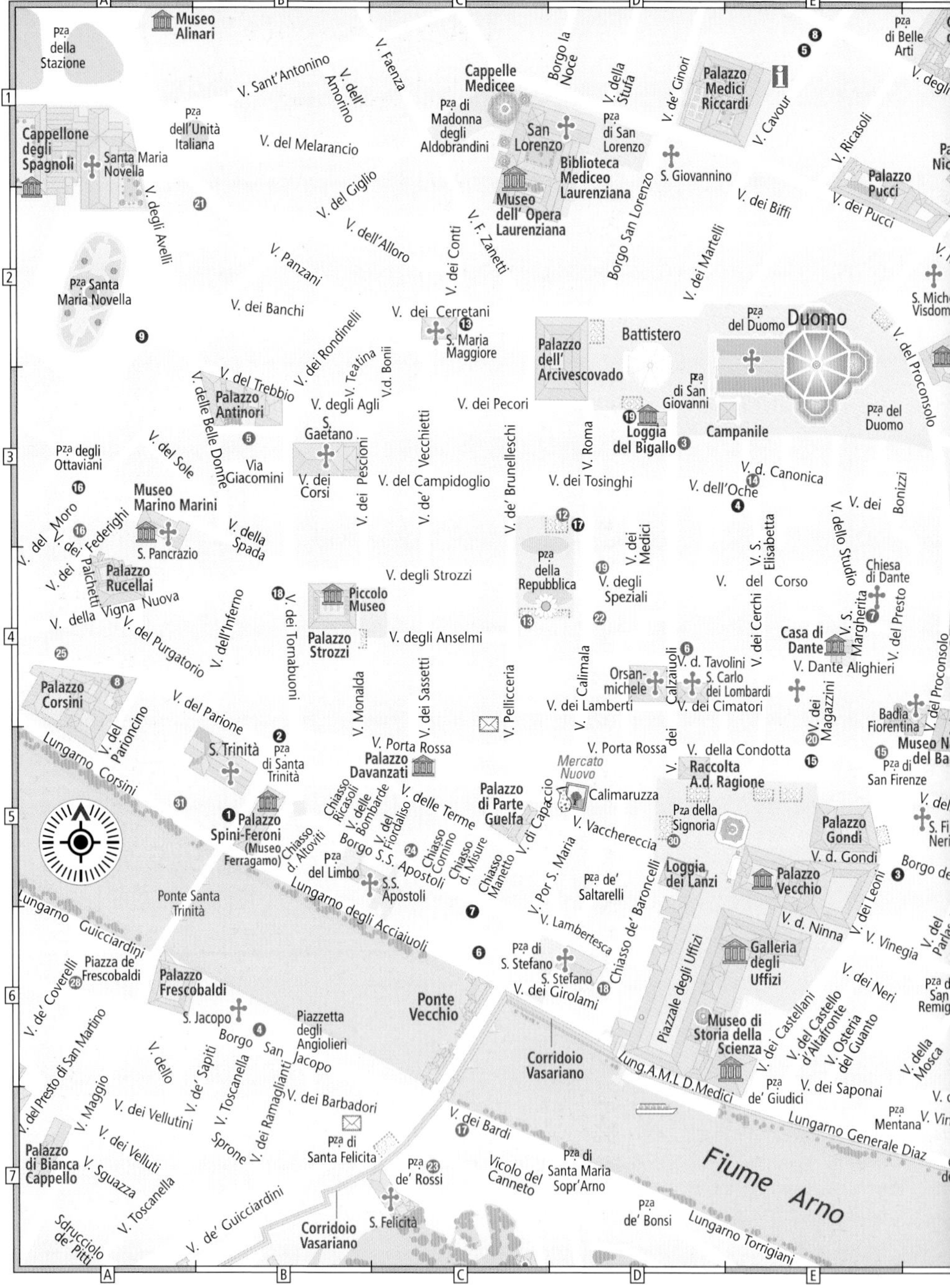

Museo Alinari
Pza della Stazione
V. Sant'Antonino
V. dell' Amorino
V. Faenza
Cappelle Medicee
Borgo la Noce
V. della Stufa
V. de' Ginori
Palazzo Medici Riccardi
Pza di Belle Arti
V. degli
Pza dell'Unità Italiana
Cappellone degli Spagnoli
Santa Maria Novella
V. del Melarancio
Pza di Madonna degli Aldobrandini
San Lorenzo
Pza di San Lorenzo
V. Cavour
V. Ricasoli
Biblioteca Mediceo Laurenziana
S. Giovannino
Palazzo Pucci
V. del Giglio
V. degli Avelli
Museo dell' Opera Laurenziana
Borgo San Lorenzo
V. dei Biffi
V. dei Pucci
V. dell'Alloro
V. dei Conti
V. F. Zanetti
V. dei Martelli
V. Panzani
Pza Santa Maria Novella
V. dei Banchi
V. dei Cerretani
S. Maria Maggiore
Palazzo dell' Arcivescovado
Battistero
Pza del Duomo
Duomo
V. del Proconsolo
V. dei Rondinelli
V. Teatina
V.d. Bonii
V. del Trebbio
Palazzo Antinori
V. delle Belle Donne
V. degli Agli
V. dei Pecori
Pza di San Giovanni
Loggia del Bigallo
Campanile
Pza del Duomo
S. Gaetano
V. del Sole
Pza degli Ottaviani
Via Giacomini
V. dei Corsi
V. dei Pescioni
V. de' Vecchietti
V. del Campidoglio
V. de' Brunelleschi
V. Roma
V. dei Tosinghi
V. d. Canonica
V. dell'Oche
V. dei
Bonizzi
Museo Marino Marini
V. del Moro
V. dei Federighi
S. Pancrazio
V. della Spada
V. dello Studio
Pza della Repubblica
V. dei Medici
V. S. Elisabetta
V. degli Strozzi
V. degli Speziali
V. del Corso
Chiesa di Dante
V. dei Palchetti
Palazzo Rucellai
Piccolo Museo
V. dei Tornabuoni
V. della Vigna Nuova
V. dell'Inferno
V. del Purgatorio
Palazzo Strozzi
V. degli Anselmi
V. dei Cerchi
V. S. Margherita
V. del Presto
Casa di Dante
V. Dante Alighieri
Palazzo Corsini
V. Monalda
V. dei Sassetti
V. Pellicceria
Calimala
Calzaiuoli
V. d. Tavolini
Orsanmichele
S. Carlo dei Lombardi
V. dei Cimatori
V. dei Lamberti
V. del Proconsolo
V. dei Magazzini
Badia Fiorentina
V. del Parione
V. del Parioncino
S. Trinità
Pza di Santa Trinità
V. Porta Rossa
Palazzo Davanzati
Mercato Nuovo
V. Porta Rossa
V. della Condotta
Raccolta A.d. Ragione
Museo N del Ba
Pza di San Firenze
Lungarno Corsini
Chiasso Ricasoli
V. delle Bombarde
V. del Fiordaliso
V. delle Terme
Palazzo di Parte Guelfa
V. di Capaccio
Calimaruzza
V. Vacchereccia
Pza della Signoria
Palazzo Gondi
V. d. Gondi
Palazzo Spini-Feroni (Museo Ferragamo)
Chiasso d. Altoviti
Pza del Limbo
Borgo S.S. Apostoli
Chiasso Cornino
Chiasso d. Misure
Chiasso Manetto
V. Por S. Maria
Pza de' Saltarelli
Loggia dei Lanzi
Palazzo Vecchio
Borgo de
S.S. Apostoli
Ponte Santa Trinità
Lungarno degli Acciaiuoli
V. Lambertesca
Chiasso de' Baroncelli
V. d. Ninna
V. dei Leoni
V. Vinegia
Lungarno Guicciardini
Piazza de Frescobaldi
Pza di S. Stefano
S. Stefano
Galleria degli Uffizi
Piazzale degli Uffizi
V. dei Neri
Palazzo Frescobaldi
V. dei Girolami
V. de' Coverelli
Ponte Vecchio
S. Jacopo
Piazzetta degli Angiolieri
Borgo San Jacopo
Corridoio Vasariano
Museo di Storia della Scienza
V. dei Castellani
V. del Castello d'Altafronte
V. Osteria del Guanto
V. della Mosca
V. del Presto di San Martino
V. dello
V. de' Sapiti
V. Toscanella
V. dei Ramaglianti
Lung.A.M.L D.Medici
Pza de' Giudici
V. dei Saponai
V. Maggio
V. dei Velluttini
V. dei Barbadori
Pza Mentana
Lungarno Generale Diaz
V. dei Bardi
V. dei Velluti
Sprone
Pza di Santa Felicita
Palazzo di Bianca Cappello
V. Sguazza
Pza de' Rossi
Vicolo del Canneto
Pza di Santa Maria Sopr'Arno
Fiume Arno
V. Toscanella
V. de' Guicciardini
Corridoio Vasariano
S. Felicità
Pza de' Bonsi
Lungarno Torrigiani
Sdrucciolo de' Pitti

Central Florence listings

❶ Sleeping

1 Antica Torre di Via Tornabuoni 1 *via dei Tornabuoni 1*, B5
2 Beacci Tornabuoni, *via dei Tornabuoni 3*, B5
3 Bernini Palace *piazza San Firenze 29*, E5
4 Brunelleschi *piazza Santa Elisabetta 3*, E3
5 Casci *via Cavour 13*, E1
6 Continentale *vicolo dell'Oro 6r*, C6
7 Gallery Hotel Art *vicolo dell'Oro 5*, C6
8 Il Guelfo Bianco *via Cavour 29*, E1
9 J.K. Place *piazza Santa Maria Novella 7*, A2
10 Morandi alla Crocetta *via Laura 50*, H1
11 Palazzo Antellesi *piazza Santa Croce 19-22*, G6
12 Palazzo Galletti *via Sant'Egidio 12*, H3
13 Perseo *via dei Cerretani 1*, C2
14 Residence Hilda *via dei Servi 40*, F1
15 Residenza d'Epoca in Piazza della Signoria *via dei Magazzini 2*, E5
16 Residenza del Moro *via del Moro 15*, A3
17 Savoy *piazza della Repubblica 7*, D3
18 Scoti *via dei Tornabuoni 7*, B4
19 Soggiorno Battistero *piazza San Giovanni 1*, D3

❶ Eating & drinking

1 Acqua al 2 *via della Vigna Vecchia 40r*, F5
2 Angels *via del Proconsolo 29/31*, F4
3 Bar Gallo *piazza Duomo 1r*, D3
4 Borgo San Jacopo *borgo San Jacopo 62r*, B6
5 Cantinetta Antinori *piazza degli Antinori 3*, B3
6 Cantinetta dei Verrazzano *via dei Tavolini 18/20r*, D4
7 Da Vinattieri *via Santa Margherita 6r*, E4
8 Florian *via del Parione 28r*, A4
9 Gastone *via Matteo Palmieri 26r*, G4
10 Gelateria dei Neri *via dei Neri 20/22r*, F6
11 Il Gelato Vivoli *via Isola delle Stinche 7*, G5
12 Gilli *piazza della Repubblica 39r*, D3
13 Giubbe Rosse *piazza della Repubblica 13/14r*, C4
14 Grom *via del Campanile 4*, E3
15 Gustavino *via della Condotta 37r*, E5
16 Il Latini *via dei Palchetti 6r*, A3
17 Il Panino del Chianti *via de' Bardi 63r*, C7
18 'Ino *via del Georgofili 3r/7r*, D6
19 L'Incontro *piazza della Repubblica 7*, D4
20 La Canova di Gustavino *via della Condotta 29*, E5
21 La Dantesca *via Panzani 57r*, B2
22 La Rinascente Cafe *piazza della Repubblica 1*, D4
23 Le Volpi e l'Uva *piazza dei Rossi 1*, C7
24 Mangiafoco Caffè *borgo Santissimi Apostoli 26r*, C5
25 Mariano *via del Parione 19r*, A4
26 Note di Vino *borgo de' Greci 4/6r*, G5
27 Oibò *borgo de' Greci 1/1a*, G6
28 Olio & Convivium *via di Santo Spirito 4*, A6
29 Osteria del Caffè Italiano *via Isola delle Stinche 11/13r*, G5
30 Rivoire *piazza della Signoria 4r*, D5
31 Rossini *lungarno Corsini 4*, A5

Tip...

Queues can get long at the Uffizi, so book in advance. If you decide to take a chance get there before they open or try at mid-afternoon, before 1530, when it is – sometimes – quieter.

Above: The Uffizi by night.
Right: Statues at the Uffizi.

Galleria degli Uffizi

Piazzale degli Uffizi, T055-238 8651, firenzemusei.it. Tue-Sun 0815-1850, Jul-Sep may open until 2200 Tue-Wed, €6.50, €3.25 EU citizens (with passport) 18-25/over 65, under 18 free; €10/€5 during special exhibitions. Pre-book on T055-294883, at ticket office or on polomuseale.firenze.it (€4 booking fee). Lift at entrance.

Uffizi means 'offices', and this enormous, strength-sapping gallery was built by Vasari to provide administrative offices for Cosimo I. His heirs began to display their enormous collection of artworks here, and the last Medici heiress left it to the city. It contains the world's finest collection of Renaissance art and is crammed with masterpieces. Allow at least three hours for a visit and accept that you just won't see everything. Work is under way to expand the exhibition space, so don't be surprised if some rooms are closed or the layout is changed when you visit.

The main rooms are all upstairs, leading off two long corridors with ceilings painted in brilliant colours and walls lined with portraits and statues. Most of the collection is arranged chronologically, showing the development of Florentine art.

Rooms 2-10 The most important works in room 2 are the three altarpieces of the *Madonna Enthroned*, by Cimabue, Duccio and Giotto. They show how artists gradually broke away from the flat, idealized images that characterized Byzantine art and began to depict their subjects as real human beings. By the time you get to Giotto's work, which probably came from Ognissanti Church (see page 120), you can see real depth and softer, more natural poses.

Room 3 contains 14th-century Sienese works, notably a gilded *Annunciation* by Simone Martini, as well as paintings by the Lorenzetti brothers. In rooms 5 and 6 you'll find works illustrating the international Gothic style, in particular Gentile da Fabriano's *Adoration of the Magi* (1423). This richly gilded painting was commissioned by a rival of the Medici for his private chapel, to show off his wealth.

Room 7 contains works of the early Renaissance, with paintings by Fra Angelico, Masaccio and a rare piece by Domenico Veneziano. His *Madonna and Child with Saints*, created for the Church of Santa

Don't miss in the Uffizi...

Giotto's *Madonna Enthroned*
The Duke and Duchess of Urbino by Piero della Francesca
Botticelli's *Birth of Venus*
Michelangelo's *Holy Family*
The Annunciation by Leonardo da Vinci
Raphael's *Madonna of the Goldfinch*
Titian's *Venus of Urbino*
Filippo Lippi's *Madonna and Child with Two Angels*

Lucia, marks a move away from gilding in its use of pastel shades and soft, natural light. Veneziano died destitute in Florence. In Room 8, all attention is on Piero della Francesca's panels depicting the Duke and Duchess of Urbino. They look extremely human There are several works by Fra Filippo Lippi, including a particularly beautiful *Madonna and Child with Two Angels* (c1465). The model is thought to have been Lucrezia Buti, a nun with whom Lippi, a monk but a notorious womanizer, was in love. He ran away with her and they set up home – their son was Filippino Lippi.

Room 9 contain works by Antonio and Piero Pollaiolo, who were willing to experiment with art. Antonio was noted for his anatomical observation.

Rooms 10-14 This is really one room, which showcases the paintings of Sandro Botticelli, most famously *The Birth of Venus* (c1484) in which Venus stands naked in a seashell being blown to land by the breath of Zephyrus. There is also *Primavera* (c1482), in which Venus stands in a wood surrounded by the three Graces, Flora, the goddess of Spring and Mercury.

Rooms 15-16 Here you can see early works by Leonardo da Vinci. There is the *Baptism of Christ in the Jordan* (c1473-8) on which he collaborated with his teacher, Andrea del Verrocchio. It's thought that he painted his *Annunciation* (c1472) while he was still working in Verrocchio's studio. In it, Mary no longer sits in her bedroom as she did in earlier Annunciations; she is now in a palace and the Angel Gabriel's wings look strong and powerful. Leonardo's other work, painted on wood, is the *Adoration of the Magi* (c1481). He never completed the work because he left for Milan in 1482. Peep into **room 16**, and the map-covered walls.

Rooms 18-24 Room 18, also known as the Tribuna, is an octagonal room that contained the Medicis' favourite works. The walls are covered

Above: Ponte Vecchio. Right: A statue from the Bargello.

with red velvet, the cupola encrusted with mother of pearl. Works within it include a richly decorated table, a sculpture known as the Medici Venus and paintings by Bronzino and Pontormo. The other rooms on this corridor contain works by artists from Luca Signorelli in **room 19** to the German masters Albrecht Dürer and Lucas Cranach in **room 20**. **Room 24** contains miniatures.

You've now reached the side of the gallery that overlooks the Arno. From the window at the far end, at the top of the next corridor, you get a great view of the Ponte Vecchio and can clearly see the roof of the **Corridorio Vasariano**. This is the covered passage, over 500 m long, designed by Vasari to link the Palazzo Vecchio to the Pitti Palace, via the Ponte Vecchio. It allowed the Medici to come and go without anyone seeing them. You can sometimes join a tour of the corridor, but you must book in advance.

At the end of this next corridor and on to the terrace, there's a café here, and even though it's expensive, the views of the Duomo and the Palazzo Vecchio are superb. If you're out here at noon you'll hear the city's bells ringing.

Rooms 25-28 Room 25 contains Michelangelo's *Holy Family* or *Doni Tondo* (1506-8), a work that inspired Mannerist artists. Not only has he departed from convention by not placing Christ on the Virgin's lap, his figures have clearly been influenced by his studies of classical statuary.

For works by Raphael go into room 26, where you can see the *Madonna of the Goldfinch* (c1505-6), an extremely gentle painting in which the infant Christ strokes the head of a goldfinch held by John the Baptist. There is also a more mature work from 1518 – the portrait *Pope Leo X with Two Cardinals*.

In **room 28**, Titian's *Venus of Urbino* (1538) reclines naked on a rumpled bed – it's the biggest selling postcard in the gallery. It was painted, apparently, as a lesson in sensuality for the young (very – she was 11) bride of the Duke of Urbino.

Rooms 31-45 Works in these rooms range from Tintoretto's *Leda and the Swan* (c1550-60) to paintings by Rubens and Rembrandt. The latter's works are in room 44, where there are also some lovely Dutch landscapes. In room 45, if you've lasted that long, you'll find some of Canaletto's unmistakable views of Venice.

Ponte Vecchio

The Old Bridge dates back to around 1345, and replaced an even older bridge built by the Romans. In 1944, when the Nazis blew up all the bridges in Florence to stall the Allies' advance, this was the only one to be spared. It retains its medieval appearance, lined with shops and apartments, giving it a pleasantly higgledy-piggledy appearance. At one time it was the haunt of butchers and tanners, but the smell became so bad in the late 16th century that they were evicted to make way for goldsmiths. The jewellers are still there today. If you cross the Arno at the next bridge up, the Ponte Santa Trinità, you'll not only get great views of the Ponte Vecchio but also escape the crowds.

Museo Nazionale del Bargello

Via del Proconsolo 4, T055-238 8606, firenzemusei.it.

Tue-Sun and 1st, 3rd and 5th Mon of each month 0815-1400, €4, €2 EU citizens (with passport)/18-25/over 65, free under 18; €7 during special exhibitions. Pre-book on T055-294883 or polomuseale.firenze.it (€3 booking fee).

Just a short walk from piazza della Signoria, the Bargello is Florence's principal museum of sculpture. A forbidding building from the outside, it dates back to 1255, when it served as the seat of the *Capitano del Popolo*, the commander of the local militia. By 1271 it was the home of the *Podestà* (the chief magistrate), and it eventually became a court, prison and torture chamber. The Medici later made it the seat of the Bargello, the chief of police. It continued to serve as a prison until 1857, after which it was completely restored, becoming a museum of sculpture in 1859. The inner courtyard makes a striking contrast to the severe exterior, with arcades, coats of arms, a romantic upper loggia and – in summer – swallows swooping overhead. It's hard to believe that it was once the site of the city's gallows.

The area opposite the entrance is used for temporary exhibitions. Upstairs on the first floor are carved ivories dating from the fifth to the 17th centuries – perhaps the most famous item is the ninth-century *flabellum*, or fan, which kept insects away from the altar during religious ceremonies. Other rooms contain majolica ware, Islamic art and 13th- and 14th-century sculptures by Arnolfo di Cambio and Tino da Camaino.

Displayed in the loggia are the Flemish sculptor Giambologna's bronze birds, made for the Medici. The main room on this level is notable for its works by Donatello. The most important sculptor of the 15th century, Donatello – who trained as a goldsmith and then worked for a while in Ghiberti's studio – combined great technical ability with enormous expressiveness. Here you can see his original *St George* (1416-17), carved for a niche on the Orsanmichele (see page 90), and the restored *Amore-Attis* (c1440) – a quirky figure wearing a thick belt, sandals and a rather wicked expression. Pride of place goes to his slim, beautiful and rather camp bronze *David* (1440s). Carved for the Medici, this was the first freestanding nude statue in Western art since classical times. Other works include the panels made by Brunelleschi and Ghiberti as entries for the competition to make the doors of the Baptistery (see page 89).

Downstairs, beside the entrance, is a room displaying works by Michelangelo, Cellini and Giambologna. Compare Michelangelo's tipsy marble *Bacchus* (1496-7), with grapes cascading from his head, with Giambologna's version.

A walking tour of Florence

Start your tour at **Sant'Ambrogio market** on piazza Ghiberti. It's where locals come to buy their fruit and vegetables and is particularly lively early in the morning. Now walk down via de' Macci, turn right down via di San Giuseppe and you'll come to **Santa Croce**, where everyone from Michelangelo to Machiavelli is buried. You should be nice and early so you can beat the crowds if you intend to go inside (but allow – at least! – 90 minutes for a visit). If you're not going in, wander on to the piazza and admire the church's dazzling façade.

Now, if you want to visit some leather workshops, leave the piazza by Borgo de' Greci – it's lined with them. Or if you fancy an ice cream, turn left down via de' Benci and right into via dei Neri, where you'll find **Gelateria dei Neri**, which even offers soya ices. Either street will eventually bring you on to via Leoni – follow this round and you'll come into the **piazza della Signoria**, the civic heart of Florence where Savaronola held his Bonfire of the Vanities. Looking over the piazza is the forbidding Palazzo Vecchio, which dates back to the end of the 13th century – you'll need to allow a couple of hours for a visit, so settle instead for a coffee at Rivoire and a look at the statues in the square, notably the copy of Michelangelo's *David*.

The Uffizi Gallery is just off piazza della Signoria, but leave it for another day (you'll need to allow at least three hours) and walk along via Vacchereccia to the **Mercato Nuovo**, where you can browse for bags and belts and rub the nose of *Il Porcellino*, the bronze boar who sits here. Walk along via Porta Rossa to the **Palazzo Davanzati** (which you can visit if you get there before lunch): it's one of Florence's lesser-known sights and gives an intriguing insight into medieval life. Continue to piazza Trinità and turn left to cross the **ponte Santa Trinità** – a great place to get photos of the **Ponte Vecchio**. For lunch you could now continue over the bridge to the **Oltrarno**, perhaps for a tasting plate at Olio & Convivium (via di Santo Spirito), or go back over the bridge and have a lunch at a café such as Mangiafoco on Borgo Santissimi Apostoli.

After lunch, time for some window-shopping along **via dei Tornabuoni**, which is crammed with designer names, then turn right at the top and walk along to the **piazza del Duomo**. The cathedral itself takes some time to explore, especially if you want to climb up inside **Brunelleschi's dome**. However, you should have time to visit the **Baptistery**, probably the oldest building in Florence. A short walk north now will take you to the **Palazzo Medici-Riccardi**, where the Medici lived before they moved into the Palazzo Vecchio. Pop in and see the frescoes in the **Chapel of the Magi**. Continue walking north, along via Cavour, and you'll come to **San Marco**, the monastic complex funded by Cosimo de' Medici. It was to here that Savonarola fled before he was arrested, and here that Fra Angelico painted delicate devotional frescoes on the walls of the monks' cells. It is one of the city's most atmospheric spots.

Before you head back into the city centre, take a walk along via Cesare Battisti to piazza Santissima Annunziata, Florence's elegant Renaissance square. The **Basilica della Santissima Annunziata** holds a special place in the hearts of local people – inside you'll find one of the most revered shrines in the city.

Left: The fountain of Neptune beside the Palazzo Vecchio. Right clockwise: The Uffizi; on the Duomo steps; detail from Ponte Vecchio.

San Marco

There's an almost constant stream of tourists to the area around piazza San Marco – all desperate to tick Michelangelo's *David* off their 'must see' list. However, a surprising number don't stay around to visit the area's other glorious sight – the Museo di San Marco, a Dominican monastery lovingly frescoed by Fra Angelico.

Galleria dell'Accademia

Via Ricasoli 60, T055-238 8612, firenzemusei.it. Tue-Sun 0815-1850, Jul-Sep may open until 2200 Tue-Thu, €6.50, €3.25 EU citizens (with passport)/18-25, free under 18/over 65; €10/€5 during special exhibitions. Pre-book on T055-294883 or polomuseale.firenze.it (€4 booking fee).

The Accademia started life as the Accademia di Belle Arti, an art school that gradually developed its own collection of artworks. Today around a million visitors a year are said to beat a path here – all to see just one statue.

Michelangelo's *David* It's strange to think that the Carrara marble from which this, probably the world's most famous statue, was carved had been rejected by other artists as unworkable – too thin, cracked and discoloured. It lay in storage, rather battered, until Michelangelo asked if he could try his hand. He was only in his mid-20s. The Opera del Duomo commissioned him and he started work in 1501. By 1504 this huge statue (over 4 m high) was completed.

It attracted controversy from the outset. This powerful-looking David, capable of defeating Goliath, symbolized the new republican Florence – recently freed from the rule of both the Medici family and Savonarola. When the statue was moved into place on the piazza della Signoria, it was attacked by mobs of Medici sympathizers. David got rather battered over the years. His left arm was smashed during a riot in 1527, and he was pounded by the elements. He was moved to the Accademia for protection in 1873, but was attacked in 1991 by an Italian painter, who smashed his toe with a hammer.

Stand beneath the mighty statue today and you're sure to be struck by David's outsize hands and rather large head. This was deliberate, as Michelangelo intended him to stand high up on the Duomo and to be viewed from far below. You might also notice that he isn't particularly well endowed. There is a theory that this too is deliberate: this David (unlike Donatello's earlier version) is not a young boy who has just killed a giant, he's an athletic man preparing for a fight, and every anatomical detail is considered to be correct – including a 'manhood' that has shrivelled with fear. A screen next to the statue allows you to view parts of it in detail, such as the unusual heart-shaped pupils of his eyes.

Recently there has been concern that the statue is in danger of cracking, due to the vibrations of the millions of feet that pass it each day. Some have suggested that it should be removed to a new site, outside the city centre; others want to insulate it at a cost of around €1m.

Head over to the Galleria dell'Accademia to see Michelangelo's *David*, the world's most famous statue.

The rest of the collection The Accademia is also home to a plaster model of Giambologna's *Rape of the Sabines* and two fascinating incomplete works by Michelangelo. Known as the *Slaves*, or *Prisoners*, they were intended for the tomb of Pope Julius II but were never completed. They clearly show how a sculpture would emerge from a piece of stone, like a prisoner escaping.

In another room, devoted to 14th-century art, there's a gilded *Tree of Life* (1310-15) by Pacino di Buonaguida, in which Christ's ancestry is lovingly portrayed. The Accademia also contains a **Museum of Musical Instruments** (turn right as you go in). If you're lucky you might happen upon an ensemble playing the instruments in rehearsal for a concert.

Museo di San Marco

Piazza San Marco 3, T055-238 8608, firenzemusei.it. Mon-Fri 0815-1350, Sat 0815-1850, Sun 0815-1900 (open 1st, 3rd and 5th Mon of each month and 2nd and 4th Sun), €4 EU citizens (with passport) €2 18-25, free under 18/over 65; pre-book on T055-294883 or polomuseale.firenze.it (€3 booking fee).

Founded in 1436, this Dominican monastery was built with generous funds from the devout Medici, Cosimo il Vecchio ('the Elder'). He engaged the architect Michelozzo to create an elegant complex for the order, which had moved here from Fiesole. The whole place exudes a gentle piety, with tranquil cloisters and walls that seem to whisper their history as you pass. The most important works are undoubtedly the frescoes painted by one of the monastery's inmates – the monk and talented artist Fra Angelico. His works were intended to inspire devotion and contemplation, and have a remarkable ethereal quality.

You come first to Michelozzo's cool, green Sant'Antonio cloister, on one wall of which you can see Fra Angelico's *St Dominic at the Cross* (c1442). The former Pilgrim's Hospice, to the right of the entrance, is filled with panel paintings by Fra Angelico, taken from churches and monasteries all over Florence. They include the *Pala di San Marco* (c1438-43) considered the prototype Renaissance altarpiece, which was commissioned by Cosimo il Vecchio for the monastery church.

Awaiting you at the top of the stairs is Fra Angelico's masterpiece – his immensely moving *Annunciation* (c1442). The Virgin and the Angel Gabriel gently bend towards one another beneath the arches of a loggia resembling that created by Michelozzo. There are more lovingly painted frescoes in the monks' cells that line the corridors. Those on the left wall are by Fra Angelico himself; the others follow his design. The first cell on the left has a *Noli mi Tangere*, in which Christ appears to Mary Magdalene in a garden – the landscape featuring prominently in the picture. The fifth 5th on the left-hand side has a *Nativity* scene and cell 6

Below: Statue in the piazza Santissima Annunziata.
Right: The piazza Santissima Annunziata.

has a luminous *Transfiguration*. If you walk along the next corridor you come to the cells occupied by Savonarola, the Dominican friar who ordered the Bonfire of the Vanities (see page 92). There are fragments of his clothes, including a black cloak, his rosary and a painting of him being burned at the stake in the piazza della Signoria. If you turn right and go to the end, you'll come to a comparatively plush set of cells reserved for Cosimo Il Vecchio . Back downstairs, the Small Refectory has a fresco of the *Last Supper* (c1479-80) on the end wall. It's by Ghirlandaio and is considered to be the twin of the one he painted in the Ognissanti (see page 120).

Piazza Santissima Annunziata

This lovely square, close to San Marco, is famed for the elegantly restrained nine-arched loggia of the Spedale degli Innocenti. This was Europe's first foundling hospital, designed by Brunelleschi around 1419. Above the arches you can see Andrea della Robbia's blue terracotta roundels depicting babies – designed to encourage charitable giving – which were added in the 1480s. Later there was a small revolving door in the wall, where babies could be left anonymously.

The Santissima Annunziata (T055-266181, daily 0730-1230 and 1600-1830, free) is surely the most extraordinary church in Florence, gilded and elaborately decorated like a dark-coloured opera house. The walls of the cloisters, which you walk through on your way in, are covered with frescoes – the earliest is a *Nativity* painted in 1460 by Alesso Baldovinetti, and there are others by Andrea del Sarto. When you go into the church it seems almost back to front, as there's an ornate shrine to the left of the entrance that looks at first like the altar. It was built to house a 14th-century painting of the Virgin that was said to have been completed by angels and was credited with many miracles.

Giardino dei Semplici

Via Micheli 3, msn.unifi.it.
Mon-Tue, Thu-Sun 1000-1300, Sat 1000-1700, may open longer in summer, €6, €3 concessions.

If you want to escape the crowds for a while, visit this botanical garden near San Marco, established by Cosimo I to research medicinal plants. Now part of the University of Florence's Natural History Museum, it makes a pleasant place to stroll and snooze. The entry price also gets you in to the other sections of the museum.

Around San Lorenzo

Squeezed between Santa Maria Novella and San Marco, this part of Florence is closely associated with the Medici: this was where they lived, where they worshipped and where they are buried. It's an immensely lively area, due not only to its proximity to the main station, but also to the presence of a busy street market and the *Mercato Centrale*, the covered food market.

Basilica di San Lorenzo

Piazza San Lorenzo, T055-264 5184.
Mon-Sat 1000-1730, Sun 1330-1730, closed Sun Nov-Mar, €3.50.

The Church of San Lorenzo is the oldest church in Florence. Founded in AD 393, it once served as Florence's cathedral – before Santa Reparata, the church now buried beneath the Duomo, took over. In later years it became the parish church of the wealthy Medici family. In 1419 Giovanni di Bicci de' Medici offered to pay for a new church and commissioned Brunelleschi to carry out the work. Brunelleschi died before he could complete it, and the building was finished by another architect, possibly Antonio Manetti. In the 16th century, the Medici Pope Leo X commissioned Michelangelo to create a grand marble façade and a plan was drawn up, but the project was later abandoned and the church remains unfinished to this day.

"Balls, Balls, Balls!"

Throughout Florence and Tuscany you'll see a distinctive coat of arms, studded with six large balls or pills (*palle*). This was the emblem of the Medici family. The number of balls varied over the years – in Cosimo's time there were seven, for instance. One theory has it that the balls refer to the family's origins as doctors or apothecaries (*medici*), another that they are coins. The colours have faded today, but the shield was originally gold and the balls red, except for the one at the top, which was blue and decorated with a fleur-de-lys. In times of danger, supporters of the Medici rallied followers with a distinctive call to arms: "*Palle, Palle, Palle!*" – or "Balls, Balls, Balls!" The ubiquity of this distinctive emblem attracted contemporary criticism: "He has emblazoned even the monks' privies with his balls," said one.

The most important works inside are the bronze pulpits, the last works of Donatello, which are carved in a free, unfinished style, like dramatic sketches. He died before he completed them and they were finished by his pupils. Donatello is buried in the church, beside his patron Cosimo il Vecchio. Then there's the Sagrestia Vecchia (the Old Sacristy), which was one of Brunelleschi's first works. It was decorated by Donatello and contains Medici tombs.

Cappelle Medicee

Piazza Madonna degli Aldobrandini, T055-238 8602, firenzemusei.it.
Tue-Sat and 1st, 3rd and 5th Sun of each month, 0815-1750 (may close earlier out of season), €6, €3 EU citizens (with passport) 18-25, free under 18/over 65; pre-book on T055-294883 (€3 booking fee).

Part of San Lorenzo, but reached by a separate entrance, the Medici Chapel is the mausoleum where many members of the family are buried. You go upstairs to the Capella dei Principi, the Chapel of the Princes. The most expensive project the

Opposite page: Tomb of Lorenzo de' Medici de Agostin at the Cappelle Medicee.
Left: Interior of the Basilica di San Lorenzo.

family ever funded, it gives the impression that they were trying to take their money with them when they died. It certainly shows that money can't buy you taste – it is a jaw-dropping mix of marble and grey stone, inlaid with coral, mother-of-pearl and lapis lazuli. Work began in 1604 and the Medici, never ones to think small, intended that the Holy Sepulchre itself would be brought here from Jerusalem and laid alongside them. The authorities in the Holy Land refused. The family continued to lavish money on their mausoleum until the last of the line died in 1743. The Chapel of the Princes wasn't completed until 1962, when the floor was finished. Unfortunately, much of it is covered in scaffolding as the chapel is undergoing renovations.

From here you come into the **Sagrestia Nuova**, the New Sacristy. This predates the Chapel of the Princes – work began in 1520 – and is decidedly more restrained. Michelangelo designed it as well as the Medici tombs inside. The most eye-catching tombs, which he worked on alone, are of those of two minor Medici: that of Lorenzo, Duke of Urbino, is topped with allegorical figures of Dusk and Dawn, while that of Giuliano, Duke of Nemours, is topped with Night and Day.

Also here is the large, unfinished tomb of Lorenzo the Magnificent and his brother Giuliano. Michelangelo intended that this should be decorated with river gods and other figures. However, he only got as far as carving the Madonna and Child before going to Rome.

Palazzo Medici-Riccardi

Via Cavour 3, T055-276 0340, palazzo-medici.it. Mon-Tue and Thu-Sun 0900-1900, €7/€4, free under 6, admission to Cappella dei Magi restricted to 8 visitors every 7 mins: book in advance by phone.

You might think this building looks unimpressive from the outside, dull even. That was deliberate: Cosimo il Vecchio was too astute to flaunt his wealth to all and sundry. He had originally asked Brunelleschi to design this, the family's first serious palace in Florence, but the architect came up with a grandiose plan that Cosimo rejected as "too sumptuous and magnificent and liable to stir envy among the populace". Cosimo turned instead to Michelozzo, who designed this restrained Renaissance residence that managed to look intimidating and yet elegant. And inside they were free to enjoy more lavish decor.

The Medici had moved to Florence from the Mugello (see page 126), and in the mid-14th century, when they were making money from banking, bought a number of properties in this area of the city. It was around 1445 that Cosimo commissioned this palace. In the 17th century it was sold to the Riccardi family, who enlarged and altered it. The courtyard, designed by Michelozzo, has columns in *pietra serena* (a grey stone) and arches festooned with carvings. You can walk from here into the quiet garden, with statues and citrus fruits.

Cappella dei Magi

The Chapel of the Magi is upstairs, and is the palace's main attraction. It was completed by Michelozzo in 1459, after which a pupil of Fra Angelico's, Benozzo Gozzoli, began to decorate the walls. He covered them with jewel-coloured frescoes, ostensibly telling the story of the *Procession of the Magi* but in reality immortalizing members of the Medici family as they took part in the annual procession of the wealthy Florentine confraternity, the Compagnia dei Magi. It's a fascinating idealized pageant set in a rocky landscape – the gentry, straight-backed on horseback, are accompanied by pages, cheetahs, wild birds and camels.

You can pick out various individuals. Most think that the young man on the east wall, wearing gold and riding a white horse, is a young Lorenzo the Magnificent. Behind him is Cosimo il Vecchio, wearing a black cloak, and just in front of him, on another white horse, Piero de' Medici, who commissioned the work. Look carefully at the crowd of followers and you can see the artist himself (his name is written on his red hat).

Other rooms upstairs in the palace are the **Sala delle Quattro Stagioni**, which gets its name from the 17th-century tapestries designed by Lorenzo Lippi, and the 18th-century **Sala Luca Giordano**, its ceiling a blue and white puff of clouds on which sit the last of the Medici. In another room is the rather more tasteful *Madonna and Child* by Filippo Lippi, painted when he was probably too old to chase women any more.

Mercato Centrale

The streets around San Lorenzo church are filled with stalls selling items such as belts and bags, sunglasses and souvenirs. The Mercato Centrale nearby is the main food market. It's a covered market built in the 19th century, and worth visiting whether you're putting together a picnic or just looking to soak up some city atmosphere. Stalls sell meat, vegetables, cheese and pasta, and there are plenty of cheap eating places nearby. Look out for the tripe sellers – it's fast food Florentine-style.

Opposite page: In the grounds of the Palazzo Medici-Riccardi.
Top left: Detail from the *Procession of the Magi*.
Above: A selection of wares at the Mercato Centrale.

Santa Croce & around

Piazza Santa Croce is one of Florence's liveliest squares – a great place to picnic and people-watch. Each year it becomes a stadium for the famous *Calcio Storico*, a no-holds-barred football match played in medieval costume. This area was particularly badly hit when the Arno flooded Florence in 1966 – you can see a mark showing the height the water reached near the corner with via de' Benci.

Basilica di Santa Croce

Piazza Santa Croce, T055-246 6105.
Mon-Sat 0930-1730, Sun 1300-1730, €5 (includes museum).

The largest Franciscan church in the world, this vast building – the burial place of Ghiberti, Galileo, Machiavelli and Michelangelo – can easily occupy two or three hours of your time. Its size reflects the fact that the Franciscans were a popular preaching order and needed a large space to accommodate their congregation. You can see the Dominican equivalent on the opposite side of the city, at Santa Maria Novella (see page 119).

Santa Croce is often known as the Pantheon of Florence. There's so much to see that it's easy to understand why the writer Stendhal was quite overcome when he visited in 1817: "Upon leaving Santa Croce my heart was beating irregularly…life was ebbing out of me and I went forwards in fear of swooning." The term Stendhal's Syndrome is now used to describe the sort of masterpiece overload that you can experience in Florence.

The most accepted date for the church's construction is 1294, though the façade wasn't completed until the 19th century. The architect was Arnolfo di Cambio, but the building was later re-modelled by Vasari, who painted over many early frescoes. The church is currently being restored and you might find that some items of interest are covered up, but there'll still be plenty to see. You enter by the side entrance, not through the main doors in the piazza.

Family chapels While it was not 'done' for wealthy families to flaunt their money in Renaissance Florence, it was acceptable for them to pay for works within a church or cathedral. This made them appear pious and benevolent – but it also gave them an opportunity to show just how rich they were, commissioning the greatest artists and sculptors of the day to decorate private chapels and tombs. To the right of the altar you can see the **Bardi Chapel** and the **Peruzzi Chapel**, both covered with frescoes by Giotto. Compare the 13th-century gilded altarpiece in the Bardi Chapel with Giotto's frescoes on the wall and you can trace the burgeoning artistic revolution. In the altar panel St Francis is portrayed in rigid Byzantine manner and the scenes around him are stylized, with the most important figures painted taller than the others, while in the fresco depicting the death of St Francis the characters are realistically proportioned, and their grief is obvious from their faces and postures.

Below: Detail from the Basilica di Santa Croce.

Tears of indignation came to Lucy's eyes…Miss Lavish…had taken her Baedeker…How could she find her way about in Santa Croce?... Now she entered the church depressed and humiliated, not even able to remember whether it was built by the Franciscans or the Dominicans.

Of course, it must be a wonderful building. But how like a barn! …Of course it contained frescoes by Giotto, … but who was to tell her which they were? She walked about disdainfully, unwilling to be enthusiastic over monuments of uncertain authorship or date." ❞

E.M. Forster, A Room with a View (1908)

To the left of the altar you should usually be able to see a wooden crucifix by Donatello (1420). The arms are inventively hinged, enabling it to serve as either a crucifixion or a deposition.

Cappella Baroncelli This chapel, at the end of the transept, has frescoes (c1332) by Taddeo Gaddi, assistant to Giotto. They include a rare night scene depicting the *Annunciation to the Shepherds*, and scenes from the *Life of the Virgin* on the main chapel wall. In the panel on the bottom right is a priest deciding who should marry Mary. Joseph brandishes a leafy branch with a dove above it, pleased that he's won her hand, while a man at the front of the picture snaps a branch beneath his foot, annoyed that he wasn't chosen. In the altar, the central panel showing the coronation of the Virgin is attributed to Giotto.

Tip...

Don't be afraid to walk on the gravestones embedded in the floor by the altar. They were placed there on purpose as a sign of humility. However, look out for the one that bears the inscription '*Noncalpestarmi*': it means 'Don't walk over me.'

Cappella Rinuccini A corridor leads to the Sacristy, which contains a *Crucifixion* by Taddeo Gaddi and a huge wooden table on which the body of Michelangelo lay in state – he died in Rome, but was brought back to Florence to be buried. Behind railings is the **Rinuccini Chapel**, which contains scenes from the *Life of the Virgin* by a follower of Giotto. The wall by the entrance is painted in imitation of marble. If you look at the bottom, in the middle, you can see that one of the artists has painted himself.

Famous tombs At the back of the church (furthest from the altar), above the tomb of Niccolini, is a statue that is believed to have been the inspiration for the Statue of Liberty. Nearby, on the south aisle, is Michelangelo's tomb, which was designed by Vasari and is topped with allegorical figures representing painting, sculpture and architecture. Michelangelo died in 1564, which was

Opposite page: The formidable Basilica di Santa Croce.
Above: Fresh porcini mushrooms for sale at Sant'Ambrogio market.

Tip...

Just a short walk north of Santa Croce, off via de' Macci, is **Sant'Ambrogio market,** surely the best place in Florence to find fabulous fresh fruit and vegetables. Look out for seasonal delicacies like huge porcini mushrooms in the autumn.

the year Galileo was born, so Galileo's tomb was placed on the opposite aisle. There is a bust of the 'heretical' scientist holding a telescope. Next to Michelangelo's tomb is Dante's, although the great writer isn't buried here but in Ravenna where he had been exiled. Carved in the 19th century, the tomb is often mocked by Florentines, who joke that Dante looks as if he is sitting on the toilet.

Beside Dante is the tomb of the poet Vittorio Alfieri, carved by Canova. Known for living the good life and occasionally tying himself to his desk to force himself to work, Alfieri ran away with Bonnie Prince Charlie's wife, the Countess of Albany. She is said to have modelled for the figure representing Italy on top of the tomb. The towers of San Gimignano form a crown on her head.

The cloister Leaving the main church through the cloister, you come to the **Cappella de' Pazzi**, which was designed by Brunelleschi for the wealthy Pazzi family of bankers and begun in the early 1440s. It's an example of harmonious design, with simple geometric forms and decorations by Desiderio da Settignano and Luca della Robbia.

Finally you come to the museum, in the former monastic refectory. Among its highlights are Cimabue's famous *Crucifix*, which was badly damaged in the floods of 1966, as well as a glorious fresco of the *Tree of the Cross and Last Supper* (c1333) by Taddeo Gaddi.

Museo Horne

Via dei Benci 6, T055-244661, museohorne.it.
Just south of piazza Santa Croce, by the Arno.
Mon-Sat 0900-1300, €5.

Housed in the Palazzo Corsi, a visit to this museum gives you a chance to see a typical wealthy cloth merchant's dwelling of the Renaissance. The house doubled as business premises, and cloth that had been dyed down in the cellars would have been hung up to dry high above the courtyard. The building was saved in the 19th century by an English art historian, Percy Horne, who restored it and filled it with a collection of artworks and quirky objects. He left it to the state when he died in 1916. Look out for features like the original glass in the windows and thick wooden shutters.

On the first floor there's *St Catherine of Alexandria* by Luca Signorelli and a painting of *Three Saints* that is an early work by Pietro Lorenzetti. Dominating one wall is an unfinished *Deposition* by Benozzo Gozzoli, one of the earliest examples of oil on canvas. Near a portrait of Percy Horne there's a *Crucifixion* by Filippino Lippi. Other rooms contain Giotto's *St Stephen* and a *cassone* or wedding chest: this wasn't just a box to store valuables but also a place to sit or lie down.

On the next floor, in a former bedroom, there's a *lettuccio* – a 15th-century day bed. It looks like a huge seat but would have been covered with a mattress and covers, which were stored in a drawer beneath.

Around piazza della Repubblica

This vast piazza, lined with famous cafés, was the site of the Roman forum and later the main marketplace. All was swept away when Florence briefly became capital in the 19th century, and the enormous triumphal arch was the first stage in the city's planned rebuilding. Nearby is the *Mercato Nuovo*, where tourists queue to rub the (very shiny) nose of the bronze boar, *Il Porcellino* – said to ensure a return to Florence.

Palazzo Davanzati

Via Porta Rossa 13, T055-238 8610.
Tue-Sat, 1st, 3rd and 5th Sun and 2nd and 4th Mon of each month 0815-1350, pre-book on T055-294883 (€3 booking fee). Partially open and free while undergoing restoration, but admission charge will apply when fully open (possibly early 2009).

A short distance from the Mercato Nuovo, the Palazzo Davanzati was built in the mid-14th century by joining together existing properties. It's a fascinating example of a medieval merchant's home and remained in the hands of the Davanzati family until the 19th century.

You step into an outer loggia, which once served as a shop. If you look up you can see spy holes, covered with wood, so that the family could see what was happening down below. The inner courtyard has a romantic Romeo-and-Juliet quality, with a stunning staircase. You'll see that while the lower section of the staircase is made of stone, the higher sections are made of wood – no point using expensive materials when only the family would see them. There's a well here too – a system of ropes and pulleys meant water could be carried to all levels of the house.

Upstairs on the first floor, the Sala Madornale preserves a brightly painted ceiling, while the Sala dei Pappagalli gets its name because its walls are covered with parrots. Further round on this floor is the Camera de Pavani, a bedroom that once had peacocks on the walls and the medieval equivalent of an en-suite bathroom.

Until the restoration is complete, the second floor can be seen only on pre-booked, guided tours. Up here, there is another wooden ceiling and signs of ancient graffiti. The bedroom is covered in paintings of the mid-14th century depicting a tragic French love story, and you can also see items of furniture like *cassoni* (marriage chests) and a *desco da parto*, or 'birthing tray'. Roundels of this kind were made to carry refreshments to a mother after she had given birth. They were often elaborately painted and hung on bedroom walls as decoration.

Via de' Tornabuoni

Just west of Palazzo Davanzati, along via Porta Rossa, is the smartest shopping street in Florence, via de' Tornabuoni. Pucci, Prada, Dior, Cartier, Armani – you name them, they're here. The huge Ferragamo headquarters occupies its own palace by the Arno, near ponte Santa Trinità. If you've got a bit of a thing about shoes, go into their museum (Wed-Mon 1000-1800, €5, free under 10/over 65) where you can see items like the original lasts and the shoes they made for film stars such as Katharine Hepburn, Marilyn Monroe and Audrey Hepburn. Make sure you pop into the nearby Church of Santa Trinita (free) in piazza Santa Trinità. It's famed for Domenico Ghirlandaio's frescoes depicting the *Life of St Francis* (c1483-6) in the Sassetti Chapel. Further along via dei Tornabuoni is **Palazzo Strozzi** (palazzostrozzi.org) the largest palace in Florence, which was built for the Strozzi banking family. Temporary art exhibitions are held here, and you can wander into the courtyard, where there's a café.

Around piazza Santa Maria Novella

This area of the city is dominated by the transport hub of Santa Maria Novella station, and it is easy to overlook its attractions as you hurry to better-known sights such as the Duomo and the Uffizi. Yet one of the city's most important churches is here, sitting with its back to the station. Its façade has recently been restored and the piazza in front has been cleaned up, enabling it to present a bright new face to the world.

Santa Maria Novella

Piazza Santa Maria Novella, T055-264 5184. Mon-Thu and Sat 0900-1700, Fri and Sun 1300-1700, €2.50; museum and Green Cloister Mon-Sat 0900-1700, Sun 0900-1400, €2.70/€2, €1 3-17.

A church stood here as early as 983AD. In 1221 it was handed to the Dominicans. Around 1240 the friars themselves started building the church you see today, and it was consecrated in 1420. By then, however, only the lower part of the façade had been completed, in Romanesque style. In the 1450s Giovanni Rucellai paid for Leon Battista Alberti to finish the work, which he did in Renaissance style.

You enter the church by a side door, reached through the graveyard. Inside you'll initially be struck by the rather severe interior – a reminder that the Dominicans were the *domini canes*, or 'hounds of God' and tended to take a rigid approach to their faith – as evidenced by Savonarola. In addition, Vasari put his stamp on the church by painting over many of the original frescoes. However, this building is filled with treasures. On the opposite wall to the entrance is Masaccio's *Trinity* (1427) which demonstrates extraordinary skill with perspective, creating a stunning *trompe d'oeil*.

Hanging in the centre of the nave is a large wooden crucifix (c1290) by Giotto, back in its original position after restoration.

Around the altar To the right, steps lead up to the frescoed **Cappella Rucellai**, which contains a statue of the *Madonna and Child* (c1350) by Nino Pisano. Closer to the altar, on the right, are chapels that 'belonged' to wealthy families. First is the **Bardi Chapel**, with lunettes frescoed by Duccio di Buoninsegna (c1285) and, beside the altar, the beautiful **Filippo Strozzi Chapel**, which contains some of Filippino Lippi's finest frescoes (c1489-1502). The chancel, behind the altar, is decorated with a fresco cycle by Domenico Ghirlandaio (c1485-90) commissioned by the banker Giovanni Tornabuoni. It depicts the lives of the Virgin and St John the Baptist. It functions as a

A fresco at Santa Maria Novella.

sort of promotional panel for the Tornabuoni family, with Giovanni's daughter dressed in gold in the scene depicting the birth of the Virgin, and Lucrezia Tornabuoni, the mother of Lorenzo the Magnificent, attending the birth of St John the Baptist on the other wall. Moving to the left of the altar you can see a crucifix by Brunelleschi. Further round is the **Cappella Strozzi di Mantova**, reached by steps, depicting scenes from Dante's *Inferno*: Paradise on the left wall and Purgatory on the right.

Museum and Green Cloister The entrance to the museum is to the left of the façade. You come into the **Chiostro Verde** (Green Cloister), which was built between 1332 and 1362. The walls are covered with early 15th-century frescoes by Paolo Uccello and his assistants, and the cloister gets its name from the green pigment they used. The best-preserved image is of *Noah and the Flood*. Walk around the cloister and you reach the **Spanish Chapel**, which got its name because the court of the Spanish wife of Cosimo I worshipped here – it had previously been the headquarters of the Inquisition. Frescoes by Andrea Bonaiuti (c1365-7) smother the walls. The right-hand wall depicts the *Allegory of the Triumph of the Church and the Dominican Order*, in which people indulge in dancing, picking forbidden fruit and being 'lusty', while disapproving Dominicans with their 'dogs of God' stand ready to force these sinners to repent. On the left of this image is a pink building, which may be how the artist imagined the Duomo would look when finished.

Last Suppers in Florence

There are a number of representations of the *Cenacolo* (Last Supper) in Florence. The most famous are Ghirlandaio's versions in San Marco and Ognissanti. But there are lesser-known ones that are worth seeking out. **Sant'Apollonia,** via XVII Aprile, has a 15th-century version by Andrea del Castagno, while **San Salvi**, via San Salvi, (about 30 minutes' walk east of the city centre near the Campo di Marte) has a dramatic 16th-century representation by Andrea del Sarto. The oldest Last Supper is Taddeo Gaddi's, now in the museum of **Santa Croce** (see page 115). It was painted shortly before the Black Death swept across the city. A 15th-century version in a former monastery, now the **Conservatorio di Foligno**, via Faenza (near the Mercato Centrale), is thought to be the work of Perugino. In the Oltrarno, the 14th-century *Cenacolo* in the **Church of Santo Spirito**, piazza Santo Spirito, was badly damaged in the 18th century. However the one in the complex of **San Giusto della Calza** (piazza della Calza, near the Porta Romana) by Franciabigio is bright and full of action. The building is now a conference centre, but they might let you look in to see it.

Detail from Ghirlandaio's *Last Supper*, at the Ognissanti.

Chiesa di Ognissanti

Piazza Ognissanti.
Daily, refectory Mon, Tue, Sat 0900-1200, free.

Ognissanti, or All Saints, church is just a short walk from Santa Maria Novella on a piazza down by the Arno. Founded in 1251 by the Umiliati, an order associated with the woollen industry, it was the parish church of the well-heeled Vespucci family. One of their members, the explorer Amerigo, gave his name to America. He's said to be buried in the church, and his image is immortalized in Ghirlandaio's fresco of the *Madonna della Misericordia* (1470s) – he is the figure whose face is immediately to the left of the Madonna. Also buried in Ognissanti is the artist Sandro Botticelli, who painted the picture of *St Augustine* here.

However the most interesting work is in the Refectory, reached through quiet cloisters just to the left of the church. Here, on the far wall, is a *Last Supper* by Ghirlandaio, painted in 1480. Similar in composition, though less formal, than the one he painted in San Marco (see page 106), it's an intriguing scene filled with symbolic images. In the background there's a palm tree for martyrdom, orange trees for heaven and cypress trees for death. On the table itself are apricots for evil and cherries for Christ's blood, while a peacock perched above symbolizes immortality. Ghirlandaio (1449-94) has been likened to a photographer because of the attention he gave to tiny details and his ability to create realistic images. He appears in this fresco himself – as the disciple at the far left end of the table.

The Oltrarno

The district on the Arno's southern bank is a great place to find buzzing bars and restaurants off the tourist trail. Traditionally a working area, it's still famous for its artisans' workshops, where you can buy anything from handmade shoes to statues. The main visitor attraction is the Pitti Palace, but it's not the only sight of note – try to make time to see the frescoes in the Brancacci Chapel and, high on a hill to the east, the church of San Miniato al Monte – which one Florentine after another declares is their favourite spot in the whole city.

Palazzo Pitti

Piazza Pitti, polomuseale.firenze.it.
The museums' opening hours vary, inclusive ticket €11.50/€5.75 (€9/€4.50 after 1600), valid for 3 days, not available during special exhibitions; pre-book on T055-294883 (€3 booking fee). Concessions for EU citizens 18-25, free EU citizens under 18/over 65 (on presentation of passport). Bus 12 or 23 from Santa Maria Novella.

The wealthy banker Luca Pitti built his palace as large as possible in an attempt to outshine the Medici, but when the Pitti fortunes declined, Cosimo I seized the opportunity to buy it for himself and made it his main residence. When Florence briefly became capital of a united Italy it became the royal residence.

The palace is divided into separate museums with separate prices and entry times. The main one is the Palatine Gallery, which takes you into the State Apartments. Extending behind the palace are the Boboli Gardens, perfect for a picnic.

Tip...

In **Santa Felicità Church**, piazza Santa Felicità in the Oltrarno, you can see **Jacopo Pontormo**'s extremely unconventional painting of the *Deposition* (1525-8). It's in the Cappella Capponi and is considered a masterpiece of **Mannerist art.**

Galleria Palatina

T055-238 8614, firenzemusei.it.
Tue-Sun 0815-1850, €8.50/€4.25, free EU citizens under 18/over 65 (on presentation of passport), includes the Galleria d'Arte Moderna (price may rise to €12/€6 during special exhibitions).

The Palatine Gallery is on the first floor of the Pitti Palace and contains the Medici's extensive collection of artworks – particularly their paintings. You'll find works here by everyone from Fra Bartolomeo to Van Dyck. They're displayed as they would have been when they were acquired, so don't expect any chronological order. The rooms in which they hang are as fascinating as the paintings, as you pass through bedrooms, private sitting rooms and the bathroom of Napoleon's sister, who once lived here: there are grandiose chandeliers, baroque ceiling frescoes and ornate plasterwork.

Among the masterpieces on display are Filippo Lippi's *Madonna with Child* and *Episodes from the Life of St Anne* (c1450) and the *Child St John* (1523) by Andrea del Sarto. There are works by Salvator Rosa, Rubens and Caravaggio, as well as Velazquez. Perhaps the best-known works are in the rooms named after Venus, Apollo, Mars, Jupiter and Saturn. Here you'll find paintings by Raphael and Titian, including Raphael's *Madonna della Seggiola* ('Madonna of the chair') and his *La Velata* ('Veiled Woman') whom Vasari said was the artist's lover. The room of Venus contains Canova's sculpture of *Venus Italica*, commissioned by Napoleon in 1810.

The gallery leads into the Royal Apartments, which show a mix of decorative styles. After the Medici left, the rooms were renovated by the Dukes of Lorraine and then by Vittorio Emanuele II. They're a lavish succession of huge chandeliers, rich brocades, tapestries and fine furniture.

Galleria d'Arte Moderna

Opening hours and prices as Palatine Gallery.

'Modern art' is 'late 18th- to early 20th-century art', as demonstrated by the works on the second floor of the Pitti Palace. The most important works are those by the Macchiaioli, the Italian division of the Impressionists: look out for landscapes and battle scenes in rooms 16 to 18. Of note is Giovanni Fattori's *Riposa* (1887), in which a farmer from the Maremma sits by the sea with his ox cart. Other rooms have paintings of the Risorgimento.

Museo degli Argenti

T055-238 8709.
Daily except 1st and last Mon of each month, Nov-Feb 0815-1630, Mar 0815-1730, Apr-May, Sep-Oct 0815-1830, Jun-Aug 0815-1930, €6/€3, free EU citizens under 18/over 65 (on presentation of passport), includes Galleria del Costume, Museo delle Porcellane, Giardino Bardini and Giardino Boboli, may rise to €10/€5 during special exhibitions.

On the ground floor of the palace, to the left of the main entrance, this is a succession of extraordinarily grand rooms that were part of the Medici summer apartments. Frescoes in the **Sala di Giovanni di San Giovanni** depict Lorenzo de' Medici giving refuge to the Muses, who have been chased from Paradise. Despite its name, the museum is not devoted to silverware but contains a range of precious (though not always pretty) objects such as ivories, glassware and amber.

Other museums covered by the same ticket are the **Museum of Costume**, with fashions from the 16th century to the present day, and the **Porcelain Museum**, on the far side of the Boboli Gardens.

Boboli Gardens

0815-dusk, prices as for Museo degli Argenti, last entry 1 hr before closing.

The Medici started laying out the Boboli Gardens around 1550, and various architects contributed to their appearance. Over the years they were extended and remodelled, with successive palace residents putting their stamp on the gardens. In the 18th century they were opened to the public.

The gardens are a formal mix of tree-lined avenues, fountains and clipped lawns dotted with classical statues and follies. Down by the palace exit you can see a statue of Cosimo's court dwarf as

Page opposite: Inside the Pitti palace.
Below left: *Nano Morgante* from the Boboli Gardens.
Below right: Another statue sits serenely within the gardens.

Bacchus, sitting on a tortoise, and the Grotta di Buontalenti – a bubbling cluster of dripping stones within which is secreted Giambologna's *Venus*. Other features include the Amphitheatre, designed so the Medici could enjoy alfresco entertainment in Roman style, and the Isolotto, an island fountain in the centre of a lake.

Less well known and less crowded than the Boboli are the **Bardini Gardens**, reached through via de' Bardi. Features include an English woodland and a baroque stairway.

Chiesa di Santa Maria del Carmine – Cappella Brancacci

Piazza del Carmine, T055-276 8224, comune.firenze.it.
Wed-Mon 1000-1700, last entry 30 mins before closing, booking essential, €4, €8 for combined ticket with Palazzo Vecchio. Time limit 15 mins, max 30 people at a time.

You walk through peaceful cloisters, then go upstairs to the Brancacci Chapel, a cordoned-off corner of the main church. The extraordinarily dramatic frescoes that cover the walls were commissioned in 1422 by a wealthy merchant, Felice di Michele Brancacci. Now restored, the brilliance of the original colours is stunning. The work was started by Masolino, who had worked with Ghiberti on the doors of the Baptistery and who essentially designed this fresco cycle, which focuses on the life of St Peter. Masolino worked alone for a while, then collaborated with a young artist, Tommaso Cassai, known as Masaccio. When Masolino left the city to work in Budapest, Masaccio continued the work alone, bringing uncompromising emotion to his painting. His panel depicting the *Expulsion of Adam and Eve*, on the left-hand wall, almost screams with their torment – contrast it with Masolino's rather courtly painting of the *Temptation of Adam and Eve* on the opposite wall, in which they look as if they're having a quiet chat under a tree.

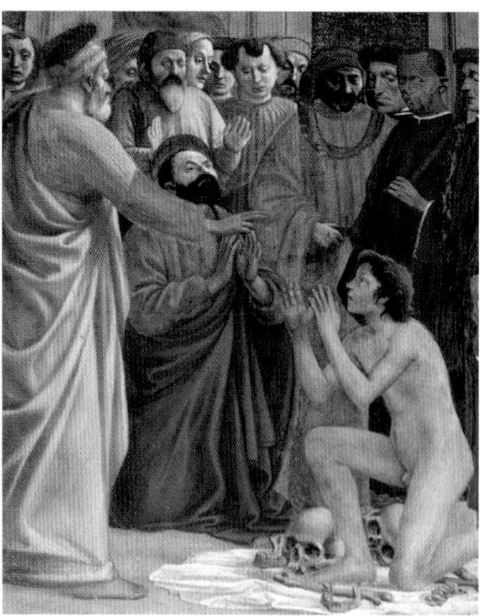

Masaccio died aged just 27, and the fresco cycle was eventually completed by Filippino Lippi in 1481-2. The works that are entirely attributed to Masaccio include *Tribute Money*, next to the *Expulsion*: in this detailed narrative Christ is asked to pay a tax to enter the city of Capernaeum; he points to a fish from whose mouth St Peter extracts a coin, with which he pays the tax at the gate. Masaccio also painted *St Peter Healing the Sick with his Shadow* (back wall panel, bottom left): it has a contemporary Florentine setting and many scholars feel it depicts contemporary characters – perhaps Donatello and Masolino.

Basilica di San Miniato al Monte

Via Monte alle Croci, T055-234 2731.
Mon-Sat 0800-1200, winter 1500-1800, summer 0800-1900, Sun winter 1500-1800, summer 0800-1900, free. Bus 13 from Santa Maria Novella.

It's well worth making the effort to visit the Church of San Miniato, which sits high above the Arno, overlooking the city. The bus from central Florence takes you up a steep, winding hill to the wide

Page opposite: Detail from Masaccio's work on events in the life of St Peter at the Brancacci. Above: The Basilica di San Miniato al Monte.

terrace of **piazzale Michelangelo** – a favourite stopping point for coach tours. Get out here and climb further uphill, and up quite a few steps, and you'll reach this much-loved church, which dates back to the 11th century. It supposedly stands on the spot where St Minias, Florence's first Christian martyr, brought his head after he had been decapitated by Roman persecutors.

A church of the Olivetan order (a branch of the Benedictines), St Miniato has a gleaming white marble façade, inlaid with green marble, which was made in the 11th and 12th centuries. Set in the centre is a rich golden mosaic of *Christ with the Virgin and St Minias*, which practically blazes under the summer sun.

The interior of the church is so full of faded frescoes, carvings and strange symbols that it could easily inspire a *Da Vinci Code*-type novel. The 13th-century floor, or pavement, in the central nave is marble and carved with signs of the zodiac. At the end of the nave is Michelozzo's unusual, freestanding **tabernacle**, embellished with painted panels by Agnolo Gaddi and terracottas by Luca della Robbia. Marble steps lead you up to the choir, where a screen is carved so delicately it looks like lace, and arched high above is another dazzling **Byzantine-style mosaic** of *Christ Pantocrator*. The sacristy is covered in frescoes painted in the 14th century by Spinello Aretino. Down in the crypt are the relics of St Minias. If you're in the church at 1730 in the summer (1630 in winter) you'll be able to hear the monks singing a magical Gregorian chant.

The piazza in front of San Miniato offers wonderful views. It's well worth walking back down into Florence from here – walk downhill, then take the steps on the left (on the other side of the road to the large Il Loggia restaurant). You'll soon come to the **Giardino delle Rose** (1 May-mid-Jun, free), a delightful rose garden where you can lie on the grass and gaze at the distant Duomo. It has to be the city's top summer picnic spot.

Fiesole & the Mugello

For centuries Fiesole has been regarded as a leafy retreat from Florence, and it still serves that purpose today. Just 20 minutes from Florence (take bus 7 from Santa Maria Novella) it has a pleasant 'village' atmosphere, interesting sights and famously fabulous views of Florence itself.

Fiesole was an Etruscan settlement (you can see the remains of the Etruscan wall, which is made up of blocks of stone so enormous it's difficult to imagine how they ever moved them). It was later settled by the Romans, who built a 3,000 seat theatre, which you can still see (summer daily 0930-1900, Mar-Oct 0930-1800, winter Wed-Mon 0930-1700, €5). The main square is **piazza Mino**, surrounded by nice little shops and cafés and dominated by the **Duomo**, which dates back to the 11th century. The artist Fra Angelico entered monastic life when he joined the monastery of **San Domenico in Fiesole** (T055-59230, sandomenicodifiesole.op.org). There's a work by him in the church of San Domenico and another in the chapterhouse of the monastery. Just outside the town is one of Tuscany's swankiest hotels, the **Villa San Michele** (villasanmichele.com) – a former monastery set in its own grounds. If your budget doesn't run to staying there, you could always treat yourself to lunch instead.

You could happily spend the day in Fiesole. But if you've got a car, you could use it as the starting point for a tour of the **Mugello**, a gorgeous corner of Tuscany characterized by fertile valleys, wooded hills and pretty hamlets – and barely explored by tourists. Drive north to **San Piero a Sieve**, where there's an 11th-century church with a font by Luca della Robbia. The Mugello was the ancestral home of the Medici, who used the area as a hunting ground, and they've left their mark everywhere. You can follow a walking trail from San Piero a Sieve to see **Trebbio Castle**, commissioned by Cosimo I (open to groups only), while another trail leads to the **Fortress of San Martino**, also built by the Medici and currently being restored. You could also visit the **Bosco ai Frati Convent** (open daily), which dates back to the 11th century. In its small museum is a crucifix attributed to Donatello.

If you now drive east you'll reach **Borgo San Lorenzo**, the main town in the region, where the Romanesque parish church contains a 13th-century Madonna attributed to Giotto. If you love fine ceramics, visit the **Chini Ceramic Museum** (villapecori.it) on the edge of the town. Housed in the elegant Villa Pecori Giraldi, it contains ceramics produced by the local Chini ceramic factory, as well as artworks by Pietro Annigoni.

Not far from Borgo San Lorenzo is **Colle di Vespignano**, where Giotto was born. The house, which is traditionally known as his birthplace, has just been turned into a museum (T055-843 9224, casadigiotto.com, Thu-Fri 1000-1500, Sat-Sun 1000-1300, 1500-1900). Vasari has it that Cimabue was walking in the Mugello when he met a young shepherd – Giotto – drawing on a stone and encouraged him to move to Florence.

A short drive further east you'll reach **Vicchio**, the birthplace of Fra Angelico. From here you can follow the course of the Sieve river, past Dicomano and on to **Rufina**. This is wine country, where you can stop off for tours and tastings of wines as well as olive oils. You can also visit the **Vine and Wine Museum** at Rufina (villapoggioreale.it) before driving back to Florence.

Tip...

Fiesole's tourist information office is at via Portigiani 3 (T055-598720/597 8373, comune.fiesole.fi.it).

Sleeping

Around piazza del Duomo

Hotel Brunelleschi €€€€
Piazza Santa Elisabetta 3, off via de' Calzaioli, T055-27370, hotelbrunelleschi.it.
Map Central Florence, E3, p96.
This hotel, tucked away in a small piazza, cleverly incorporates a former church and a sixth-century watchtower. If you fancy a 'loo with a view', book room 420 – it has a stunning view of the Duomo. The hotel even has its own museum in the basement, where you can see part of a Roman *caldarium*, or hot bath.

Hotel Perseo €€
Via dei Cerretani 1, T055-212504, hotelperseo.it.
Map Central Florence, C2, p96.
Very close to the Duomo, Hotel Perseo takes up two floors of an old building (there is a lift). Reception is dazzling orange, but the rooms (recently refurbished) are light and contemporary, with good, sparkling bathrooms. Modern artworks are dotted around, there's free Wi-Fi access and a selection of books on loan.

Palazzo Galletti €€
Via Sant'Egidio 12, T055-390 5750, palazzogalletti.it.
Map Central Florence, H3, p96.
The extremely good-sized rooms at this high quality residence, on the first floor of a historic building, are ranged around an internal courtyard. They have high ceilings, good modern bathrooms and flat screen TVs. There are nine rooms at the time of writing (with two new suites due to open in 2009), some with lavish frescoes. Breakfast is a buffet downstairs in the former kitchen, which dates back to 1550.

Soggiorno Battistero €€
Piazza San Giovanni 1, T055-295143, soggiornobattistero.it.
Map Central Florence, D3, p96.
You really can't get much closer to the Duomo than this simple B&B, which has seven rooms, on the floor above the small Leonardo museum. Some rooms have views. There are no frills and the rooms are simply furnished, but clean. You take breakfast on a tray in your room.

Around piazza della Signoria

Gallery Hotel Art €€€€
Vicolo dell'Oro 5, T055-27263, lungarnohotels.com.
Map Central Florence, C6, p96.
With its white sofas and walls, this hotel exudes a determinedly minimalist style. The contemporary art on the walls changes every couple of months, and the restaurant offers Eastern-inspired fusion food. If you really want to treat yourself, go for the Palazzo Vecchio penthouse suite, where there's a terrace with an outdoor bed. (Yes, you get one inside too.)

Tip...

Florence has a confusing street numbering system, with commercial premises like restaurants numbered separately with a small red 'r' (for rosso) and non-commercial ones in blue, or sometimes black. So there may be two of the same number in the same street: 4r (a business) and 4. Confusingly, hotels and B&Bs are often not numbered in red!

Hotel Continentale €€€€
Vicolo dell'Oro 6r, T055 27262, lungarnohotels.com.
Map Central Florence, C6, p96.
Situated across from the Gallery Hotel Art, this is even more self-consciously stylish. The public areas are broken up into separate 'break out' rooms, with white-cushioned seats and chaises longues, and a pink and white breakfast bar. There's even a glass lift with banquette seats. Some rooms have views of the Arno, there are white-curtained beds and lots of bleached oak.

Hotel Bernini Palace €€€
Piazza San Firenze 29, T055-288621, baglionihotels.com.
Map Central Florence, E5, p96.
The location for this plush hotel couldn't be bettered: it's just a minute's walk from the Uffizi and about three minutes from Santa Croce, the Duomo and the Ponte Vecchio. Rooms are quiet and comfortable, with gleaming bathrooms. Those on the exclusive Tuscan floor are

decorated in Renaissance Florentine style, with beamed ceilings and canopied beds. You breakfast in the frescoed Sala Parlamento – where the Italian Parliament met during Florence's spell as capital.

Residenza d'Epoca in piazza della Signoria €€€
Via dei Magazzini 2, T055-239 9546, inpiazzadellasignoria.com.
Map Central Florence, E5, p96.
A rather chic residence, with 10 rooms and three self-catering apartments. The style is uncluttered and traditional with a contemporary twist – the rooms have plasma screen TVs on easels, free Wi-Fi access and modern bathrooms. Breakfast is taken round a long wooden table – though you can ask to have it in your room.

San Marco

Four Seasons €€€€
Borgo Pinti 99, T055-26261, fourseasons.com/Florence.
Map Florence, G3, p84.
As much a museum as a hotel, the Four Seasons is the latest – and most luxurious – addition to the Florentine scene. It comprises two Renaissance palaces, which took nearly eight years to restore, and over 4.5 ha of private gardens: the largest green space in the city. The most stunning rooms are those on the 'noble' floor, adorned with lavish frescoes, chandeliers and silk wall coverings. There's a separate spa with a large gym and a heated outdoor pool. Perfect for honeymooners.

Hotel Regency €€€€
Piazza Massimo d'Azeglio 3, T055-245247, regency-hotel.com.
Map Florence, H3, p84.
On a cool, leafy square just a few blocks from Sant'Ambrogio market is this classy hotel in a 19th-century villa. The atmosphere is friendly and welcoming and there's a lovely courtyard garden – ideal for relaxing in after a hard day's sightseeing. Rooms have large beds and gleaming bathrooms and are well equipped. There's a private garden suite.

Hotel Morandi alla Crocetta €€€
Via Laura 50, T055-234 4747, hotelmorandi.it.
Map Central Florence, H1, p96.
This welcoming, family-run hotel is housed in a former convent. Rooms have plenty of historic features – original frescoes in room 29, for example. Bathrooms are a bit small and dated, but the rooms are comfortable, with plasma screen TVs and computers with internet access. Antiques, books and prints are dotted around and it's on a quiet street. It's one floor up and there's no lift .

Antico Dimora Johlea €€
Via San Gallo 80, T055-463 3292, johanna.it.
Map Florence, F2, p84.
There's a real home-from-home feel at this classy little B&B. The rooms, decorated in bold colours with antiques and prints, all have four-poster beds and plasma screen TVs/DVDs. There is a lovely little terrace, reached by a short flight of stairs, which has stunning views of the Duomo.

Il Guelfo Bianco €€
Via Cavour 29, T055-288330, ilguelfobianco.it.
Map Central Florence, E1, p96.
Just a couple of minutes from the Accademia, this friendly, smallish hotel (40 rooms) has retained plenty of the original features of its 16th-century building. They serve aperitifs each evening in the little bar.

Residenza Johlea €€
Via San Gallo 76, T055-463 3292, johanna.it.
Map Florence, F1, p84.
Part of a small chain run by Lea Gulmanelli and Johanna Vitta, this boutique B&B offers excellent value for money. There are nine rooms, all stylishly furnished and with private bathrooms in white Carrara marble. There's a table in the hallway where you can help yourself to coffee, tea and fruit.

Self-catering

Residence Hilda
Via dei Servi 40, T055-288021, residencehilda.it.
Map Central Florence, F1, p96.
Slick, modern apartments in the heart of the city: Residence Hilda has 12 serviced apartments furnished in crisp, minimalist style, with white walls, wooden floors, sparkling bathrooms and well-equipped kitchens. Excellent value, from €230 per day.

Around San Lorenzo

Hotel Casci €€
Via Cavour 13, T055-211686, hotelcasci.com.
Map Central Florence, E1, p96.
The 24 rooms are all different and have flat screen TVs, DVDs and free Wi-Fi access. There are original frescoes on the ceiling of the breakfast room and a small bar serving drinks and coffees. Many visitors return again.

Residenza Johanna 1 €
Via Bonifacio Lupi 14, T055-481896, johanna.it.
Map Greater Florence, E1, p84.
This was the first in the reliable Johlea & Johanna chain of chic B&Bs, which really set the standard for stylish and affordable accommodation in Florence. It's a bit hard to find, upstairs in a 19th-century palazzo, but once there you'll find bright rooms with high ceilings, marble or polished wood floors and private bathrooms. You breakfast in your room – they provide you with a basket of goodies.

Santa Croce & around

Palazzo Antellesi
Piazza Santa Croce 19-22, T055-244456, florencerentals.net or sacoapartments.co.uk.
Map Central Florence, G6, p96.
This 16th-century palace in the heart of the city offers a taste of grand living. It's divided into 10 apartments (with a further four in an annexe), all furnished in different styles, some with original frescoes. Some look on to piazza Santa Croce, while Belvedere has a quiet private terrace. The smallest, Annigoni, sleeps two and was the eponymous painter's studio. From €1,850 per week, minimum stay six nights.

Around piazza della Repubblica

Hotel Savoy €€€€
Piazza della Repubblica 7, T055-27351, hotelsavoy.it.
Map Central Florence, D3, p96.
For style and luxury in the heart of the city, you can't beat this sleek retreat. Styled by Olga Polizzi, it has spacious contemporary rooms, in shades of cream and oatmeal, marble bathrooms, plasma screen TVs, broadband – all a refreshing change from the ornate gilding that adorns many Italian hotels.

Antica Torre di Via Tornabuoni 1 €€€
Via dei Tornabuoni 1, T055-265 8161, tornabuoni1.com.
Map Central Florence, B5, p96.
Beside the Arno, on one of Florence's smartest streets, is this gorgeous residence in a medieval tower. There are three apartments (with kitchens) and 12 rooms, with TVs, Wi-Fi, marble bathrooms and some private balconies. You can take breakfast on the top-floor terrace, which has glorious views across the city. Room 4, overlooks the river.

Hotel Beacci Tornabuoni €€€
Via dei Tornabuoni 3, T 055-212645, tornabuonihotels.com.
Map Central Florence, B5, p96.
This historic, family-run hotel fills the top floor of a Renaissance palace. The public rooms have an

air of grandeur, with chandeliers, antiques and tapestries. Some of the rooms are decorated with original 18th-century frescoes, and all are slightly different. There's a roof garden where you can have breakfast or drinks.

Hotel Scoti €€
Via dei Tornabuoni 7, T055-292128, hotelscoti.com.
Map Central Florence, B5, p96.
This welcoming small hotel has just 11 rooms. It's on the second floor of a former palazzo on one of Florence's smartest streets. Inside are *trompe l'oeil* frescoes from the 18th century, tiled floors and comfy chairs. The rooms are simply furnished and overlook a little courtyard. You take breakfast on a tray in your room.

Around piazza Santa Maria Novella

J.K. Place €€€€
Piazza Santa Maria Novella 7, T055 264 5181, jkplace.com.
Map Central Florence, A2, p96.
This sleek celebrity hideaway has just 20 rooms in an elegant, white-painted townhouse opposite Santa Maria Novella Church. Bedrooms are super-stylish, with large mirrors and gleaming bathrooms – one has a bath in which you can sit and look over to the Duomo.

Residenza del Moro €€€€
Via del Moro 15, T055-290884, residenzadelmoro.com.
Map Central Florence, A3, p96.
This residence, on the first floor of a 16th-century palace, offers sumptuous rooms and suites. All are different but have features such as original frescoes, chandeliers and marble bathrooms. The owners are collectors of art, and modern works mingle with antiques. There's a garden where you can take breakfast in the summer.

The Oltrarno

Palazzo Magnani Feroni €€€€
Borgo San Frediano 5, T055-239 9544, florencepalace.it.
Map Florence, C5, p84.
An elegant residence in a 16th-century palace in the Oltrarno. There are 12 suites, all furnished with antiques and works of art from the owners' collection. The smallest suite's walls are covered in frescoes. All bathrooms are stocked with Bulgari products, and public rooms have Murano glass chandeliers and flowers. The top-floor terrace has views of the Duomo and Campanile.

Camping

Camping Michelangelo
Viale Michelangelo 80, T055-681 1977, ecvacanze.it.
Map Florence, G7, p84.
There are great views over the city from this campsite close to piazzale Michelangelo and the glorious church of San Miniato al Monte. You can rent a tent from €15.50 per night and there are pitches for campervans and caravans. There's a shop, bar and internet access.

> My favourite view of Florence is from piazzale Michelangelo. Go there at sunset for a wonderful sky – people sometimes cry it's so beautiful. There's a small rose garden down the steps nearby – it's a piece of paradise.
>
> *Lara from Florence*

Around Florence

Collefertile €€€
Via Arliano 37, Località La Sughera, Montegiovi, T055-849 5201, collefertile.com.
This 19th-century hunting lodge sits in the heart of the Mugello, 33 km northeast of Florence, surrounded by chestnut woods and meadows. It's been in the hands of the same family for three generations and makes an ideal rural retreat. There's an outdoor swimming pool and a tennis court, and the restaurant serves hearty Tuscan fare.

Villa Campestri €€€
Via di Campestri 19/22, Vicchio di Mugello, T055-849 0107, villacampestri.it.
This tastefully restored villa 38 km northeast of Florence is a real treat. It dates back to the 13th century and belonged to an aristocratic Florentine family for over 700 years. The present owner bought it from them and has retained its original features: you feel as if you're staying in a Renaissance palace. There are extensive grounds, an excellent restaurant and an oleoteca where you can do tutored olive oil tastings.

Casa Palmira €€
Via Faentina, Località Feriolo, Polcanto, T055-840 9749, casapalmira.it.
Set in quiet countryside just 9 km from Fiesole and 16 km from Florence, this is the friendliest B&B imaginable. Assunta and Stefano make you feel immediately welcome, helping you with your luggage, offering you drinks and showing you their pretty garden and swimming pool. Guests can make themselves hot drinks in the large kitchen/dining room and relax by the log fire on chilly nights. They'll make you dinner if you ask in advance – lovely Tuscan food. They have many repeat visitors, so book well ahead. No credit cards.

Villa Corte Armonica €€
Via Bosconi 22, Fiesole, T055-59334, cortearmonica.it or uniquehomestays.com.
This lovely B&B nestles into the side of a hill on the outskirts of Fiesole and has fabulous views of the Florentine valley from the terrace. Owned by Elisa, a friendly former goldsmith, the house was built in the 1960s. There are just two comfortable guest rooms and breakfast is taken around a large wooden table in Elisa's kitchen. There's an outdoor swimming pool and lovely gardens, where Elisa grows salads, vegetables and fruit – often eaten by marauding porcupines.

Eating & drinking

Around piazza del Duomo

Angels €€€€
Via del Proconsolo 29/31, T055-239 8762, ristoranteangels.it.
Daily 1200-1500, 1930-2300.
Map Central Florence, F4, p96.
Trendy but pricy candlelit restaurant situated in a historic building. During the winter there's a piano bar that serves a wide range of cocktails from 1800. Dishes might include seafood risotto with saffron, homemade pasta with crab sauce, or beef with porcini.

Cantinetta dei Verrazzano €
Via dei Tavolini 18/20r, T055-268590.
Mon-Sat 0800-2100.
Map Central Florence, D4, p96.
This cantinetta functions as a deli/café and is a great place for a quick lunch. Join locals for a plate of cheeses, cold meats, breads and wine from the cantinetta's own vineyards. There are a few seats in one corner, as well as a wooden bench where you can perch. An ideal place to pick up picnic supplies.

Da Vinattieri €
Via Santa Margherita 6r.
1000-0100 (can vary).
Map Central Florence, E4, p96.
The sign reads "*Trippa e Lampredotto*" and there are few places like this left in Florence. Just a hole in the wall, a counter with a couple of stools outside and a chance to sample the local speciality: tripe. Panini with tripe are €3.50, while *lampredotto* (cow's stomach) is a bit more. Do as the regulars do and wash it down with red wine.

Cafés & bars

Bar Gallo
Piazza Duomo 1r, T055-219251, b-gallo.it.
Daily 0800-0100 (sometimes closed Tue).
Map Central Florence, D3, p96.
This funky bar/lounge attracts everyone, from young Florentines out for cocktails to tired tourists taking a break. Just by the Baptistery, it has a contemporary interior, seats outside and a private room upstairs where the likes of Gucci hold exclusive gatherings. The menu offers everything from crêpes with Nutella to steaks. Come early evening for a champagne cocktail (€15) or at lunchtime for a sandwich.

Grom
Via del Campanile 4, T055-216158.
Daily Apr-Sep 1030-2400, Oct-Mar 1030-2300.
Map Central Florence, E3, p96.
Tucked away on the corner of a back street, just a couple of minutes from the Duomo, Grom, say locals, has the best ice cream in Florence. And it really is superb: no artificial colourings or additives, organic eggs, rich cream. You can have a cone for €2 – a scoop of extra dark chocolate, plus one of milk and mint, makes a winning combo. There are a few seats inside.

> "For me, you get the best ice cream in Florence in Grom, the best pizza in Dantesca and the best Florentine steak in Il Latini."
>
> *Francesco, local policeman*

Around piazza della Signoria

Gustavino €€€€
Via della Condotta 37r, T055-239 9806, gustavino.it.
Daily 1900-1130, also Sat-Sun 1230-1530.
Map Central Florence, E5, p96.
Sophisticated Gustavino, with its silvery chairs, high arched ceilings and glass-fronted kitchen, attracts a fashionable crowd, who come for Tuscan food with a modern twist. The menu might feature homemade *pici* pasta with guinea fowl ragù spiced with chocolate and Parmesan cheese, and beef fillet with onion marmalade. The wine list features wines from the family's own estate.

La Canova di Gustavino €€
Via della Condotta 29, T055-239 9806, gustavino.it.
Daily 1200-2400.
Map Central Florence, E5, p96.
Situated next door to its sister restaurant Gustavino, La Canova has a cosier, more traditional atmosphere and serves classic Tuscan dishes, many of which require longer, slower cooking. As well as dishes such as ossobuco in tomato sauce, you can also find light lunch options such as Tuscan bread with lardo and honey, and Cinta Senese cold cuts.

'Ino €
Via dei Georgofili 3r/7r, T055-219208, ino-firenze.com.
Mon-Sat 1100-2000, Sun 1200-1700.
Map Central Florence, D6, p96.
Tucked away near the Uffizi is this lovely little wine and sandwich bar. You can sit inside and have wine and a tasting plate of fresh cheeses and meats for €4-7, and they'll also make up panini for you to take away. Worth seeking out when you want lunch on the run, or picnic supplies.

Cafés & bars

Gelateria dei Neri
Via dei Neri 20/22r, T055-210034.
Daily 1100-2400 (may be shorter hours in winter).
Map Central Florence, F6, p96.
Handmade ice creams in enticing flavours such as pistachio and chilli or strawberry pie – there are even soy and yoghurt versions too. It's in a back street between the Palazzo Vecchio and piazza Santa Croce, and a favourite with locals.

Rivoire
Piazza della Signoria 4r, T055-214412, rivoire.it.
Tue-Sat 0730-2400.
Map Central Florence, D5, p96.
OK, you can spend over €5 on a coffee here, but Rivoire, which dates back to 1872, is a Florentine institution. Seats on the outdoor terrace offer peerless views of the Palazzo Vecchio and it's a great place just to sit and soak up the city's atmosphere. In winter, snuggle inside with a hot chocolate and admire the grand turn-of-the-century interior.

San Marco

Cibrèo €€€€
Via Andrea del Verrocchio 8r, T055-234 1100.
Tue-Sat 1250-1430, 1900-2315, closed Aug.
Map Florence, G5, p84.
Situated right beside Sant'Ambrogio market, Cibrèo is a long-established Florentine restaurant serving sophisticated versions of classic Tuscan dishes. On the opposite corner is Cibrèo Caffè, which offers the same dishes in a less formal setting. Nearby Teatro del Sale (via de' Macci 111r) is a private members' club under the same ownership. Join as a non-resident for €5, then have access to their buffet breakfasts and lunches, as well as their dinner buffets, which are followed by performances.

Taverna del Bronzino €€€€
Via delle Ruote 27r, T055-495220.
Mon-Sat 1230-1400, 1930-2200, closed 3 weeks in Aug.
Map Florence, E1, p84.
This restaurant is the sort of place that's popularly described as 'fine dining'. Behind a huge wooden door you'll find an air of calm, with tables set under a white canopy, cream linen tablecloths and deep green

seats. Dishes tend towards Italian classics, with *primi* such as creamy risotto with ricotta and spinach, and *secondi* such as ossobuco with rice and saffron.

Osteria Pepo €€
Via Rosina 6r, T055-283259, pepo.it.
Daily 1230-1430, 1900-2230, closed Sun in summer.
Map Florence, E3, p84.
This relaxed osteria is just off the bustling Central Market. It has an informal, rustic feel at lunchtime – then morphs into something more sophisticated at night, with candles and crisp white tablecloths. Food and wine are Tuscan, and offer good value.

Santa Croce & around

Gastone €€€
Via Matteo Palmieri 26r, T055-263 8763, gastonefirenze.it.
Mon-Sat 1200-1500, 1900-2300, bar open Mon-Sat 1100-2400.
Map Central Florence, G4, p96.
Trendy Gastone only opened in 2008 but is already a favourite with locals. The décor is light and bright, with blue-painted wooden floors and prints on the walls. It's a great place for pre-dinner drinks, or a post-sightseeing pick-me-up. The menu changes twice a month and features dishes such as fish ravioli, sea bass or duck breast with berries. Wines featured come from across Tuscany.

Acqua al 2 €€
Via della Vigna Vecchia 40r, T055-284170, acquaal2.it.
Daily 1930-0100.
Map Central Florence, F5, p96.
Close to the Teatro Verdi, the walls of this restaurant are hung with plates signed by performers. It can get extremely busy, though that should be eased when they expand in 2009. The longish menu ranges from pastas to steaks, with some dishes – such as couscous – appearing on a seasonal basis.

Il Pizzaiuolo €€
Via de' Macci 113r, T055-241171.
Mon-Sat 1230-1415, 1930-2400.
Map Florence, G5, p84.
This busy pizzeria is close to Sant'Ambrogio market and offers a wide range of pizzas, cooked in a wood oven. You might have to queue and share a table – both locals and tourists come here, and service can be brusque.

Bistrot Baldoria €
Borgo Allegri 4r/via San Giuseppe 18r, T055-234 7220.
Daily 1100-1600, 1830-2400.
Map Florence, G5, p84.
This friendly trattoria attracts plenty of locals, and there are a few tables squeezed on to the street outside. Come for large plates of sheep's cheese with pears and nuts, homemade pasta and a wide selection of Tuscan wines. Unusually for Florence, there's no cover charge.

Osteria del Caffè Italiano €
Via Isola delle Stinche 11/13r, T055-289368, caffeitaliano.it.
Tue-Sun 1230-1430, 1930 till late.
Map Central Florence, G5, p96.
You could easily walk straight past this little pizzeria, which adjoins the Caffè Italiano restaurant. However, it does some of the best pizzas in the city – made in a, wood-fired oven. There are only four tables and you have a choice of just three toppings – but they're delicious and made with fresh ingredients. Gets busy with queues for takeaways.

Cafés & bars

Il Gelato Vivoli
Via Isola delle Stinche 7, T055-292334.
Closed Mon.
Map Central Florence, G5, p96.
Vivoli is the most famous gelateria in Florence, dating back to 1929 – many guidebooks claim it's also the best. There are always queues of tourists, scooping up spoonfuls of ice cream from little tubs – you don't get cones here.

Note di Vino
Borgo de' Greci 4/6r, T055-218750, notedivino.it.
Map Central Florence, G5, p96.
There's not much more than a hole in the wall and a small counter at this busy *enoteca*. Everyone sits at the wooden tables lined along the street outside, and there's a selection of aperitifs early in the evening. Wines include Tuscan classics such as Brunello di Montalcino and sparkling prosecco.

Oibò
Borgo de' Greci 1/1a, T055-263 8611, oibo.net.
Daily 0800-0200.
Map Central Florence, G6, p96.
Oibò functions as a café during the day and a lively cocktail bar after 1900. The bar is all lit up in blue, there's loud music and a small seating area upstairs. Try a *copa gabana* – a mix of gin, bitter orange and apricot brandy.

Around piazza della Repubblica

L'Incontro €€€€
Piazza della Repubblica 7, T055-27351, hotelsavoy.it.
Daily 1230-1500, 1930-2230.
Map Central Florence, D4, p96.
Soft music, contemporary art and modern Tuscan food make L'Incontro a stylish dining option. It's the restaurant of the Hotel Savoy and a place to see and be seen. Come at lunchtime, nibble on a Caesar salad or some artichoke and saffron risotto, and watch the crowds strolling around the piazza. Booking advised in the evening.

Rossini €€€€
Lungarno Corsini 4, T055-239 9224, ristoranterossini.it.
Thu-Tue 1230-1430, 1930-2230.
Map Central Florence, A5, p96.
Gourmet food on the Arno: this restaurant, in a former palazzo, is the place to come for a treat. Under the high arched ceiling you can work your way through a six-course €100 tasting menu. If you blanch at that price, the two-course 'light lunch' is €35 including wine and coffee. The cellar contains around 600 wines, from all over Italy.

Mangiafoco Caffè €€
Borgo Santissimi Apostoli 26r, T055-265 8170.
Mon-Sat 0900-2130.
Map Central Florence, C5, p96.
This is as much a wine bar as a café. Have a light lunch such as bruschetta, or go for a tasting plate of Tuscan cheeses and cured meats. Come in the early evening for aperitifs and you can help yourself to the free buffet and snacks.

Mariano €
Via del Parione 19r, T055-214067.
Map Central Florence, A4, p96.
This popular bar gets packed with locals at lunchtime. Panini are freshly made in front of you and cost as little as €2, crammed with salads and cured meats. There are also a few seats (if you can find one). It's a great choice for a takeaway lunch, though you will have to fight for attention.

Cafés & bars

Caffè Florian
Via del Parione 28r, T055-284291, caffeflorian.com.
Mon-Thu 0830-1930, Fri-Sat 0830-2000.
Map Central Florence, A4, p96.
This is a Florentine outpost of the famous Florian in Venice. Tucked away in a back street near the Arno, it's a small but chic retreat. As well as serving coffees it also sells chocolates, pastries, jams and liqueurs.

Gilli
Piazza della Repubblica 39r, T055-213896, gilli.it.
Wed-Mon 0730-0100.
Map Central Florence, D3, p96.
Once a meeting place for artists and writers, Gilli now attracts everyone from tourists to well-heeled locals. It's one of the grand old cafés of Florence, with a marble bar, lots of dark polished wood and mirrors.

Giubbe Rosse
Piazza della Repubblica 13/14r, T055-212280, giubberosse.it.
Daily 0830-0200.
Map Central Florence, C4, p96.
There's an air of faded grandeur about this historic café. Founded in the 19th century, it was once a meeting place for the German community, and later became a favourite haunt of Florence's literati. Today there are arty prints on the walls, lots of dark wood fittings and seats out on the piazza.

La Rinascente Caffè
Piazza della Repubblica 1, T055-219113, rinascente.it.
Mon-Sat 1000-2000, Sun 1030-1900.
Map Central Florence, D4, p96.
Who cares about the coffee with views like this? This café, on the fifth floor of La Rinascente department store, has an outdoor terrace with mesmerising views of the Duomo (so close you feel you could almost touch it). Come for coffee or an early evening glass of wine.

Around piazza Santa Maria Novella

Cantinetta Antinori €€€€
Piazza degli Antinori 3, T055-292234, antinori.it.
Mon-Fri 1230-1430, 1930-2230.
Map Central Florence, B3, p96.
Set inside the courtyard of an old palazzo, with just a discreet wooden sign outside, this cantinetta simply oozes wealth. Inside are sharp-suited staff, shiny wooden tables and cream walls. Dishes range from delicious fillet of fresh turbot to pasta with mussels and fresh white beans.

Il Latini €€€
Via dei Palchetti 6r, T055-210916, illatini.com.
Tue-Sun 1230-1430, 1930-2230, closed Mon.
Map Central Florence, A3, p96.
Locals consistently mention this as one of their favourite restaurants. It's family run and has a rustic, Tuscan look, with hams hanging from the ceiling and black and white photos on the walls. The food is similarly Tuscan, and it's the place to try meaty dishes such as *trippa alla fiorentina* and roast lamb. It gets busy, so it's best to book.

Caffè San Carlo €
Borgo Ognissanti 32/34r, T055-216879, caffesancarlo.com.
Mon-Sat 0730-2400.
Map Greater Florence, B4, p84.
A cheerful, friendly café: contemporary red and white colour scheme, seats outside on the street, and glasses of wine from €3. Come for fast panini at lunchtime or pasta in the evening. They also serve aperitifs and cocktails.

La Dantesca €
Via Panzani 57r, T055-212287.
Daily 1200-1500, 1830-2330.
Map Central Florence, B2, p96.
No frills at this place near the railway station. It has pink-washed walls, a TV set above the door, a large wood-fired oven, and busy staff serving delicious thin and crispy pizzas, which many locals reckon are some of the best in the city. Other dishes include Florentine fried rabbit, or gnocchetti with Gorgonzola.

The Oltrarno

Borgo San Jacopo €€€€
Borgo San Jacopo 62r, T055-281661, lungarnohotels.com.
Wed-Mon 1930-2400.
Map Central Florence, B6, p96.
Style-conscious dining at the Lungarno Hotels' restaurant on the Arno. You might find first courses such as gnocchi with quail sauce, and mains such as fillet of beef with asparagus. The most highly prized tables are those on the little terrace, right on the river – there are only four, so book early if you want one.

Nove €€€€
Lungarno Guicciardini, T055-230 2576, ristorantenove.it.
Daily 1930-2330.
Map Florence, C5, p84.
Newly opened restaurant offering a contemporary Tuscan menu with an Eastern influence. Fish features prominently, with dishes such as tagliatelle with cuttlefish or black cod. There's an outdoor terrace beside the Arno.

Enoteca le Barrique €€€
Via del Leone 40r, nr Piazza del Carmine, T055-224192, enotecalebarrique.com.
Tue-Sun evenings.
Map Florence, B6, p84.
Light wood tables, high ceilings and relaxed dining at this trendy *enoteca*. The menu isn't divided into courses – choose whatever you want, whether it's fresh pasta with herbs, pumpkin ravioli or squid with cannellini beans.

Filipepe €€€
Via San Niccolò 39r, T055-200 1397, filipepe.com.
Daily 1900-2400.
Map Florence, F7, p84.
This place has a quirky, theatrical feel, the food is modern Italian, and fish is a speciality. You'll find salt cod with chickpea and pistachio mousse; pasta with sardines, fennel and pine nuts; and monkfish with courgettes, apples and capers. They have two gourmet menus at €50 and €60, each offering six courses for a minimum of two people.

Olio & Convivium €€€
Via di Santo Spirito 4, T055-265 8198, conviviumfirenze.com.
Tue-Sat 1000-1500, 1800-2230, Mon 1000-1500.
Map Central Florence, A6, p96.
A deli with a difference, the upmarket shop stocks all sorts of gourmet Tuscan foods from ham to olive oil, but also has dining tables. Tasting plates, which include wine and dessert, are €18. Check out the daily specials, which can range from risottos to homemade pasta with monkfish and tomatoes.

Borgo Antico €€
Piazza Santo Spirito 6r, T055-210437, borgoanticofirenze.com.
Daily 1200-2400.
Map Florence, C6, p84.
Convenient if you've been to the Pitti Palace, this popular trattoria attracts a lively mix of young locals and tourists. There are plenty of seats on the piazza, and it's a place for relaxed dining – wooden tables, paper placemats and drinks in tumblers. Come for pizzas, or hearty dishes such as gnocchi with blue cheese and chicory or salt cod with chickpeas.

Rifrullo €€
Via San Niccolò 55r, T055-234 2621, ilrifrullo.com.
Daily 0700-0100, may close for 2 weeks in Aug.
Map Florence, F7, p84.

This café/restaurant/wine bar is a long-established favourite. It always seems busy, but it has a pleasantly laid-back atmosphere and a pretty garden at the back. Come for coffee, a quick lunch or a more substantial evening meal, such as sea bass with tomato and olive sauce or beef fillet with green pepper sauce. Aperitifs are served from 1900: for €5-7 you can have a drink and help yourself to the buffet.

Antica Porta €
Via Senese 23r, T055-220527.
Tue-Sun 1930-2400.
Map Florence, A7, p84.
This simple pizzeria, just outside the Porta Romana, is a favourite with local diners. The pizzas are made in a traditional wood-fired oven, and homemade pasta dishes are posted on a daily blackboard menu. Desserts, like tiramisù, are freshly made too.

Cafés & bars

Il Panino del Chianti
Via de' Bardi 63r, T055-239 8831.
Daily 1045-2130 (longer at weekends).
Map Central Florence, C7, p96.
Just beside the Ponte Vecchio, this tiny bar/*enoteca* has just one table, and a good choice of Tuscan wines that you can purchase by the glass for €2-9. You can also get panini, and there are aperitifs after 1800.

Le Volpi e l'Uva
Piazza dei Rossi 1, T055-239 8132, levolpieluva.com.
Mon-Sat 1100-2100.
Map Central Florence, C7, p96.
This busy *enoteca* attracts a loyal following. It should be on any wine lover's itinerary, as they stock a wide range of little-known wines, sourced from small producers across Italy. You can enjoy local cheeses and meats while you're there.

Entertainment

For more festivals see pages 52-55. For listings of concerts, films and other events, buy Firenze Spettacolo (firenzespettacolo.it) or the English-language paper *The Florentine* (theflorentine.net).

Children

Children are widely welcomed in Florence, and state museums offer free admission to under-18s, but they can quickly get bored if overloaded with visits to cultural sights. The best child-centred tours are at the Palazzo Vecchio, where tours run by costumed guides really help to bring the palace alive. They're run by the **Associazione Musei dei Ragazzi** (T055-276 8224, museiragazzifirenze.it) based in the palace, which also offers some visits to other attractions, such as the Brancacci Chapel. Older ones should enjoy the challenge of climbing to the top of the Duomo or the Campanile, and the Boboli Gardens and Parco delle Cascine (west of the city centre, bus 17) offer them a chance to let off steam. Football fans will welcome a trip outside the city centre to the **Museo del Calcio** (viale Aldo Palazzeschi 20, Coverciano, T055-600526, museodelcalcio.it, Mon-Fri 0900-1300, 1600-1800, Sat 0900-1300, €3/€1.50, bus 17).

Cinema

Goldoni

Via Serragli 109, T055-222437.
Around €7.
Shows original language films on Wednesday or Thursday.

Odeon Cinehall

Piazza Strozzi 2, T055-295051, cinehall.it.
Closed Aug, around €7.20.
Shows original language films on Monday and Tuesday.

Clubs

If you love aperitifs and a cool Italian crowd, there are a couple of bars/clubs that should hit the spot. Noir (lungarno Corsini, T055-210751), has a great view of the Ponte Vecchio and a 20/30-something, well-dressed crowd. Come for a martini at aperitif time and stay to dance. Colle Bereto (piazza Strozzi, T055-283156) is an über-trendy place with a designer-clad 30-something crowd with cash to flash. There's a VIP area and a very plush terrace.

Central Park

Via Fosso Macinante 2, Parco delle Cascine, T055-333505.
Entry around €20-25.
A popular commercial summer dance venue, with outdoor dancefloors.

Girasol

Via del Romito 1, T055-474948, girasol.it.
Out by the Fortezza, this is a popular and lively Latin bar with plenty of live music.

Tenax

Via Pratese 46, nr Peretola Airport, T055-308160, tenax.org.
Thu-Sat, closed in summer, entry from €20 on Sat. Bus 29 or 30 (or get a taxi).
Lively place that doubles as a club and live-music venue. Noted for its famous DJs, and great dance floor. Attracts international acts. Thursday is student night, disco on Friday and cool clubbing on Saturday.

Universale Firenze

Via Pisana 77r, Oltrarno, T055-221122, universalefirenze.it.
Thu-Sun, closed Jun-Sep.
Trendy dance venue in a flashily converted cinema, with a large bar, sweeping staircase and restaurants and clubbing area.

YAB

Via dei Sassetti 5r, T055-21560, yab.it.
Oct-May Mon-Sat, restaurant Thu-Sat 2100-2300, entry around €15, meal/disco €25.
Long-established glamorous club with a sheeny disco feel. There's a restaurant, lots of mirrors and a huge dance floor. Monday is hip-hop night and attracts a lively 20-something crowd; Friday is house.

Shopping

Music, theatre & dance

Jazz Club
Via Nuova de' Caccini 3, off Borgo Pinti, T055-247 9700, jazzclubfirenze.com.
Tue-Sat from 2100, membership (join at door) €5.
Long-established jazz venue that attracts acts on the up, and those at the top. Big names like Joe Diorio, Marco Tamburini and Sandro Gibellini have all appeared here. It attracts a knowledgeable crowd, many coming for the Tue/Wed jam sessions, and has a laid-back atmosphere and food and wine.

Mandela Forum
Viale Pasquale Paoli 3, T055-678841, mandelaforum.it.
East of the city centre – take bus 17, 10 or 20.
Major venue for big-name international acts.

Teatro Communale
Corso Italia 16, T055-277 9350, maggiofiorentino.com.
The city's main performance space, and home to its orchestra, L'Orchestra del Maggio Musicale Fiorentino. The Teatro del Maggio Musicale Fiorentino mounts concerts here throughout the year, as well as the summer festival.

Teatro della Pergola
Via della Pergola, T055-226 4353, pergola.firenze.it.
Lovely old theatre staging classic productions, plus some opera and chamber music.

Teatro Verdi
Via Ghibellina 99, T055-212320, teatroverdifirenze.it.
This large theatre hosts musicals, dance and music concerts.

Art & antiques

L'Ippogrifo
Via Santo Spirito 5r, T055-213255, stampeippogrifo.com.
Mon-Sat 1000-1900, closed Sat in summer.
Husband-and-wife team Gianni Raffaelli and Francesca Bellesi, have worked here in their studio in the Oltrarno for over 10 years. They create delicate, handmade etchings using traditional techniques and will take on commissions too. You can watch them working in the studio, though it's best to call in advance to check.

Pietra di Luna
Via Maggio 4, T055-265 8257, biancobianchi.com.
Tue-Sat 1000-1300, 1530-1930.
One of the fascinating traditional crafts of the Oltrarno is *scagliola*

– a decorative technique that was once used to imitate marble and the costly inlaid work known as *pietra dura*. The Bianchi family have revived the art: mixtures of moonstone dust, dyes and glue are etched into stone, moonstone or marble to create brightly coloured patterns. You'll find full-sized tables as well as inlaid boxes and paperweights – and you might sometimes see someone demonstrating the art.

Galleria Romanelli
Borgo San Frediano 70, T055-239 6047, raffaelloromanelli.com.
Mon pm and Tue-Sat 0900-1900.
This studio in the Oltrarno is crammed with marble, bronze and plaster sculptures, giving it the look of a small museum. Six generations of the same family have worked here and the pride they take in their work is evident. They'll take on commissions, and have a workshop on site.

Books & stationery

Abacus
Via de' Ginori 28r, T055-219719, abacusfirenze.it.
Mon 1500-1900, Tue-Fri 0930-1330, 1400-1930, Sat 0930-1345, 1500-1900.
As well as being bookbinders and restorers, working with fine leather, Abacus also stock items such as leather-bound address books and photo albums, which make great gifts. Their workshop is next to their shop.

Giulio Giannini & Figlio
Piazza de' Pitti 37r, T055-212621, giuliogiannini.it.
Daily 1000-1900.
The Giannini family have been working as bookbinders in this part of Florence since 1856. They also make marbled paper and stationery items. Their workshop, tucked away in the Oltrarno by the Pitti Palace, is worth a visit. Call first to check it's convenient.

Paperback Exchange
Via delle Oche 4r, T055 293460, papex.it.
Mon-Fri 0900-1930, Sat 1030-1930.
This English-language bookshop is a great place to pick up translations of Italian titles, as well as all sorts of new and used books with an Italian theme. If you forgot to bring your copy of *A Room with a View*, here's where you'll find it. The friendly chap behind the counter also seems to do a great line in giving directions to bewildered tourists.

R. Vannucchi
Via Condotta 26/28r, T055-216752.
Mon-Sat 1000-1930.
Florence is famous for its handmade paper, and it makes a great gift to take home. The paper here is some of the best – and you'll also find greetings cards and other stationery, pens, and leather wallets and diaries.

Clothing & shoes

Antonio Gatto
Piazza de' Pitti 5, T055-294725.
Tue-Sun 0900-1900, Mon pm.
Antonio is a tailor and former costume designer. Here, in his shop in the Oltrarno, he makes clothes for both men and women. You can buy off the peg or have something made to measure. He also makes a wide selection of women's hats.

Stefano Bemer
Borgo San Frediano 143r, T055-222558, stefanobemer.it.
Mon-Fri 0900-1300, 1500-1930, Sat 0900-1300.
Tucked away in the Oltrarno is this specialist shoe shop, selling made-to-measure shoes – mainly for men, but with some styles for women. You'll need to return two to three months after your first visit to have a fitting. It will cost €300 to have a last made, then €1,800 for a pair of men's shoes, €1,500 for ladies. The price, you'll be glad to hear, does fall if you order more.

Ceri Vintage
Via dei Serragli 26r, T055-217978.
Mon 1530-1930, Tue-Sat 1000-1230, 1530-1930.
Dressing-up heaven at this store in the Oltrarno, which sells men's and women's vintage clothes and accessories. Items date back to the 19th century and up to the 1980s. They also stock a few new lines from Denmark.

Grevi
Via della Spada 11/13r, T055-264139, grevi.com.
Mon-Sat 1000-1300, 1400-2000.
You'll find hats galore at this specialist shop near piazza Santa Maria Novella. There are handmade ladies' hats in a huge range of styles, and gloves as well if you want to match.

Food & drink

Bacco Nudo
Via de' Macci 59/61r, T055-243298, bacconudo.it.
Mon-Sat 0900-1315, 1600-2015.
Close to Sant'Ambrogio market, this shop has a wide selection of Tuscan wines, as well as the best-known Italian wines and grappa. Some wines are available from vats – they'll fill up a bottle for you. They also do tastings.

Dolcissima
Via Maggio 61r, T055-239 6268.
Tue-Sat 0800-2000, Sun 0900-1400.
This pasticceria in the Oltrarno sells a selection of cakes, chocolates and croissants.

La Buca del Vino
Via Romana 129r, T055-233 5021, labucadelvino.it.
Mon 1600-2000, Tue-Sat 1000-1330, 1600-2000.
This wine and oil shop in the Oltrarno offers an introduction to wines from selected small-scale producers in Tuscany. ome in and taste the wine, then watch as they fill up a bottle for you from one of the huge barrels. It's an inexpensive way of purchasing wine – they'll ship some home if you wish. The olive oils they sell are also high quality.

Jewellery

Amber Line
Piazza de' Pitti 6, T055-288519.
Mon-Sat 1000-1800, Sun 1100-1900.
This shop opposite the Pitti Palace sells a wide range of amber jewellery. The amber, from Russia and Scandinavia, comes in many colours including deep red and even green.

Penko
Via Ferdinando Zannetti 14-16r, T055-211661, penkofirenze.it.
Tue-Sat 0900-2100 (but closed Sat pm in Jul), Mon pm.
There's a long tradition of handmade gold jewellery in Florence, and Paolo Penko keeps the craft alive in his workshop

Tip...

The Oltrarno is famous for its crafts. The tourist office has a useful leaflet, Craftsmen of the Oltrarno.

near the Duomo. He makes reproductions of famous pieces of jewellery and old designs, and will take on commissions. You can ask for a demo – he's often working away in the shop.

Markets

Mercato Centrale
Piazza Mercato Centrale.
Mon-Sat 0700-1400 and Sat pm in winter.
The city's largest permanent food market is lively and colourful. Whether you're looking for fruit, fish, cheese or meat, you should find it here.

Sant'Ambrogio
Piazza Ghiberti.
Mon-Sat 0700-1400.
Fabulous fruit and vegetables, along with a few stalls selling cheese, bread and oils. This is a real locals' market and the produce is excellent.

Madam, I simply refuse to sell you this scarf. The colour doesn't go with your hair. ”

A trader to a lady with grey hair in the Mercato Nuovo

Mercato Nuovo
Off via Porta Rossa.
Summer daily 0900-2000, winter Tue-Sun 0900-1930.
Always crammed with visitors having their photos taken rubbing the nose of *Il Porcellino*, the bronze wild boar, Mercato Nuovo is essentially an accessories market selling bags, scarves and wallets.

San Lorenzo
Piazza San Lorenzo and around.
Summer daily 0900-2000, winter Tue-Sun 0900-1930.
Leather market selling items such as bags, belts and souvenirs.

Cascine
Viale Lincoln, Parco delle Cascine.
Tue 0800-1300.
On the edge of the city centre, this weekly market sells everything from clothes to food.

Mercato delle Pulci
Piazza dei Ciompi.
Summer daily 0900-2000, winter Tue-Sun 0900-1930.
You can hunt for a variety of antiques and bric-a-brac in this small flea market, which grows much larger on the last Sunday of each month when the stalls extend down the side streets around the piazza.

Pharmacies

Bizzarri
Via Condotta 32r, T055-211580, bizzarri-fi.biz.
Tue-Sat 0930-1300, 1500-1930.
Florence has a number of historic herbalists and this one is fascinating. It dates back to 1842 and has lovely old wooden cabinets, which contain everything from herbal remedies to linseed oil. Cash only.

Officina Profumo-Farmaceutica di Santa Maria Novella
Via della Scala 16, T055-216276, smnovella.com.
Daily 0900-2000.
This historic pharmacy was founded in the 13th century, turning medicinal herbs into remedies. It opened to the public in 1612. Inside are dark wooden display cases, ceramic storage jars and 14th-century frescoes. You can buy elixirs, pot-pourri, soaps and candles.

Activities & tours

Cultural

Isango (UK)
T+44 (0) 203-355 1240, isango.com.
They offer a range of guided tours and cultural experiences in Florence and Tuscany, ranging from a Segway tour of the city centre to a cheese and wine tasting tour. You can also have excellent private guided tours, such as one of Chianti and the Tuscan hill towns. Prices range from £15.40 per person for a central sightseeing tour to £144 or more for a full-day tour of Chianti. They can also arrange cookery courses.

Cycling

Florence By Bike
Via San Zanobi 120r, T055-488992, florencebybike.it.
An established bike rental company (you can hire city bikes by the hour), it also suggests self-guided tours and offers a guided Chianti Bike Tour for around €70.

I Bike Italy
T347-638 3976, ibikeitaly.com.
They offer one- and two-day cycling tours of Tuscany: the two-day tour goes from Florence to Siena.

Golf

Circolo del Golf dell'Ugolino
Via Chiantigiana 3, Grassina, T055-230 1009, golfugolino.it.
About 20 mins' drive from central Florence (take the SP222 past Grassina).
This is an 18-hole course (green fee €70). It's not always open to non-members, so check in advance and reserve a tee-time.

Walking

Artviva
Via dei Sassetti 1, T055-264 5033, italy.artviva.com.
This established company offers a wide range of walking and cycling tours. Their Original Florence Walk lasts three hours and costs €25.

Transport

Regular trains to Pisa (1 hr 5 mins), Pistoia (40 mins), Arezzo (45-90 mins). To reach Grosseto, travel via Pisa or Livorno (2 hr 53 mins). Regular buses to Siena (1 hr 15 mins), also buses to Volterra (1 hr 10 mins).

Siena & around

Contents

Introduction

It takes only a moment to be seduced by Siena, but once you've succumbed you're under its spell for good. It's a Gothic gem and has everything you want from a medieval city: stern palaces, intimate alleyways and timeless churches, all grouped around a theatrically beautiful piazza – the Campo. Were it not for the Renaissance glories of its near neighbour and ancient rival, Florence, Siena would be the star of Tuscany. The city's heyday was in the 13th and 14th centuries, when it spawned a clutch of Gothic buildings and a dazzling school of art. Today it is the most individual of places, clinging to traditions – such as the Palio horse race – that form a vigorous and vital part of its daily life. It's worth a few days on any itinerary, and as it sits in the very heart of Tuscany it makes a great base for exploring. Just an hour away is the beguiling town of San Gimignano, a medieval dream of soaring towers that attracts a multitude of visitors each year. To the north lie the sleepy hamlets and pretty villages of Chianti, which boasts quiet woodlands of oak, chestnut and fragrant pine as well as its world-famous vineyards.

What to see in…

…one day
Start at the **Campo**, then go into the **Palazzo Pubblico** to admire the frescoes and nip up the **Torre del Mangia** for views of the city. After a coffee on the Campo, head down via del Porrione to explore the medieval streets. then make for the **Duomo**, followed by the Santa **Maria della Scala** complex opposite to see the frescoes in the **Pilgrims' Hall**. There should be just enough time for shopping on via Banchi di Sopra.

…a weekend or more
Visit the **Crypt** behind the **Duomo** and the **Museo dell'Opera del Duomo**. Then perhaps a trip to the **Pinacoteca** if you're an art lover, or the *Biccherne*, the painted book covers in the **Palazzo Piccolomini**. You could also take in some historic churches such as the **Basilica di San Francesco** or **San Domenico**. You'll also have a chance to visit some of the artisan workshops and the quieter corners of the various *contrade*.

Siena

In the heart of the city, ancient buildings stand testament to medieval power struggles, the lofty tower of the civic Palazzo Pubblico rising cockily above the colossal, jazzily striped Duomo. Meanwhile, down steeply sloping lanes and darkened, eerie alleyways lurks a compelling, hidden city, quiet and full of secrets. Traditions are alive here, a vigorous and vital part of daily life. The Palio is not just costumed spectacle but a manifestation of the rivalries that shape Siena's distinct identity.

Piazza del Campo

All life in Siena converges on Il Campo, the scallop-shaped piazza that's the heart of the city and links the *terzi*, or thirds, into which the city is divided. It's a magical medieval amphitheatre, paved in rosy-red bricks sloping gently towards the Palazzo Pubblico. It's the first stop for cone-licking day-trippers and the natural gathering place for locals and visitors. The Campo's enclosed by a towering ring of ancient palaces, giving it an insular atmosphere all of its own – and keeping its splendour a secret until the last minute. Neutral territory, not belonging to any *contrada*, it's the setting for the Palio and bulges when crowds pour in to watch the race. Built on the site that was once the forum of the Roman settlement Sena Julia, the Campo was designed by the Council of Nine, who ruled the city from 1287-1355. It was in their honour that the piazza was divided into nine segments by marble strips. Today, cafés and bars encircle it.

The three *terzi*, home to the city's *contrade*, radiate out from the Campo. Each has a different character. The *Terzo di Città* is the oldest: a tightly meshed labyrinth of back streets and lanes (*vicoli*), home to treasures like the Duomo and Santa Maria della Scala. *Terzo di Camollia* covers the area north of the Campo and includes the smartest shopping street, via Banchi di Sopra. At its end is the Porta Camollia, the gate that faced the city's great enemy, Florence. The *Terzo di San Martino* runs southeast from the Campo and is characterized by its Renaissance buildings.

The Campo – its name means 'field' – was completed in the 1340s. In medieval times all manner of activities took place here: bullfights, boxing matches, the Palio, trading – even executions. The design was carefully planned. In 1297 the authorities decreed that the frontages of any buildings should harmonize with the Palazzo Pubblico, the seat of government, and although alterations have taken place over the years the impression is still remarkably medieval. The Campo is home to the **Fonte Gaia** ('fountain of joy'), a favourite photo-stop with visitors. It's a 19th-century copy of the original fountain, constructed by Jacopo della Quercia in 1419. A pool surrounded by reliefs of Adam, Eve and allegorical figures, it was intended to be a key feature of the Renaissance in Siena, rivalling Florence's celebrated Baptistery doors by Ghiberti. The original fountain is now displayed in the Spedale di Santa Maria della Scala (see page 160).

The Fonte Gaia replaced an earlier fountain topped by a statue of Venus. However, after the Black Death in 1348 religious leaders decided that God was punishing the Sienese for displaying this pagan statue. Venus was promptly destroyed. But they didn't let the pieces go to waste – they buried them in Florentine territory, hoping to pass the curse to their enemy.

Below: Palazzo Pubblico.
Right: *Contrada* members entering the Campo during a parade.

S. Sepolcro
Stazione F.S.
Pza. Guido Saracini
Vle. Sardegna
V. Piave
V. Malta
V. B. di Montluc
Vle. Don Giovanni Minzoni
V. Nino Bixio
Vle. Giuseppe Mazzini
V. Rutilio Manetti
Ple. Francesco di Giorgio
V. Simone Martini
V. Malta
S. Piero alla Magione
V. di Camollia
V. Campansi
V. del Pignatello
TERZO DI CAMOLLIA
Pass. Staz. Vecchia
V. V. Gioberti
Vle. Don Giovanni Minzoni
Vle. Lippo
V. Lorenzo Memmi
Maitani
V. del Vecchietta
Fontegiusta
V. Biagio di Montluc
V. Monte Grappa
Costa Paparoni
ISTRICE
Campansi
S. Bartolomeo
Vle. Nazario Sauro
V. Montluc
Villa Rubini
LUPA
V. Domenico Beccafumi
V. Simone Martini
V. Duccio di Boninsegna
V. F. Valdambrino
V. d. Romitorio
V. Campansi
V. di Camollia
Barriera S. Lorenzo
Chiesa Inglese
Vle. Armando Diaz
Pal. di Giustizia
Pza. del Sale
S. Sebastiano
BRUCO
Porta Ovile
Fonte d'Ovile
V. A. Lorenzetti
Cadorna
Vle. Rinaldo Franci
Giuseppe Garibaldi
S. Stefano
V. della Stufa Secca
V. del Pian d'Ovile
V. d. Pian d'Ovile
V. A. Federighi
Fosso d'Ovile
La Lizza
La Lizza
S. Andrea
Fonte Nuova
S. Rocco
V. Baldassarre Peruzzi
Vecchia
Vle. Cesare Maccari
Pza. Antonio Gramsci
V. dei Montanini
Piccolo Teatro
Pza. d'Ovile
V. del Comune
V. di Vallerozzi
V. di Mezzo
V. degli Orti
S. Francesco
La Lizza
Vle. dello Stadio
DRAGO
Stadio Comunale AC Siena
V. Federico Tozzi
V. Malavolti
Pza. Fabio Bargagli Petrucci
Vic. d. Orbachi
S. Donato
V. dei Rossi
Pza. S. Francesco
V. d. Baroncelli
Oratorio S. Bernardino e Museo Diocesano d'Arte Sacra
V. Baldassarre Peruzzi
Vle. XXV Aprile
Pza. Giacomo Matteotti
S. Maria d. Nevi
V. dell' Abbadia
Pal. Tantucci
S, Pietro a Ovile
V. del Giglio
Vle. dei Mille
Vle. dello Stadio
TAXI
Ortorio d. Suore
Pza. Salimbeni
Pal. Salimbeni
V. P. Salvani
V. d. Vergini
GIRAFFA
Vle. Curtatone
V. del Paradiso
Pal. Spannocchi
V. d.
Banchi di Sopra
Pza. Provenzano Salvani
S. Maria di Provenzano
Biblioteca Comunale degli Intronati
Pal. Tolomei
S. Messe
Pza. S. Domenico
V. d. Sapienza
V. d. Pittori
Pza. Tolomei
V. Sallustio Bandini
CIVETTA
S. Domenico
OCA
V. S. Caterina
Santuario e Casa di S. Caterina
Vic. d. Fontani
V. d. Terme
Termini
V. d. Galluzza
Loggia d. Mercanzia
S. Vigilio
Universitá d. Studi di Siena
Fonte di Foilonica
Fonte Branda
V. di Fonebranda
Pza. Indipendenza
Banchi di Sotto
S. Giovannino della Staffa
Pal. Piccolomini
Porta Fontebranda
Rozzi
Fonte Gaia
Logge del Papa
V. di Pantaneto
LEOCORNO
Pal. d. Magnifico
AQUILA
Pza. del Campo
Torre del Mangia
Museo Civico
Santo Spirito
V. del Costone
V. Esterna di Fontebranda
Pza. S. Giovanni
Museo dell'Opera dell Duomo
V. di Città
Pal. Chigi Saracini
Palazzo Pubblico
S. Martino
S. Giorgio
Vic. di Finimondo
Pza. Santo Spirito
SELVA
V. d. Vallepiatta
V. Franciosa
V. d. Fusari
Duomo
V. d. Sotto
Sinagoga
V. del Porrione
TORRE
V. dei Pispini
V. dell' Oliviera
Pzetta. d. Selva
Pza. del Duomo
Pza. J. d. Quercia
Rinnovati
V. del Rialto
V. San Martino
V. di Pantaneto
V. di Fieravecchia
Raimond
Pza. del Mercato
V. dell'Oro
S. Sebastiano
Prefettura
V. d. Fosso d. S. Ansano
V. d. Capitano
V. di Salicotto
V. Roma
Pal. S. Galgan
Pal. Bianchi
Spedale Santa Maria della Scala
V. di Città
Casato di Sopra
V. d. Lombarde
V. G. Dupre
S. Giacomo
V. del Sole
TERZO DI CITTA
Pza. di Postierla
V. di S. Pietro
Pinacoteca Nazionale (Pal. Buonsignori)
V. di Porta Giustizia
S. Girolamo
V. delle Cantine
V. d. Servi
Pza. Alessandro Manzoni
PANTERA
Pza. delle Due Porte
V. Stalloreggi
V. di Castelvecchio
Pza. del Conte
S. Pietro
S. Giuseppe
VALDIMONTONE
V. Val di Montone
V. Paolo Mascagni
S. Quirico
V. di S. Quirico
V. S. Agata
V. di Fontanella
S. Maria dei Servi
V. Ettore Bastianini
Piano dei Mantellini
V. Tommaso Pendola
Vic. della Tartuca
V. Tito Sarrocchi
V. delle Cerchia
Prato S. Agostino
S. Agostino
Porta Laterina
Pal. Pollini
Museo di Storia Naturale
ONDA
Convitto Tolomei
Universitá degli Studi di Siena
V. del Nuovo Asilo
S. Niccolò al Carmine
V. della Diana
S. Lucia
Orto Botanico
577

Siena listings

Sleeping

1 Antica Residenze Cicogna *via dei Termini 67*
2 Antica Torre *via di Fieravecchia 7*
3 Grand Hotel Continental *via Banchi di Sopra 85*
4 Palazzo Ravizza *pian dei Mantellini 34*
5 Porto Romana *via E.S Piccolomini 35*
6 Relais Campo Regio *via della Sapienza 25*
7 Santa Caterina *via E.S. Piccolomini 7*

Eating & drinking

1 Antica Osteria da Divo *via Franciosa 29*
2 Caffè Diacceto *via Diacceto 14*
3 Cane e Gatto *via Pagliaresi 6*
4 Carla e Franca *via di Pantaneto 6*
5 Enzo *via Camollia 49*
6 Fiorella *via di Città 13*
7 Fori Porta *via C Tolomei 1*
8 Gelateria Super Panna *via Banchi di Sotto 27*
9 I Terzi *via dei Termini 7*
10 Il Grattacielo *via dei Pontani 8*
11 Il Papei *piazza del Mercato 6*
12 Il Vinaio dell'Eremita *via delle Cerchia 2*
13 Key Largo *via Rinaldini 17*
14 La Chiacchera *costa di Sant'Antonio 4*
15 La Costarella *via di Città 33*
16 La Sosta di Violante *via Pantaneto 115*
17 Le Logge *via del Porrione 31*
18 Nannini *via Banchi di Sopra 24*
19 Nello *via del Porrione 28*
20 Osteria del Coro *via di Pantaneto 85*
21 Taverna di San Giuseppe *via Giovanni Duprè 132*

Essentials

Getting around Siena is small enough to explore on foot – which is handy because the historic centre is pedestrian only. Even bikes are banned from the centre. The small bus, Pollicino, run by Tra.in (trainspa.it), covers a few streets in the centre. Car parks are located on the outskirts (there's a large one near the Fortezza). Taxi ranks are on piazza Matteotti and by the train station (T0577-49222).

Bus station The main bus station is on piazza Gramsci

Train station The train station is 2 km from the bus station.

ATM There are ATMs on via Banchi di Sopra.

Hospital Siena's main hospital is Le Scotte, outside town at viale Mario Bracci, T0577-585111.

Pharmacy Pharmacies include Antica Farmacia Parenti (via Banchi di Sopra) and Ceccherini, on the Campo.

Post office The main Post Office is on piazza Matteotti 37.

Tourist information Piazza del Campo 56, T0577-280551, terresiena.it, daily 0900-1900.

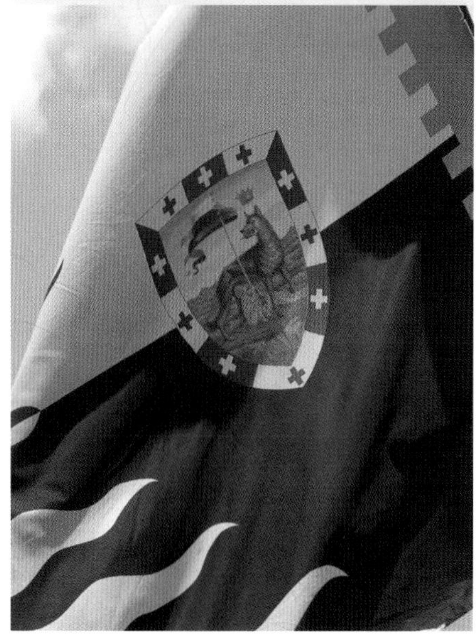

Il Palio

Intrigue, pageantry, bribery and brutality – the Palio has it all. The origins of this spectacle possibly go back to the 13th century, when a feast and horse race were held to give thanks to the Madonna for Siena's victory at the Battle of Montaperti in 1260 (see page 32). The first documented Palio was in 1310, and the race has evolved over the centuries. It's a bareback horse race – bitterly contested between the various *contrade* in which old scores are settled and anything goes. It's held in the Campo and involves three circuits of the 'shell'. There are actually two Palios: one on 2 July and the second on 16 August, and 10 out of the 17 contrade take part in each (there's no room for more). Seven are guaranteed a place if they missed the July race in the preceding year; the other three are drawn by lots. A week before the race the Campo is covered with earth (*la terra in piazza*) to create the track. In the run-up to the race a lot of dealing – and double dealing – goes on. The jockeys are all outsiders, often from the Maremma, and can earn large sums of money. Captains of the *contrade* negotiate to get the best riders, but jockeys also do deals between one another. Ten horses are also chosen. Three days before the race there is a public draw to assign the horses from the pool to the competing districts: once allotted they can't be changed. The horses are led to special stalls within their *contrada*, and placed under 24-hour guard to prevent doping. The jockeys, who aren't held in much respect by the locals, are also kept under close watch. On the day of the race each horse and jockey is blessed in the relevant *contrada* church. The race is preceded by a parade, with *contrada* members dressed in medieval costumes, waving flags and beating drums. The Campo fills with people and tension mounts. The jockeys continue making deals between themselves even on the starting line – and scramble for position. Once the race begins it's a mêlée: riders can beat one another and their horses, and if jockeys fall off it doesn't matter – it's the horse that finishes first that wins. Although mattresses are placed at certain points to provide protection – notably at the tight San Martino curve – the race is dangerous, particularly for the horses. Injured horses receive good veterinary care, but around 50 have died in the last 30-odd years.

Although crime hardly exists in Siena (the *contrada* system sees to that), fights often break out on race days, generally between members of rival *contrade*, and a lot of alcohol is consumed. Married couples from different *contrade* tend to stay away from one another at the Palio – it avoids tension.

Once the race is over – and it lasts only around 90 seconds, the celebrations begin. The next best thing to winning the race is seeing your rival lose it. The winning *contrada* becomes the 'baby' and members wear dummies round their necks. The one that hasn't won for longest becomes the *nonna*, or grandmother. A dinner is held by the winning *contrada* – at which the horse is the star guest. In the months after the race, victory dinners continue to be held outdoors and preparations begin for the next Palio. Yet for all the pageantry the race is just the tip of the iceberg, it is the *contrade* that are the soul of Siena, not the Palio.

Palazzo Pubblico & Museo Civico

Piazza del Campo, T0577-292614 , comune.siena.it. Daily, Nov-mid Mar 1000-1800 (approx), mid Mar-end Oct 1000-1900 (last entry 45 mins before closing), €7.50 without reservation, €6.50 with reservation, €3.50/4.50 concessions, free under 11/over 65; €11 joint ticket with Santa Maria della Scala, €12 joint ticket with Torre del Mangia.

Occupying almost the whole of the south side of the Campo, the Palazzo Pubblico is a monumental Gothic building, constructed in the late 13th century as the seat of the Sienese government. It was built to impress – a symbol of the city's independence and power – and still succeeds. Today, as well as being the home of the city authorities, it houses the Museo Civico, a series of frescoed rooms and grand halls evoking medieval life.

The first few rooms contain a jumble of paintings from the 16th to 18th centuries. If you're short of time, skip them to reach the **Sala del Risorgimento** on the first floor, which is covered in colourful 19th-century frescoes celebrating the unification of Italy and Vittorio Emanuele II, its first king. Scenes include his meeting with Garibaldi and allegorical depictions of Italy.

Turn left out of here to climb the stairs to the Loggia, a wide terrace built to enable the Council of Nine to get some fresh air during the months when they were unable to leave the palace. There are great views to the surrounding countryside.

Back downstairs is the **Anticamera del Concistoro**, with a fragment of a fresco attributed to Ambrogio Lorenzetti. This leads to the **Anticappella**, decorated with frescoes by Taddeo di Bartolo in the 15th century, and the **Cappella del Consiglio**, surrounded by an elaborate wrought-iron screen by Jacopo della Quercia. The altarpiece, *La Sacra Famiglia con San Leonardo* (The Holy Family with St Leonard), was painted around 1530 by Giovanni Antonio Bazzi (Il Sodoma). Spare some time for the inlaid wooden choir stalls, too, carved by Domenico di Niccolò between 1415-28. They're said to be the first example of conceptual art.

Look at the basin for holy water by the chapel entrance. There's a small metal ring beside it, into which single Sienese girls have traditionally inserted their ring fingers hoping it will bring them a husband. Look closely on the opposite wall and you can see medieval graffiti scratched into the fresco.

Sala del Mappamondo One of the most important rooms in the palace is the richly decorated Sala del Mappamondo, once used as the law court and named after a rotating wheel map of the world painted by Ambrogio Lorenzetti (c1344). Now all that remains are the marks where it was fixed to the wall. Above is the fresco of *Guidoriccio da Fogliano all'Assedio di Montemassi* (Guidoriccio da

The Palazzo Pubblico.

> “The finest example of 14th-century vernacular architecture in the known world.”
>
> *Will Self on the Palazzo Pubblico,* The Independent, *2004.*

The *Contrade*

Siena is split into 17 *contrade*, legally chartered districts that date back at least as far as the 13th century. Each has its own traditions, church, museum, bar and club, symbol (such as a snail, wave or turtle), colours and fountain.

The *contrada* is like a large family and loyalties are fierce – people are born into one and they can't change it. Sienese babies are baptized twice: first into the church and then into the *contrada*, when they're given their *fazzoletto* or contrada scarf. Many men wear gold rings on the third finger of their right hands, leading to comments that they're married to their *contrada* rather than their wife.

For historical reasons, most long forgotten, most *contrade* have an enemy. Ten of the 17 take part in the Palio each year, and open-air dinners are held to celebrate not only their own victories, but also their enemies' losses. Yet while most attention is focused on the Palio, it's just the tip of the iceberg; it's the *contrada* system itself that keeps Siena going.

Fogliano at the Siege of Montemassi) in which da Fogliano, a Sienese army leader, and his horse – both draped in golden cloth – ride across newly conquered territories dotted with castles and tents. It is a work surrounded by controversy. Dated 1328, it was attributed to Simone Martini, although a number of academics now doubt this, saying that the castle style points to it being a 16th-century fake; others believe it was simply restored by later artists. Beneath it is a newly revealed fresco of two men engaged in the purchase of a fenced castle. The oldest fresco in the palace, it had been covered with plaster for years. Recent studies attribute it to Duccio di Buoninsegna.

Opposite is one of Simone Martini's finest works, the *Maestà* (1315), in which Mary sits on a gilded throne under a canopy supported by apostles, rather as if she's attending a medieval tournament. It was the first in Siena to show Mary against a sky-blue background, rather than regal gold, making her appear much more human. The picture – one of the most important in Siena – symbolizes the ideal of a good and just governor and was a reminder for leaders to govern fairly and not take advantage of their power. On the beams above the *Maestà* you can see a hand peeping out on either side. These would once have held curtains that framed the painting.

Sala della Pace The Sala della Pace, the meeting room of the Council of Nine, contains some of Europe's most important medieval secular frescoes: the *Allegories of Good and Bad Government*. Painted by Ambrogio Lorenzetti between 1337 and 1339, they were commissioned by the remarkably enlightened Council of Nine as a constant reminder of the need to use their power wisely. On one wall a bearded Good Government sits enthroned, attended by figures including Justice, Wisdom and Charity. Beside them, a vibrant panorama shows the city that flourishes under such a regime – Siena, as observed by Lorenzetti from the palace windows. You can see contented citizens going about their business while masons construct new buildings. Outside, by the Porta Romana, a well-dressed party of falconers ride their horses into safe and fertile countryside. You can even spot a man leading a Cinta Senese: a distinctive black and white Sienese pig. On the other wall, Bad Government is represented by a devil, aided by Vice who has unceremoniously squashed Justice. The effects are dramatic and the accompanying panorama depicts a threatening landscape – dry, bare and full of robbers; the city is ruined and violence reigns. The message is clear: behave, or else.

Torre del Mangia

Piazza del Campo, T0577-292223, comune.siena.it. Nov-mid Mar 1000-1600 (approx), mid Mar-end Oct 1000-1900, €7 joint ticket with museum without reservation; tickets can be pre-booked. Closed for safety reasons during rain.

Turn left when you enter the palace to climb the thigh-tightening 388 steps of this 102-m tower, which gives outstanding views of the city. Topped with an enormous bell, it once dominated the Sienese skyline, a symbol of the Republic's

Tip...

Save money by buying a joint ticket that covers the Duomo, Museo dell'Opera, Cripta, Battistero and Oratorio di San Bernardino, €10.

Visitors flock to the Duomo.

authority over any competing religious and aristocratic powers. It gets its name from one of the first bellringers – a lazy, fat man nicknamed *Mangiaguadagni* ('Eat the profits').

Duomo

Piazza del Duomo, off via di Città, T0577-283048 operaduomo.siena.it.
Mar-Oct Mon-Sat 1030-1930, Sun 1330-1930, Nov-Mar Mon-Sat 1030-1830, Sun 1330-1730, €6 when floor is uncovered (late Aug-end Oct, dates vary, phone to book), otherwise free.

Siena's cathedral justifies the term 'jaw-dropping'. Consecrated in 1179, it continued to grow over the years, becoming increasingly ornate in the process. Early visitors on the Grand Tour found it stunning – and sometimes shocking: John Ruskin, who had a headache at the time, described it as "absurd…a piece of costly confectionery". The lower part of the façade was lavishly carved by Giovanni Pisano in the late 13th century; although his original statues have now been moved to the **Museo dell'Opera del Duomo** (see page 89) to protect them, the copies that replace them mean that none of the effect is lost. The upper half of the façade was begun later, and the mosaics at the top weren't added until the 19th century. The humbug-striped bell tower was built around 1313.

The Duomo was meant to be even larger. Early in the 14th century the Sienese decided to make their cathedral the largest in Christendom. But work had to be abandoned when the Black Death of 1348 decimated the population and sparked an economic crisis. The Museo dell'Opera del Duomo is now housed in what would have been the right nave, and the frame of the façade is nearby.

The *pavimento* The interior is visually stunning and surprisingly colourful; it's hard to know where to look first. The plan is like a Latin cross, with three enormous aisles. The columns and walls are covered with black and white zebra stripes, the ceiling and arches are decorated too; the faces of 172 former popes peer down at you from on high, and the floor – known as the *pavimento* – is made up of 56 inlaid marble squares decorated with *sgraffito*. Work on these began in 1367 and continued for 200 years, involving many of Siena's finest artists, such as Pinturicchio, Beccafumi and Matteo di Giovanni. In black and white with touches of yellow and red, these magnificent mosaics tell stories from the Old Testament and from mythology – one scene shows the Sienese she-wolf surrounded by an elephant, a lion and a unicorn – and they are extremely detailed: look closely and you'll see carefully crafted snails, frogs and tortoises. In order to preserve it, most of the floor is covered except for a few weeks between late August and early October (dates vary).

Piccolomini Library The Piccolomini Library, off the left aisle of the cathedral, is like a jewel box. It was built in 1495 to celebrate the life of Enea Silvio

Inside the stunning Museo dell'Opera del Duomo.

Piccolomini, who became Pope Pius II, on the orders of his nephew, Cardinal Francesco Todeschini Piccolomini, then Archbishop of Siena, and it is richly decorated with a cycle of frescoes by Pinturicchio depicting episodes from the life of the pope.

To the left of the library is the Piccolomini altar. Most of its statues of saints are by Michelangelo but one, *St Francis*, is by Sebastiano Torrigiani, who gained notoriety for breaking Michelangelo's nose.

In the **Cappella di San Giovanni Battista** is a statue of St John in rags, by Donatello (1457). The tomb of Cardinal Riccardo Petroni opposite is by the Sienese artist Tino di Camaino. On the left, behind the altar, inlaid choir stalls depict lifelike birds, streets and buildings.

Pisano's pulpit The marble pulpit is a masterpiece, sculpted by Nicola Pisano (father of Giovanni Pisano, who carved the façade) between 1265 and 1268. He was the first 'modern' sculptor in Italy, giving emotion to his subjects. The figure of Christ on the cross is portrayed as a suffering man rather than a triumphant divine figure. There are 300 human figures on the pulpit, and all the faces are different. Look at the columns in this part of the cathedral: at one point the zebra stripes become much more widely spaced. This indicates an early extension to the original building.

Tip...

For stunning city views, don't miss the Panorama dal Facciatone: 70 narrow spiral stairs lead on to the walls of the abandoned cathedral extension – vertigo sufferers beware.

Cappella della Madonna del Voto This chapel, designed by Bernini, is adorned with lapis lazuli and contains a medieval picture of the Virgin that is said to grant miracles. Hanging beside it are all sorts of offerings. They range from cycle helmets and baby shoes to *contrade* scarves and horses' bits – the latter giving thanks for 'miraculous' Palio victories.

Museo dell'Opera del Duomo

Piazza della Quercia, by the Duomo, T0577-283048, operaduomo.siena.it.
Daily, Mar-end May and Sep-end Oct 0930-1900, Jun-end Aug 0930-2000, Nov-end Feb 1000-1700, €6.

Occupying what was intended to be the nave of the extended Duomo, this museum houses much of its art collection. Among the works displayed here are the original sculptures from the façade and, most famous of all, Duccio's *Maestà*. On the second floor you can see icons and altarpieces, including a Byzantine work, *Madonna degli Occhi Grossi* ('of the Big Eyes'), which was painted early in the 13th century and was the cathedral's original altarpiece. The Sienese prayed in front of it to ask the Virgin for protection before the Battle of Montaperti in 1260. They won, and the Virgin became their patron saint.

Sala il Duccio The most important room is the Sala il Duccio, on the first floor, which contains Duccio di Buoninsegna's masterly *Maestà*, a double-sided work painted on wood for the Duomo's high altar. It took three years to complete, and in 1311 it was carried ceremoniously from Duccio's workshop to the cathedral, attended by virtually everyone in the city. Considered one of the most important paintings in medieval art, it is richly gilded and depicts the Madonna and Child on a marble throne, surrounded by saints and angels. The back is covered with scenes depicting the Passion of Christ. Drawing on Byzantine tradition mingled with lyrical elements of humanity and narrative, it essentially founded the Sienese school of painting. Not all the panels are here, though. Other works include Duccio's *Madonna di Crevole* (1283) and Pietro Lorenzetti's *Birth of the Virgin*. The lower floor is dedicated to statues, including those carved by Giovanni Pisano that would once have covered the façade of the Duomo. The figures seem to loom over you, fingers raised, sizing you up with unseeing eyes. You leave the museum through the high baroque Church of San Niccolò in Sasso, adorned with lavish stuccowork and an inlaid floor.

Cripta di San Giovanni

Piazza della Quercia, T0577-283048, operaduomo.siena.it.
Mar-May, Sep 0930-1900, Jun-Aug 0930-2000, Oct 0930-1800, Nov-Feb 1000-1700, €6.

Tucked behind the back of the Duomo at the top of the steps leading down to the Baptistery, it would be easy to miss this little treasure. The term *cripta* (crypt) is a misnomer, since it was more probably a hall leading to the pilgrims' entrance to the Duomo. Having followed the via Francigena, tired and hungry pilgrims would first enter this hall to prepare themselves for their devotions. Here they could wash, purify themselves and have something to eat before going into the Duomo. However, it was filled with rubble and sealed up when the Baptistery was built, and was only rediscovered in 1999 by a workman swinging a pickaxe.

The walls are covered with brilliantly coloured, and perfectly preserved, 13th- and 14th-century frescoes depicting stories of the Old and New Testament. Among the artists involved were Guido and Renaldo da Siena and Guido di Graziano. On the ground, covered by glass, are the remains of an eighth-century food store, while the walls are dotted with medieval graffiti. You can also see the arch that supports the pulpit in the cathedral above.

Battistero di San Giovanni

Piazza San Giovanni, T0577-283048, operaduomo.siena.it.
Mar-May, Sep-Oct 0930-1900, Jun-Aug 0930-2000, Nov-Feb 1000-1700, €3.

The gorgeous Baptistery, also called San Giovanni, was built between 1316 and 1325 by Camaino di Crescentino, father of Tino di Camaino. It is underneath the choir of the Duomo and is reached by a long set of marble stairs – look for the one marked with a cross, where St Catherine is said to have fallen and broken her tooth. Every surface seems to be covered with jewel-bright frescoes, painted in the 15th century by Lorenzo di Pietro (Il Vecchietta) and Michele di Matteo.

The star is the baptismal font, to which all the major Italian Renaissance sculptors contributed. Commissioned in 1416, it took 20 years to complete. It's decorated with gilded bronze panels depicting the life of the Baptist, and includes Ghiberti's *Baptism of Christ*, Jacopo della Quercia's *Annunciation of the Baptist to Zacharias* and an extremely vivid *Herod's Feast* by Donatello.

Santa Maria della Scala

Piazza del Duomo, T0577-224811, santamariadellascala.com.
Daily 1030-1830 (may close earlier in winter), €6 (€5.50 if booked in advance),€3.50/€3 student, free under 11/over 65.

Stretched across the piazza opposite the Duomo, this was once the city's hospital. It was one of the first in Europe, and was still treating patients in the 1980s. Now it has been turned into a museum complex, with unmissable examples of secular art.

Legend dates it to the ninth century when a cobbler named Sorore opened a hostel for travellers. In fact, it was set up by the cathedral canons to provide hospitality for pilgrims on the via Francigena. It also took in *gettatelli* (abandoned children). Donations to it have been recorded as early as 1090 and by the 14th century it came under control of the city rather than the church. The building incorporates the **Church of Santa Maria Annunziata** (left at entrance, free), which dates back to the 13th century. Above the altar there's a painting of a miraculous healing, *Probatica Piscina* (1730), by Sebastiano Conca. There's also a signed bronze of the *Risen Christ* by Il Vecchietta.

Sala del Pellegrinaio The hospital complex was further developed in the 14th and 15th centuries. The most important room is the Sala del Pellegrinaio, an unlikely ward that was still in use in the 1980s. Its walls are smothered with frescoes that lovingly record the daily life and legends of the hospital. Painted between 1440 and 1444 by Il Vecchietta, Domenico di Bartolo and other artists, they were the brainchild of Rector Giovanni di Francesco Buzzichelli and their secular content makes them unique: food is given to the poor, a bishop distributes alms, the sick are tended. The most famous part is *Il Governo e la Cura degli Infermi* (1440-1), by Domenico di Bartolo, an intense and busy scene in which a man with a bad gash on his thigh is being washed gently, while doctors carefully examine a specimen of urine and a monk hears a man's confession.

The via Francigena

The pilgrims' route known as the via Francigena was first documented in the year 990 by Sigeric, then Archbishop of Canterbury, who was obliged to travel to Rome to receive the *pallium* (a symbolic woollen stole) from the Pope. The record of his journey, listing the places at which he stopped, is now preserved in the British Library.

The road evolved over the years and alternative routes were established, eventually creating a trans-European highway for pilgrims and merchants.

It could be an arduous and dangerous journey, and once travellers reached the north of Italy they risked malarial swamps to the west, and robbers and bandits in the mountains to the east. The safest route was through Siena. Hospitals offering both hospitality and healthcare – such as the Spedale di Santa Maria della Scala – sprang up along the way. By the Middle Ages pilgrimages had become big business: they were almost medieval package tours, with itineraries featuring churches and holy relics instead of today's art treasures and Armani. With no rivers, Siena could neither work materials nor easily transport goods, so the via Francigena provided an economic lifeline. The city grew wealthy by providing hospitality and banking facilities – something that made it very attractive to its rival city-state, Florence.

Santa Maria della Scala

To the left of the Sala del Pellegrinaio are two medieval hospital wards, used from the end of the 13th century. You can see where the beds would have stood and, on one wall, the word "SILENTIUM".

Museum tour The complex also contains the restored Cappella del Manto, which was built to house the hospital's precious relics and contains a fresco by Domenico Beccafumi, and the Sagrestia Vecchia, the old sacristy, in which you can see a fresco cycle depicting the *Articles of the Creed.*

Downstairs, there's an exhibition on the restoration of the Fonte Gaia, the original fountain from Il Campo (see page 151). Turn right at the bottom of the stairs and there's a gloomy corridor leading to the Oratorio di Santa Caterina della Notte, a grim, oppressive and extremely creepy chapel where St Catherine used to come to pray. Continue downstairs and you come to a 12th-century chamber once used by the lay council of the hospital. Right down in the bowels of the building is the Museo Archeologico, where shadowy tunnels cut into the tufa are filled with artefacts and finds from excavations around Siena, including some from tombs of the sixth century BC.

Palazzo Piccolomini & Museo delle Tavolette di Biccherna

Via Banchi di Sotto 52, T0577-247145.
Entrance across courtyard on left (door signed Archivio di Stato), 4th floor.
Guided tours Mon-Sat 0930, 1030, 1130, free.

Most visitors bypass this 14th-century palace, which houses the dull-sounding state archives. Yet they're missing a treasure: an unusual collection of over 100 beautifully illustrated ledgers. The *Biccherne*, as they're known, are decorated wooden covers made to protect the city's accounting sheets. The first was commissioned in 1257, and they were produced until the 17th century.

The finest Sienese artists were entrusted with this work (including Ambrogio Lorenzetti, Sano di Pietro and Benvenuto di Giovanni) and the resultant paintings are little masterpieces. What's most interesting is the subject matter – the daily life of the city. The earliest covers show monastic treasurers counting money, a man washing his hands, a wedding and the Duomo.

The Biccherne gradually became more sophisticated, depicting significant events in Siena such as the time of the *terremoto* (earthquake) of 1467. Historical events were also recalled, such as the coronation of Pope Pius II in 1460, or the Spanish destroying the walls of Siena. Over time they became paintings hung on the office walls, rather than book covers. They grew in size but lacked the integrity of the earliest works. The archive also houses illuminated manuscripts, 60,000 scrolls and thousands of books.

Around via di Pantaneto

At the top of via di Pantaneto – the name comes from *pantano*, the old local word for mud or bog – is the Logge del Papa, a striking white loggia. Commissioned by Pope Pius II, it is the most important Renaissance monument in Siena and was designed in 1462 by Antonio Federighi. To the right of it, on via del Porrione, is the Chiesa di San Martino (0930-1230, 1800-1900). Despite its 17th-century façade, this is one of the oldest churches in the city; it has been altered many times over the years. The high altar is adorned with marble angels and there's a 16th-century painting of the Madonna protecting the city.

Via di Pantaneto is lined with old palaces, such as the 15th-century Palazzo di San Galgano. Today it's the heart of student Siena. It runs down into via Roma, at the bottom of which is the Porta Romana, the most imposing gate in the city walls. Completed around 1330, it was later decorated with a fresco (now gone) by the Sienese painter Sassetta (1394-1450), who became ill while carrying out the work; the illness killed him.

Linking via di Pantaneto and via del Porrione is an atmospheric little lane called Vicolo delle Scotte. Once part of the Jewish Ghetto, it's home to the Synagogue, built in the late 18th century. The Jewish community is now very small but you can visit the Synagogue (T055-234 6654 or 0577-284647, sienaebraica.com; Sun 1000-1300, 1400-1700 approx, guided tours only, book ahead).

Basilica di Santa Maria dei Servi

Piazza Alessandro Manzoni.
Daily, 0830-1230, 1530-1830, free.

Down near the Porta Romana is this enormous church, one of Siena's most significant. Building began in 1235 but continued until well after it was consecrated in 1533, and the façade was never completed. From outside it there is a lovely view of the city. Inside it's wide and airy, supported by rows of columns, and with side chapels containing many important paintings. To the right of the entrance is *Madonna and Child with Two Angels*, painted in 1261 by Coppo di Marcovaldo. A Florentine artist, he was taken prisoner at the Battle of Montaperti by the Sienese, who then cunningly demanded that he paint this picture in return for his freedom. Other works include two gruesome versions of *The Slaughter of the Innocents*, one by Matteo di Giovanni (c1430-95) and another by Pietro Lorenzetti (c1280-1348), and a fresco of *The Banquet of Herod*, also by Lorenzetti.

Convento di San Girolamo

Piazzetta San Girolamo, off via dei Servi.
Mon-Sat during the day.

Not far from the Basilica di Santa Maria dei Servi, this little convent dates back to 1470. Ring the bell, and once she's peeped at you through the window, a nun will let you in. The lavish church contains Francesco Vanni's painting of *St Catherine drinking the blood of Christ*, and an *Annunciation* by Rutilio Manetti. In an alcove in the passage outside is a vibrant fresco by Fungari.

Pinacoteca Nazionale

Via San Pietro, T0577-281161.
Mon 0830-1330, Tue-Sat 0830-1915, Sun 0815-1315, €4.

The city's art gallery is devoted to Sienese art from the 13th century, with a dazzling array of paintings embellished with gold leaf – a legacy of the Sienese school's adherence to the Byzantine tradition. Comprehensive though it is, this gallery is less likely to absorb the casual visitor than the specialist, so if you feel you've seen enough religious painting, don't feel guilty about giving it a miss. Among the most important works is the tiny *Madonna dei Francescani*, by Duccio, probably painted in 1285, pre-dating his *Maestà* for the Duomo. Other works include Simone Martini's *Madonna and Child*, Pietro Lorenzetti's *Madonna Enthroned*, *The Adoration of the Magi* by Taddeo di Bartolo and works by Il Sodoma, Sassetta, Beccafumi and Guido da Siena. Look out for two charming and extremely detailed landscapes, *A City on the Sea* and *A Castle on the Shore*. Said to be the first examples of pure landscape painting, they were originally thought to be the work of Ambrogio Lorenzetti, but have now been attributed to Sassetta. The gallery also contains cartoons by Beccafumi, some of which were designs for panels in the floor of the Duomo (see page 87).

Palazzo Chigi Saracini

Via di Città 89, T0577-22091, reservations 0577-286300, chigiana.it.
Guided tours Mar-Nov Fri-Sat 1030-1930, Sun 1030-1330, advance booking essential, €7.

This palace dates back to the 12th century, but was remodelled in later years by a succession of Siena's most powerful families. It's now the seat of the prestigious Fondazione Accademia Musicale Chigiana (see page 183), founded in 1932 by Count Guido Chigi Saracini. The **Library** contains a shelf-breaking 70,000 volumes, including rare sheet music. The **Musical Instrument Museum** fills three rooms, and contains everything from violins to mandolins and rare harpsichords, including instruments by Stradivari, Amati and other famous makers. The palace itself has a stunning art collection, with paintings from the 13th to 19th centuries as well as ceramics, porcelain and silver.

The Golden Age

Gilded paintings of the Madonna characterize Sienese art. The Virgin Mary was particularly important here from early medieval times: the citizens believed she was their protector and had been responsible for their victory at the Battle of Montaperti, which sparked a production line of paintings. A Florentine artist, Coppo di Marcovaldo, had been taken prisoner at Montaperti, and the Sienese demanded a painting as a ransom. It took him a year to do (you can see it in the Basilica di Santa Maria dei Servi) and during that time he met and influenced local artist Guido da Siena. Up to then, Sienese artists – always more conservative than those in Florence – had followed the Romanesque tradition, which had strong Byzantine roots. Figures were flat, with emphasis on their eyes and hands and, rather than natural settings, artists used gold leaf for backgrounds – suggesting that their subjects were bathed in divine light.

Guido began to relax this rigidity, and was followed by Duccio di Buoninsegna, the acknowledged father of the Sienese school. Duccio skilfully combined Byzantine tradition with Northern European, Gothic influences. His painting of the Madonna and Child, the *Maestà*, produced for the high altar of the Duomo, still has the Byzantine gilding, but there's more movement: faces turn in various directions, it's not so flat, and Christ looks more childlike. Duccio's pupil, Simone Martini, introduced an even more relaxed Gothic style and gave a human dimension to his religious subjects. More emotional works followed with the Lorenzetti brothers, Ambrogio and Pietro. The former painted the political frescoes in the Palazzo Pubblico, which not only show secular figures, but also landscapes.

The Lorenzetti brothers died in the Black Death, which decimated Siena's population. Important artists such as Domenico Beccafumi and Il Sodoma followed, but the Golden Age of Sienese painting was essentially over.

Chiesa di Sant'Agostino

Prato di Sant'Agostino.
1100-1300, 1400-1730 (closed Oct-mid-Mar), €2.

By the square where the *Contrada della Tartuca* (Turtle) hold their celebratory dinners, this Gothic church was nearly burnt to the ground in the 18th century and was rebuilt by Luigi Vanvitelli. The church is no longer used for services, just occasional concerts. It justifies its entrance fee with a flamboyant marble altar, frescoes by Ambrogio Lorenzetti in the Cappella Piccolomini and a lovely *Epiphany* by Il Sodoma. Most unusual are the recently restored monochrome frescoes in the Cappella Bichi. They've been attributed to the Sienese artist Francesco di Giorgio Martini (1439-1502). There is also work by Luca Signorelli, and the floor is covered with painted majolica tiles.

Orto Botanico

Via Pier Andrea Mattioli 4, T0577-232874/235415.
Mon-Fri 0800-1230, 1430-1730, Sat 0800-1200, free.

Part of the university, this botanical garden provides a rare cool, green haven within the city walls. It is laid out in terraces, dotted with seats, and contains Tuscan plants, orchids, mosses and trees such as *Ginkgo biloba*, fig, peach and persimmon. Walk down to the bottom and you'll reach a tranquil patch of grass by an old stone pool and a section of old city wall – a good spot for a picnic. It's said that the garden is haunted by the ghost of Giacomo del Sodomo ('Giomo'), a monk and painter who is said to wander around making noises and throwing things at people.

Museo di Storia Naturale

Piazzetta Silvio Gigli 2, by via Pier Andrea Mattioli, T0577-232940, accademiafisiocritici.it.
Mon-Wed, Fri 0900-1300, 1500-1800, Thu 0900-1300, free.

There's a somewhat 'dusty', old-fashioned feel to this traditional collection of fossils, rocks, stuffed animals and skeletons owned by the university. The large beaked skeleton of a fin whale in the courtyard might satisfy younger kids on a wet day.

The Basilica Cateriniana di San Domenico.

Basilica Cateriniana di San Domenico

Piazza San Domenico, basilicacateriniana.com. Daily, Mar-Oct 0900-1830, Nov-Feb 0830-1800, admission free.

Perched on a steep escarpment above the Fontebranda Valley, this enormous brick church was built by the Dominicans in the 13th century. There was once an ambitious plan to bridge the valley, linking the church to the cathedral on the other side, but it never went ahead. It's vast and empty inside, and its most important works of art focus on St Catherine, who was said to have performed some of her miracles here. The **Cappella di Santa Caterina** is covered with frescoes of her life by Il Sodoma, the artist who introduced the Leonardo style of painting to Siena. Rather alarmingly, it also contains a holy relic: her preserved head in a glass case. Her famous broken tooth – she fell on the steps by the Baptistery – is clearly visible. Other cases contain one of her fingers and the whip with which she beat herself. To the right of the door is Andrea Vanni's *Portrait of St Catherine*: it is the only work completed in her lifetime, and is thought to be a realistic likeness.

Santuario e Casa di Santa Caterina

Costa di Sant'Antonio, T0577-247393/280801. Daily 0915-1230, 1500-1900, free.

St Catherine's home was turned into a sanctuary in the 15th century. On one side is the **Oratorio del Crocifisso**, built in Rococo style to house the Pisan painting in front of which St Catherine was said to have received the stigmata. Opposite is the family's old kitchen, now an oratory; the fireplace is under the altar. The floor is covered with faded blue and yellow majolica tiles. Downstairs is **St Catherine's cell**, now covered with 19th-century frescoes of important episodes in her life – including the time she cut off her long hair. Another painting of her, with Mary, shows the switch with which she regularly beat herself. The tiny bedroom contains holy relics.

Via Banchi di Sopra

Once part of the via Francigena, this is now the city's smartest street, with shops like Max Mara and the famous Nannini café/bar. This is where the evening *passeggiata* takes place – the see-and-be-seen stroll that happens in all Italian cities.

Siena's ascetic saint

The Sienese have enormous respect for their patron saint, Catherine of Siena (1347-1380), not to be confused with the Roman martyr who's remembered with Catherine Wheels. Caterina di Benincasa was one of 25 children and, from a very early age, showed signs of being distinctly different from other children. She began having visions when she was very young and at around seven declared she would remain a virgin. When her family tried to marry her off in her teens, she flatly refused – cutting off her hair in protest.

Against her parents' will Catherine entered the Dominican order and for three years lived like a hermit in her own home. Her life was ascetic in the extreme: she regularly flagellated herself, had a stone for a pillow and apparently survived for years eating only communion wafers. Her visions continued, including one in which she married Christ, and she eventually rejoined the world and began to care for the needy.

When she received the stigmata in 1375, her fame spread. She became increasingly political and corresponded with the most powerful people in Europe – dictating her letters since she was illiterate. In 1378 she went to Avignon and persuaded the Pope to move the papal court from France back to Rome. She died in Rome aged 33 and was later canonized by the Sienese Pope, Pius II. She's now patron saint of Italy (together with St Francis), a patron saint of Europe and – an unusual honour for a woman – a Doctor of the Church.

Many fine old buildings and palaces line the street, and reminders of the glory days are everywhere – not many branches of Benetton have 16th-century frescoes on the ceiling. The oldest Gothic palace is the **Palazzo Tolomei**, which dominates piazza Tolomei. It was once the seat of one of the city's most powerful families of merchants and bankers. At the junction with Banchi di Sotto there's the **Loggia della Mercanzia**, the court of the city's merchants, where the daily rate of exchange was set. It was here that pilgrims had to choose whether to continue along via Banchi di Sotto to Rome, or turn down via di Città to Siena's cathedral. The faces of the statues on the columns all look north, up via Banchi di Sopra, inviting pilgrims to break their journey in Siena.

Partway up the street is **Palazzo Salimbeni** (Piazza Salimbeni, T0577-294111, mps.it, visits by appointment only). This is the headquarters of the Monte dei Paschi Bank, founded in 1472 and probably the oldest in the world. The bank grew from the practice of charging shepherds to graze their sheep on the pastures (*paschi*) in the Maremma region. The money was then used to make loans, and the banking trade grew thanks to the thousands of foreign visitors who arrived on the via Francigena. Many moneylenders charged very high interest, but the Monte dei Paschi bank charged less. It began a long tradition of commissioning and purchasing works of art and now has a fine collection. It sponsors cultural events in the city and often contributes to building restoration. Most Sienese still bank here.

Fonte Branda.

Tip...

Near here is the Fonte Branda, one of the largest fountains in the city, which dates back to at least 1081 and is mentioned by Dante in *The Divine Comedy*. The water would have flowed into four basins: the first for drinking, the second for animals, the third for washing and the fourth for industry.

Basilica di San Francesco

Piazza San Francesco, end of via dei Rossi.
Daily 0730-1200, 1530-1900, free.

You don't appreciate the scale of this church until you're inside. Built in the late 14th century, it was later badly damaged by fire. It contains works by the Lorenzetti brothers. In the adjoining cloisters, which are part of the university, you can see the Tolomei stairs: under them, tradition has it, are buried 18 members of the Tolomei family, who were murdered by the rival Salimbeni family at a picnic, after a feud over money: "...the tablecloth, perfumed with lavender, became red..."

Oratorio di San Bernardino & Museo Diocesano d'Arte Sacra

Piazza San Francesco, T0577-283048, operaduomo.siena.it.
Mar-Oct 1030-1330, 1500-1730,€3.

This oratory marks the spot where St Bernardino prayed and preached while in Siena. There are two chapels. The lower one was frescoed by leading 17th-century Sienese painters, while the upper chapel is an example of High Renaissance art, the walls covered with frescoes illustrating stories of the Virgin by Beccafumi, Il Sodoma and Girolamo del Pacchia (1477-c1533).

The museum contains important works such as the *Madonna del Latte* (a breastfeeding Madonna) by Ambrogio Lorenzetti, and the Byzantine-style *Madonna* with particularly large eyes by Maestro di Tressa, from the early 13th century.

I Bottini

Tours start from Fonte Gaia, Il Campo, or Fonte Nuova, off via del Pian d'Ovile.
Tours Sat-Sun, each limited to 8 people, no children under 6, booking essential around 6 months in advance: apply in writing to Associazione La Diana, T0577-41110, ladianasiena.it (specify if you need an English-speaking guide), €8.

It's a fact...

The first Italian bankers worked from a bench (*banco*) in the street. If the city decided to stop them trading the bench was broken (*rotto*) – hence the term *bancarotta*, or bankrupt.

These atmospheric tunnels are the hidden face of Siena – they featured in the James Bond film *Quantum of Solace*. Unlike many major cities, Siena is not built on a river and has no natural water supply. It needed one to grow successfully, but the Sienese didn't want to build aqueducts – their enemies could have sabotaged them too easily. The people believed there was an underground river, called La Diana, but excavations failed to find anything. Instead they made their own river, building tunnels (*bottini*) to channel water from the distant hills to large fountains in the city.

Work began in the early 13th century and continued for 200 years – the network covers 25 km. The water was so precious that the fountains were under 24-hour armed guard. Both men and women carried out the work, men doing the tunnelling and women removing the rubble. The medieval workmen had only basic equipment but were highly skilled, and the tunnels still work efficiently. Ironically, they also provided an efficient method of spreading the plague, which ravaged the city in the 14th century.

You'll certainly see another side to Siena if you join a tour, and the guides, all of whom are volunteers, are knowledgeable. The walls of the tunnels you explore on the Fonte Nuova tour contain tiny fossilized seashells and stones from prehistoric times. If you go deep into the tunnels you might even be able to make out crosses that workers cut into the walls as protection against the dangerous creatures that they believed lived underground. Tours from the Fonte Nuova must always return the way they came in, so they are less popular but you're more likely to get places on one. The tunnels can be wet – you're expected to provide your own wellies and torch.

San Gimignano & around

The towers that characterize the hilltop town of San Gimignano have justly made it one of the most celebrated places in the world. Of the original 72, 14 of the towers remain: stone skyscrapers that give the place a romantically menacing air. Unfortunately, a trip here is number one on everyone's Tuscan tick-list, and visitors swarm over it from around Easter to October. Sometimes it feels a bit like a living museum: a place that everyone visits but where no one lives. To get the best from the town, try to visit in the off-season or stay overnight.

Collegiata

Piazza del Duomo, T0577-940316.
Apr-Oct Mon-Fri 0930-1930, Sat 0930-1700, Sun 1200-1730, Nov-Mar Mon-Sat 0930-1700, Sun 1230-1700, closed mid-Jan-Feb and mid-end Nov, €3.50, €5.50 combined ticket with Museo d'Arte Sacra.

Modelled on Siena's cathedral, this Romanesque collegiate church is simply covered with wonderfully lively frescoes. The **Cappella di Santa Fina**, a masterpiece of Renaissance architecture, contains works by Domenico Ghirlandaio illustrating scenes from the short life of the town's patron saint. The left aisle, as you face the altar, contains scenes from the Old Testament painted in the 1360s by Bartolo di Fredi: the creation of Adam and Eve is particularly charming. The opposite wall, telling the New Testament story, is thought to be from the studio of Lippo Memmi. There are also two wooden statues by Jacopo della Quercia, and some particularly gruesome Last Judgment scenes by the Sienese painter Taddeo di Bartolo: *Inferno* and *Paradiso* are on opposing sides near the exit.

Palazzo Comunale

Piazza del Duomo, T0577-990312.
Mar-Oct 0930-1900, Nov-Feb 1000-1700, €5.

This medieval palace, beside the Collegiata, houses the **Museo Civico** and the **Pinacoteca**, and gives you access to the **Torre Grossa**, reached by 218 stairs. It's the tallest tower in the city. The **Sala di Dante**, opposite the ticket office, is where Dante held a meeting with the council. It contains a copy of Simone Martini's *Maestà* in Siena's Palazzo Pubblico: it was done by his brother-in-law Lippo Memmi – but isn't as good. The Pinacoteca is filled with works by Tuscan and Umbrian painters, including Taddeo di Bartolo, Coppo di Marcovaldo, Pinturicchio and Filippino Lippi. The liveliest frescoes – showing a couple on their wedding night – are in the **Camera del Podestà**, painted by Memmo di Filippuccio in the 14th century.

Tip...

You can buy a combined ticket for San Gimignano, which gets you into all the civic museums. It costs €7.50. The Collegiata is not included.

Museo d'Arte Sacra

Piazza del Duomo, T0577-940316.
Opening times as for Collegiata, €3, €5.50 joint ticket with Collegiata.

Devoted entirely to religious art, this small museum has items such as embroidered copes, chalices and paintings, including *The Madonna of the Rose*, part of a triptych by Bartolo di Fredi, in which the Christ child holds a rose to the Madonna's face. There's a wooden throne from the late 15th century.

Chiesa di Sant'Agostino

Piazza Sant'Agostino.
Nov-Mar 0700-1200, 1500-1800, Apr-Oct 0700-1200, 1500-1900, free.

In a quiet square on the edge of the town, this church attracts fewer visitors but is worth the short walk. Built in the 13th century, it was later embellished with fine Renaissance frescoes. The high altar has a painting of *The Coronation of the Madonna* by Piero del Pollaiuolo, while the surrounding walls contain a fresco cycle depicting *The Life of St Augustine* that is filled with glimpses of

Left: A view of the town.

Towering ambition

Fortified houses were common in medieval Tuscany. Towns and families were often divided between the Guelph and Ghibelline factions, and towers provided both a refuge and a place from which to bombard enemies. But they were also a status symbol – and everyone wanted a big one. Towers grew higher and higher as wealthy families tried to outdo one another. In the end it got out of hand and the authorities imposed a limit on their height. If a family fell out of favour, their tower would be demolished.

After the Black Death, the population of San Gimignano fell, and buildings began to be deserted and fall into disrepair. It became a sleepy backwater. Ironically this preserved the architecture: while more successful Tuscan towns were pulling down their towers, San Gimignano remained in a time warp. The town's tallest tower is the Torre Grossa, which soars over 60 m. If you're feeling energetic you can climb to the top for a panoramic view of the countryside. On a clear day they say you can see the Apuan Alps – just.

15th-century life; it is the work of Benozzo Gozzoli and his pupils (1464-5). The chapel dedicated to St Bartolo contains the saint's tomb, and has a terracotta floor by Andrea della Robbia. To the left of the altar a door leads to a peaceful cloister filled with roses and potted plants.

Museo Archeologico, Spezeria di Santa Fina & Galleria d'Arte Moderna

Via Folgore di San Gimignano, T0577-940348.
Daily 1100-1730, €3.50.

This is a strange mix of museums squeezed into one building. At entry level there are items from a 13th-century pharmacy, moved from its original location in the city – you see the fragrant kitchen where potions were prepared. Other rooms contain archaeological exhibits, including Etruscan pots and funerary urns. Upstairs you jump a few centuries to 19th- and 20th-century paintings, including landscapes and works by Giannetto Fieschi (b 1921).

Above: The towers of San Gimignano.

Tip...

One of the best ways to enjoy the town is to take a walk along the quieter streets, such as via Berignano, and around the walls.

Museo del Vino

Villa della Rocca, T0577-941267.
Daily in summer 1130-1830, may close Tue and/or Wed in winter, free.

Set in part of the Rocca, the old fortress built in the 14th century, this small museum has displays on wine production, as well as an *enoteca* where you can taste a selection of wines – notably the local Vernaccia. Tastings cost €6 for four wines; you can also buy wine by the glass for €3-5. Even if you're not into wine, it's still well worth walking up here, as there are wonderful views of San Gimignano's towers from the fortress. There are also plenty of quiet spots for a picnic.

Southeast of San Gimignano

Colle di Val d'Elsa

The rivers round here made Colle an early industrial town. Glass was produced from Roman times, and in later centuries paper factories grew up. It's the place to come to buy crystal, both factory and handmade. There's a large shop in the lower town and a CALP factory on the outskirts. The **Museo**

del Cristallo (Via dei Fossi 8, T0577-924135, cristallo.org, Easter-Oct 1000-1200, 1600-1930, Nov-Easter Tue-Fri 1500-1900, Sat-Sun 1000-1200, 1500-1900, €3) tells you everything you could want to know about the history of crystal and its association with Colle and has some fine pieces.

The town's divided in two: Colle Bassa, the workaday lower part, and Colle Alta, the medieval part up on the hill. It's a steep climb to the top but once there you can mooch round the pretty streets and enjoy the views. Look for the via delle Volte – a section of underground road built when the townsfolk needed protection. Colle was the birthplace of Arnolfo di Cambio, the architect who designed Florence's Palazzo Vecchio.

Sienese and Florentine works spanning the 12th to the 20th centuries are on show in the **Museo Civico** (Via del Castello, T0577-923888, May-Sep Tue-Sun 1030-1230, 1630-1930, Oct-Apr Tue-Fri 1030-1230, 1530-1830, €3). It includes a *Maestà* by a 12th- to 13th-century artist known as Maestro di Badia a Isola, created for a church near Monteriggione, and a rare eucharist vessel, the Tesoro di Galgognano from the 6th century.

Above and right: Views of Monteriggioni.

Monteriggioni

Small but perfectly formed best describes this medieval fortification, which is as perfectly preserved as an ant in amber. It was built in 1203 by the Sienese to defend their northern border against the stroppy Florentines. A massive structure, it's easily seen from the road and instantly recognizable: a ring of walls studded with 14 towers. Dante mentions it in his *Inferno*, describing the towers as giants surrounding hell's abyss. The relevant quotation is carved on a plaque above the gate. Inside there's a tiny hamlet with a church, hotel and restaurant.

Chianti

Although it's sprinkled with pretty villages and has a generous share of castles and churches, there's nothing you feel obliged to see in the Chianti area – making it a pleasant antidote to treasure-filled cities like Florence and Siena. It's enough just to wander off the beaten track following the network of unsurfaced *strade bianchi* ('white roads') that lace the rugged, wooded countryside. Stop when you see something you like, enjoy lazy lunches and drop in to vineyards offering tastings of the local wine.

Around the region

The wine draws loads of visitors. Chianti Classico is a DOCG wine, and the S222, the main road generally known as the Chiantigiana, forms a natural wine route. You need a car to get about, or you can go by bike – the *strade bianchi* make great cycle trails. The main centres fill up in the summer, while spring and autumn are quieter. Go at harvest time for fresh porcini on the menu, newly pressed olive oil, trees turning gold and the scent of wood smoke lingering in the air.

Quercegrossa

Close to Siena, this village is mainly known as the birthplace of the great sculptor Jacopo della Quercia (c1367-1438). On the main road, the Chiesa di Santi Giacomo e Niccolò contains a late 15th-century painted wood *Pietà* by Francesco di Giorgio Martini that's recently been restored.

Castellina in Chianti

One of the most important centres in Chianti, Castellina is a hill town with a historic fortress in the centre and an Etruscan tomb on the outskirts. It's an excellent base, with some good places to eat and medieval streets in which to wander. Via delle Volte is an underground street with secret hideouts.

Radda in Chianti

Generally known as the capital of Chianti, Radda is a well-preserved hill village bearing the remains of ancient fortifications. The Palazzo del Podestà, its façade covered with coats of arms, is due to open to the public. On the first floor there's a 16th-century fresco of the Florentine school that's recently been restored. San Niccolò Church is medieval but was given an unusual *stile-Liberty* façade when it was rebuilt at the turn of the 20th century.

Volpaia

An ancient fortified village high in the hills, traditionally allied with Florence. It's hard to distinguish the village from the castle, as they're essentially the same. You find low arches in the street, built to thwart assailants on horses, and the cemetery is inside the castle. The village was on the via Francigena, and pilgrims would stop here on their way to Rome. Look above the door of Casa Selvolini and you can make out a square cross in the stone – the sign of the Knights of Malta.

Gaiole in Chianti

The village started life as a marketplace and hasn't grown much since. It's not far from several imposing castles – which are also wine producers.

Castello di Cacchiano

Near Monti in Chianti, T0577-747018.
Tue-Sat, morning and afternoon, call first.

This 11th-century Florentine fort has panoramic views from its terrace – you can see the Val d'Orcia and the peak of Monte Amiata, Tuscany's highest peak. It's been producing wine for 500 years and now offers tastings and tours of the cellars.

Castello di Meleto

Località Meleto, 2 km south of Gaiole, T0577-749217, castellomeleto.it.
Guided tours Mon 1500 and 1630, Tue-Sat 1130, 1500 and 1630, Sun 1330, 1600 and 1700.

The history of this castle goes back to the early Middle Ages, when it was founded by Benedictine monks. In 1269 it became the property of the aristocratic Ricasoli family, who owned it for 800 years. Take a guided tour and taste the Chianti wines and olive oils produced on the estate.

Castello di Brolio

Località Madonna a Brolio, near Brolio village, T0577-731919, ricasoli.it.
Tours daily 1000-1730 in summer, shorter hours in winter. Shop Apr-Oct Mon-Fri 0900-1930, Sat-Sun 1100-1830, Nov-Mar Mon-Fri 0900-1300, 1400-1730.

This is the home of the Ricasoli family and has been since the 12th century. It was here in the 19th century that Baron Bettino Ricasoli revived the local wine industry and established the 'formula' used to make Chianti Classico. Today you can take tours of the castle, as well as specialist wine tours – and tastings – of the estate's produce. There's a well-stocked shop too, as you might expect.

Castelnuovo Berardenga

The closest of the Chianti towns to Siena, this was another fortified village. It is now surrounded by soft vine-studded countryside, full of restored villas. The church in the main square contains a *Madonna and Child with Angels* by Giovanni di Paolo (1426). It's also the site of the Villa Chigi (T0577-355500, Sun 1000-1700 winter, 1000-2000 summer, free), the home of the founder of Siena's musical academy (see page 183).

West of the town, at Pievasciata, is the Parco Sculture del Chianti (T0577-357151, chiantisculpturepark.it, daily Apr-Oct 1000-sunset, call before visiting in winter, €7.50/5). Covering 13 ha of woodland, it is an outdoor 'gallery' displaying sculptures and installations from all over the world.

Greve in Chianti

This is the largest town in Chianti. The main square is the piazza Matteotti. The town hosts a large wine fair, the Rassegna del Chianti Classico, each autumn, on the second weekend in September. A short drive (2 km) west from Greve is the little village of Montefioralle, which claims to be the birthplace of Amerigo Vespucci – the explorer who gave his name to America (though the more accepted view is that he was born in Florence).

Castello di Verrazzano

Via San Martino in Valle 12, Greti, near Greve in Chianti, T055-854243, verrazzano.com, 20 km from Florence.
Wine tour and tasting Mon-Fri 1000, booking essential, €18.

Chiantishire

Chianti was once the promised land for the British. The landscape is craggy and hard to farm, and after the Second World War local people left in droves. In the 1960s the British middle classes began snapping up the ruined farmhouses and converting them into fashionably rustic second homes – now worth small fortunes. Many incomers settled for good and were followed by others chasing the Tuscan dream. The area became known as 'Chiantishire' – a term used in John Mortimer's book *Summer's Lease* – which still seems appropriate today, with British accents outnumbering Italian in some places. Almost all the properties have now been restored; whole hamlets have been turned into hotels, and tourism is thriving.

There has been a settlement on this hilltop since Roman times, and the present building dates back to the 12th century. The castle is most famous as the birthplace of the navigator Giovanni da Verrazzano. Winemaking on the large estate dates back centuries, and they produce a fine Chianti Classico. You can take a wine tour, which includes the historic castle cellars and tastings of four wines, as well as oil, balsamic vinegar and Vin Santo. The direct sale shop is just off the SR222.

Pieve di San Leolino

About 9 km south of Greve on SS222.

This beautiful church dates back to the 10th century. Inside are two glazed terracotta tabernacles by Giovanni della Robbia. Make sure you visit the immaculate cloisters, built in the 14th century. The terrace outside the church offers striking views of the countryside, with seats under the trees providing a peaceful picnic spot.

Sleeping

Siena

Tip...

The city walls mean that Siena just can't expand to accommodate all the tourists who want to stay in high season, so book well in advance. The busiest times are Easter, around the Palio – 2 July and 16 August – and in autumn when the Duomo floor is uncovered.

Grand Hotel Continental €€€€
Via Banchi di Sopra 85, T0577-56011, royaldemeure.com.
Situated in a suitably plum location on Siena's smartest street for this swish five-star hotel with 51 rooms. Once a rich family's villa, it's now been restored with exuberant frescoes, chandeliers and lashings of gilt. Room 138 has a terrace, and suite 135 offers the best view of the Palio parade. This is one for special occasions.

Hotel Certosa di Maggiano €€€€
Strada di Certosa 82, T0577-288180, certosadimaggiano.com.
Built in the 14th century, this former monastery 2 km southeast of the Campo is the last word in luxury – it even has a helipad. It's beautifully secluded, with lovely gardens that supply fresh produce to the restaurant. There's nothing monastic about the 17 rooms or the service.

Relais Campo Regio €€€
Via della Sapienza 25, T0577-222073, camporegio.com.
You get great views of the Duomo from the terrace of this lovely B&B in a 16th-century building. There are six rooms, all furnished in different styles, but featuring antique furniture and drapes. You can take breakfast on the terrace on fine days.

Palazzo Ravizza €€€
Pian dei Mantellini 34, T0577-280462, palazzoravizza.it.
In this elegant former Renaissance palace some rooms have countryside views and many are decorated with frescoes. Antiques are dotted around, and the public areas have comfy chairs and ornate ceilings. Best of all is the tranquil garden – breakfast is taken outside in summer. The hotel has its own parking.

Hotel Antica Torre €€
Via di Fieravecchia 7, T0577-222255, anticatorresiena.it.
An ancient tower dating back to the 16th century, this hotel's as tall and narrow as you'd expect. Rooms and bathrooms are small but clean. They're furnished simply and the whitewashed walls are dotted with photos and prints, while the ceilings have thick wooden beams. Steep stone stairs run down to a tiny breakfast room; it feels a little like a prison cell. Breakfast is €5 extra.

Frances' Lodge €€
Strada di Valdipugna, T0577-281061, franceslodge.it.
This farmhouse B&B is in a peaceful location on the eastern outskirts of Siena, with vineyards, olive groves and a pretty garden. The lodge has a small pool and serves good breakfasts with homemade preserves. There's a minimum stay of two nights.

Hotel Porta Romana €€
Via E.S. Piccolomini 35, T0577-42299, hotelportaromana.com
About 30 minutes' walk from the Campo, this former farmhouse has a fresh, rustic feel, and some of the rooms have views across the valley.

Hotel Santa Caterina €€
Via E.S. Piccolomini 7, T0577-221105, hscsiena.it.
There's a real home-from-home feel at this lovely hotel in an elegant villa by the Porta Romana. Staff are consistently friendly and helpful, and about half the 22 air-conditioned rooms overlook a gorgeous Tuscan valley. Breakfast is excellent, and in summer you can have it in the pretty little garden; in winter in the conservatory.

Antica Residenze Cicogna €
Via dei Termini 67, T0577-285613, anticaresidenzacicogna.it.
Excellent value at this small B&B on the first floor of a historic building in the heart of Siena. There are five recently restored rooms, all with private bathrooms, high ceilings and original features, including *stile-Liberty* frescoes.

Self-catering

Villa Agostoli
Strada degli Agostoli 99, T0577 44392, gardenhotel.it.
Just under 5 km west of the city. Lovely self-catering villas and apartments. Set among olive and pomegranate trees and with a swimming pool, there are 10 to choose from, sleeping from two to seven people. They're attractively furnished with well-equipped kitchens and their own patios. Rentals are weekly (from €1014 in high season) and prices vary seasonally.

San Gimignano & around

L'Antico Pozzo €€
Via San Matteo 87, T0577-942014, anticopozzo.com.
Plenty of history at this townhouse hotel, which dates back to the Middle Ages – there are two wells inside and some atmospheric cellars. In the 18th century, parties were held here. It's less decadent today but still atmospheric, with frescoes and four-poster beds in some rooms – others are more modern. Rooms are air-conditioned and have satellite televisions.

Leon Bianco €€
Piazza della Cisterna, T0577 941294, leonbianco.com.
You couldn't get a more convenient base than this established, family-run hotel in the main square. About half the 25 rooms have views over the surrounding countryside– more expensive than those on the square. There's an attractive terrace where the breakfast buffet is served on fine days.

La Locanda di Quercecchio €
Via Quercecchio 15, T0577-907172, sangiroom.it.
This historic family residence has just six comfortable bedrooms, all different and all with private bathrooms. Breakfast isn't provided but you can take it the family's bar in piazza del Duomo. They also have a self-catering apartment that sleeps two.

Chianti

Borgo San Felice €€€€
Località San Felice, T0577-3964, borgosanfelice.com.
Closed Nov-early Apr.
This is a whole medieval hamlet that has been transformed into a hotel complex 6 km west of Castelnuovo Berardenga. It has its own chapel, tennis courts,

swimming pool, beauty salon and restaurants. There are 43 rooms, some in the main house, others in outbuildings. It's perfect for honeymooners.

Castello di Spaltenna €€€
Località Pieve di Spaltenna, Gaiole in Chianti, T0577-749483, spaltenna.it.
You get secluded bliss and discreet service in this charming old castle, with its swimming pools (one indoor, one outdoor), sauna, gym and tennis court. It even has its own medieval church. Many of the 30 rooms and eight suites have four-poster beds. There are also two self-catering apartments in an ancient tower.

Villa Bordoni €€€
Via San Cresci 31/32, Località Mezzuola, Greve in Chianti, T055-854 7453/884 0004, villabordoni.com.
A stylish hotel combining modern luxury with quirky charm. Rooms have flat screen TVs, DVD players and large, comfy beds. Bathrooms are colourful and contemporary – some with showers that can accommodate two. There's a restaurant, swimming pool, well-kept gardens and two welcoming golden retrievers.

Le Pozze di Lecchi €€
Località Mulinaccio, Gaiole in Chianti, T0577-746212, lepozzedilecchi.it
Plenty of rustic charm at this beautifully converted 15th-century mill 4 km southwest of Gaiole in Chianti, set in peaceful grounds. There are 14 rooms, all with different features such as private terraces, wrought-iron beds or whirlpool baths. The swimming pool is particularly charming, with a waterfall and natural spring.

Podere Terreno €€
Via della Volpaia, Radda in Chianti, T0577-738312, podereterreno.it.
There's a comfortable, rustic atmosphere at this welcoming 16th-century farmhouse. Everyone dines together at night (it's half board only) – either round the long table in the kitchen or outside on the terrace. The food is very good and fresh, and the wine comes from the family's vineyards.

Villa Curina Resort €€
Località Curina, Castelnuovo Berardenga, T0577-355630, villacurina.it.
You'll find brick and beam ceilings, antique furnishings and contemporary comforts at this 17th-century villa 4.5 km west of the village. It makes a good choice for families, as there's a swimming pool, tennis court, and lovely garden. They also have a number of self-catering apartments with one or two bedrooms (from €1,050 per week).

Self-catering

Castello di Fonterutoli
Fonterutoli, 5 km from Castellina in Chianti, book through Stagioni del Chianti, T055-265 7842, stagionidelchianti.com.
There are five charming apartments in this pretty medieval village, owned since 1435 by the Mazzei family. The smallest is Carpentiere, which sleeps two (from €690 per week);

the largest, Limonaia, sleeps seven. A small, shared swimming pool has views of Siena. There are no shops or restaurants in the village, so come prepared.

Residence Catignano
Località Catignano, T0577-356744, villacatignano.it.
Closed Jan-Mar and Nov-mid Dec.
The Sergardi family have lived here for over 400 years and the estate, 8 km northeast of Siena, has a relaxed atmosphere, with cats lazing around the classical Italian garden. Buildings have been beautifully converted into apartments that sleep from two to six, and cost from €525-1,155 per week. From the swimming pool you can see the towers of distant Siena.

Podere San Giuseppe
Via Val di Sambra 6, Castelnuovo Berardenga, T0577-353133/355436, vacanzesangiuseppe.it.
A striking villa converted into three immaculate, roomy and tastefully furnished apartments, sleeping four to six (from €1,020 per week). They have power showers, panoramic views, a swimming pool and a large terrace. They can provide a breakfast basket if you wish.

Eating & drinking

Siena

Cane e Gatto €€€€
Via Pagliaresi 6, T0577-287545.
Fri-Wed 2000-2200, sometimes open for lunch.
Husband-and-wife team Sonia and Paolo offer a five-course 'tasting meal' (€60), as well as a fine selection of wines. There's no menu, but typical dishes are ravioli with ricotta and spinach in a truffle sauce, or veal with tarragon. If you don't want all five courses they'll adjust the price. Booking advised.

Le Logge €€€€
Via del Porrione 31, T0577-48013, osterialelogge.it.
Mon-Sat 1200-1500, 1900-2300.
Doors open onto the street revealing old prints, antiques, walls lined with bottles of wine and the buzz of serious diners. It's one of the best-known places in the city serving lots of local meat like lamb and beef in sophisticated sauces. The wide selection of wines includes a distinctive Brunello di Montalcino.

Antica Osteria da Divo €€€
Via Franciosa 29, T0577-284381, osteriadadivo.it.
Wed-Mon 1200-1430, 1900-2230.
Troglodyte dining at this excellent restaurant set in a series of atmospheric caves. The cuisine is creative Tuscan and reflects the seasons. You might find a delicious risotto served from a whole pecorino cheese, black tagliatelle with cuttlefish sauce or main courses like pigeon in Vin Santo with grapes. Sophisticated but relaxed.

Enzo €€€
Via Camollia 49, T0577-281277.
Mon-Sat 1200-1430, 2000-2230.
This is slightly off the beaten track, but worth seeking out for imaginative dishes such as pecorino flan or gnocchi with black cabbage and Parmesan. They do a five-course Tuscan set menu, as well as meat and fish tasting menus (veggies are catered for with advance warning), and wonderfully calorific desserts.

Nello €€€
Via del Porrione 28, T0577-289043, toskana-online.de/nello.
Mon-Sat 1200-1500, 1900-2200.
The contemporary black tables and metal seats make a welcome antidote to the ubiquitous 'rustic Tuscan' look, and the food's imaginative too. Veggies have an excellent choice from dishes such as chickpea and artichoke pie or goats' cheese and aubergine risotto with courgette flowers.

Fori Porta €€
Via C. Tolomei 1, T0577-222100.
Daily 1230-1430, 1930-2230, about 5 mins' walk outside the Porta Romana.
Not many tourists make it to this authentic neighbourhood trattoria, as it's just outside the city walls, but it offers delicious dishes like steak with rosemary or *cappellacci al dragoncello* (pasta with tarragon). Leave room for some fig and walnut tart or their delicious chocolate cake. You can walk it off on the way back.

I Terzi €€
Via dei Termini 7, T0577-44329, enotecaiterzi.it.
Mon-Sat 1230-1500, 1930-2300.
This sophisticated *enoteca* gets its name from the fact that it's situated at the meeting of the *terzi*, or 'thirds' of Siena. As well as doing a good line in aperitifs, it has a daily changing blackboard menu, which might feature homemade *pici* pasta or Chianina beef, and a wide range of Tuscan wines.

Il Papei €€
Piazza del Mercato 6, T0577-280894.
Tue-Sun 1200-1500, 1900-2230, evenings only Nov-Mar.
Cheery trattoria, down in the marketplace, with plenty of tables outside. The service is always courteous even when they're busy – which they often are. Yellow cloths and red bentwood chairs make for laid-back dining. Dishes might include pappardelle with wild boar sauce, or breasts of chicken. Try a traditional *torta della nonna* for dessert.

La Sosta di Violante €€
Via Pantaneto 115, T0577-43774, lasostadiviolante.com.
Closed Sun.
It's always busy at this lively trattoria, which serves hearty dishes such as traditional *pici* pasta with cheese, or vegetable nests with beef and apple vinegar. It's popular with young locals as well as visitors.

Osteria del Coro €€
Via di Pantaneto 85, T0577 222482, osteriadelcoro.it.
Tue-Sun 1230-1500, 1900-2300.
Cosy osteria, with buttery yellow walls and a comfortable bustle. Come for homemade pasta, local cheeses (pecorino wrapped in walnut leaves) and good range of wines. Dishes are filling like potato and porcini pie, cinta senese with beans or tagliatelle with pork and grapes. Desserts include an indulgent ricciarelli mousse and a delicious pear tart.

Taverna di San Giuseppe €€
Via Giovanni Duprè 132, T0577-42286, tavernasangiuseppe.it.
Mon-Sat 1200-1430, 1900-2200.
With frescoes on the walls by the entrance and brick-vaulted ceilings, there's an atmospheric and intimate feel to dining at this traditional taverna. Lots of Tuscan dishes to choose from, including *trippa alla senese*, gnocchi verdi with herbs, beef with *lardo di Colonnata* and chicken with porcini.

Carla e Franca €
Via di Pantaneto 138, T0577-284385.
Thu-Tue 1130-1430, 1700-2230.
Simple but popular pizzeria that also does takeaways. Brown paper placemats, tumblers, no frills. Pizzas are thin, crispy and freshly made, and there are around 40 types to choose from. Good value.

Il Grattacielo €
Via dei Pontani 8, T0577-289326.
Mon-Sat 0800-1500, 1730-2000.
Ironically called 'the skyscraper' due to its low ceiling, this osteria practically bulges at lunchtime. The owners serve the best they can find each day and dish out heaps of potatoes, beans, slices of prosciutto and olives from behind the counter. It's cheery, chaotic and great value.

La Chiacchera €
Costa di Sant'Antonio 4, T0577-280631.
Wed-Mon 1200-1530, 1900-2300.
Excellent value (no cover charge) and rustic Tuscan food. They don't serve fripperies like coffee, but you can try good *penne al pomodoro*, and traditional sausage and beans. Be prepared to share a table; if you're outside

the waiter will stick a block under your seat to stop it wobbling.

Il Vinaio dell'Eremita €
Via delle Cerchia 2, T0577 49490.
Mon-Fri 1100-1500, 1900-2300; Sat 1130-1430, 1900-2330.
There's a suitably intimate, rustic feel to this tiny osteria down in the *Contrada della Tartuca* (Turtle). They specialize in ancient Sienese cuisine. You can start with hearty crostone slathered with porcini or ricotta and spinach, try spelt soup, various cured meats or strong pecorino cheese.

Cafés & bars

Caffè Diacceto
Via Diacceto 14, T0577-280426.
Mon-Sat 0700-2230.
It's a café as well as a bar, but is most popular at aperitif time, when a 20-something crowd meets here and spills on to the street outside.

Fiorella
Via di Città 13, T0577-271255.
Mon-Sat 0700-1930.
If you want a quick coffee or a snack, this friendly little café/bar is considered to offer the best in Siena. It's a bit of a squeeze to find room at the wooden counter sometimes, but that's part of the charm.

Gelateria Super Panna
Via Banchi di Sotto 2.
Daily 1100-0100 summer, 1100-2100 winter.
New kid on the block attracting local acclaim for its delicious ices and unusual flavours. Look out for chocolate with peppers and cherries, ricotta with Nutella and even chocolate and beer.

Key Largo
Via Rinaldini 17, T0577-236339.
Daily Oct-Mar 0700-2200, Apr-Sep 0700-2400.
Do as the locals do and pop in for an espresso and a pastry. Its best feature is the secret balcony reached by a narrow stairway on the upper floor: the views of the Campo are superb.

Nannini
Via Banchi di Sopra 24, T0577-236009.
Mon-Sat 0730-2300, Sun 0800-2100 (2000 in winter).
A Sienese institution, this is where people come for pre-work cappuccino or a shot of espresso to sustain them while shopping. It's also a popular early evening stop for cocktails, wine and nibbles. There are seats at the back, but if you want to fit in simply prop up the counter.

San Gimignano & around

Arnolfo €€€€
Via XX Settembre 50, Colle di Val d'Elsa, T0577-920549, arnolforistorante.com.
Thu-Mon 1300-1500, 2000-2400, closed mid-Jan-end Feb, end July-mid-Aug.
New-wave Tuscan cookery and views at this acclaimed restaurant with rooms. The menu changes frequently and might feature Crete Senesi goat with apples, or beef from the Chianina Valley. There's a comprehensive, but pricey, wine list.

Dulcis in Fundo €€€
Vicolo degli Innocenti 21, T0577-941919, dulcisinfundo.net.
Thu-Tue 1230-1430, 1930-2145.
On a quiet street that looks over the countryside, this restaurant serves Tuscan dishes with a modern twist. You might find Cinta Senese, the local pork, with roast potatoes, or meat served with blue cheese, walnuts and honey. Desserts range from *cantucci* with vin santo, to a cake made with pumpkin, vanilla, chocolate and saffron.

Trattoria Chiribiri €€
Piazzetta della Madonna 1, T0577-941948.
Daily 1100-2300.
You could easily miss this excellent trattoria, as it's tucked away in a side street near Porta San Giovanni. The menu changes all the time, but might include traditional dishes such as ossobuco, tagliatelle with porcini mushrooms, and beef in Chianti.

Cafés & bars

Caffè delle Erbe
Via Diacceto 1, T0577-907083.
Summer 0830-2300, winter 0830-2000.
Pleasant, contemporary café behind the Duomo serving panini, coffees and snacks.

Gelateria di Piazza
Piazza della Cisterna 4, T0577 942244.
Daily 0900-2300, closed mid-Nov until a fortnight before Easter.
San Gimignano is nearly as famous for its ice creams as its architecture, thanks to the Gelateria di Piazza, which regularly scoops (sorry) international awards. Famed for their saffron flavour, they also do a delicious raspberry and rosemary, as well as one made with the local Vernaccia wine.

Chianti

Al Gallopapa €€€€
Via delle Volte 14, Castellina in Chianti, T0577-742939, gallopapa.com.
Tue-Sun 1230-1400, 1930-2130.
Squeezed under the arches that ring the village of Castellina, this well-known restaurant is a bit like a medieval cavern. It has over 400 wines to choose from and dishes might include red

beetroot gnocchi paired with ragù and a pecorino fondue, or pigeon with cocoa beans.

La Bottega del 30 €€€€
Via Santa Caterina 2, Castelnuovo Berardenga, T0577-359226, labottegadel30.it.
Thu-Mon 2000-2130, Sun 1300-1430, 2000-2130.
Think upmarket rustic and you'll get the picture. The food's Tuscan with French influences, and the menu might include ravioli stuffed with wild boar with chocolate pasta, or duck with vin santo. There's a multi-course tasting menu for €65.

La Bottega €€€
Piazza della Torre 2, Volpaia, T0577-738001.
Mid-Mar-Jan, Wed-Mon 1200-1500, 1900-2130.
Carla produces wonderful food using vegetables from the family garden and other local produce. Try the handmade ravioli, *ribollita*, or rabbit with porcini, and her mother's speciality dessert, a light chocolate cake. Across the square is sister Paola's friendly café/bar, which also serves good local food.

L'Alto Chianti €€€
Via della Croce 5, Località Castagnoli, Gaiole in Chianti, T0577-731068, laltochianti.com, off SS 408 from Gaiole.
Mar-Dec daily 1200-1530, 1700-2230, closed Tue in winter.
The views from the terrace of this family restaurant would grace any picture postcard. Sebastian is the chef, along with his mother, and his father is the waiter. The menu changes regularly and might feature ravioli with fresh porcini, or thick Florentine steaks.

La Torre €€€
Piazza del Comune, Castellina in Chianti, T0577-740236.
Sat-Thu 1210-1430, 1930-2130.
The Stiaccini family have run this trattoria since 1920, and it's popular with locals. Steaks are a speciality, but you can also try traditional tripe, local Cinta Senese pork, ravioli with truffles, homemade pasta and lovely fresh desserts, as well as a large selection of Chianti wines.

Ristorante Giovanni da Verrazzano €€€
Piazza Giacomo Matteotti 28, Greve in Chianti, T055-853189, albergoverrazzano.it.
Daily in summer 1200-1430, 1915-2200, closed Sun evening and Mon in winter.
Try to grab a seat on the terrace here, as it overlooks the town's main square. The menu features Tuscan classics such as *ribollita* and braised beef in Chianti.

Cantinetta di Rignana €€
Località Rignana, outside Greve in Chianti, T055-852601, lacantinettadirignana.it.
Wed-Mon 1230-1430, 1930-2200.
There are glorious views from the terrace of this restaurant. They're famous for their grilled meats and homemade pasta, and make their own wines, which you can sample in the restaurant – and buy in their nearby farm, where they also produce olive oil.

Il Borgo €€
San Piero in Barca, near Castelnuovo Berardenga, T0577-363029.
Thu-Tue 1200-1430, 1900-2200, shop opens at 0700.
There's a real neighbourhood feel to this friendly little shop/ *enoteca*/restaurant. The menu changes daily and often features Chianina beef as well as other local produce. You can eat outside on the terrace on fine days.

Ristorante Semplici €
Via Roma 41, Radda in Chianti, T0577-738010.
Thu-Tue lunch only.
No menu, just whatever's cooking that day at this no-frills family eatery. Good sliced meats, beans and pasta forno – a typical pasta stuffed with cheese. It's very good value and a favourite with locals.

Entertainment

For more festivals see pages 52-55.

Siena

Cinema
Siena has several cinemas, which often show foreign films in the original language. Tickets (around €6.70/€5.20) are sometimes cheaper for afternoon showings.

Cinema Nuovo Pendola
Via San Quirico 13, T0577-43012, mymovies.it.
Arthouse films.

Metropolitan
Piazza Giacomo Matteotti, T0577-47109, mymovies.it.

Moderno
Via Calzoleria 44, just off Piazza Tolomei, T0577-289201.
A short film on the Palio is shown here from April to October, Monday to Saturday. It lasts 20 minutes and screenings take place in several languages.

Odeon
Via Banchi di Sopra 31, T0577-42976, mymovies.it.
The place to catch the new releases from Hollywood.

Clubs
Il Barone Rosso
Via dei Termini 9, T0577 286686, barone-rosso.com.
Mon-Sat 2100-0300.
There's live music at weekends, and dancing, Guinness and late-night snacks at this youthful bar in the centre of the city.

Il Bombo
Monteroni d'Arbia, T0577-372185, about 20 mins' drive south of Siena.
Fri-Sat evenings till late.
Disco and dining is the idea here, and most dress to impress. They have some separate bars serving rum and wine.

The Tea Room
Cosy, arty little hangout squeezed behind the Piazza del Mercato. They often have live music and cabaret nights.

Festivals & events
Fiera di San Giuseppe (Feast of St Joseph)
19 Mar
Celebrating the patron saint of the *Contrada dell'Onda* (Wave), this is an outdoor fair with stalls selling traditional fritters and handmade toys. The focus is on the children of the *contrada*.

Il Palio
2 Jul
The first of the Palios takes place at 1930 in the Campo, and ten *contrade* race in it. Trials are run on 29 June at 1930, 30 June at 0900 and 1930, 1 July at 0900 and 2 July at 0900. There is a dress rehearsal on 1 July at 1930. At 1530 on 2 July is the blessing of the horse in each *contrada*'s church; the pageant begins around 1600 and enters the Campo at 1720.

Il Palio
16 Aug
The second Palio takes place at 1900. Trials are held on 13 August at 0900 and 1900, 14 August at 0900 and 1900, 15 August at 0900 and 16 August at 0900. The rehearsal is on 15 August at 1900. On 16 August at 1900 the blessing of the horses takes place and the procession enters the Campo.

Fiera di Santa Lucia (Feast of St Lucia)
13 Dec
Celebrations focus on the *Contrada della Chiocciola* (Snail), and the streets are filled with stalls selling food and crafts.

Tip...

Look out for Manfred, the German with the red hat, who entertains diners on the Campo most days during the summer months. He's been going to Siena for years.

Music & dance

Accademia Musicale Chigiana
Siena's most prestigious musical establishment is housed within the medieval Palazzo Chigi Saracini (see page 162) and was founded in 1932 by Count Guido Chigi Saracini. Its concert season runs from November to March, and is known as the *Micat in Vertice* – after the Saracini family's motto. It also organizes the *Settimana Musicale Senese*, which is a week of classical concerts in July, and other concerts during the summer.

Teatro dei Rozzi
Book online at comune.siena.it. Both contemporary and classical dance works are staged here.

Chianti

Festivals & events

Chianti Festival
Jul
A 10-day art festival in the towns of Castellina in Chianti, Castelnuovo Berardenga, Gaiole in Chianti and Radda in Chianti.

Shopping

Siena

Art & antiques

Alvalenti
Via di Beccheria 7, T0577-286888, alvalenti.it.
Usually open daily.
Popular cartoon *contrade* posters. The artist will also do personalized works.

Biale Cerruti Art Gallery
Via di Città 111, T0577-223793, bialecerrutiarte.it.
Mon-Sat 1030-2000.
Features contemporary art from all over Italy, including works by Tuscan artists.

Books & stationery

Il Papiro
Via di Città 37, T0577-284241.
0930-1930.
Lovely books and diaries made from handmade paper.

Libreria Senese
Via di Città 64, T0577-280845.
Mon-Sat 0900-2000, Sun 1000-2000.
Lots of English-language books and newspapers, as well as a good selection of Italian works.

Clothes

Cortecci
Via Banchi di Sopra 27, T0577-280096 (0930-2000) and *Il Campo 30, T0577-280984* (1000-1300, 1530-2000), *cortecci.it.*
Designer heaven, with enough labels to please the Beckhams.

Dolci Trame
Via del Moro 4, off Piazza Tolomei, T0577-46168.
Tue-Sat 1000-1300, 1530-1930, Mon 1530-1930.
Friendly staff and a good range of quirky designer clothes for women – ideal for something a bit different.

Il Telaio
Chiasso del Bargello 2, T0577-47065.
Mon-Sat 0930-1930.
Classic clothes with a twist. The name means 'the loom', and dresses, jackets, coats and scarves are all woven by hand.

Ragno
Just off via di Calzoleria.
Tue-Sat.
Old-fashioned little shop stuffed with all sorts of loose buttons, braiding, sequins and the like. Be prepared for long queues: it's very popular with local women.

Stefano Veneziani
Via dei Montanini 86, T0577-45860.
Tue-Sat 0930-1300, 1530-1930, Mon 1530-1930.
Smart men's clothes store, stocking things like cashmere jumpers.

Tessuti a Mano
Via San Pietro 7, T0577-282200.
Mon-Fri, sometimes Sat, 1030-1900.
Lovely shop with all sorts of handwoven items, like jumpers, hats and ponchos, in silk, mohair and wool. They also stock perky little bags.

Crafts & ceramics

Alessandro Marchionni
Via San Pietro 22.
Handmade ceramics: some with *contrade* symbols, some inspired by the floor of the Duomo.

Ceramiche di Santa Caterina
Via di Città 74/76, T0577-283098.
Daily 1000-2000.
Good quality ceramics: many customers come in to buy the same cups that were used in the film *Mrs Doubtfire.*

Luciana Staderini
Via Monna Agnese, T0577-43316.
Open when it's open.
Studio of a local sculptress, tucked behind the Duomo.

Vetrate Artistiche
Via della Galluzza, T0577-48033.
Mon-Fri 0900-1300, 1500-1800.
Fascinating stained-glass workshop. They do commissions for a variety of buildings, and also sell small items such as earrings, photo frames and bracelets.

Food & drink

Antica Drogheria Manganelli
Via di Città 71-73, T0577-280002.
Mon-Sat 0900-1945.
An ancient pharmacy, now a swish food shop. The old glass-fronted cabinets are filled with wines and chandeliers hang from the ceiling.

Consorzio Agrario Siena
Via Pianigiani 9, T0577-47449.
Mon-Sat 0800-1930.
Deli/supermarket with a good range of Sienese and Tuscan produce. Lots of wine, honey, biscuits, and dried porcini – as well as basics for a picnic.

Enoteca Italiana
Fortezza Medicea, Bastione San Francesco, T0577-288497, enoteca-italiana.it.
Mon-Sat 1200-2000, often later in summer.
Italy's largest wine collection. Around 1,500 wines are stored here and you can taste some of them and buy to take home.

Il Magnifico
Via dei Pellegrini 27, T0577-281106.
Mon-Sat 0700-1430, 1600-1930.
Bakery where you can pick up delicious and freshly made *panforte* and *ricciarelli*.

Morbidi
Via Banchi di Sopra 73, T0577-280268.
Mon-Fri 0900-2000, Sat 0830-2000.
Exclusive food shop selling all sorts of tasty cheeses, pastas and meats, as well as lovely honey, olive oil and treats to take home.

Markets

General Market
Viale XXV Aprile, in front of the Fortezza.
Wed 0730-1400.
Lively weekly market packed with stalls selling everything from olives to overcoats.

Antique Market
Piazza del Mercato.
3rd Sun of every month except Aug and Easter, dawn to dusk.
Also known as Collector's Corner, with traders selling antiques and collectibles. It's good for browsing if not bargains.

Chianti

Food & drink

Antica Macelleria Falorni
Piazza Giacomo Matteotti 71, Greve in Chianti, T055-853029, falorni.it.
Mon-Sat 0800-1300, 1530-1930, Sun 1000-1300, 1530-1900.
This shop is famed for its meats – especially its salamis, made from Cinta Senese and wild boar. They've been making them since 1729.

Casa Porciatti
Piazza IV Novembre, Radda in Chianti, T0577-738055.
Apr-Oct daily 0800-1300, 1600-2000, Nov-Mar Mon-Sat.
Celebrated grocery shop bursting with dozens of local meats, over 50 types of cheese, wines, honeys, chocolate and loads of other goodies.

Le Cantine di Greve in Chianti
Galleria delle Cantine 2, Greve in Chianti, T055-854 6404, lecantine.it.
Daily 1000-1900.
Wine-loving Florentines often drive out to this historic shop in Greve, as they consider it offers an excellent choice of wines and oils at prices that are hard to beat. Shipping home can be arranged.

Activities & tours

Siena

Cookery classes

Scuola di Cucina di Lella
Via Fontebranda 69, T0577-46609, scuoladicucinadilella.net.
Classes Mon-Sat at 1000 and 1600.
Lella demonstrates typical Tuscan dishes. Classes last 3 hours, you'll get hands-on and end by eating what you've prepared. You can join a group or have a tailor-made session. From €45-150 per person.

Cycling

You can follow two long-distance cycling routes around Siena. The **Eroica Loop** is 200 km and takes in Chianti as well as the Crete Senese. The **Tour** is a 350-km circular route taking in all the Sienese countryside. The local tourist board has more details and produces a useful brochure called **Terre di Siena in Bici** (terresienainbici.it).

Amici della bicicletta di Siena (via Campansi 32, Siena, T0577-45159) has more information on cycling in Tuscany. Go to **Perozzi** (via del Romitorio 5, Siena, T0577-280839, perozzi.it) for mountain bike hire.

Chianti

Walking

Cor Magis Travel
Via della Sapienza 98, Siena, T0577-222684, sienapoint.com.
They offer guided walking trips in Chianti, as well as horse riding, cycling and hang gliding. Prices vary according to the activity. Available April-October.

Wine tours

Isango
T+44 020-3355 1240, isango.com.
Offers wine and food tours as well as other specialist tours.

Transport

Trains regularly go to Florence, via Empoli (1 hr 30 mins); for Pisa, change at Empoli (1 hr 45 mins); for Rome, change at Chiusi (2 hrs 50 mins).

SITA (sitabus.it) operate buses roughly every 30 mins between Florence and Siena (1 hr 15 mins). Buses also run regularly to San Gimignano (1 hr) and Colle di Val d'Elsa (40 mins).
Train Spa (trainspa.it) operate a bus service between Pisa airport and Siena. Buses leave twice a day (1 hr 55 mins). SENA (sena.it) operate a bus service between Siena and Rome (2 hrs 45 mins).

Eastern Tuscany

Contents

Introduction

The eastern corner of Tuscany has plenty to offer the visitor who's keen to discover the region's hidden corners. Traversed by the busy A1 autostrada that links Rome to the north, it's a combination of busy industrial districts and outlet shops with quiet hill towns and gloriously tranquil forests. Arezzo, about an hour by train from Florence, is the main centre and the springboard for a trail of works by Piero della Francesca, the acclaimed early Renaissance painter who was born in nearby Sansepolcro and spent most of his life in this part of Tuscany.

South of Arezzo is Cortona, a deliciously picturesque town with pre-Etruscan origins and steep, winding streets, which attracts legions of tourists in summer. It's set on a hill that rises steeply from the reclaimed marshes of the Valdichiana, the flat agricultural plain on which Chianina beef cattle are raised.

To the north of Arezzo are quiet hill towns such as Poppi and Bibbiena, and the extensive woodlands of the Casentino, a protected area that offers excellent possibilities for walking and cycling.

What to see in...

...one day
If you've got a car, do a whistle-stop version of the Piero della Francesca trail. Starting in **Arezzo**, make your first call **San Francesco Church** to see his *Legend of the True Cross* frescoes. Stroll round the piazza Grande, then on to the **Duomo** to see Piero's Mary Magdalene. After lunch, drive to **Monterchi** to see the famous Madonna del Parto. Your final stop is **Sansepolcro**, Piero's birthplace.

...a weekend or more
You have time to enjoy both the main centres. Spend a day in **Arezzo**, visiting sights such as the 12th-century **Pieve Santa Maria** and the **Ivan Bruschi museum**, as well as Piero della Francesca's frescoes. Next day, take a train to picturesque **Cortona**, where you can take a stroll round the shops, visit the **Etruscan Museum** (MAEC) and the **Museo Diocesano**, which is the home of Fra Angelico's Annunciation.

Arezzo listings

❶ Sleeping

1 Antiche Mura *piaggia di Murello 35*
2 Continentale *piazza Guido Monaco 7*
3 Patio *via Cavour 23*
4 Vogue *via Guido Monaco 54*

❶ Eating & drinking

1 Buca di San Francesco *via San Francesco 1*
2 Caffè dei Costanti *piazza San Francesco 19*
3 Coffee o'Clock *corso Italia 184*
4 Enoteca Bacco & Arianna *via Cesalpino 10*
5 Fiaschetteria de'Redi *via de' Redi 10*
6 Gastronomia Il Cervo *via Cavour 38/40 (on corner of piazza San Francesco)*
7 I Tre Bicchieri *piazzetta Sopra I Ponti 3-5*
8 Il Gelato *via Madonna del Prato (on corner by via di Tolletta)*
9 L'Agania *via Mazzini 10*
10 La Curia *via di Pescaja 6*
11 O Scugnizzo *via de' Redi 9*
12 Paradiso *piazza Guido Monaco*

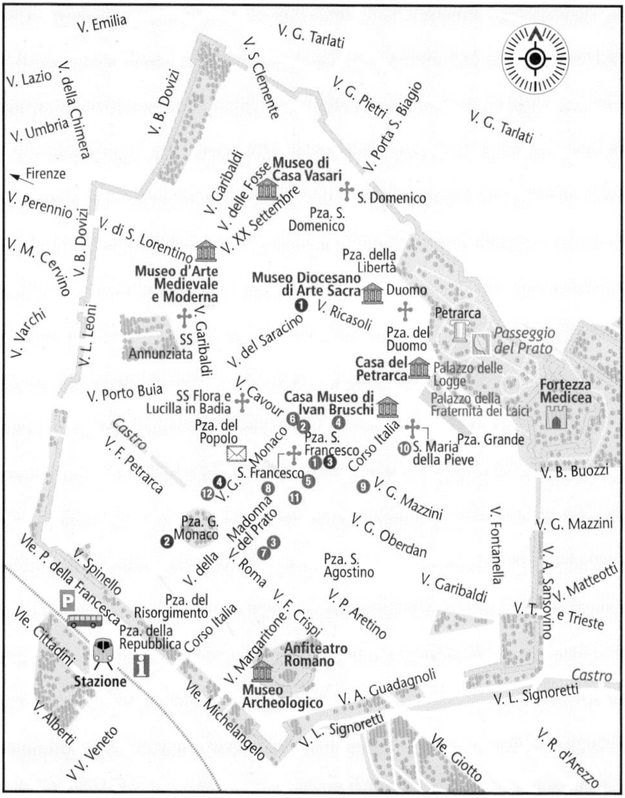

V. Emilia
V. G. Tarlati
V. Lazio
V. della Chimera
V. B. Dovizi
V. S Clemente
V. G. Pietri
V. Porta S. Biagio
V. Umbria
Firenze
V. Perennio
V. Garibaldi
V. delle Fosse
V. XX Settembre
Museo di Casa Vasari
S. Domenico
Pza. S. Domenico
V. M. Cervino
V. di S. Lorentino
Museo d'Arte Medievale e Moderna
Pza. della Libertà
Museo Diocesano di Arte Sacra
Duomo
V. Ricasoli
Petrarca
Passeggio del Prato
V. Varchi
V. L. Leoni
SS Annunziata
V. del Saracino
Pza. del Duomo
Casa del Petrarca
Palazzo delle Logge
Fortezza Medicea
V. Porto Buia
SS Flora e Lucilla in Badia
V. Cavour
Casa Museo di Ivan Bruschi
Palazzo della Fraternità dei Laici
Pza. del Popolo
Pza. S. Francesco
Corso Italia
S. Maria della Pieve
Pza. Grande
Castro
V. F. Petrarca
V. G. Monaco
S. Francesco
V. G. Mazzini
V. B. Buozzi
Pza. G. Monaco
Madonna del Prato
V. G. Oberdan
V. Fontanella
V. G. Mazzini
Vle. P. della Francesca
V. Spinello
V. della
V. Roma
Pza. S. Agostino
V. A. Sansovino
V. Garibaldi
V. Matteotti
V. T. e Trieste
Pza. del Risorgimento
Pza. della Repubblica
V. F. Crispi
V. P. Aretino
Vle. Cittadini
Stazione
V. Margaritone
Anfiteatro Romano
Museo Archeologico
V. A. Guadagnoli
Castro
V. L. Signoretti
V. Alberti
V V. Veneto
Vle. Michelangelo
V. L. Signoretti
Vle. Giotto
V. R. d'Arezzo

Arezzo

Arezzo is a prosperous working city with Etruscan origins. The lower part is busy and modern, the upper part well tended and medieval. Once a month it fills to bursting with thousands of Italians, attracted by the large antiques market that spills out of the main square into the surrounding streets. This is fun if you want to browse among the stalls and experience local life, but best avoided if you're on a whistle-stop artistic pilgrimage, as it's frustratingly hard to move around the city.

Basilica di San Francesco

Piazza San Francesco, T0575-352727/299071, apt.arezzo.it.
Nov-Mar Mon-Fri 0900-1730, Sat 0900-1700, Sun 1300-1700, Apr-Oct Mon-Fri 0900-1900, Sat 0900-1730, Sun 1300-1730. Entry to frescoes on the hour and half hour, €4 plus €2 booking fee (booking essential in high season, booking office next to church), free 5-18/EU citizens/over 65, but booking fee applies; church free.

This huge Franciscan church is most people's first stop in Arezzo, as it's the home of some of Piero della Francesca's most famous works. But the church would be worthy of a visit even without their presence: the walls are covered with fascinating fragments of frescoes, which were painted as a sort of 'bible of the poor' to make the Christian story accessible to the illiterate. The oldest of them date from the 1380s. There's also a huge 13th-century wooden crucifix over the altar, the work of an Umbrian artist. It's noteworthy as an early example of a depiction of Christ as a suffering man, rather than simply a divine being.

Just beside the ticket barrier, near the altar steps, is an unusual 15th-century tomb on the wall. It is credited to Michele da Firenze, who had worked as an assistant in Lorenzo Ghiberti's workshop while he was creating the north doors of the Baptistery in Florence. The tomb is made in *coccio pesto*, a kind of stucco made from crushed terracotta, which gives it

Essentials

Getting around Arezzo and Cortona are both small enough cities to explore on foot – and both are closed to tourist traffic anyway. There's a car park near the railway station in Arezzo, and others just outside the walls of Cortona (but spaces are very hard to find in high season). There are regular trains between Arezzo and Cortona-Camucia. Buses also run between the cities. Many of the streets in Cortona are extremely steep and would be difficult for anyone with mobility problems to negotiate.

Bus/train station Arezzo station is by Piazza della Repubblica, and buses also stop nearby. Cortona's railway station, Camucia, is about 6 km out of the city centre. Buses stop at piazza Garibaldi.

Hospital Ospedale San Donato, viale Alcide de Gasperi 17/via Pietro Nenni, Arezzo, T0575-2551.

Pharmacy Farmacia Centrale, Corso Italia 120 and Farmacia Merelli, Corso Italia 157, both in Arezzo.

Post office Main Post Office, via Guido Monaco 34, Arezzo.

Tourist information Arezzo: piazza della Repubblica 28, T0575-377678, apt.arezzo.it, daily 0900-1300, 1500-1900 (shorter hours out of peak season). Cortona: via Nazionale 42, T0575-630352, May-Sep Mon-Sat 0900-1300, 1500-1900, Sun 0900-1300, winter closes at 1800 Mon-Sat and closed Sun.

Tip...

Save money and buy a combined ticket for Arezzo's four state museums: €12 (€10 plus €2 booking fee) covers the frescoes in San Francesco, the Museo Archeologico, the Museo Statale Medievale e Moderna and Casa Vasari. You can buy it at any of the participating museums.

Piero's *Legend of the True Cross*: the panels

1. The death of Adam. His son Seth plants a sprig from the Tree of Knowledge in his mouth.
2. The Queen of Sheba kneels before the wood. She shakes hands with Solomon symbolizing hopes for unity between the Western and Orthodox churches.
3. The beam of wood is buried.
4. Constantine's dream.
5. Constantine goes into battle (he's on the white horse, holding a cross) and defeats Maxentius.
6. Judas the Levite is tortured and reveals where the Cross is hidden.
7. The Cross is discovered. The town in the background is medieval Arezzo, here representing Jerusalem.
8. Heraclius defeats Chosroes, who had stolen the Cross.
9. The Cross returns to Jerusalem.
10. The Annunciation.

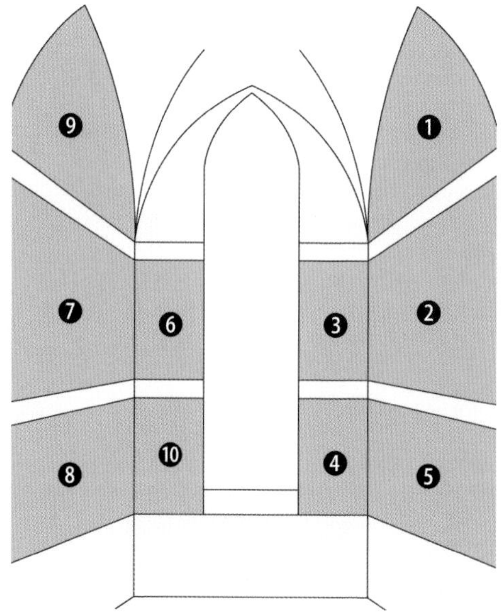

a distinctive salmon colour. It was used by the Romans to make pavements, as it could withstand high temperatures, and da Firenze revived the technique. You can see other examples in the **Santissima Annunziata** in via Garibaldi and on a lunette above a doorway outside the cathedral.

The frescoes Behind the altar are Piero della Francesca's frescoes illustrating the *Legend of the True Cross*, which were painted some time between 1452 and 1466. This was a time when the Christian West felt threatened: the Ottoman Turks had taken Constantinople, causing the collapse of the Byzantine Empire, and the frescoes reflect some of those contemporary fears.

Piero della Francesca (c1412/20-92) was born in Borgo San Sepolcro (now Sansepolcro) and spent much of his life in the environs of that little town. He served some time as an apprentice painter in Florence, where he worked with Domenico Veneziano. He was an academic artist, particularly interested in perspective and geometry – on both of which he wrote respected treatises. He was invited to carry out the work in San Francesco after the original artist, Bicci di Lorenzo, died. (You can see di Lorenzo's work on the ceiling.)

The frescoes were badly damaged by damp and it took 15 years – and a great deal of money – to restore them. Work began in 1991. To get a proper look at them you need to go beyond the altar steps, and for that you have to buy a ticket. The panels don't follow a narrative order but are arranged to be most aesthetically appealing: structure, symmetry and geometry were important to Piero. So you have to jump from one to another to follow the story, which was taken from a 13th-century text by Jacopo da Varazze: *Legenda Aurea*.

The tale starts at the top with Adam's death, and a seed planted on his grave growing into the tree that eventually made the Cross. It moves down to show the Queen of Sheba kneeling before a beam that she recognizes as part of this holy tree – and which she realizes will form the Cross of the Crucifixion. Solomon orders the wooden beam to be buried. One of the most famous panels is on the back wall, bottom right, in which Emperor Constantine has a dream in which an angel tells him that he will defeat his enemies by giving up his weapons and fighting under the sign of the Cross. Constantine sleeps under a tent, which appears to be softly illuminated (the effect is rather more obvious if you stand back, near the altar). It's one of the first night scenes by an Italian painter.

Panels on the other side wall include one in which a man is dropped down a well to force him to say where the Cross is buried; and one in which, out of three possibilities, the True Cross is discovered when it resurrects a dead man. The last one, at the top of this wall, shows the Cross returning to Jerusalem.

Piazza Grande

The town's medieval piazza is an unusual trapezoidal shape, with a distinct slope. On one side is a 16th-century **arched loggia** designed by local man Giorgio Vasari: it's essentially the first shopping mall, with swish apartments above and shops underneath. It was reserved for the wealthy, and a sign remains reminding members of the lower orders that they'd be subjected to the local equivalent of the stocks if they were found under the hallowed arches. Now some smart restaurants mingle with antiques shops, which, along with those on via di Seteria, look like antiques themselves.

Above: The Piazza Grande. Right: Pieve di Santa Maria.

Tip...

To the side of the church, in via di Seteria, you can see a door that has part of an earlier ninth-century church above it. Look among the geometric shapes and you can see the face of Christ.

Pieve di Santa Maria

Oct-Apr 0800-1200, 1500-1800, May-Sep 0800-1300, 1500-1900, free.

You enter this church, which backs on to the piazza Grande, from corso Italia. Built in the 12th century, it was originally the town's cathedral. Steps by the altar lead to the choir, where there's a painted cross dating from 1262 and a polyptych by Pietro Lorenzetti, painted in 1320. The façade has three tiers of columns, which get closer together and smaller. Some, in an early example of recycling, are Roman. Sculptures above the door show scenes from each month of the year – May is represented by soldiers going to war: apparently it was the favoured season for fighting.

Duomo

Piazza del Duomo, T0575-23991.
Daily 0630-1230, 1500-1900, free.

Although the cathedral was started in 1277, work carried on for centuries (the bell tower wasn't completed until 1936). It's noted for its **stained glass windows** (1516-25) by Guillaume de Marcillat, a French Dominican friar, and they're distinctive, with architectural backgrounds, bright colours and flesh tones in the people's faces. In one, depicting Christ driving the money-lenders out of the temple, there's a man in a red hat who seems to be running straight at you, no matter where you stand. (It's on the right hand side as you look at the altar.) Near the tomb of Pope Gregory is a small fresco of *Mary Magdalene* (c1459) by Piero della Francesca, in which he demonstrates his knowledge of perspective. She's holding an opaque apothecary's jar – a local tradition always depicts her as a bearer of myrrh. The church also contains the ornate **tomb of San Donato**, Arezzo's patron saint. A neighbouring column, topped with an oil lamp, is said to be the one on which he was beheaded.

La Casa Museo di Ivan Bruschi

Corso Italia 14, T0575-354126, fondazionebruschi.it. Tue-Sun 1000-1300, 1500-1900 (summer 1000-1800), €3, €2 6-8/over 65.

The home of a famous antiquarian (1920-1996 – who started the local antiques fair) contains his enormous collection of antiques and oddities from around the world. It's spread over three floors and includes everything from Etruscan urns to African statues. There are displays of his stamps (arranged in patterns stuck into albums), household items, glassware, books and gold coins. Be sure to go up to the terrace on the very top floor: it allows you to see the detail on the columns of the Pieve opposite.

Tip...

If you're in the mood for shopping make for corso Italia, the main street. Arezzo's the centre of Italian gold production, but there aren't as many jewellers as you'd expect: most of the work goes on in factories out of town.

Chiesa di San Domenico

Piazza San Domenico.
Daily 0800-1900, free.

This church was mostly constructed in the 13th century. You can see fragments of later frescoes on the walls. It's most famous for a **crucifix by Cimabue**, Giotto's teacher. The work, dating from 1260–5, at first looks Byzantine, but then you see that Cimabue has departed from convention by depicting Christ as a suffering man: you can see the tensed muscles in the body, and the blood coming from the wounds realistically coagulating. A few drops have even fallen on to the golden frame.

Below: Detail from the main room of Casa Vasari.
Right: *Madonna del Parto* by Piero della Francesca.

Museo Archeologico

Via Margaritone 10, T0575-20882.
Daily 0830-1930 (though may be closed in low season), €4, free under 18/EU citizens over 65.

On the edge of town, this museum is next to the **Roman amphitheatre**, which is thought to date from the second century AD. Some estimates suggest it could have held 13,000 people. You can view it for free. The museum itself contains important finds, including a vase attributed to the Greek painter Euphronius and Etruscan and Roman artefacts including bronzes and jewellery. Don't miss the coral-coloured ceramic vases, which were produced in workshops in Arezzo during Roman times and were widely exported.

Fortezza Medicea & Prato

Viale Bruno Buozzi.
Daily, free.

Not far from the Duomo, a public park leads to this fortress. It was built in the 16th century by the Florentines, who destroyed houses, churches and lanes in the process. It's generally quiet and gives good views of the town and the distant mountain. The park makes a great picnic spot. There's a kiosk café/bar, which opens intermittently.

Casa Vasari

Via XX Settembre 55, T0575-409040.
Mon and Wed-Sat 0830-1930, €2, free under 18/ EU citizens over 65.

This was the home of Giorgio Vasari (1511-74), who was born in Arezzo and became an influential artist and architect. He was court painter to Cosimo de' Medici and has often been called the first art historian: he wrote *Lives of the Most Excellent Painters, Sculptors and Architects*, in which he traces the development of art from the time of Cimabue. He designed this house and decorated it himself with lavish frescoes.

Monterchi

Museo della Madonna del Parto

Via Reglia 1, Monterchi, T 0575 70713.
Apr-Sep Tue-Sun 0900-1900, Oct Mon-Fri 0900-1300, 1400-1900, Sat-Sun 0900-1900, Nov-Mar Mon-Fri 0900-1300, 1400-1700, Sat-Sun 0900-1700, €3.10, free under 14/ pregnant women.

A rather unremarkable former school in the small village of Monterchi is the home of one of the most unusual paintings in Western art: Piero della Francesca's *Madonna del Parto* (1450-68). It depicts Mary while pregnant, with angels parting the curtains around her as if she's on a stage. You almost expect them to cry 'Ta-ra!' The church used to disapprove of such a human depiction of the Madonna, but they've come round to the idea now. Some think it was a homage to the artist's mother, who was born in Monterchi.

The fresco used to be in a church in the town, but was detached and moved to another chapel in the 18th century. It was eventually restored in 1992 at a cost of over €100,000 and is now displayed alone in a glass case. Other rooms in the museum are given over to detailed descriptions of the restoration. The painting has become a point of pilgrimage and women hoping to have a child will often come here to pray before it.

Sansepolcro

Museo Civico

Via Niccolò Aggiunti 65, T0575-732218.
Mid-Jun-mid-Sep daily 0930-1330, 1430-1900, mid-Sep-mid-Jun 0930-1300, 1430-1800, €6, €3 10-18, free under 10.

The town was the birthplace of Piero della Francesca, and the former town hall is now a museum containing some celebrated examples of his work. There's the *Madonna della Misericordia* (1445-61), an early polyptych, richly gilded and displaying his distinctive geometric forms. There's also his fresco of the *Resurrection of Christ* (1458-74), which depicts Christ standing in a landscape with one raised foot resting on the edge of his tomb; soldiers sleep beneath him, one of whom, dressed in brown, is said to resemble the artist. Aldous Huxley once declared this painting "the best picture in the world", and his description saved it (and Sansepolcro) from destruction by the Allies in the Second World War, because the officer who was to order the bombardment had read Huxley's essay. Other works in the museum include a large ceramic *Nativity* by della Robbia: look closely and you'll see that it was made as a 'jigsaw'.

Aboca Museum

Via Niccolò Aggiunti 75, T0575-733589.
Oct-Mar Tue-Sun 1000-1300, 1430-1800, Apr-Sep 1000-1300, 1500-1900, €8, €4 10-14.

A former palace that's been turned into a fragrant museum of herbalism – a pleasant change if you've had your fill of high culture. There are carefully illustrated old herb books, huge majolica storage jars, masses of dried herbs, an old apothecary's shop and a 'poison cell', where toxic remedies were tucked behind an iron grille. Pick up one of the informative brochures before you look round, as the labelling's in Italian.

Duomo

Via Matteotti.
Daily early-1200, 1530-1830, free.

Sansepolcro's cathedral had its origins in the 11th century and is in Romanesque-Gothic style. The most striking feature of its façade is a fine rose window – when you stand inside you can see the panes of alabaster with which it is glazed.
The cathedral contains a gilded 14th-century

Right: Views across Cortona.
Below: Detail from the cathedral interior.

polyptych of the *Resurrection*, attributed to Niccolò di Segna: the central figure of Christ stands in a pose so similar to Piero della Francesca's in the Museo Civico that many feel Piero must have studied this painting. There's also a 10th-century woodcarving of *Christ on the Cross*.

Cortona

There are enough museums and works of art in Cortona to occupy you for a couple of days at least – Fra Angelico and Luca Signorelli are the stars. It's also a good base for exploring the villages of the Valdichiana and nearby Lago Trasimeno. However, it's much more commercialized than Arezzo. It's been besieged by visitors ever since American author Frances Mayes set up home here in the 1990s and wrote about her experiences in *Under the Tuscan Sun*, which was later made into a film. Late spring and summer are particularly busy. Not all the locals approve of visitors on this modern literary trail. They did, as one said, "have Fra Angelico long before Frances Mayes".

Museo dell'Accademia Etrusca (MAEC)

Palazzo Casali, Piazza Signorelli 9, T0575-637235, cortonamaec.org.
Apr-Oct daily 1000-1900, Nov-Mar Tue-Sun 1000-1700, €7. To arrange visits to the tombs, ask at the museum or T0575-630415/612565.

You can't miss the prize exhibit here: an **Etruscan bronze oil lamp** from the fourth century BC, hanging from the ceiling of its own little temple on the first floor. It was probably designed for an important sanctuary and looks much like a chandelier. It's covered with ornate carvings of goddesses and priapic satyrs, with a gorgon at the centre. The rest of the floor is filled with cases displaying serried ranks of Etruscan bronzes – all the more mysterious because they're not labelled. There's a swaddled baby, horses, a delicately worked swan and mice nibbling at ears of corn. At the end are paintings by Luca Signorelli and his nephew. For great views of the countryside, go on to the terrace, which links two parts of the upper floor.

At the time of writing the museum was being extended, with six new rooms due to open by 2009. Plans include a reconstruction showing the historic development of Cortona. Other exhibits cover everything from Egyptian artefacts –

Fra Angelico

One of the most celebrated of the early Renaissance artists, Fra Angelico was born Guido di Pietro near Fiesole in around 1387. He became a Dominican friar in 1407, together with his brother, taking the name Giovanni. A talented artist, influenced by Giotto, his works were intended to stimulate prayer and meditation. He prayed before starting work and his paintings are notable for their tenderness and glorious colours. It was said that he was so devout that tears would pour down his face as he painted.

He initially trained as an illuminator. John Ruskin said he was "not an artist … [but] an inspired saint" and Vasari called him "humble and modest". When he had completed the Annunciation, now in Cortona's Museo Diocesano, he said: "When I saw this work, I nearly fainted dead from shock and love of it. I could not have done it alone. I sighed and wept." He spent four years in Cortona, and worked all over Tuscany as well as in Rome. Known in Italy as *Beato Angelico* (the 'blessed' Angelico), he died in 1455 and is buried in Rome. His epitaph contains the words: "The deeds that count on Earth are not those that count in Heaven. I, Giovanni, am the flower of Tuscany." He was beatified in 1982.

including a wooden funerary boat – to Tuscan paintings. From the Roman era there's a mosaic pavement and a *glirarium* – a shelved urn used for breeding and fattening dormice, a favourite Roman dish. On the lower floor are finds from Melone del Sodo, the Etruscan tomb just outside the town. They include an exquisite gold panther and delicate jewellery, and a scale model of the tomb gives some idea of its sophistication. MAEC's website shows two routes you can follow – one inside and one outside the city – to see this and the other main archaeological sites.

Museo Diocesano

Piazza del Duomo, T0575-62830.
Apr-Oct daily 1000-1900, Nov-Mar Tue-Sun 1000-1700, €5, €3 6-14.

Made out of two former churches, this museum contains some stunning works of art. Turn right when you enter to see Fra Angelico's superbly delicate, gilded *Annunciation* (c1430), painted when he lived in Cortona for a few years. On the wall to the right is another of the master's works, a triptych of the *Madonna with Child and Four Saints*. Other artists represented in the museum include Sassetta, Pietro Lorenzetti and Luca Signorelli. On the ceiling of the Lower Oratory downstairs are frescoes of Old Testament scenes designed by Vasari. Twentieth-century works by the Futurist artist Gino Severini, born in Cortona, line the stairs.

Chiesa di San Domenico

By piazza Garibaldi.
Daily but sometimes closed, free.

The sun is fading one of this Gothic church's most precious items: a lunette above the door frescoed by Fra Angelico (*c* 1433-34). Inside is a 16th-century altarpiece by Luca Signorelli.

Chiesa di Santa Margherita

Piazzale Santa Margherita, T0575-603116.
Winter daily 0830-1200, 1500-1800, summer 0730-1200, 1500-1930, free.

There's been a church on this site since 1297, built in honour of St Margaret of Cortona. The present church was built in the 19th century. It's got an eye-catching blue ceiling and a rose window made by Giovanni Pisano. In pride of place is the intact body of St Margaret, set in a glass coffin. Should you wish to, you can press a switch to light it up. You can walk to the church from Cortona by following the **viale Santa Margherita**. It joins an ancient track, possibly used by medieval pilgrims, along which are the *Stations of the Cross* decorated with mosaics by the artist Gino Severini.

Left: Chiesa di San Domenico.
Above: The cathedral at Cortona.

Tip...

If you want to see another site associated with St Francis, visit **La Verna** (T0575-5341, santuariolaverna.org) near Bibbiena in the Casentino. This monastic complex is where he received the stigmata.

Around Cortona

Convento delle Celle

3.5 km east of Cortona, T0575-603362, lecelle.it.
0830-1200, 1530-1830, free.

Set in a peaceful hollow beside a gushing stream, this monastery was built by St Francis in 1211 and enlarged over the centuries. Built in creamy stone on the craggy slopes of Monte Sant'Egidio, it's immensely evocative. You can visit the original chapel and St Francis' tiny cell, with its wooden bed and wooden pillow. He used to stop here regularly on his travels and visited just four months before he died in 1226.

Frantoio Landi

Località Cegliolo 71, Mezzavia, T0575-612814, frantoiolandi.it.
A 15-min drive from Cortona.

If you fancy some olive oil, take a trip out to Frantoio Landi, a family-run olive mill. Olives are collected and pressed between granite stones in the traditional way – they'll give you a tour of the factory – and in season (November/December) you can watch the pressing. The family's own oil is for sale.

Sleeping

Arezzo

Hotel Vogue €€€

Via Guido Monaco 54, T0575-24361, voguehotel.it.
Not only does this hotel have contemporary rooms, they boast original bathroom features: Leoparda has a freestanding bath behind the bed, and Michelangelo has a double 'massage' shower. Each room has TVs, high-quality fittings and a careful blend of historic features and up-to-the minute style.

Hotel Continentale €€

Piazza Guido Monaco 7, T0575-20251, hotelcontinentale.com.
Clean and comfortable, with a central location, pleasant staff and a lovely terrace with views of the cathedral. The hotel is gradually being refurbished; at the time of writing rooms on the first floor are fresh and bright, with newly tiled bathrooms. At the very top are three new suites (€€€€), decorated in French style with contemporary bathrooms.

Hotel Patio €€

Via Cavour 23, T0575-401962, hotelpatio.it.
This stylish small hotel has quirky Bruce Chatwin-themed suites, featuring different aspects of the great writer's travels. Baalbek, for example is pink and yellow, with a mosquito net over the bed, while Wu-Ti is red and cream. Two new rooms are contemporary and uncluttered in shades of beige, and feature chromotherapy baths. There's Wi-Fi access in all rooms.

Antiche Mura €

Piaggia di Murello 35, T0575-20410, antichemura.info.
Six light, stylish rooms at this friendly new B&B, set on the first floor of a 13th-century building. On the top floor is a room with a panoramic view of the city. Breakfast is included in the price, but taken in the nearby Bar Il Duomo – space is reserved for you in their pretty courtyard.

Self-catering

Agriturismo Montemiliano

Località Borgacciano, near Monterchi, T0575-709030, montemiliano.it.
You'll get glorious views of historic Monterchi when you stay at this farm estate. Outbuildings have been carefully converted into rooms and apartments, sleeping two (from €600 per week) to six. You can also take the whole property, which accommodates up to 14, or choose B&B (€) – with homemade cake and jam for breakfast. The owners are extremely helpful, there's a swimming pool and plenty of lovely country walks.

Casa Pippo

Località Lignano, T0575-365555/910251, casapippo.it.
Immaculate and beautifully furnished, this traditional stone house is set in the countryside near Arezzo. It's divided into two apartments that can be linked: the whole house (€3400 per week) sleeps eight, or 10 using a sofa bed, and the small apartment is suitable for two. There's a heated swimming pool and a gym, and the friendly owners take great care of you. It's a good base for riding and walking. Overnight stays (€€) are possible in the low season.

Podere La Foce

Monterchi, T+44(0)7989-864976, lafoce.co.uk.
May-Oct.
A recently renovated 18th-century farmhouse sleeping up to 11 and set in 15 ha of land overlooking Monterchi, La Foce has three double bedrooms and a twin (with space for a cot) in the house, and another double bedroom in the converted barn. All bedrooms have en-suite marble bathrooms, traditional terracotta floors and chestnut-beamed ceilings. There's a well-equipped kitchen, a dining room and terrace, and a swimming pool in the garden. From €1560 per week; shorter stays and out-of-season lets are possible on request.

Il Trebbio
Località Ossaia 24, T0575-67002, villailtrebbio.it.
This 17th-century farmhouse is divided into three apartments sleeping 4-6 people. It can also be rented as a whole. The apartments have plenty of character, with rustic beamed ceilings, tiled floors and original fireplaces. Il Trebbio has a swimming pool and well-tended grounds in which to relax, as well as a tiny chapel. €820-2500 per week in high season.

Cortona

Il Falconiere €€€€
Località San Martino 370, T0575-612679, ilfalconiere.it.
Just a few kilometres outside Cortona, this hotel offers peaceful and elegant accommodation. There are 20 rooms, some in the original villa and others in outlying buildings, decorated in grand country-house style with antiques, four-poster beds and freestanding baths. There's a swimming pool, a restaurant and even a cookery school.

Hotel San Michele €€€
Via Guelfa 15, T0575-604348, hotelsanmichele.net.
There's plenty of character at this central hotel, which offers good-sized rooms with period features. Suite 214 has a private terrace, and all rooms have air conditioning. Unusually for Cortona, the hotel also has its own garage, which you can use for an extra €20 per night.

Villa Marsili €€€
Viale Cesare Battisti 13, T0575-605252, villamarsili.com.
On the edge of the old city, this restored 17th-century villa manages to combine elegance and comfort. The cast of *Under the Tuscan Sun* stayed here when filming. Many original features have been preserved, and antiques and Murano glass chandeliers add to the stylish interiors. Most rooms are a good size, and many have lovely views.

Casa Bellavista €€
Località Creti, T0575-610311, casabellavista.it.
At this family-run B&B around 15 km from Cortona you can get a real taste of living the Tuscan dream and enjoy lovely views of the countryside. There are four pretty rooms, all furnished in different styles. Breakfast features homemade jams, cakes and fresh cheese and meat – and guests eat together round a large table. Simonetta, the owner, also runs cookery courses, so you can learn how to make your own pasta or Italian bread.

Casa Chilenne €€
Via Nazionale 65, T0575-603320, casachilenne.com.
A steep flight of stairs leads to this light and clean B&B, which opened in 2008 in a medieval building in the heart of Cortona. It's owned by American Jeanette Wong, and there are five rooms, all with freshly tiled bathrooms with refreshingly powerful showers, plasma screen TVs and air conditioning. There's also a small, light rooftop room, where you can make yourself tea or coffee and relax with a book.

Eating & Drinking

Relais San Petro in Polvano €€

Località Polvano 3, Castiglion Fiorentino, T0575-650100, polvano.com.
Open Mar-Nov.
Castiglion Fiorentino is a former Etruscan settlement 12 km north of Cortona, and this lovely hotel is a tastefully converted farmstead in tranquil countryside nearby. The rooms embody rural chic: wooden shutters, tiled floors and wrought-iron bedsteads. You can dine on the terrace on fine days – dishes feature local produce, including the hotel's own olive oil. Take a dip in the pool or wander in the hotel's gardens.

Self-catering

I Pagliai

La Montalla, contact Terretrusche, vicolo Alfieri 3, Cortona, T575-605287, terretrusche.com.
This company's properties, dotted around the countryside near Cortona, are reasonably priced and beautifully restored. I Pagliai is a converted farm with both apartments and rooms available (the whole property, sleeping 20, can also be rented). Breakfast can be provided on request and there's an old wood-fired pizza oven outside. An apartment for four costs €950 per week; two-night stays are also possible.

Arezzo

I Tre Bicchieri €€€€

Piazzetta Sopra i Ponti 3-5, T0575-26557, itrebicchieri.it.
Mon-Sat and first Sun in the month 1200-1400, 1945-2200.
Tucked away in a tiny courtyard just off the main shopping street, this restaurant run by brothers Stefano and Leonello has an excellent reputation for the quality of its food and its extensive wine list.

Buca di San Francesco €€€

Via San Francesco 1, T0575-23271, bucadisanfrancesco.it.
Wed-Sun 1200-1430, 1900-2130, Mon 1200-1430, closed 2 weeks in Jul.
The menu features typical Tuscan fare, including thick ribollita, homemade pasta and the local Chianina beef.

La Curia €€€

Via di Pescaja 6, T0575-333007, ristorantelacuria.it.
Fri-Tue 1230-1430, 1930-2200, Wed, Thu closed.
Formal, refined restaurant with gold walls and gilded chairs. Dine in a hushed atmosphere on dishes like pecorino fondue with truffles, porcini risotto, and fillets of Cinta Senese.

Enoteca Bacco and Arianna €€

Via Cesalpino 10, T0575-299598.
Daily 1000-1900, Thu-Sat open for dinner till around 2200.
This *enoteca* has a frescoed ceiling and old fittings. During the day you come and taste cheeses and wines, while dinner features seasonal food and traditional specialities.

L'Agania €€

Via Mazzini 10, T0575-295381, agania.com.
Tue-Sun 1200-1500, 1900-2300, open Mon in Aug.
Red and white tablecloths and walls give this trattoria a vibrant look. It serves hard-to-find Tuscan dishes and cuts of meat like pigs' trotters and veal cheeks, as well as rabbit, duck and boar.

Gastronomia Il Cervo €

Via Cavour 38/40 on corner of Piazza San Francesco, T0575-20872.
Tue-Fri 0730-1500, 1700-2100, Sat 0730-2300, Sun 1000-1500, 1730-2000.
Whether you want provisions for a picnic or an informal meal, you'll find it here. Choose what you want from the shop downstairs, then take it away or eat upstairs in the little dining area. Portions are large and fresh.

Il Cantuccio €
Via Madonna del Prato 76, T0575 26830, il-cantuccio.it.
Thu-Tue 1200-1430, 1900-2230, closed Wed.
Cosy dining at this cellar restaurant. Service is swift and friendly, the pasta is home-made and you can choose from a selection of pasta sauces.

O Scugnizzo €
Via Redi 9.
Tue-Sun 1930-2330.
"Only beer and pizza, is that okay?" says the waitress in this busy pizzeria. And it is when it's this good. The beer menu offers around 180 beers, including Trappist beers from Belgium, and there's plenty of choice of pizza toppings. As well as standard-size pizzas they also serve them 1 m wide – to share of course.

Cafés & bars

Caffè dei Costanti
Piazza San Francesco 19, T0575-1824074, caffedeicostanti.it.
Wed-Sun 0800-2200 or later.
The walls of this historic café are lined with mirrors. As well as locals drinking espressos at the bar, you'll also find lots of tourists, as the café featured in the film *Life is Beautiful*.

Coffee o'Clock
Corso Italia 184, T0575-333067, coffeeoclock.com.
Daily 0800-2000.
Refreshing contemporary café with stripped floors, shiny counters and a large table strewn with papers and magazines. It serves snacks at lunchtime and has Wi-Fi access at €3 per hour.

Fiaschetteria de'Redi
Via de' Redi 10, T0575-355012.
Tue-Sun 1200-1500, 1930-2230.
Map Arezzo, p192.
A lively wine bar that also offers dishes such as bruschetta and salads. Good for a light lunch.

Il Gelato
Via Madonna del Prato, on corner by via di Tolletta.
Thu-Mon 1100-2400, shorter hours in winter.
A good choice of ice creams at this back-street gelateria.

Paradiso
Piazza Guido Monaco, T0575-27048.
Apr-Oct daily 1100-2300, more erratic in winter.
A gelateria serving some of the best ices in town.

East of Arezzo

Il Convivio €€
Via Traversari 1, Sansepolcro, T0575-736543.
Open for lunch and dinner, closed Tue.
With friendly staff and a good selection of traditional local dishes, this restaurant is well worth trying. You might find dishes such as Tuscan onion soup, *la soppressata* (calf cheeks), or *taglionini* pasta with porcini. They also offer a special vegetarian platter.

La Locanda al Castello di Sorci €€
Anghiari, T0575-789066, castellodisorci.it.
2 km from Monterchi. Closed Mon.
This restaurant is set in the grounds of a medieval castle, and is a good place to stop if you're on the Piero della Francesca trail. It has a relaxed atmosphere and on Sundays you're likely to find Italian families enjoying lunch. The pasta is all homemade and the menu changes daily: gnocchi, polenta and *ribollita* could feature.

Cortona

Hosteria La Bucaccia €€€
Via Ghibellina 17, T0575-606039, labucaccia.it.
Apr-Nov daily, lunch from 1230, dinner from 1930, closed Mon in winter.
Thick stone walls, old wine barrels and plenty of character at this friendly family restaurant on a steep street in Cortona. There's an excellent selection of pecorino cheeses aged from 15 to 180 days, as well as tasty crostini and homemade pasta served with seasonal produce such as truffles or porcini.

La Locanda nel Loggiato €€
Piazza di Pescheria 3, T0575 630575, locandanelloggiato.it.
Thu-Tue 1230-1500, 1930-2300.
A picturesque setting in the centre of Cortona makes this a favourite place for tourists to eat. You can dine inside or sit out under the romantic loggia. The menu's imaginative, with options like spelt with chicory and Parmesan and Valdichiana steak with pepper and rosemary. In late autumn you might find polenta with white truffle cream.

Osteria del Teatro €€
Via Maffei 2, T0575-630556, osteria-del-teatro.it.
Thu-Tue 1230-1430, 1930-2130, closed Wed.
A historic building, intimate dining areas and walls hung with photos of old theatrical productions make this one of the loveliest places to eat in town. Locals come for special occasions. The food is Tuscan with an imaginative twist, so you might find ravioli filled with pumpkin flowers or beef with *lardo di Colonnata* and plum sauce. There's an extensive wine list and a good choice of vegetarian dishes. Booking recommended.

Croce del Travaglio €
Via Dardano 1, T0575-62832.
Fri-Wed, 1200-1430, 1915-2200.
Locals reckon the pizzas here are some of the best in town. They're certainly good value, starting at

€4.50. You can dine in the courtyard on fine days.

Trattoria Dardano €
Via Dardano 24, T0575-601944, trattoriadardano.com.
Thu-Tue 1200-1500, 1900-2200, open daily Jul-Aug.
With plain whitewashed walls hung with family photographs, there's a relaxed feel to this simple, busy eatery. The menu consists of uncomplicated Italian and Tuscan dishes – with many of the ingredients produced on the family's farm.

Cafés & bars

Caffè degli Artisti
Via Nazionale 18, T0575-601237.
Daily 0730-2300, closed Thu Oct-Mar.

Central bar/café attracting everyone from locals to tourists who come in for cocktails, Chianti and glasses of beer.

Gelateria Snoopy
Piazza Signorelli 29, T0575-630197.
Daily 1000-2400, closed Nov-Jan/Feb.
Fabulous creamy ices close to Cortona's cathedral. You can have a cone with four flavours for under €2 and eat it on a seat outside. Try the fresh strawberry, refreshing peach and orange or the rich crème caramel.

Taverna Pane e Vino
Piazza Signorelli 27, T0575-631010, pane-vino.it.
Tue-Sun 1200-1400, 1900-2300.
There are over 900 wines to choose from at this relaxed taverna off the main piazza. You can buy wine by the glass from €2.50, perhaps accompanied by local cheese or bruschetta.

Tuscher
Via Nazionale 43, T0575-62053, caffetuschercortona.com.
Tue-Sun 0800-2100, daily till 2400 in summer (food 1200-1500 only).
A lovely café in a historic building, furnished in restrained, contemporary style. Pop in for delicious fresh pasta or bruschetta for lunch. They also serve cocktails and wine by the glass and there's often live music.

Entertainment

For more festivals see pages 52-55.

Arezzo

Clubs

La Vispa Teresa
lavispateresa.it.
Outside Arezzo, exit Valdichiana off A1, marked Bettolle (SI).
Slick bar and club: check website for special dance nights.

Le Mirage Disco
Viale di Santa Maria delle Vertighe 34, Monte San Savino, T0575-810215, lemirage.it.
South of Arezzo, just off A1, take Monte San Savino exit.
Various dance anthems and some live music.

Music & theatre

Teatro Petrarca
Via Guido Monaco 10, T0575-23975.
Classical and jazz concerts.

Teatro Comunale Pietro Aretino
Via della Bicchieraia 32, T0575-302258/377503.
Music, plays and theatre.

Cortona

Music & theatre

Teatro Signorelli
Piazza Signorelli, T0575-601882, teatrosignorelli.com.
Wide variety of music, opera, dance, theatre and cinema.

Shopping

Arezzo

Art & antiques

Fiera Antiquaria (Antiques Fair)
T0575-377993, arezzofieraantiquaria.com.
This takes place on the first Sunday of every month and the preceding Saturday. It's a huge event with more than 500 exhibitors spread throughout the streets and squares of Arezzo. It seems to attract everyone from far around.

Clothes & textiles

Busatti
Corso Italia 48, T0575-355295, busatti.com.
Tue-Sat 0900-1300, 1530-1930, Mon 1530-1930.
Lovely hand-woven linens – locals come here to stock up on sheets, tablecloths and napkins. You can also visit their workshop out of town at Anghiari (via Mazzini 14, T0575-788013/788424).

Vintage Shed
Via San Lorentino 63, T329-323 9035.
Mon-Sat 1000-1300, 1800-2000.
Tucked away near Porta San Lorentino, this men's clothes shop is crammed with vintage clothes and accessories.

Designer outlets

Dolce e Gabbana
Località Santa Maria Maddalena 49, Plan dell'Isola Rignano sull'Arno, T055-833 1300.
Mon-Sat 0900-1900, Sun 1500-1900. By train, nearest station is Rignano sull'Arno.

Prada (Space)
Località Levanella, Montevarchi, T055-91901/978 9481.
Mon-Sat 0930-1900, Sun 1000-1300, 1400-2000 (hours subject to change). Nearest station is Montevarchi.

Pratesi
Via Dante Alighieri 83, Ambra, shoes-pratesi.com.
Apr-Oct Mon-Sat 0900-1930, Nov-early Jan Mon-Sat 0900-1230, 1530-1900, closed Jan-end Feb, 30 mins' drive west of Arezzo.
For shoes.

The Mall
Via Europa 8, Leccio Reggello, T055-865 7775.
Mon-Sat 1000-1900, Sun 1500-1900. By public transport, train from Arezzo to Montevarchi, then a taxi.
Outlet shops here include Gucci, Armani, Ferragamo, Yves St Laurent and Fendi.

Tip...

Visit one of the designer discount outlet stores, (outlet-firenze.com), where you can pick up off-season bargains. They're easily reached by car from Florence and Arezzo.

Valdichiana Outlet Village
Località Le Farniole, Foiano della Chiana, T0575-649926, valdichianaoutlet.it.
Mon 1400-2200, Tue-Sun 1000-2200. Off A1 at Valdichiana exit, signs to Foiano della Chiana.
Less upmarket (and more affordable) than other retail outlets, this mall houses around 200 discount stores including Nike, Stefanel, Calvin Klein and Sergio Tacchini.

Food & drink

Canto de' Bacci
Corso Italia 65, T0575-355804, cantodebacci.com.
Daily 0800-2000.
This salumeria stocks all sorts of Tuscan specialities to take home, as well as cheeses, olives, sandwiches and salamis if you want to put together a picnic.

Enoteca Bacco and Arianna
Via Cesalpino 10, T0575-299598.
Daily 1000-2000.
There are 900 different wines for sale here. They'll show you the cellars if you wish, and you can taste Tuscan wines by the glass.

Activities & tours

Cycling & walking

Parco Nazionale delle Foreste Casentinesi
parcoforestecasentinesi.it.
The Casentino Forest is in the northern part of Arezzo province, north of Poppi, and stretches into Emilia-Romagna. The national park encompasses woodlands where wolves and wild boar roam. It's great for walkers, as there's a maze of paths to follow, varying from lengthy 'excursions' to nature trails that are more suited to families. There are also mountain bike trails. Visitor centres focus on different aspects of the park: the one at Badia Prataglia (via Nazionale 14a, T0575-559477, open all year) concentrates on the relationship between man and the forest. Other centres include Premilcuore (via Roma 34, T0543-956540), which is just over the border into Emilia and focuses on the park's wildlife, and Castagno d'Andrea (via della Rota 8, T055-837 5125), which looks at the story of Monte Falterona.

Transport

Arezzo

Regular train service to Florence (journey 40-60 mins); less frequent service to Camucia, (nearest station to Cortona, 25 mins) where you can pick up a bus into the town (or a taxi if the bus is late). Terentola is Cortona's other railway station, a bit further from town.

Buses run direct to Siena (approx 1 hr 30 mins), Cortona (1 hr) and Sansepolcro (1 hr). A few buses stop in Monterchi (30 mins).

Cortona

Regular train service from Camucia to Florence (journey 1 hr 15 mins), and Arezzo (as above). Buses also run direct to Siena.

Contents

Northern Tuscany

Introduction

Northern Tuscany is wonderfully varied, encompassing top tourist sights as well as remote hills and valleys. Yet many visitors pause here only briefly, beating a path from Pisa airport to the famous Leaning Tower, taking a few photos, buying a cheesy souvenir, then making straight for Florence. But do that and you'll miss so much. Here you'll find one of Tuscany's gems, the medieval city of Lucca, as perfectly preserved inside its medieval walls as an ant entombed in amber. The birthplace of Puccini, it's an easy city to explore on foot or by bike – and a great place to shop for olive oil and regional delicacies.

From Lucca you can drive into the chestnut covered hills of the Garfagnana, a barely explored rural region that's rich in wildlife and laced with walking trails. You can drive into the mountains where marble has been quarried for centuries, buy contemporary works of art in Pietrasanta or dance the night away at coastal resorts like Viareggio – party central in Tuscany. Travel a little further east and you'll find Pistoia. An undeservedly neglected city, squeezed between Lucca and Florence, it has a fine historic centre and a clutch of artistic treasures. Take your time in this region – you'll be rewarded.

What to see in...

...one day
See the main sights in **Pisa** (the **Leaning Tower**, the **Duomo** and the **Baptistery**), then catch a train to **Torre del Lago** on the coast, to visit the **Puccini Villa** or go on to **Viareggio**, famed for its *stile-Liberty* architecture. Or, spend a day exploring the lovely walled town of **Lucca** – essentials here are **San Martino Cathedral**, shopping on via **Fillungo**, a stop for some photos of the **piazza dell'Anfiteatro** and a walk (or cycle ride) around the ramparts.

...a weekend or more
Spend a day in **Pisa**, followed by a day in **Lucca**. Or – and perhaps more rewarding – spend one day in Lucca followed by a day's exploration of the **Garfagnana**, one of Tuscany's quietest corners. To take in **Pistoia** you'll need another day, especially if you want to drive to **Vinci** to see Leonardo's birthplace.

Pisa

Pisa is now synonymous with just one thing: the Leaning Tower. Yet in medieval times it was a powerful maritime republic. Its decline began with its defeat by the Genoese at Meloria (1284) and continued as the Arno silted up – losing it vital access to the sea. In 1406 it was conquered by Florence, and the Medici rulers put their stamp on the city. They established its university, where the Pisan-born Galileo once taught.

Essentials

Getting around Pisa is easy to explore on foot. Buses from the airport and railway station stop just beside the Campo dei Miracoli, so you can see the main sights even if you're just in the city for a couple of hours.

Train and bus stations Pisa's main station is Pisa Centrale at piazza della Stazione. It's about a 20-min walk to the Campo dei Miracoli. Buses from the airport stop opposite the station, and others come to nearby piazza San Antonio. You can also get trains from the airport to Pisa Centrale.

ATM Corso Italia, piazza Garibaldi and via Oberdan.

Hospital Ospedale di Santa Chiara, via Roma 67, T050-992111/996111.

Pharmacy Farmacia Comunale 5, via Niccolini 6a, near Campo dei Miracoli (24 hrs), and Salvioni, via Oberdan 3.

Post office Piazza Vittorio Emanuele 11 (near station) and via Vecchia di Barbaricina (near Campo dei Miracoli).

Tourist information Piazza Vittorio Emanuele 11, T050-42291, pisaturismo.it, Mon-Fri 0900-1900, Sat 0900-1330, and piazza Arcivescovado (by Campo dei Miracoli), T050-560464, daily 1000-1700.

Campo dei Miracoli

The 'Field of Miracles' is the name given to the grassy expanse that is the ecclesiastical heart of Pisa. At one time this was a rather marshy area, between two rivers: the (now invisible) Auser and the Arno. It was the site of an early Christian cathedral. It's here that you'll find the famous Leaning Tower, as well as the Duomo, the Baptistery, the Camposanto and two museums – the Museo delle Sinopie and the Museo dell'Opera del Duomo. These snowy marble buildings appear almost blindingly white in the sunshine. One edge of the Campo is lined with stalls selling an extraordinary range of tourist tat – look out for 'light-up' models of the Leaning Tower and 'leaning' mugs. You'll also see everyone taking their turn to do the 'comedy photo' – standing with the tower behind them, their hands poised as if they're holding it up.

Duomo

Nov-Feb Mon-Sat 1000-1300, 1400-1700, Mar 1000-1800, Apr-Sep 1000-2000, Oct 1000-1900, Sun opens at 1300 all year.

Building of this magnificent cathedral began in 1064, when victory over the Saracens had brought Pisa enormous wealth. It was a statement to the world that this was a city to be reckoned with. Construction continued until the 13th century.

The cathedral represents the finest Pisan Romanesque style. The first architect, Buscheto, is buried in the wall on the left of the façade – an ornate construction built in the 12th century, which mixes Italian and Moorish influences. The three portals are topped with four tiers of colonnades and there are inlaid mosaics, stones and marble.

Inside, the cathedral is laid out in the shape of a Latin cross. It's a mix of styles, as a fire in the 16th century destroyed much of the original interior. There are Moorish black and white striped marble columns, a Byzantine-style gilded mosaic in the apse – which Cimabue completed in 1302, paintings by artists such as Beccafumi, and a 17th-century fresco in the dome. In the centre of

Tip...

Tickets are available at the ticket office at the Museo delle Sinopie, or the central ticket office by the tourist office near the Tower. They are rather complicated. Admission to the Leaning Tower is €15 (€17 if you pre-book online at opapisa.it), and entry is only by guided tours, every 30 minutes or so. No children under eight and no bags, only cameras. For the other attractions, tickets are €2 for the Duomo (free Nov-Mar), and €5 for each of the other sites if purchased individually. For any two attractions, including the Duomo, the cost is €6 and for all five it is €10. Children under 10 go free, except for the Tower.

Bus 3 goes from the airport to Pisa station and then on past the Campo dei Miracoli. Get out at piazza Manin.

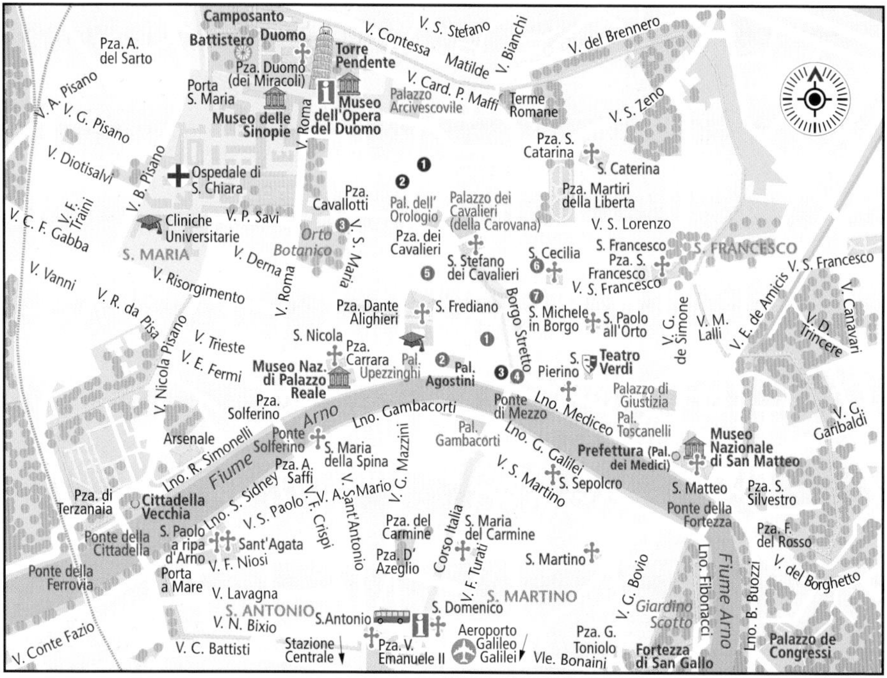

Camposanto
Battistero
Duomo
Torre Pendente
Pza. Duomo (dei Miracoli)
Pza. A. del Sarto
Porta S. Maria
Museo delle Sinopie
Museo dell'Opera del Duomo
V. Roma
V. Contessa Matilde
V. S. Stefano
V. Bianchi
V. del Brennero
V. Card. P. Maffi
Palazzo Arcivescovile
Terme Romane
V. S. Zeno
V. A. Pisano
V. G. Pisano
V. Diotisalvi
V. B. Pisano
Ospedale di S. Chiara
Pza. S. Catarina
S. Caterina
Pza. Martiri della Liberta
V. S. Lorenzo
V. F. Traini
V. C. F. Gabba
Cliniche Universitarie
V. P. Savi
Pza. Cavallotti
Pal. dell' Orologio
Palazzo dei Cavalieri (della Carovana)
Pza. dei Cavalieri
Orto Botanico
S. MARIA
V. Derna
V. S. Maria
S. Stefano dei Cavalieri
S. Cecilia
S. Francesco
Pza. S. Francesco
S. FRANCESCO
V. S. Francesco
V. Vanni
V. Risorgimento
V. Roma
Borgo Stretto
V. E. de Amicis
V. Canavari
V. D. Trincere
V. R. da Pisa
Pza. Dante Alighieri
S. Frediano
S. Michele in Borgo
S. Paolo all'Orto
V. G. de Simone
V. M. Lalli
V. Trieste
S. Nicola
Pza. Carrara
Pal. Upezzinghi
Pal. Agostini
S. Pierino
Teatro Verdi
V. E. Fermi
V. Nicola Pisano
Museo Naz. di Palazzo Reale
Pza. Solferino
Ponte di Mezzo
Lno. Mediceo
Palazzo di Giustizia
Pal. Toscanelli
Fiume Arno
Lno. Gambacorti
Pal. Gambacorti
Lno. G. Galilei
Museo Nazionale di San Matteo
Prefettura (Pal. dei Medici)
V. G. Garibaldi
Arsenale
Lno. R. Simonelli
Ponte Solferino
S. Maria della Spina
Pza. A. Saffi
V. G. Mazzini
V. S. Martino
S. Sepolcro
S. Matteo
Pza. S. Silvestro
Pza. di Terzanaia
Cittadella Vecchia
Lno. S. Sidney
V. S. Paolo
V. F. Crispi
V. A. Mario
V. Sant'Antonio
Pza. del Carmine
Corso Italia
S. Maria del Carmine
Ponte della Fortezza
Pza. F. del Rosso
Ponte della Cittadella
S. Paolo a ripa d'Arno
Sant'Agata
V. F. Niosi
Pza. D' Azeglio
V. F. Turati
S. Martino
V. Bovio
Lno. Fibonacci
Lno. B. Buozzi
V. del Borghetto
Ponte della Ferrovia
Porta a Mare
V. Lavagna
S. ANTONIO
S. MARTINO
S. Domenico
V. G. Giardino Scotto
S.Antonio
V. N. Bixio
V. Conte Fazio
V. C. Battisti
Stazione Centrale
Pza. V. Emanuele II
Aeroporto Galileo Galilei
Pza. G. Toniolo
Vle. Bonaini
Fortezza di San Gallo
Palazzo de Congressi

Pisa listings

Sleeping

1. Di Stefano *via S. Apollonia 35*
2. Hotel Relais dell'Orologio *via della Faggiola 12/14*
3. Royal Victoria Hotel *lungarno Pacinotti 12*

Eating & drinking

1. Antica Trattoria il Campano *via Cavalca 19*
2. De'Coltelli *lung. Pacinotti 23*
3. Dolce Pisa *via S. Maria 83*
4. La Bottega del Gelato *piazza Garibaldi 11*
5. Osteria dei Cavalieri *via San Frediano 1b*
6. Osteria del Tinti *vicolo del Tinti 26*
7. Osteria la Grotta *via San Francesco 103*

the coffered ceiling you can see the Medici coat of arms. To the right-hand side of the altar is the mummified body of the city's patron saint, Ranieri, wearing a silver mask; to the left is the tomb of the Holy Roman Emperor Henry VII.

The most important work is the marble pulpit (1302-10), which was sculpted by Giovanni Pisano. It is supported by the Virtues, Faith, Hope and Charity, and is covered with reliefs vividly depicting episodes from the New Testament. It is a masterpiece, the last of the great series of Pisano pulpits. After the fire it was dismantled and put into storage, and was eventually re-assembled in the early 20th century – though no-one can be completely certain that everything went back the way it was originally intended.

Torre Pendente

Daily Nov-Feb 1000-1700, early Mar 0900-1800, late Mar 0830-2030, Apr-mid-Jun and Sep 0830-2030, mid-Jun-Aug 0830-2300, Oct 0900-1900. Tours only, advance booking essential in summer, recommended at other times.

Construction of this, the cathedral's bell tower, started in 1173. Due to the unstable, silty soil on which it was built and its shallow foundations, it began to lean before the third storey was completed – though it originally leaned the

Tip...

Stand at a central point at the back of the cathedral, facing the altar, and look at the large bronze lamp that hangs above the main aisle. Raise your eyes to the rope and compare it with the structure of the cathedral – you'll be able to see that the building is slightly off centre, leaning to the right.

Inside the Duomo.

opposite way. Attempts were made to counteract this, and building then halted for 100 years. It continued in fits and starts until around 1350, with various architects, including Tommaso Pisano, attempting to correct the tilt – which now went the other way. The tower continued to tilt and by 1990 had reached a dangerous angle: experts estimated that if nothing were done it would collapse within 10 years. The tower was closed and a sophisticated programme of adjustment began. Rings of steel were placed around it, lead ingots were used as counterweights and soil was dug out from underneath the northern side. These measures were successful and the tower now leans only as far as it did in 1838 – decidedly tipsy, but no longer dangerously drunk. It reopened in 2001.

The trip to the top involves climbing a narrow spiral staircase with – puff – 294 steps. The steps can seem slippery, as they slope so much in parts, and it can feel claustrophobic. However, it is a great way to truly appreciate the extent to which the tower leans.

Tip...

To get the best view of the tower's tilt, go to the corner of the Campo dei Miracoli by via Cardinale Maffi.

Battistero

Daily Nov-Feb 1000-1700, Mar 0900-1800, late Mar-Sep 0800-2000, Oct 0900-1900.

The dazzling marble Baptistery was begun in 1152 and is the largest in Italy. Its shape resembles that of the Church of the Holy Sepulchre in Jerusalem. The first architect was Diotisalvi, but in the 13th century Nicola and Giovanni Pisano modified the building, which was eventually completed in the 14th century. It has a distinctive double dome, with an inner and outer cone, and fine acoustics. At busy times, on the hour and the half hour, attendants will shut the doors and demonstrate the echo. (Don't try it yourself, they'll tick you off.)

There is a large 13th-century font with inlaid marble panels, designed so that people could be baptised by total immersion. Most striking of all is Nicola Pisano's pulpit, which he completed in 1260. It was the first of the Pisano pulpits and was clearly influenced by Roman art.

It's (not) a fact...

Legend has it that Galileo conducted an experiment, dropping two objects of differing mass from the top of the tower to show that they reached the bottom at the same time – disproving Aristotle's theory that they would fall at different speeds. However, this appears to be nothing more than a good story.

Camposanto

Opening hours as for the Baptistery.

Enclosed by long marble cloisters, the Camposanto or Holy Field is a walled cemetery, built on a site said to have been a burial area since Etruscan times. After the Third Crusade, at the end of the 12th century, the land was reputedly enriched with sacred soil brought from the Holy Land, and it was

Dickens at the Leaning Tower

When Charles Dickens saw the Leaning Tower for the first time he was disappointed, declaring in *Pictures from Italy* : "it was too small". However he warmed to it the next day when he climbed it, saying that when at the top, "it gives one the sensation of being in a ship that has heeled over, through the action of an ebb-tide. The effect upon the low side, so to speak – looking over from the gallery and seeing the shaft recede to its base – is very startling; and I saw a nervous traveller hold on to the Tower involuntarily, after glancing down, as if he had some idea of propping it up."

said that bodies buried here would decompose within 24 hours. Construction of the cloister itself began in 1278, and Roman sarcophagi, which had been re-used as tombs for wealthy Pisans (an early example of recycling), were brought here – you can see them as you walk around the cloisters.

At one time, the walls of the cloisters were covered with frescoes so stunning that they became an important sight on the Grand Tour. But the building was bombed in the Second World War, and the resultant fire melted the lead on the roof – which ran down the walls and destroyed most of the frescoes. You can see the survivors in the Frescoes Room: Buonamico Buffalmacco's lurid 14th-century cycles of *The Triumph of Death*, painted after the Black Death had swept through Tuscany, and *The Last Judgment*.

Take a look at the lamp that hangs under an arch in the cloisters. It is known as Galileo's Lamp and it is said that it once hung in the cathedral. Galileo, legend has it, observed it moving in the breeze, timed it with his pulse – and realized that it took the same number of beats to complete a swing no matter how far it moved. A pendulum, he concluded, could be used to measure time.

Left: The Torre Pendente. Below: The Camposanto.

Piazza dei Cavalieri.

Tip...

A popular picnic spot is piazza Alighieri, a short walk from piazza dei Cavalieri.

Museo delle Sinopie

Opening hours as for the Baptistery.

This museum, on the opposite side of the Campo to the Camposanto, contains the preliminary sketches, known as *sinopie*, for the frescoes that lined the cloisters of the Camposanto. These were revealed after the paintings were destroyed by the bombing and were later detached and displayed here. They got their name as they were made using paint pigmented with red earth from Sinope in Turkey.

Museo dell'Opera del Duomo

Opening hours as for the Baptistery.

This museum, housed in an ex-convent near the Leaning Tower, contains statues and treasures from the main buildings in the Campo. There are carved tombstones, richly jewelled reliquaries, engravings and Roman and Etruscan objects. The most important work is a *Madonna and Child* (c1298) carved from ivory by Giovanni Pisano.

Piazza dei Cavalieri

A few streets away from the Campo is this airy piazza, the historic seat of Pisan government. The most striking building, the *sgraffito*-covered Palazzo della Carovana (also known as the Palazzo dei Cavalieri), was remodelled by Giorgio Vasari in the 16th century. It housed an order of knights, the Cavalieri di Santo Stefano, established by the Medici ruler Cosimo I. They acted much like authorized pirates, frequently robbing ships of precious items. It is now a university, founded by

Napoleon, specializing in maths and physics. Outside you can see a statue of Cosimo, his foot crushing a dolphin – symbolizing his victory over this maritime city.

On the corner of the square, with an archway and clock, is the **Palazzo dell'Orologio**. The tower to the right of the clock is often known as the **Torre della Fame** (the Hunger Tower). This was where the Pisan Count Ugolino della Gherardesca was walled up, together with his sons, and left to starve, because the Pisans suspected him of treachery leading to their defeat at the Battle of Meloria. Dante describes the episode in his *Inferno* – according to him, the count ate the bodies of his children to stay alive.

From here you can walk down via Ulisse Dini and on to via Oberdan and Borgo Stretto: this is Pisa's slickest shopping street, lined with arcades and home to Salza, the city's historic *pasticceria*. Look out for the arresting frontage of the **Church of San Michele in Borgo**. Eventually you'll reach the Arno and the ponte di Mezzo. If you cross the river here the road becomes Corso Italia, a busy – but less pricey – shopping street. Turn left and you can walk along the Arno to the **Museo Nazionale di San Matteo** (Tue-Sat 0830-1900, Sun 0830-1330, €5/€2), which houses a large collection of Tuscan art. Turn right, and you'll come to the **Museo Nazionale di Palazzo Reale** (Mon-Fri 0900-1430, Sat 0900-1330, €5/€2.50), a 16th-century palace that was the seat of the Medici court during the winter months. As well as portraits and tapestries, it houses a large collection of items associated with the annual Gioco del Ponte (see page 53). Not far from here is the **Orto Botanico**, Pisa's botanical garden – a lovely refuge in the heart of the city.

A view of the Duomo, as seen from the leaning tower.

Tip...

At night, avoid the dark narrow lanes in Pisa – particularly around the piazza di Vettovaglie.

Viareggio & the coast

From both Pisa and Lucca, it is easy to take a train to spend a day at the coast. Viareggio is the liveliest and most famous of Tuscany's seaside resorts, the golden sand almost invisible under the endless rows of sun loungers. Famous today for its carnival, it was a fishing village until the 16th century, when it became the Republic of Lucca's only coastal base. By the late 19th century Viareggio was growing as a seaside resort, reaching its heyday in the 1920s and 1930s. As you walk around you can see the *stile-Liberty* buildings erected in that era – though some of them now look neglected.

Just 6 km south of Viareggio – you can take a bus from piazza d'Azeglio – is **Torre del Lago**. This was, for many years, the home of Giacomo Puccini. The great composer lived in an elegant villa by Lake Massaciuccoli, where he had peace and quiet and could indulge his love of shooting: he claimed his rifle was his "second favourite instrument". **Museo Villa Puccini** (T0584-341445, giacomopuccini.it, Tue-Sun, Apr-May 1000-1230, 1500-1800, Jun-Oct 1000-1230, 1500-1830, Dec-Mar 1000-1230, 1430-1730, €7, € 6-13, guided tours last around 40 mins) is filled with Puccini's original furnishings, musical instruments, rifles and memorabilia. It was here that he composed most of his operas, including *La Bohème*, *Tosca* and *Madama Butterfly*. In 1921 he moved to Viareggio, where he lived until his death in 1924. He is buried in the chapel at Torre del Lago.

This part of the coast is much less developed than Viareggio, with fragrant pine forests and rich birdlife. The lake is part of the **Parco Regionale di Migliarino, San Rossore, Massaciuccoli** (parks.it) and there are a number of visitor centres (T0584-975 5677) where you can arrange birdwatching trips, guided walks and boat trips.

Tip...

Italian resorts have bagni: private bathing establishments with their own section of beach, a bar and often a restaurant – you must pay if you want to sit on a sun bed, which also gives you access to the other facilities.

It's a fact...

It was at Viareggio, in 1822, that the body of the poet Percy Bysshe Shelley was washed up. He had drowned in a boating accident, aged 29. His body was cremated on a beach a little way along the coast, in the presence of his friends Lord Byron, Edward Trelawny and Leigh Hunt.

Page opposite: Viareggio.
Top: Resort antics.
Above: A *stile-Liberty* building.
Left: Carnival time.

Lucca

Lucca, the birthplace of Puccini, is a delightful place to visit – the historical centre is immaculately preserved within its city walls. Despite its small size, Lucca was once a significant force in Tuscany. It was the capital of the Lombard Duchy of Tuscia, which was more important in its time than Florence, and continued to be a powerful centre under the Frankish rulers. In fact the Duchy of Lucca (as it became) remained essentially independent until Napoleon's era, and the city today radiates a confidence born of centuries of power. Lucca is still extremely prosperous and has a large British community.

Essentials

Getting around Most of the historic centre of Lucca is pedestrianized – the locals buzz around on bicycles. You can get buses or taxis from the railway station that will take you within the city walls. To explore the Garfagnana you really need a car.

Train and bus stations The railway station is just outside the city walls at piazza Ricasoli. You can get buses or taxis from here into the centre.

ATM Piazza San Michele.

Hospital Campo di Marte, via dell'Ospedale, T0583-9701.

Pharmacy Farmacia Alliance, piazza Curtatone 9 (24 hrs), Farmacia Massagli, piazza San Michele 36, and G. Giannini, piazza San Frediano 1.

Post office Via Vallisneri 2.

Tourist information Piazza Santa Maria 35, T0583-919931, luccaturismo.it, daily, Apr-Oct 0900-2000, Nov-Mar 0900-1300, 1500-1800.

Detail from the Duomo.

It's a fact...

For a great view of Lucca, climb the 200-odd steps to the top of the **Torre Guinigi**, via Sant'Andrea, a fortified tower attached to the Guinigi ancestral home. You can't miss it – a huge holm oak tree is growing out of the top. Watch out for the pigeons though – they have a very accurate aim.

Duomo di San Martino

Piazza San Martino, museocattedralelucca.it. Daily, summer 0830-1800, winter 0900-1200, 1500-1700, free. Sacristy Mon-Fri 0930-1645, Sat 0930-1845, Sun 0900-0950, 1120-11.50, 1250-1750, €2, €6 joint ticket with Museo della Cattedrale and San Giovanni.

Lucca's magnificent cathedral was founded way back in the sixth century, though the present building is largely medieval. The façade is eye-catching as it's not symmetrical – it was built on to an earlier bell tower, dating from 1060, which sits at the right-hand corner of the façade. It makes a striking sight – a fine example of Pisan Romanesque style, with three tiers of ornate marble columns sitting above a portico. This is filled with carvings created by Lombard sculptors in the 13th century, including a *Deposition from the Cross* and an *Adoration of the Magi* by Nicola Pisano – essentially the first of the great Tuscan sculptors.

The Holy Face Once inside the cathedral you can see its most important treasure, a wooden crucifix known as the *Volto Santo* (Holy Face). Made of cedar of Lebanon, the face is said to be a true portrait of Christ, which was carved by Nicodemus – and finished by an angel – in the Holy Land. Nicodemus was a witness to the Crucifixion. In fact the work is said to be a 13th-century copy of an earlier carving. The Holy Face is thought to have miraculous powers – King William Rufus of England literally swore by it: *"Per sanctum vultum de Luca"* was his customary

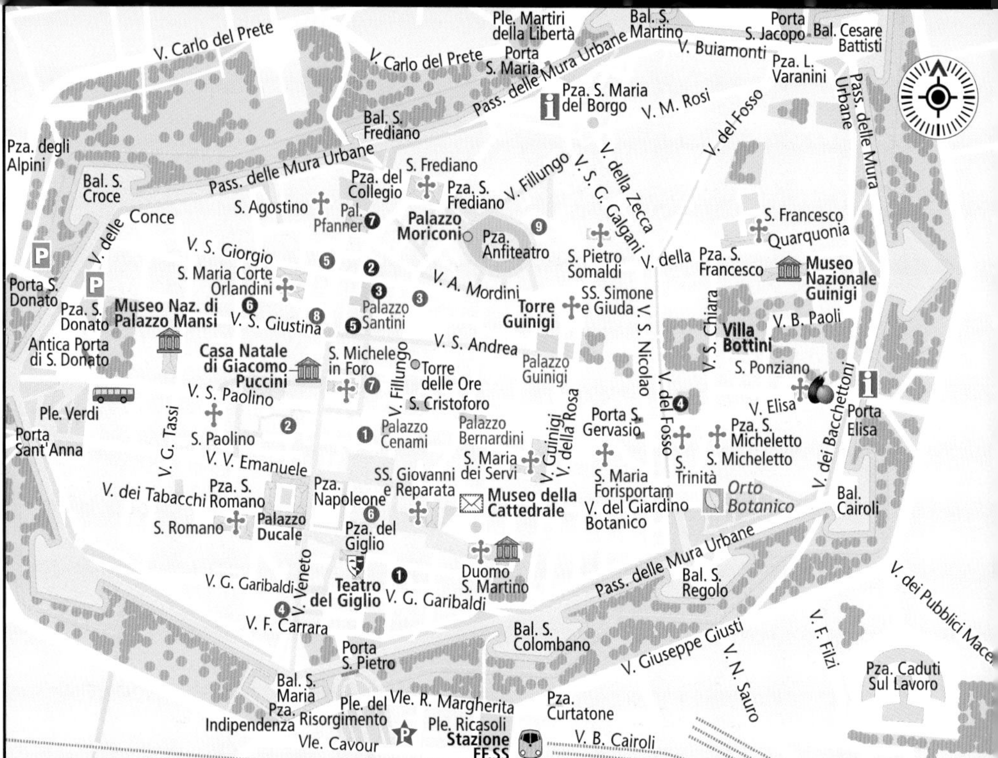

Lucca listings

❶ Sleeping

1 Albergo San Martino *via della Dogana 9*
2 Alla Corte degli Angeli *via degli Angeli 23*
3 Guest House San Frediano *via degli Angeli 19*
4 Ilaria *via del Fosso 26*
5 La Boheme *via del Moro 2*
6 Palazzo Alexander *via S. Giustina 48*
7 Palazzo Tucci *via Cesare Battisti 13*

❶ Eating & drinking

1 Antica Locanda dell'Angelo *via Pescheria 21*
2 Buca di Sant' Antonio *via della Cervia 1/3*
3 Caffè Di Simo *via Fillungo 58*
4 Gelateria Veneta *via V. Veneto 74*
5 Locanda di Bacco *via S. Giorgio 36*
6 Ristorante Giglio *piazza del Giglio*
7 Taddeucci *piazza S. Michele 34*
8 Trattoria da Leo *via Tegrimi 1*
9 Vineria I Santi *via de Anfiteatro 29*

Lucca's Villas

Lucca is a wealthy city, partly due to silk (it was noted for the quality of its underwear) and olive oil, and it's surrounded by grand villas that were built as summer homes by wealthy merchants between the 15th and 19th centuries. You can easily spend a day touring these villas, some of which are within a short distance of the city. The gardens alone are well worth seeing.

One of those closest to Lucca is the **Villa Reale** (Marlia, T0583-30108, parcovillareale.it, Mar-end Nov, gardens only 1000-1300, 1400-1800, sometimes guided tours only), which once belonged to Napoleon's sister. The violinist Paganini, her court composer, played here, and John Singer Sargent painted the grounds. Further on is **Villa Mansi** (Segromigno, T0583-920234, Tue-Sun summer 1000-1230, 1500-1900, shorter hours in winter, €7), a former silk merchant's house, and the baroque **Villa Torrigiani** (Camigliano, T0583-928041, daily Mar-Nov, grounds only €6, grounds and villa €9), built in the early 16th century by the Buonvisi family. It was later bought by the Marquis Nicola Santini, who was Lucca's ambassador at the court of the Sun King, Louis XIV of France. Santini had the garden transformed, with a parterre and ornamental ponds. He also added grottoes and *giochi d'acqua* – surprise water features, which would soak unsuspecting guests.

oath. It was said to have journeyed to Lucca all by itself, by boat and then on a cart pulled by oxen, and its presence in Lucca made the cathedral an important pilgrimage site during the Middle Ages. This, of course, brought considerable wealth to the town. The Holy Face is kept in an ornate shrine within the cathedral, and every September there are celebrations in its honour: there is a procession through the city and the figure of Christ is dressed in an embroidered tunic and gold crown.

The Sacristy In the Sacristy you can see a beautiful early Renaissance carving, the **tomb of Ilaria del Carretto** (1407). The second wife of a local nobleman, Paolo Guinigi, Ilaria died in childbirth aged just 24, and this work was created in her memory by Jacopo della Quercia. She lies, sculpted in marble, on top of the tomb – a delicate figure who looks as if she's sleeping, with a dog at her feet as a symbol of fidelity. The Sacristy also contains a *Madonna and Child Enthroned* by Ghirlandaio.

Museo della Cattedrale

Piazza San Martino, T0583-490530, museocattedralelucca.it.
Mar-Nov daily 1000-1800, Nov-Mar Mon-Fri 1000-1400, Sat-Sun 1000-1700, €4 or joint ticket as above.

Across the square from the cathedral, this museum contains the cathedral's treasures displayed in a medieval building. Among them are the richly jewelled items with which the *Volto Santo* is dressed each year: his shoes, his crown and a silver girdle. There are also illuminated texts and a Limoges enamel box depicting the martyrdom of St Thomas à Becket.

Chiesa di Santi Giovanni e Reparata

Piazza San Martino, museocattedralelucca.it.
Mar-Nov daily 1000-1800, Nov-Mar Sat-Sun 1000-1700, €2.50 or joint ticket as above.

On the other side of the cathedral square, this church was Lucca's original cathedral. It was built in the fourth century, but has been altered many times since then. Excavations have revealed a number of ancient structures beneath the church, including a Roman mosaic floor, a Roman bath and an early Christian baptistery.

San Michele in Foro

Piazza San Michele.
Daily summer 0800-1200, 1500-1800, winter 0900-1200, 1500-1700, free.

San Michele rather outshines Lucca's Duomo, so lavish is its façade and so lively its location. The piazza on which it sits is the historical heart of the city – the former Roman forum. A church stood here in the eighth century, though this building dates from the 11th century on. The medieval façade is an extraordinary confection of twisted

A statue in the Palazzo Pfanner gardens.

columns and rich carvings. Look carefully (not easy, as it's several storeys high) and you'll see it's decorated with allegorical scenes, wild birds and animals and topped with a winged statue of St Michael the Archangel.

Inside it's surprisingly restrained. The large cross by the altar was made by local artists around 1200 (pre-Giotto), and there's a terracotta by Andrea della Robbia by the door. The most important work is Filippino Lippi's painting of *Four Saints*.

Note how small the windows are: this church is Romanesque in style, with rounded arches, in which most of the weight has to be borne by the walls. The later Gothic style employed pointed arches, which are more stable than rounded ones and can bear weight themselves. This allowed Gothic churches to have larger windows, making them lighter inside.

Museo Casa Natale di Giacomo Puccini

Corte San Lorenzo 9, off via di Poggio, T0583-584028.
Closed for restoration but due to reopen in 2009.

Lucca was the birthplace of one of Italy's most famous composers, Giacomo Puccini (1858-1924) and the house where he was born has been turned into a museum. It's small but stuffed with sheet music, letters and other memorabilia. In pride of place is the grand piano on which he composed his last opera, *Turandot*; he died before he could complete it. A statue sits in the square nearby.

Museo Nazionale di Palazzo Mansi

Via Galli Tassi 43, T0583-55570.
Tue-Sat 0900-1900, Sun 0900-1400, €4, €2 under 18.

This former aristocratic home, dating back to the 16th and 17th centuries, is now a museum and art gallery. It's worth visiting just to see the utter grandeur of the rooms, decorated with frescoes and hung with rich tapestries. Most striking is the Baroque honeymoon suite, a confection of gold, carved woods and silk. There are paintings by Tintoretto, Bronzino and a portrait by Pontormo of Alessandro de' Medici, who was murdered in 1537.

Piazza Anfiteatro

It's hard to stop taking pictures of this elegant piazza, which was once a Roman amphitheatre, built in the second century. Although the original buildings have been replaced by private houses, the distinctive curved shape remains, giving the

Round the ramparts

Built in the 16th century to defend the city against hostile neighbours, Lucca's walls are almost perfectly preserved and have not only limited the town's size but have also helped to preserve its ancient buildings and Roman street patterns. The effect is even said to have rubbed off on its people, as the *Lucchese* (those born and bred inside the walls) are said to be particularly conservative.

The town has an ancient history and has built a succession of defensive walls – each enclosure being wider and more elaborate than the last. The earliest walls, built by the Romans, have largely disappeared today, but remnants can still be seen inside the Church of Santa Maria della Rosa. A larger circle of walls was built during medieval times, and these were extended and strengthened during the 16th century, so as to withstand bombardment by the most up-to-date missiles – cannon balls. However, the work took so long that by the time the new walls were completed they were no longer needed.

Today the walls still seem to act as a barrier – only this time to the modern world rather than invaders. They're broad and lined with trees, providing a convenient cycling, walking and jogging track (a 4-km circuit), used by locals and tourists alike. You can easily get on to the walls from any of the bastions and the tourist office has details of bike hire.

place an air of drama. Today it's a great spot to chill out, as it's full of shops, bars and cafés, with tables spilling out on to the piazza. It's tucked away off the north end of **via Fillungo**, one of Lucca's main shopping streets. Some of the shops are rather like museums in themselves, especially **Carli**, a jeweller that dates back to 1655. You'll also find **Caffè di Simo**, which has original *stile-Liberty* décor and once boasted Puccini as one of its customers.

Basilica di San Frediano

Piazza San Frediano, T0583-493627.
Daily summer 0900-1200, 1500-1700, winter 0900-1200, 1500-1800, free.

The façade of this church, which dates back to the 12th century, is covered with a stunning gilded mosaic in Byzantine style, depicting Christ with his Apostles. The interior is impressive too, with fragments of frescoes adorning the walls. Look out for the enormous baptismal font, to the right of the entrance, richly decorated with carvings depicting stories from the Old and New Testaments – including Moses crossing the Red Sea. In a side chapel is the uncorrupted body of St Zita, a 13th-century saint, which is brought out once a year for people to touch. The basilica was built on the site of a sixth-century church founded by St Fredian, an Irish monk who rose to become Bishop of Lucca.

Palazzo Pfanner

Via degli Asili, T0583-954029, palazzopfanner.it.
Apr-Oct daily 1000-1800, €3 garden, €4.50 garden and palace.

A local family of silk merchants built this 17th-century palace, which was bought in the 19th century by an Austrian brewer, Felix Pfanner. It has a grand staircase that sweeps up to some equally grand rooms (only part of the palace is open to the public). Loveliest of all are the gardens, filled with roses, citrus trees and statues – if you think it looks like a film set you'd be right: the gardens featured in *The Portrait of a Lady* (1996), which starred Nicole Kidman. You get a great view of the gardens from the city ramparts.

Puccini statue.

The Garfagnana & the marble mountains

The Garfagnana is a glorious area. It's the mountain valley of the Serchio River – a land of thick chestnut forests, little towns, country churches and sleepy hamlets, where few tourists come. There are lots of possibilities for walking and wildlife watching, and if you've got a car the winding roads (watch the hairpin bends) lead you through some stunning scenery. You can explore some of it in a day from Lucca, but to really appreciate its quiet charm it's better to take a couple of days.

The SS12 from Lucca shadows the river to **Diecimo** (the name comes from the fact that it was 10 Roman miles from Lucca), near which you can see one of the oldest churches in the valley, which has been populated since Paleolithic times. From here you can continue to **Celle dei Puccini** (where the composer's family once lived) and the **Museo del Castagno** at Colognora (T0583-358159, museodelcastagno.it, weekend afternoons). Chestnuts have long been immensely important to the local economy: they are ground into flour and used in both sweet and savoury dishes.

Continue north and you reach **Borgo a Mozzano**, where the 14th-century Devil's Bridge spans the river. The name comes from a legend that says the devil built the bridge in return for the soul of the first to cross it: the villagers sent a dog and 'outwitted' him (though who says dogs don't have souls?).

The road soon branches, going east to **Bagni di Lucca**, a fashionable spa town in the 19th century, or heading north towards **Barga**. This ancient hill town is a great place to stop for an hour or so. Its cathedral (free) dates back to the ninth century and stands on the town's highest point, offering glorious views across to the Apuan Alps. Inside is a magnificent marble pulpit, which stands on columns supported by two lions and a crouching man. Outside, look above the portal to the left of the entrance to see a famous carving of a feast. Barga has extremely strong links with Scotland, and you'll hear many Scottish accents there. Local people migrated to Glasgow in the 19th century, some selling plaster statues of saints, others seeking work in the shipyards. They settled, and were followed by friends and family, many of whom started businesses making ice cream or frying fish and chips. Famous Glasgow Italians include the actress Daniella Nardini, whose family originally came from Barga.

From Barga you could cross the valley and head west to visit the **Grotta del Vento** (grottadelvento.com, daily tours hourly from 1000-1800, €7.50-17), or Cave of the Wind. These caves are filled with stalactites, stalagmites, secret passages and underground lakes. Various tours are available, lasting from one to three hours. Otherwise, you can drive on to **Castelnuovo di Garfagnana**, the main town, where you can pick up plenty of information and maps on walking in the region.

From here you can follow the roads northeast, high into the mountains, to **San Pellegrino in Alpe**, where there's a museum devoted to rural life. Alternatively, take the **Cipollaio road** that leads southwest, crossing the mountains and down to the coast. This was an ancient route used by pilgrims and has a wild, lonely feel. You'll pass **Isola Santa**, a medieval village that was deserted when a hydroelectric dam was created there in 1949. After this the scenery changes, the mountains look bare and forbidding and you enter marble country. The Romans started quarrying for marble here and it continues today – marble from **Carrara** is famous throughout the world. You will pass an abandoned marble quarry, drive through a tunnel and come down to **Seravezza** – where Michelangelo was sent by the Medici Pope Leo X to find the best marble he could for the church of San Lorenzo in Florence. He didn't like the area, considering it wild and rough. The air is filled with marble dust.

You can drive from here to the coast and **Forte dei Marmi**, or turn off to **Pietrasanta**, a chic little walled city that has long been a magnet for sculptors and has a thriving artistic community. Contemporary sculptures are displayed in the lively piazza del Duomo and there's a bronze of a warrior by Fernando Botero in piazza Matteotti. The Duomo was built in the 14th century and has a stunning rose window – and marble fish floating in the font. Take a look at the pulpit – the staircase that leads to it was made by Andrea Boratta in the 17th century from a single block of marble. Pietrasanta has plenty of studios and workshops open to the public – it's a great place to pick up original artworks. Check out the Associazone Artigianart website for addresses: artigianart.org.

Top: Scenes from the marble mountains and the crumbling cloisters at Ai Frati. Page opposite: In a village of the Garfagnana.

Pistoia & around

Pistoia is one of Tuscany's best-kept secrets, a small city with a rich history and a fine medieval square. It sits surrounded by fertile countryside dotted with plant nurseries and mountain villages, but because of its strategic position (squeezed between Lucca and Florence), life was not always so tranquil. The city folk once had a reputation for violence: in the 13th century the Guelphs here divided into rival factions: the Blacks and the Whites.

Pistoia was a Roman settlement, and some think that the city's name comes from the *pistores*, the Latin name for the many bakers who worked here. Another theory gives the name Etruscan roots, from *pist oros* – 'mountain gate' – as the city lies at the foot of the Appenines. Visitors are often disappointed not to find lots of shops selling pistols, as some say a *pistole* was once a type of dagger, and its name was later given to a locally made firearm.

The city was put on the map in the 12th century when a relic of St James was brought here and it became a stop on the via Francigena. Its striking medieval piazza del Duomo is much larger than you'd expect, with buildings representing ecclesiastical and secular power taking equal precedence.

The Duomo di San Zeno.

Duomo di San Zeno

Piazza del Duomo.
Daily 0830-1230, 1530-1900, free, €2 to get close to the silver altarpiece.

This cathedral dates back to AD923, though it was remodelled in Pisan Romanesque style from the 12th century, as you can see from the zebra-striped marble and tiered arcades. Before you go in, take a look at the statue on the top right of the façade, wearing the red cloak – it is St James wrapped in a pilgrim's mantle. In the archway above the entrance are colourful tiles by Andrea della Robbia.

The cathedral interior Inside, to the right of the entrance, is the tomb of Cino da Pistoia – a poet and a friend of Dante. Then you come to the most outstanding work in the cathedral, the **Altarpiece of Saint James**, tucked into a side chapel. This silver altar was made to hold the holy relic and is decorated with over 600 figures, with scenes from the Old and New Testaments, the life of St James and the apostles. It was started in 1287 and not completed until the 15th century. Over 40 artists and craftsmen were involved in its creation, including a young Brunelleschi. You have to pay to see it up close, but it's worth it, as only then can you appreciate the details, the progression in artistic styles and the gleaming gemstones inlaid into the silver.

Also in the cathedral is a 13th-century gilded wooden crucifix, of the school of Cimabue. The colours are bright: gold, turquoise and lapis lazuli. In the chapel to the left of the altar is a painting, the *Madonna di Piazza*, which is said to be the only signed work by Andrea del Verrocchio (c1435-88), an artist at the Medici court who had Leonardo da Vinci as a pupil. It is thought that he started the work, but it was completed by Lorenzo di Credi.

Around piazza del Duomo

Beside the Duomo is the **Bell Tower** (tours at weekends 1100-1200 and 1600-1700, book at the tourist office). It was built as a watchtower. Look at the crenellations on top: the swallowtail shape is a sign that this was a Ghibelline town: Guelph walls had square crenellations. However, given how often loyalties changed, architectural details were not always accurate indicators.

On the other side of the Duomo is the wall of the former **Palazzo dei Vescovi** (Bishop's Palace). It houses the tourist information office and the **Museo di San Zeno** (Tue, Thu-Fri 1000-1300, 1500-1700, guided tours 1000, 1130 and 1530, €4), which contains the reliquary of St James. If you venture downstairs you can see remains of the Roman town.

The Pisano pulpits

There are four particularly famous pulpits in Tuscany, all carved by members of the Pisano family. Nicola Pisano (c1220/5-84) is considered the first great Tuscan sculptor. He came from Apulia, in southern Italy, and trained in the court workshops of Emperor Frederick II. He moved to Tuscany in the mid-13th century and around 1255 accepted a commission to create a pulpit for the **Baptistery in Pisa**. This, the first of the Pisano pulpits, represented a break with the past – it was no longer square, but a free-standing hexagon covered with relief panels. Look carefully at these and you can see how he drew on the traditions of ancient Rome but added life to his figures in characteristic Gothic style. In the nativity scene, you can see the Madonna leaning on her elbow and looking outward, looking rather like a Roman woman at a feast expecting to be fed grapes at any moment. Lions support the columns that hold the pulpit – one of them shows an interesting biological confusion: it has teats like a lioness, but the mane of a male lion.

After his success in Pisa, Nicola received a commission for another pulpit – this time for the **Duomo in Siena**. He worked on this with help from his son Giovanni, completing it in 1268. It's similar in design to the first but larger and even more magnificent. There are 300 figures on the panels and all have different faces. Although you can still see the classical influence, there is more drama and life here and the figures show emotions.

The third pulpit is in the **Church of Sant'Andrea in Pistoia** and was carved by Giovanni Pisano between 1298 and 1301. The panels here, notably the *Massacre of the Innocents*, are full of movement and energy; there is no central figure, but a tangle of characters all interacting. Here, well before Michelangelo, is an emotional depiction of suffering. Even the lionesses supporting the columns are more realistic – they don't have manes any more and one gently feeds her cubs.

The final pulpit is in **Pisa's Duomo** and is a masterpiece of the Italian Gothic. Carved by Giovanni in the early 14th century, it shows the extent to which he has been influenced by the Gothic style. Now the Madonna looks at her child rather than out to the viewer, and there is real desperation in the figures writhing in the *Massacre of the Innocents* panel. The series of pulpits provides a fascinating illustration of the evolution of sculpture in medieval Tuscany.

Opposite the Duomo is the 14th-century **Baptistery** (Wed-Sun 0930-1330, 1500-1800), a black and white striped marble octagon designed by Andrea Pisano. **Via di Straccerie** is an atmospheric street that was the heart of medieval commercial life in Pistoia. You can still see the rustic-style porticoes and wooden shutters on the shops. It leads on to **piazza della Sala**, the heart of daily life in the city, where the market is held. **Vicolo della Torre** is another interesting city street, connecting the Bishop's Palace to piazza della Sala.

Chiesa di San Giovanni Fuorcivitas

Via Cavour.
Daily 0730-1830 – though often closed.

This church, once outside the city walls (*fuorcivitas*), is notable for the green and white marble stripes that cover its north wall. Inside is a large pulpit, carved by a pupil of Nicola Pisano, while the basin holding the holy water is by Giovanni Pisano. To the left of the door is a *Visitation* by Luca della Robbia. One of his earliest works, it is in white glazed terracotta and depicts Elizabeth, pregnant with John the Baptist, kneeling at the feet of Mary.

Chiesa di Sant'Andrea

Via Sant' Andrea, T0573-21912.
Daily 0930-1300, 1500-1900.

The foundations of this church date back to the eighth century, though the present building is largely 12th century. Above the door is a Romanesque relief of the *Journey of the Magi*, while inside is one of Pistoia's greatest treasures, a marble pulpit carved by Giovanni Pisano, the third in the series of the great Pisano pulpits.

Near here is the **Ospedale del Ceppo** (Piazza Giovanni/via del Ceppo). Founded in the 13th century, this is still a functioning hospital. It's named after the offertory box (*ceppo*) in which alms were collected for the sick. The building is notable for its fine portico, which was decorated with a frieze in the 16th century. It depicts all the functions a hospital would then have fulfilled.

Montecatini Terme & around

You can get a train from Pistoia to this historic spa town. Development really began in the 18th century and Montecatini soon became a fashionable health resort. At the beginning of the 20th century, extravagant buildings were constructed around the springs at Parco delle Terme. The most impressive is **Tettuccio**, where you can buy a day ticket to taste the waters. There are four waters on offer here, flowing from different taps. Each has its own name and characteristics: Leopoldina is very strong and laxative, so be warned ("It will work in 20 minutes," declares an attendant. "We have 600 toilets.") Regina is considered full of calcium and good for the liver; Tettuccio is salty, considered good for lowering cholesterol. These three fountains are turned off in the afternoon, but Rinefresco, the lightest water, is available all day. (For information on the spas, T0572-772244 montecatiniturismo.it and T0572-7781, termemontecatini.it.)

Allow time to take the funicular railway (daily Apr-Oct, €6) uphill to the original medieval settlement of **Montecatini Alto**. It bumps upward through olive groves and thick trees, and you get superb views at the top. The square has a number of restaurants. (The funicular stops for lunch between 1300 and 1430. Check the times: if you get stuck at the top a taxi would cost around €20.)

If you have a car visit some of the hill towns near Montecatini. There're not full of 'sights', but the atmosphere and views are very pleasant. West of Montecatini at **Colle di Buggiano**, for instance, you can see San Lorenzo Church, which contains a 14th-century wooden crucifix, while at **Buggiano Castello** there is 11th-century San Nicolao Church, which contains an *Annunciation* (1442) attributed to Bicci di Lorenzo. There's a great picnic spot just here – a bench near the church with stunning views. **Montevettolini** (southeast of Montecatini, near Monsummano Terme) is another pretty village, with a 13th-century town hall and a café/

Signposts mark footpaths near Vinci.

enoteca on the main piazza. The Medicis built a mansion here. There's a good, family-run restaurant at **Monsummano Alto**: La Foresteria (T0572-520097, ristorantelaforesteria.it).

Vinci

Surrounded by silvery olive groves, a few kilometres south of Pistoia, Vinci is famous as the birthplace of the ultimate Renaissance man, Leonardo da Vinci. There's a wooden model of his *Vetruvian Man* on the town's panoramic terrace. The sights are low key but the countryside is deliciously tranquil, with plenty of walking trails to follow.

Pop into the **Chiesa di Santa Croce** in the village, as this is where Leonardo was baptised. You can walk from Vinci to Anchiano, 2 km away, to visit the **Casa Natale di Leonardo** (daily Mar-Oct 0930-1900, Nov-Feb closes 1800, free).

This three-roomed house is where Leonardo was born in 1452. Inside, there's little to see, just an exhibition on the great man and some lovely views.

Museo Leonardiano

Palazzina Uzielli, T0571 933251, museoleonardiano.it.
Mar-Oct daily 0930-1900, rest of year closes at 1800, €6, €3 6-14, under restoration at time of writing so changes are likely.

The museum is essentially split between two sites (the other is the Castello dei Conti Guidi nearby) and focuses on Leonardo's extraordinary inventions, with scale models of the machines he invented – ranging from an automatic weaving loom to a flying machine.

Sleeping

Pisa

Hotel Relais dell'Orologio €€€€

Via della Faggiola 12/14, T050-830361, hotelrelaisorologio.com.
This 14th-century fortified house has been turned into a five-star hotel with plush rooms. Some feature frescoes, others coffered ceilings, and all are very comfortable – though very small. There's a courtyard garden and the hotel is very close to the Leaning Tower.

Bagni di Pisa €€

Largo Shelley 18, San Giuliano Terme, T050-88501, bagnidipisa.com.
The poet Shelley once stayed at this 18th-century villa, which evokes the grandeur of a more elegant age. Only 20 minutes by train from Pisa, it makes a relaxing base for exploring the city and nearby coastline. They have a rooftop swimming pool and spa facilities – on arrival you're asked for your shoe and clothing size, so they can provide you with slippers and a robe. The buffet breakfast is excellent.

Di Stefano €€

Via Sant'Apollonia 35, T050-553559, hoteldistefano.it.
The best rooms at this hotel are in the recently renovated 11th-century tower house. They have a contemporary Tuscan look, with some original features and fresh, clean bathrooms – some with Jacuzzi baths. Facilities include flat screen satellite televisions and air conditioning. Room 401, the top floor single room, has a cracking view of the Leaning Tower from its bathroom.

Royal Victoria Hotel €€

Lungarno Pacinotti 12, T050-940111, royalvictoria.it.
This riverside hotel seems to have changed little since it first opened in the early 19th century. The rooms have heavy, dark wood furniture and iron bedsteads, and some have frescoes. Bathrooms need a facelift. But the public areas are hung with fascinating photos, it has plenty of character and the rooms overlooking the Arno have fabulous views.

Viareggio

Principe di Piemonte €€€€

Piazza Giacomo Puccini 1, T0584-4011, principedipiemonte.com.
Lots of *stile Liberty* and Murano glass at this plush hotel. Each floor is furnished in a different style, with the fifth floor being the most modern. There's an outdoor rooftop pool and a good quality restaurant.

Hotel Plaza e de Russie €€€

Piazza d'Azeglio 1, T0584-44449, plazaederussie.com.
This hotel, in a late 19th-century building not far from the harbour, has comfortable bedrooms, marble bathrooms and a rooftop terrace restaurant with great views.

Camping

There are two campsites near Viareggio: **Viareggio** (via dei Comparini 1, T0584-391012, campingviareggio.it), open mid-Mar-end Sep, and **Camping Paradiso** (via dei Tigli, T0584-392005, campingparadiso.com).

Lucca

Palazzo Tucci €€€
Via Cesare Battisti 13, T0583-464279, palazzotucci.com.
You'll feel as if you're staying in your own private palace at this gorgeous residence on the first floor of an 18th-century palace. Just a discreet brass doorbell proclaims its presence; inside are three large rooms and three suites, all with original features such as flamboyant frescoes. Bathrooms are large, there is elegant period furniture, and one room has a small terrace. The ballroom makes it a great venue for a small wedding.

Albergo San Martino €€
Via della Dogana 9, T0583-469181, albergosanmartino.it.
All nine rooms at this friendly three-star hotel have recently been refurbished. They're small and clean, decorated in pastel colours with private bathrooms, all with showers. In summer you can breakfast outside on the little street-side terrace, and it's very close to the Duomo.

Alla Corte degli Angeli €€
Via degli Angeli 23, T0583-469204, allacortedegliangeli.com.
Spread over three floors, this B&B has 13 small but clean rooms – and plenty of character. Each room is different, many have newly painted frescoes.

Hotel Ilaria €€
Via del Fosso 26, T0583-47615, hotelilaria.com.
Situated close to the city walls, this four-star hotel makes a comfortable base for exploring the city and its surroundings (it has private parking). There's a pleasant lobby with comfy sofas, free Wi-Fi and complimentary hot drinks and snacks. Rooms are clean and light, with flat screen TVs and tea and coffee making facilities. There's a terrace with sun beds placed under the trees, and free bicycle hire.

La Boheme €€
Via del Moro 2, T0583-462404, boheme.it.
There are just 5 rooms at this friendly, central B&B. One room has a four-poster bed. Bathrooms are small but clean, and there is air conditioning. The breakfast room is light and fresh – though you can breakfast in your room if you prefer.

Palazzo Alexander €€
Via Santa Giustina 48, T0583-583571, palazzo-alexander.it.
There's a touch of 18th-century gilded grandeur to the rooms and suites in this historic residence, with its period furniture, swagged curtains, shiny wood floors and gold bedcovers. Bathrooms can be small but are modern and clean, with marble fittings and hairdryers. Breakfast is an elegant affair: a buffet of dainty pastries, fresh fruit and yoghurts. The staff are consistently friendly and helpful – always a bonus.

Guest House San Frediano €
Via degli Angeli 19, T0583-469630, sanfrediano.com.
This small, friendly B&B has six well-kept rooms, with original features such as beamed ceilings. Not all have private bathrooms and you take breakfast in your room. There's a guest sitting room with scarlet walls and some quirky features.

The Garfagnana

Fortezza di Monte Alfonso €
Piazzetta Ariosto 1, 55032 Castelnuovo di Garfagnana, T0583-643201, montalfonso.it.
This fortress is gradually being converted into a welcome centre for the Garfagnana, and has six hostel-type rooms in converted outbuildings. These are very clean, have bunk beds and sleep from two to eight people. There's also a restaurant where you can have breakfast.

Palazzo Guiscardo €€€
Via Provinciale 16, Pietrasanta, T0584-792914, palazzoguiscardo.it.
This *stile-Liberty* building has been transformed into a small hotel, with just nine rooms. Bathrooms are fitted with local marble and furnishings are plush, with period pieces, plump cushions and rich colours.

Self-catering

Ai Frati
Località ai Frati 19, 55036 Pieve Fosciana, T0583-65378, agriturismoaifrati.com.
This is a 14th-century monastery, converted into an *agriturismo*. The five small apartments (€620 per week) have been created out of monks' cells. It's surrounded by grounds and has a pool. Most atmospheric are the cloisters, with their crumbling walls. There is also a bedroom that can be rented by the night (€).

I Cedri
Località Alla Villa, 55020 Albiano, T0583-765270, agriturismoicedri.it.,
La Filanda is a former silk factory, on the I Cedri estate about 10 minutes' drive from Barga. There are well-tended grounds and an outdoor pool, and the views of distant Barga are glorious. The estate produces wine and olive oil. Three apartments are available at €1100 (sleeps four) to €1300 (sleeps six) per week.

Pistoia

Il Convento €€
Via San Quirico 33, Pontenuovo, T0573-452651, ilconventohotel.com.
3 km from Pistoia.
This former monastery makes a fascinating place to stay. The bedrooms were originally monks' cells but obviously they're rather more luxurious now. There are comforts such as televisions, and you can dine on the terrace in the evening. There's a pool outside.

Tenuta di Pieve a Celle €€
Via Pieve a Celle 158, T0573-913087, tenutadipieveacelle.it.
On the outskirts of Pistoia is this excellent *agriturismo* in an elegant villa set in its own grounds. The immaculate rooms all have private bathrooms, and there's a comfortable lounge with fresh flowers and lots of books and magazines. The owners use produce from their organic garden for breakfast (and dinner, which they cook on request). There's a swimming pool, vineyard and free bike hire.

Canto all Porta Vecchia €
Via Curtatone e Montanara 2, T0573-27692, dormireintoscana.it.
Map Pistoia, p239.
Press the brass bell, go up three flights of stairs and you're in this lovely B&B run by Anna Bresci. There are just four rooms, only one with its own bathroom, but they're lovely and clean with original frescoes, a tiny terrace and stunning views from the lounge. Friendly and central.

Le Pòggiola €
Via Treggiaia 13, T0573-51071, lepoggiola.com.
Just 10 minutes from the centre of Pistoia is this lovely farmhouse. They have double rooms (minimum three nights' stay) – some with shared bathrooms – as well as one self-catering apartment sleeping four (€750 per week). Lisa, the charming owner, can give cookery lessons if you wish and organize tours of the farm, with oil and wine tastings. There's a swimming pool too. Lisa also has a separate self-catering residence, Il Vallone, in Monsummano Terme (tenutailvallone.it).

Self-catering

ArteMura Residence
Via Pietro Bozzi 6/8, T0573-366698, artemuraresidence.com.
Map Pistoia, p239.
There are 20 beautifully furnished apartments in this former palace. All are different – the most unusual is the Tower Room – and they vary in size, sleeping two (€891 per week) to six (€1980). The residence also has a lovely secluded garden.

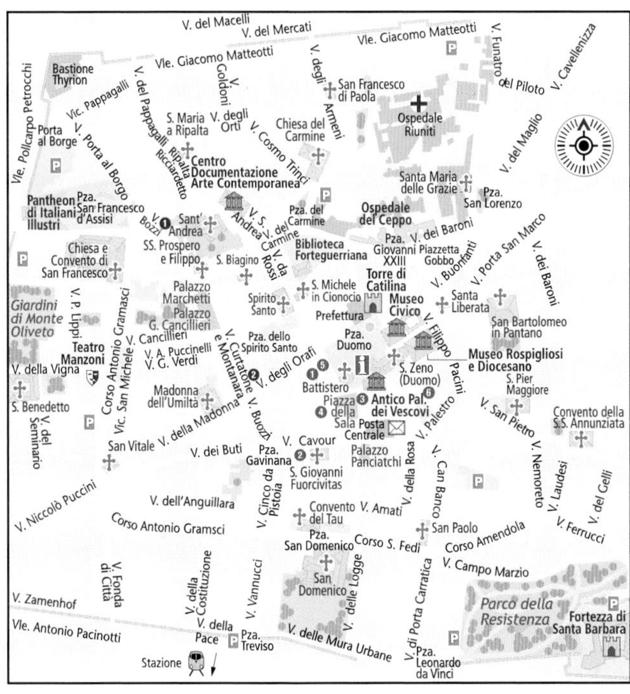

Pistoia listings

❶ Sleeping

1 ArteMura Residence *via P. Bozzi 6/8*
2 Canto all Porta Vecchia *via Curtatone e Montanara 2*

❶ Eating & drinking

1 CacioDivino *via del Lastrone 13*
2 Caffè Valiani *via Cavour 55*
3 CapaTosta *piazza della Sala*
4 Da Ale *via S. Anastasio 4*
5 La BotteGaia *via del Lastrone 17*
6 Lupulula *vicolo de'Bacchettoni 10*

Casa Carbonaia

San Lucia, via di S. Lucia 11, near Anchiano T0571-993252, casacarbonaia.com.
Just a few minutes' drive from Leonardo's birthplace is this country farmstead, converted into 7 apartments. They make a great choice for families. There's a pool and plenty of walking and cycling routes nearby. Minimum stay 3 nights, prices from €875-1199 per week.

Nido del Merlo

Via Montalese 67, T0573-479602, nidodelmerlo.it.
The Bindini Family don't speak English, but they're so friendly and welcoming it doesn't matter. They have two self-catering apartments sleeping up to six (€90-150 per night) and four simply furnished B&B rooms (€). It's not a quiet retreat but a slice of Italian life. There's a small pool, you can borrow bikes and bus 19 will take you into Pistoia.

Around Pistoia

Self-catering

La Porta di Mignana,

Via Mignana 67, Vitolini, T0571-584726, casavacanzelaporta.it.
This rustic Tuscan building a short drive from Vinci has been converted into five self-catering apartments sleeping two to four (€900-1150 per week). It's a popular choice with families. There is also a swimming pool.

Eating & drinking

Pisa

Antica Trattoria Il Campano €€€

Via Cavalca 19, T050-580585, ilcampano.com.
Fri-Tue 1230-1500, 1900-2300, Thu 1900-2300.
This trattoria in the market is in a medieval building with a vaulted ceiling and has some seats outside. Come for homemade pasta, with truffles or wild boar, and a good choice of wines.

Osteria dei Cavalieri €€

Via San Frediano 16, T050-580858, osteriacavalieri.pisa.it.
Mon-Fri 1230-1400, 1945-2200, Sat 1945-2200.
Fine Tuscan food, served with an imaginative twist, at this popular osteria. Dishes include courgette pudding, gnocchi with squash flowers and pistachio nuts, and Tuscan tripe. There are some four-course set menus, including a vegetarian one for €26.

Osteria la Grotta €€

Via San Francesco 103, T050-578105, osterialagrotta.com.
Mon-Sat 1200-1430, 1945-2230.
Resembling a dark cave inside, with puppets of witches hanging on the walls, this osteria offers starters like toast with *lardo* and figs, filling soups and unusual pasta dishes like pistachio ravioli.

Osteria del Tinti €€

Vicolo del Tinti 26, T050-580240, osteriadeltinti.com.
Thur-Tue 1900-2400, Sun also 1230-1500.
Good local food, tucked away down a side street. Their pasta dishes include *testaroli* with pecorino and olive oil, and they also do gnocchi with monkfish and lemon sauce.

Cafés & bars

De' Coltelli

Lungarno Pacinotti 23, T050-541611.
Daily 1130-0100 (shorter hrs in winter).
Delicious ices on the Arno.

Dolce Pisa

Via Santa Maria 83, T050-563181.
Sat-Thu 0730-2000.
Not far from the Orto Botanico, this is a good place to stop for lovely pastries and espresso.

La Bottega del Gelato

Piazza Garibaldi 11, T050-575467.
Daily, summer 1100-0100, closes earlier and on Wed in winter.
Many locals rate this as the best gelateria. Prepare to queue.

Viareggio

Bagno Ristorante la Rondine €€€€

Terrazza della Repubblica 33, T0584-53130.
Daily 1230-1430, Thu-Sat 2000-2230.
At the far end of the seafront, at the Citadelle di Carnevale end, this quality restaurant specializes in locally caught fish. Specialities include tagliatelle with *bottarga*, and mixed fried fish.

Cabreo €€€

Via Firenze 14, T0584-54643.
Lunch and dinner. Closed Mon.
In a quiet side street, with its own little courtyard, this restaurant offers a variety of fish dishes – such as gnocchi with lobster sauce. You can also find pasta dishes like tagliatelle with beef.

La Darsena €€€

Via Virgilio 150, T0584-392785, trattorialadarsena.it.
Mon-Sat 1200-1430, 1945-2230.
This fish restaurant by the harbour area offers dishes such as seafood risotto and spaghetti with clams. Their mixed grill is a speciality. Desserts include homemade cakes.

Lucca

Antica Locanda dell'Angelo €€€
Via Pescheria 21, T0583-467711, locandadellangelo.it.
Tue-Sat 1200-1430, 1930-2200, Sun 1200-1430.
This family-run restaurant is tucked away on a side street near piazza Napoleone. A courtyard terrace at the back means you can dine outside. There are two set menus – 'creative' and 'Tuscan', and you can also order à la carte – ravioli with sea bass and celery cream perhaps, or swordfish with tomato and mint.

Buca di Sant'Antonio €€€
Via della Cervia 3, T0583-55881, ristorantilucca.it.
Tue-Sat 1230-1500, 1930-2200, Sun 1230-1500.
Dating back to 1782, this is Lucca's most famous restaurant – Puccini used to eat here and it still attracts the great, the good, locals and visitors. The interior is full of character, with copper pans hanging from the ceiling, and the food – traditional Lucchese – is consistently good.

Locanda di Bacco €€€
Via San Giorgio 36, T0583-493 1363, locandadibacco.it.
Wed-Mon 1200-1530, 1900-2230.
Intimate restaurant with dark wood interiors, offering typical food of the region. Dishes include pork with cannellini beans and rosemary, and tortelli lucchese – meat-filled pasta with ragù. There's a five-course tasting menu too. A few doors down, at number 26, is its cheaper sister restaurant, Osteria Via San Giorgio.

Vineria i Santi €€€
Via dell'Anfiteatro 29a, T0583-496124, vineriaisanti.it.
Thu-Tue 1230-1500, 1930-2300.
This stylish vineria, its walls lined with wine bottles, is behind the Anfiteatro. It offers contemporary versions of traditional dishes, such as fusilli pasta with Chianina beef ragù or stuffed rabbit with potatoes and spinach. Desserts might include a walnut and fig tart. Around 400 Tuscan wines to choose from too.

Ristorante Giglio €€
Piazza del Giglio 2, T0583-494058, ristorantegiglio.com.
Thu-Mon 1200-1430, 1930-2200, Wed 1930-2200.
You'll find queues at this restaurant, which offers pasta and dishes such as bean soup with spelt, and rabbit with olives and corn mash. There are tables outside; eat inside and you'll be surrounded by flamboyant frescoes – the building was a palace in the 18th century.

Trattoria da Leo €
Via Tegrimi 1, T0583-492236, trattoriadaleo.it.
Mon-Sat 1200-1430, 1930-2230.
This established trattoria attracts both locals and tourists, who come for the lively atmosphere and hearty dishes such as pasta with meat sauce and fried chicken with vegetables. Plenty of seats outside – but no credit cards accepted.

Cafes & bars

Caffè di Simo
Via Fillungo 58, T0583-496234.
Daily 0930-0030.
This is the best known of all Lucca's cafés, worth seeing for its turn-of-the-century interior of dark wood with marble and glass fittings. Locals come in to play chess and chat.

Gelateria Veneta
Via Vittorio Veneto 74, T0583-467037, gelateriaveneta.net.
Daily 1000-0100 in summer, closed Nov-Feb.
Lucca's most famous gelateria.

Rewine
Via Calderia 6, T0583-48427.
Tue-Sat 0800-2200, Mon evening and 3rd Sun in month.
This contemporary bar does a good range of aperitifs, ideal for an early evening drink.

Taddeucci
Piazza San Michele 34, T0583-494933, taddeucci.com.
This café proudly proclaims that Prince Charles is a former customer. It's famed for its *buccellato* (aniseed and sultana bread) and also does unusual tarts, such as a sweet vegetable tart with pine nuts and spices.

The Garfagnana

Enoteca Marcucci €€€
Via Garibaldi 40, Pietrasanta, T0584-791962, enotecamarcucci.it.
Tue-Sun evenings.
Lively family-run *enoteca*, with communal wooden tables, candlelight and a cellar stocked with around 2000 wines. The food is good as well – they are noted for their steaks.

L'Osteria di Riccardo Negri €€
Piazza Angelo 13/14, Barga, T0583-724547.
1200-1500, 1900-2200.
Sunflowers on the terrace make this osteria in the centre of Barga bright and welcoming. The menu changes daily, but you might find nettle ravioli, ravioli filled with spinach and ricotta, or grilled beef. For dessert, try a homemade cake.

Al Laghetto €
Località Pontaccio, Turrite Cava, Gallicano, T0583-75798.
Wed-Mon 1200-1500, 1900-2300.
They're noted for their meats at this large restaurant set among the trees. Try a mixed grill, or delicious potatoes cooked very simply in ashes in the wood-fired oven. They also do excellent flatbreads with different fillings.

Osteria Vecchio Mulino €
Via Vittorio Emanuele 12, Castelnuovo Garfagnana, T0583-62192, ilvecchiomulino.com.
Tue-Sun 0730-2030.
You could easily pass by this excellent osteria, perched on a corner. Inside are original wood fittings, wooden tables and Andrea Bertucci, the owner, encouraging you to try his home-cured meats, local cheeses and bread. Desserts are freshly made – perhaps a chestnut torte or ricotta cake.

Ristorante Molino della Volpe €
Località Molino della Volpe, Gello, Pescaglia, T0583-359045, off Diecimo-Pescaglia road, by sign to Celle dei Puccini.
Mon-Tue, Thu-Sun 1900-0100, also Mon and Sat-Sun 1200-1430.
This is a charming countryside restaurant in a converted mill. The seasonal menu uses typical products of the Serchio Valley, such as mushrooms, pumpkins and chestnuts. If you ask in advance, they can prepare some old recipes using chestnut flour.

Rita e Rinaldo €
Focchia 9, 55060 Pescaglia, T0583-357728, off Pascoso-Diecimo road.
Thu-Tue.
Just a handwritten wooden sign directs you to this little country restaurant, run for over 40 years by Rita and her husband Rinaldo. Tables outside give views over the valley, and dishes might include tortelli pasta with ragù, rabbit with olives and *sformato di verdure* – vegetable pie.

Cafés & bars

Caffè Capretz
Piazza Salvo Salvi 1, Barga, T0583-723001.
Tue-Sun 0745-approx 2200.
Historic café that once played host to Garibaldi. There is outdoor seating – the terrace at the back has the best views.

Pistoia

CacioDivino €€
Via del Lastrone 13, T0573-194 1058, cacio-divino.it.
Mon-Sat 1000-1500, 1800-2300.
Light blue walls and cheery napkins give this place a youthful feel. There's a blackboard menu and an excellent selection of tasting plates. The *crostone* make a good light lunch.

La BotteGaia €€
Via del Lastrone 17, T0573-365602, labottegaia.it.
Tue-Sat 1030-1500, 1830-0100, Sun 1830-0100.
A lovely osteria where you can just drop in. Come for tagliatelle with beef, or beans and rosemary, or *panzanella* with greens.

Lupulula €€
Vicolo de' Bacchettoni 10, T0573-23331, lupulula.it.
Tue-Sun 1230-1415, 2000-2400, Mon 1230-1415.
This taverna serves delicious pasta dishes such as basil tortelli with pumpkin flowers, and main courses like *baccalà* (salt cod) with green beans.

Da Ale €
Via San Anastasio 4, T0573-24108.
Daily 1930-2430, closed Mon in winter.
This pizzeria, set in a former church, is quite small and gets very busy. There are paper placemats and no frills, but the pizzas are delicious.

Cafés & bars

Caffè Valiani
Via Cavour 55, T0573-23034.
Daily 0730-1930.
This historic café is set in a former oratory – you can see frescoes on the wall above the counter. Past customers include Verdi, Rossini and Puccini.

Tip...

Look out for confetti – white sweets made of sugar and almonds, which were given to pilgrims in Pistoia. They sell them in Caffè Valiani.

Entertainment

CapaTosta
Piazza della Sala, T0573-308240.
Daily 0700-0100.
Contemporary wine bar that's very popular with locals – especially at aperitif time.

Gelateria Monerosa
Via Dalmazia 397, T0573-402075.
Take Viale Europa exit off ring road.
Mon-Tue and Thur-Sat 1530-2300, Sun 1030-late.
Arrigo Merlini makes his ice creams on the premises and locals like them so much they drive here to sample them.

For more festivals see pages 52-55.

Pisa

Festivals & events

Gioco del Pont
Jun
Celebrations for Pisa's patron saint: on 16 June the façades of all the palaces along the Arno are illuminated with candles; on 17 June there is a boat race on the river, and on the last Sunday in the month rival *contrade* take part in the Gioco del Ponte.

Viareggio & the coast

Clubs

The coastline around Viareggio is noted for its nightlife – head for Forte dei Marmi, Viareggio and Marina di Pietrasanta. The gay scene is lively on the coast at Torre del Lago.

Nightspots include **Twiga** (viale Roma 2, Marina di Pietrasanta, T0584-21518, twigaclub.it), Fri-Sat; **La Canniccia Club** (via Unita d'Italia, Marina di Pietrasanta, T0584-23225), Sat from 2300; **La Capannina di Franceschi** (Forte dei Marmi T0584-80169, lacapanninadifranceschi.it); **Mama Mia** (Torre del Lago, T389-626 2642, mamamia.tv), Apr-Sep daily 2400-0400, Oct-Mar Fri-Sun 2100-0200; BK2 **Balena 2000** (Lungomare Margherita, via Modena, Viareggio T0584-44045, balena2000.net) and **Seven Apples** (viale Roma 108, Marina di Pietrasanta, T0584-20458, sevenapples.it), Fri-Sun. Many clubs close in winter.

Lucca

Children

Parco di Pinocchio
Collodi, T0572-429342, pinocchio.it.
Mar-Nov daily 0830-sunset, €11 park, €20 park, gardens and butterfly house, €8 and €16 3-14/over 65.
In the birthplace of Carlo Lorenzi, the creator of *Pinocchio*, this amusement park 15 km east of Lucca is dedicated to the puppet. You can also visit the formal gardens of Villa Garzoni.

Festivals & events

Lucca Film Festival
T0583-390597, vistanova.it.
Mid-Oct
Young international festival with a focus on experimental cinema.

Music

Lucca is great for music, with concerts staged outdoors and in churches and theatres. Contact the tourist office for details. Contemporary acts come to the city in July during the Summer Festival (T0584-46477, summer-festival.com), while concerts focused on Puccini are often held at San Giovanni Church (puccinielasualucca.com).

Shopping

Pisa

Food & drink

Il Vecchio Forno
Via Domenico Cavalca, corner of Vicolo del Tidi, Piazza del Campano, T050-580488.
Daily 0900-1400, 1600-2000.
All sorts of lovely handmade sweets and cakes, such as Pisanini buns and cantucci.

Market
Piazza Vettovaglie
Daily 0730-1330.
Pisa's food market, where you can buy picnic supplies and bottles of olive oil to take home. It sells fruit, vegetables, cheese and more.

Pistoia

Market
Sala Square
Mon-Sat 0800-1300, 1500-1900, closed afternoons in Jul and Aug.
The main market in Pistoia, full of fruit and vegetable stalls.

Viareggio

Market
Via Antonio Fratti/via Battisti, and piazza Cavour.
Daily.
You can buy anything at these market stalls and small shops, whether you want fresh fruit, bread or a pair of shoes. There are also clothing outlets nearby.

Lucca

Books

Edison
Via Roma 20, T0583-492447, edisonlucca.it.
Daily 0900-2400.
This bookstore, set in the former Palazzo Cenami, has a good range of English-language as well as Italian books.

Clothes

Santi Guerrieri
Via Calderia 7, T0583-491352.
Closed Sun.
This shop, established in 1870, is famous for its hats – including a range of panamas. You'll also find hat boxes and hat stretchers.

Vispateresa
Via Santa Lucia 5, T0583-051136.
Tue-Sat 0930-1300, 1530-1930 (1600-2000 in summer), Mon afternoons only.
This small shop stocks unusual and stylish ladies' clothes made in Italy and Spain.

Food & drink

Antica Bottega di Prospero
Via Santa Lucia 13.
Mon-Sat 0900-1300, 1600-1930, closed Wed afternoon in winter, Sat afternoon in summer.
You'll find wines, fruit, local salami and good quality olive oil at this well-stocked food shop.

Antica Farmacia Massagli
Piazza San Michele 36, T0583-496067, massagli.com.
Mon-Sat 0900-1300, 1530-1930 (1600-2000 in summer).
This pharmacy is famed for its Elixir di China, a mix of aromatic herbs and bark that was formulated in 1855 as a cure for malaria. It's also said to act as a digestive and locals come in each morning for a measure.

Antica Pasticceria Fonte della Rocca
Piazza Ariosto 1, Castelnuovo Garfagnana. T0583-62190.
Tue-Sun 0730-1300, 1500-1930.
This pasticceria stocks cakes and tarts, made using butter, lots of chocolate and local flour.

Tip...

A short drive northwest of Vinci, in Lamporecchio, you'll find **Carli** (piazza Francesco Berni 20, T0573-82177, closed Wed), a pasticceria famed for its *brigidini*, snacks flavoured with aniseed.

Enoteca Vanni
Piazza San Salvatore 7, T0583-491902, enotecavanni.com.
Tue-Sat 0900-1300, 1600-2000, Mon 0900-1300.
Excellent selection of wines at this *enoteca*, with bottles ranging from under €10 to €18,000. Make sure you go downstairs to see the cellars. Tutored tastings are available (book in advance).

Forno a Vapore
Via Santa Lucia 18/20, T0583-496285.
Mon-Tue and Thu-Sat 0700-1300, 1600-1930, Wed 0700-1300.
Bakery established in the early 1900s. Perfect for picnic supplies of delicious focaccia and cakes. Look out for *buccellato grande*, a large, local fruit and aniseed loaf.

Homewares

L'Erbario Toscano
Via Santa Lucia 17, Lucca T0583-464567.
Tue-Sat 0930-1300, 1600-2030, Mon 1600-2030.
All sorts of items for the home, such as tablecloths and napkins, hand-woven in the nearby Serchio Valley. They also stock soaps and candles.

Jewellery

Chiocchetti
Via Fillungo 20/24, Lucca, T0583-493179, gioielleriachiocchetti.net.
Tue-Sat 0930-1300, 1530-1930, Mon 1530-1930, summer 1600-2000, may close Sat afternoon in Jul-Aug.
Gorgeous interiors with chandeliers and wooden fittings; a good place to find jewellery.

Activities & tours

Cycling

Toscana in Tour
Via San Giuseppe 5, Pisa, T0583-991 1006, toscanaintour.it.
Offers mountain bike and scooter hire in Pisa.

Food & wine

Sapori e Saperi
T339-763 6321, sapori-e-saperi.com.
Heather Jarman offers food and wine tours of Northern Tuscany, meeting local producers and growers, and dining in little-known restaurants.

Treno dei Sapori
pontineltempo.it.
Special steam train services, which leave Livorno, stop at Pisa and Lucca and then go into the Garfagnana, are associated with seasonal events such as the chestnut harvest.

Walking

The Alpi Apuane (Apuan Alps) can easily be reached from Lucca and the coast. A protected regional park, they have plenty of walking trails, and you can book guided tours. Contact the visitor centre in Seravezza (T0584-075 6144, parks.it). The Garfagnana is great for walkers. The visitor centre in Castelnuovo Garfagnana (Piazza delle Erbe, T0583-644242) provides maps and information on guides and activities.

Toscana Adventure Team
tateam.it.
This company, based in Vinci, can offer a good variety of walking, cycling and climbing tours in northern Tuscany.

Transport

Frequent trains go from Pisa to Florence (1 hr 20 mins), Lucca (20 mins) and Viareggio (18 mins). Trains also go to Pistoia (1 hr 16 mins), sometimes requiring a change at Lucca. There are slow, irregular trains from Lucca to Barga (36 mins) but Barga station is outside the town and you will need to take a taxi.

Southern Hill Towns

Contents

COME BENEDETTO FA PORTARE IL CORPO DI CRISTO
SOPRA AL CORPO DEL MONACO
CHE LA TERRA NON VOLEVA RICEVERE

Introduction

This is quintessential Tuscany – a rolling landscape dotted with immaculately preserved hill towns and ancient abbeys, punctuated with cypress trees that pierce the sky like dark green daggers. Here is Pienza, Pope Pius II's ideal Renaissance town, and here too is the abbey of Monte Oliveto Maggiore, famed for its frescoes. The area was once ravaged by power struggles between the Sienese and the Florentines, but now it's deliciously tranquil. The pace of life is slow, and most people make their living from olives, wine or tourism – sometimes all three. The fabric of life seems remarkably unruffled by the 21st century, and people still feel great allegiance to their village or hamlet.

There are two distinct landscapes: the Val d'Orcia, which is soft and picturesque, fertile and rather dreamy; and the Crete Senese, which is starker with smooth waves of clay soil rippled by *calanchi* (rivers of erosion), long curvy roads and cheery fields of sunflowers. It's the sort of scenery that has you pulling out your camera every few minutes. It can get busy in high summer, so it's better to come in spring or autumn. Many visitors come to sample the fine red wines, the star being Brunello di Montalcino.

What to see in...

...one day
If you're driving out from Siena you can do one of two routes. One option is to drive to **Montepulciano**, where you can call in to some of the hill town's famous wine cellars, stroll around the picturesque streets and visit the most stunning church, **San Biagio** on the edge of the town. In the afternoon, make for **Pienza**, Pope Pius II's ideal Renaissance town. Alternatively, drive to the other famous wine town, **Montalcino**, continue to the baths at **Bagno Vignoni** then drive back via **San Quirico d'Orcia** and the glorious **Abbazia Monte Oliveto Maggiore**.

...a weekend or more
You can do both the itineraries above – and if you have a third day you could include the **Abbazia di Sant'Antimo** and some of the quieter villages such as **San Giovanni d'Asso**.

Montepulciano

This beautifully preserved hill town, about 43 km south of Siena, sits at the junction of the southern part of the flat Valdichiana and the Val d'Orcia. The strategically important site has certainly been settled since Roman times, and the town's name comes from the Latin Mons Politianus,: the local people are known as *Poliziani*. Wealthy Florentines would come to spend the summer here, and there are plenty of Renaissance buildings to admire. The main artery, the Corso, runs the length of the town, with steep streets stretching to either side. The highest point is the piazza Grande.

Wine cellars

Wine's the big attraction here, of course: the town's most famous product is Vino Nobile di Montepulciano, and there are plenty of places to try it – and buy it. There are two particularly famous cellars:

Azienda Agricola Contucci (Palazzo Contucci, via del Teatro, T0578-757006, contucci.it, Mon-Fri 0830-1230, 1430-1830, longer in summer) is the historic wine cellar of the aristocratic Contucci family, who produce Vino Nobile, Rosso di Montepulciano and Sansovino, among others. You can visit the cellars, taste the wine and have bottles shipped home – and meet Adamo, the friendly wine master who kisses all the ladies' hands.

Not far away is Cantina del Redi (via di Collazzi, T0578-716092, cantinadelredi.com, 1030-1300, 1500-1900), the best-known and most photographed wine cellars in Montepulciano. They're reached by a long flight of steps and are full of atmosphere – worth visiting whether you want to buy wine or not.

Duomo

Piazza Grande.
Daily, free.

The Duomo's façade is unfinished, which makes it look rather un-enticing, but inside it's a different story. The eye-catching altarpiece is a masterly *Assumption of the Virgin* created in 1401 by Taddeo di Bartolo. It's a triptych, painted on wood and lavishly gilded. Look carefully at the figures surrounding the virgin's tomb in the centre: the figure facing you, on the right, is a self-portrait – the artist representing himself as St Thaddeus. There's also work by Andrea della Robbia (1435-1525) and fragments of the tomb of Bartolomeo Aragazzi by Michelozzo (1396-1472).

The Duomo is the main sight on piazza Grande, which, as its name suggests, is the main square. It's ringed by imposing palaces – such as the Palazzo Comunale and the Palazzo Tarugi – and contains the town's old well.

Essentials

Tourist information

Montepulciano: Piazza Don Minzoni 1, T0578-757341, prolocomontepulciano.it.
Pienza Corso Rossellino 30, T0578-749905.
San Quirico d'Orcia: Via Dante Alighieri 33, T0577-897211, ufficioturistico@comunesanquirico.it.
Montalcino: Costa del Municipio 8, T0577-849331, prolocomontalcino.it.

Above: Wooden cross inside the Temple of Saint Biagio, Montepulciano

Museo Civico

Via Ricci 10, T0578-717300, north of piazza Grande.
Tue-Sun summer 1000-1300, 1500-1900, winter 1000-1300, 1500-1800, €4, €2.50 under 18.

Situated in the ancient Palazzo Neri-Orselli, the town museum is part art gallery and part archaeological museum. The gallery has a wide range of works by Tuscan painters from the 14th to 17th centuries, among them *The Holy Family* by Il Sodoma, and a *Madonna and Child* attributed to a follower of Duccio. There are also some terracotta works by Andrea della Robbia. Among the ancient stonework and pieces of pottery, you'll find a silver *Funeral Mask of St Agnes*.

Nearby via di Gracciano nel Corso is the most important shopping street: stop to look at the covers of Etruscan tombs on the outside of Palazzo Bucelli.

Tempio di San Biagio

Via di San Biagio.
Daily, free.

If you're going to visit one church in town make it this one, which is one of the finest Renaissance monuments in Italy. About 15 minutes' walk from the centre, it seems to cling to the hillside and was the masterpiece of Antonio da Sangallo the Elder. Built over an earlier chapel, it was designed as a pilgrimage church for a fresco depicting the *Madonna with Child and St Francis*, in which people were said to have seen the Madonna's eyes moving. The work is within the altar. The church was inaugurated in 1529, although it was not completed until 1533. It's designed in the form of a Greek cross. Sangallo was influenced by Bramante's designs for the reconstruction of St Peter's in Rome – though they did not go ahead as planned.

Montepulciano.

Pienza

A visit here is a trip to Utopia – at least one man's idea of it. The tiny village of Corsignano was transformed in 1459 by Pope Pius II, who had decided to turn his birthplace into an ideal Renaissance city. The Florentine architect Bernardo Rossellino cleverly redeveloped the centre without destroying the medieval layout. The project went around 500% over budget, which did not please the Pope. "You did well, Bernardo, in lying to us about the expense," he said, although he loved the 'glorious structures' that were the result.

Corsignano was later renamed Pienza after Pius himself, and it's still the most memorable of places. Italians often come for Sunday lunch and a stroll around the walls, from which you get spectacular views to Monte Amiata.

The People's Pope

If ever there was a Renaissance man it was Pope Pius II (1405-64), often known as the first Humanist. Enea Silvio de' Piccolomini was born in the Val d'Orcia to a noble but poor family, the eldest of 18 children. He studied in Siena, then embarked on a successful diplomatic career. He moved first to Switzerland, then to Scotland, where he was ambassador to James II. Later he became secretary to the Holy Roman Emperor Frederick III, who made him poet laureate. He was a free thinker; he loved nature and the arts, and was a prolific author, writing poetry and books – including a vivid autobiographical diary. He also loved women, fathering at least two illegitimate children.

At 40 he dramatically changed his life and became a priest. He was no less successful at that – he was soon made a cardinal and by the age of 53 he was Pope. After Constantinople fell to the Ottoman Turks he called for Europe to unite and embark on a crusade to free it – but the expedition never got further than Ancona, where Pius, by then an old man, fell ill and died. Stunning frescoes of episodes in his life adorn the walls of the Piccolomini Library in Siena's cathedral.

Via delle Case Nuove, near the Church of San Carlo in Pienza, contains small, neat houses that were built specifically for working people. It was part of Pius' humanist vision of the ideal city – a small forerunner of model British industrial towns such as New Lanark and Bournville.

Duomo

Piazza Pio II.
Daily, free.

The crack in the wall of the cathedral clearly illustrates the fact that it's gradually slipping downhill. It started sinking shortly after it was built and, despite attempts to halt it, still moves a bit every year. It's light and bright inside, as the Pope wanted it to be a *domus vitrea* (house of glass) to symbolize intellectual enlightenment. He commissioned paintings from skilled Sienese artists, which still hang here today, including a masterly *Assumption* by Il Vecchietta.

Museo Diocesano

Corso Rossellino 30, T0578-749905.
Mid-Mar-Oct Wed-Mon 1000-1300, 1500-1800, Nov-mid-Mar, Sat-Sun 1000-1300, 1500-1800, €4.10, €2.60 under 12.

This museum houses an eclectic mix of medieval paintings, sculptures and other treasures. Look out for a *Madonna and Child* by Pietro Lorenzetti and the cope, embroidered in England, that belonged to Pope Pius II: it is covered with intricate scenes from the lives of the Virgin and Saints Catherine of Alexandria and Margaret of Antioch.

Palazzo Piccolomini

Piazza Pio II 2, T0577-286300, palazzopiccolominipienza.it.
Tue-Sun, mid-Mar-mid-Oct 1000-1830, mid-Oct-mid-Mar 1000-1630, €7 plus €1 booking fee, free under 6, guided tours only.

Commissioned by Pius, this was his summer residence and remained home to members of his family until 1962. It was modelled on the Palazzo Rucellai in Florence and was designed to make the most of the stunning views. It's a building that symbolizes the ideal harmony between man and nature. The tour takes you round the state apartments, including the Pope's rather lavish bedroom and library. There's also an ornate courtyard and gorgeous hanging gardens with views right across the Sienese valleys.

Tip...

Pienza's renowned for its pungent pecorino cheese, a sheep's cheese that's often drizzled with honey. It can be eaten fresh, when soft and white, or aged, when it's hard, creamy coloured and full flavoured. Look out for it in shops and restaurants.

San Quirico d'Orcia

Don't be put off by the dull modern outskirts – the centre of this village in the Val d'Orcia is charming. Its origins are Etruscan but its heyday was in medieval times; 40 km from Siena, it was an important stopping place on the busy via Francigena. The village's Romanesque church, the Collegiata, is its greatest attraction.

La Collegiata

Piazza Chigi, off via Corso.
Daily, free.

The 12th-century Collegiata was built on the site of an eighth-century parish church and has three impressive entrances embellished with Lombard-influenced carvings: all of them faced the via Francigena, encouraging pilgrims to stop and take a look. Lions support telamons at each side of one portal, and creatures that look like crocodiles hover entwined above another.

Inside there's a slightly incongruous Rococo altarpiece, and inlaid wooden choir stalls behind the altar that were originally made by Antonio Barili for Siena's Duomo. Unfortunately it's hard to see them. To one side of the altar there's a gilded triptych by the Sienese painter Sano di Pietro, a pupil and follower of Sassetta – put 50 cents in the box to illuminate it.

Near the church is the **Palazzo Chigi**, which was badly damaged in the Second World War and is now gradually being restored. Another church, the **Chiesa della Madonna di Vitaleta**, on the main square, has a sculpture of the Madonna on the high altar by Andrea della Robbia. Just off the main square is a Renaissance garden, **Horti Leonini** (Porta Nuovo, 0800-2000 summer, closes earlier in winter, free), which was created in 1580 and has formal box hedges and statues.

Chiesa di Santa Maria

Via Dante Alighieri.
Daily, free.

Also known as Santa Maria ad Hortos, because it was once surrounded by orchards, this small Romanesque church dates back to the 11th century. There are two entrances: one very simple, the other – which faces the via Francigena – ornate. On the opposite side of the road is a former hospital where pilgrims could shelter.

Tip...

The picturesque hamlet of **Lucignano d'Asso** lies about 5 km southeast of San Giovanni d'Asso. This was the family seat of the wealthy Piccolomini dynasty, whose most famous member was Pope Pius II, who created Pienza. You can see the family's coat of arms high on a wall.

Villa Malintoppo

Strada delle Fornaci, T0577-898244, simonellisanti.com, just outside San Quirico.
Daily.

This elegant villa, owned by the Simonelli-Santi family, is a good place to come to try the local Orcia DOC wines and organic olive oil. Tastings and guided tours are on offer.

Around San Quirico d'Orcia

Bagno Vignoni

4 km southeast of San Quirico d'Orcia on SS2.

The great and the good once came here, not to pray but to bathe in the steaming waters of the pool that fills the hamlet's main square. The hot springs were known to the Etruscans, but it took those professional bathers, the Romans, to transform the area into a spa. In medieval times travellers following the via Francigena stopped here to treat their aching limbs in the sulphurous water. St Catherine of Siena and Pope Pius II both took the waters, and Lorenzo de' Medici was so keen he built the Renaissance loggia.

You can't bathe in the central pool – the water reaches 45ºC – but there are a couple of hotels: the **Posta Marucci** (T0577-887112, hotelpostamarcucci.it), allows non-residents day passes to use its spa (Fri-Wed 0900-1300, 1430-1800, Thu 0900-1300, €12), while **Le Terme** (T0577-887150, albergoleterme.it) has facilities for residents only. If you want to indulge in a whole range of treatments, the enormous new hotel/spa **Adler Thermae** (T0577-889001, adler-thermae.com), on the outskirts of the village, offers everything from facials to hot stone therapies.

Buonconvento

17 km northwest of San Quirico d'Orcia.

Few people stop in Buonconvento, as it initially looks unappealingly industrial. Yet at its heart is a pretty walled medieval village that feels pleasantly untouched by tourism, with bustling shops and a friendly family-run restaurant. It once served as a defensive outpost for the Sienese – they built the town's walls. In 1313 the Holy Roman Emperor Henry VII died here – fever, probably malaria, is generally cited. The **Chiesa dei Santi Pietro e Paolo** dates back to the 14th century and contains a painting of the *Madonna Enthroned with Child and Two Angels* by Matteo di Giovanni.

The main attraction is the **Museo d'Arte Sacra** (via Soccini 18, T0577-807190, museoartesacra.it, Apr-Oct Tue-Sat 1000-1300, 1500-1800, Nov-Mar Sat- Sun 1000-1300, 1500-1700, €3.50, free under 12). This museum, set in a *stile-Liberty* building, is a good place to see some great art without the crowds. The collection, much of it taken from churches in the region, includes a *Madonna and Child* by Duccio di Buoninsegna and another by Pietro Lorenzetti. There's also a *Madonna and Child with Angels* by Matteo di Giovanni.

If you want to know more about the social history of the region, there's the **Museo della Mezzadria** (piazza Garibaldi 10, T0577-809075, museomezzadria.it, Apr-Oct Tue-Sun 1000-1300, 1400-1800, Nov-Mar Tue-Fri 1000-1300, Sat-Sun 1000-1300, 1400-1800). It focuses on rural life in Tuscany, with photographs, artefacts and reconstructed interiors.

Museo del Tartufo, San Giovanni d'Asso

Piazza Gramsci, San Giovanni d'Asso, T0577-803101/803268, museodeltartufo.it, beside the Castello, 16 km north of San Quirico d'Orcia.
Apr-Nov, Fri-Sun 1030-1300, 1500-1800, €3/€1.50.

San Giovanni's famed for its truffles, particularly the white variety (the type that, a few years ago, a London restaurant bought for thousands of pounds, then left in the fridge to rot while the head chef went on holiday). This new museum covers the history and folklore of the famed fungus – once considered the food of witches. There's a film on truffle hunting, traditionally done with dogs (pigs can also sniff out truffles but tend to eat them as well) as well as some scratch-and-sniff displays. The village holds an annual truffle festival in November (see page 55).

The Orcia Valley.

Tip...

On the SS2 going southeast, 4 km from San Quirico d'Orcia and just by a bridge, is a small group of cypress trees breaking the smooth landscape of the Crete Senesi; they're the ones that feature on all the postcards.

Monte Oliveto Maggiore abbey.

Tip...

Arrive early to try and beat the tour buses – the abbey gets incredibly busy. There's a good restaurant/café, La Torre.

Abbazia di Monte Oliveto Maggiore

Asciano, T0577-707611, monteolivetomaggiore.it, 30 km south of Siena.
Daily 0915-1200, 1515-1730 (1800 in summer), free.

A fragrant tree-lined path leads to this gloriously isolated Benedictine abbey, founded in 1313 by Sienese nobleman Giovanni Tolomei, who took the religious name Bernardo. He is said to have taken to the religious life after he was struck blind – and then miraculously recovered his sight. He and two fellow nobles retreated to the quiet of the countryside, and their hermitage soon began to attract devout followers. Just six years later the Pope approved them as an order, known as Olivetans or White Benedictines. They lived extremely simply at first, following the strict rule of St Benedict. Bernardo and his fellow Olivetans nursed the sick and dying during the plague epidemic of 1348, and Bernardo died the same year.

The Church Despite their ascetic origins, the Olivetan order grew incredibly wealthy and the charm of humble living faded somewhat. Building of the monastery began in 1319 and the development continued into the 16th century. The gateway to the complex, decorated with della Robbia terracottas, hints at the grandeur to come.

In the church, which dates back to the 15th century but was remodelled in the 18th, there are choir stalls inlaid by Giovanni da Verona in 1505 – the first examples of this kind of mosaic to be done in wood (known as intarsia). They depict birds, musical instruments and landscapes. Mass is still sung daily in Gregorian chant (Mon-Fri 0700 and 1815, Sun 0800, 1100 and 1800; hours can change).

The refectory is decorated with colourful 17th-century frescoes and there's also an imposing arched library and an old pharmacy, filled with majolica storage urns.

Il Sodoma

Giovanni Antonio Bazzi (1477-1549) was one of Siena's more flamboyant characters. Born in Lombardy, he moved to Siena as a young artist, where he acquired his nickname 'Il Sodoma' – the sodomite. Some think it was a corruption of a family name, Sodona, but Giorgio Vasari, evidently not a fan, described him in a contemporary account as eccentric and self-indulgent, surrounding himself with "boys and beardless youths of whom he was inordinately fond". The artist married and had children, but was noted for painting androgynous figures. He good-humouredly adopted the nickname and used it to sign his work.

He was influenced by Leonardo when young and was later invited to Rome to paint the bedroom of the Sienese banker Agostino Chigi. He was certainly individual, dressing gaudily, cracking jokes, composing bawdy poems – and keeping a menagerie of exotic pets that Vasari disapprovingly referred to as a 'Noah's ark' of "badgers, squirrels, apes, dwarf asses." Vasari considered him extremely lazy: when he got older he stopped bothering to make cartoons (preparatory drawings) for his frescoes and just painted straight on to the walls. Most of his best work is in Siena, where he died in the hospital on St Valentine's Day.

You can see more of Il Sodoma's works at **Sant'Anna in Camprena** (via Don Flori, T0578-748037, camprena.it, 20 km southeast of Monte Oliveto beyond San Giovanni d'Asso). The frescoes at this 15th-century Benedictine monastery were his first major work. It is now an *agriturismo* with simple rooms, some of which were formerly monks' cells. Various art and culture groups run courses there, and there's an Italian language school nearby.

Life of St Benedict fresco cycle The main draw is the cloisters, whose walls are smothered with 15th-century frescoes depicting the life of St Benedict. The earliest, showing scenes from his later life, are by Luca Signorelli; the remaining 27 are by Il Sodoma and one, showing St Benedict in Sicily, is by a pupil of Il Sodoma: Bartolomeo Neroni, known as Il Riccio. The cycle as a whole shows how the saint leaves Rome, becomes a hermit, is tempted to leave religious life and eventually founds 12 monasteries, establishing the Benedictine order.

The works by Signorelli are less secular than Sodoma's. The first scene he painted is of God's revenge on Florentius, a priest who opposed Benedict, which takes the form of crushing his house. You can also see two monks eating at an inn (rather going against the strict monastic rule), and St Benedict meeting Totila, the king of the Goths.

In Sodoma's works the combination of landscapes, narrative and attention to detail is compelling. One, showing St Benedict mending a broken trough, includes a self-portrait of Il Sodoma wearing white gloves, with his pet badgers at his feet. Others show a monk being scourged, St Benedict supervising building projects, and prostitutes tempting the monks.

Frescoes at the Monte Oliveto Maggiore abbey.

Montalcino & around

Wine lovers all over the world have heard of Montalcino, home of the famous – and famously expensive – Brunello di Montalcino. It's aged for four or more years before going on sale. The town sits high on a hilltop, surrounded by vineyards and glorious countryside. It was the last of the towns in the Sienese Republic to surrender to the might of the Medici and Florence, only admitting defeat in 1559, four years after Siena itself.

La Fortezza

Piazzale Fortezza, T0577-849211, enotecalafortezza.it.
Apr-Oct daily 0900-2000, Nov-Mar Mon-Sat 1000-1800.

The town's dominant feature, this 14th-century fortress is a reminder of Montalcino's strategic position on the via Francigena. It was Siena's greatest ally. Now it's been turned into a pleasant *enoteca* (see page 271), with a wide choice of wines and olive oils to taste and buy. It's well worth walking up on to the old ramparts (€4/€2): there are head-spinning views of the Val d'Orcia.

Museo Civico e Diocesano d'Arte Sacra

Via Ricasoli 31, T0577-846014.
Tue-Sun 1000-1300, 1400-1740, €4.50 (€6 combined ticket with La Fortezza).

This museum features a fine collection of Sienese artworks, including some of the very earliest examples of the school, such as an anonymous painted crucifix from the late 12th century, which once hung in the abbey church at Sant'Antimo (see next page). There are pieces by Bartolo di Fredi, who worked on many of Montalcino's churches in the 14th century, and works by Lorenzetti and Sano di Pietro. Other artists represented are Il Vecchietta, and Girolamo and Giovanni Benvenuto.

There are valuable painted wooden sculptures, early majolica mugs and some illuminated texts – notably a 12th-century Bible, on the top floor. On a neighbouring wall you will find a bronze crucifix by Giambologna.

Above: Vineyards at Montalcino.
Below: The town's main street.

Tip...

If your budget won't stretch to Brunello, try some of the other local wines, which are excellent and a lot cheaper: Rosso di Montalcino is a good bet.

Abbazia di Sant'Antimo

Castelnuovo dell'Abate, T0577-835659, antimo.it, 10 km south of Montalcino.
Mon-Sat 1015-1230, 1500-1830, Sun 0915-1045, 1500-1800, free.

Set in lush green countryside, this soft, honey-stone abbey was reputedly founded by Charlemagne in AD781, as thanks for his troops escaping disease. However, it seems more likely that an early religious house was already in existence here when Charlemagne visited and gave it his seal of approval – and perhaps also donated to it relics of the Roman martyr St Anthimus, which Pope Hadrian I had previously given him. The religious community grew up on the site of a Roman villa and a nearby spring, which was thought to have healing properties. This early monastic settlement thrived and grew wealthy, as it was on the via Francigena, the busy pilgrim path to Rome.

The present Romanesque church was built in 1118 after a wealthy nobleman left the community a fortune. The then abbot determined that they should have the finest building in Europe, and engaged architects from France. It was constructed of stone, in French style, and the design is unique in Tuscany. This is evident in the ambulatory – a walkway round the altar that allowed pilgrims to pray at the martyrium containing the relics of the saint – from which chapels radiate out. The church contains a 12th-century wooden crucifix, and there is a carving of Daniel in the lions' den on the capital of one of the columns, the work of a sculptor known as the Master of Cabestany.

The abbey flourished for many years, but eventually suffered both financial and moral decline. Pope Pius II suppressed it in 1462 and it was eventually abandoned. The buildings were saved only after a long programme of restoration, which began in the 19th century. Mass is still sung in Gregorian chant (times are available from the abbey).

Take a walk...

There's an easy walk from Sant'Antimo along an old Roman road. A brown sign in the abbey car park indicates the start, with red and white flashes on trees along the way. Walk to a stone hut, then fork left through quiet woods and olive groves. Go right at the next fork and you'll eventually climb uphill to La Magia farmhouse. Turn right and walk into Villa a Tolli, a lovely sleepy hamlet with several wineries. Friendly locals will often show you around. From here you can continue to Montalcino or walk back to the abbey.

Abbazia di Sant'Antimo.

Detail from the remains of the abbey.

Tip...

In summer the abbey is often used as a setting for classical music and operatic concerts. Details from **Operafestival** (T055-5978309, festivalopera.it) or the helpful tourist office at San Galgano (T0577-756738, prolocochiusdino.it).

Abbazia di San Galgano

Val di Merse, 30km southwest of Siena on SS73, nearest village Palazzetto.
Abbey always open, chapel daily 0900-1930, closes earlier in winter, free.

This is one of Tuscany's most celebrated and most romantic spots: the ruined Cistercian Abbey of San Galgano. It was built in the 12th century in honour of St Galgano, a dissolute young nobleman from Chiusdino who renounced worldly ways and his life as a knight after he had a vision of St Michael. In a reverse of the Arthurian legend, it's said that he thrust his sword into a stone, forming the sign of the Cross with its hilt and symbolically renouncing his former life.

The abbey flourished and grew in both size and influence, but was sacked in the late 14th century by *condottiere* Sir John Hawkwood, the English mercenary who's commemorated in an equestrian fresco in the Duomo in Florence. It gradually fell into ruin, the roof collapsed in the 18th century, and it was eventually deconsecrated. The ruin makes an impressive sight and provides a dramatic setting for musical events.

From the abbey a track leads uphill to the Chapel of Montesiepi, built over the spot where Galgano had his hermitage until he died in 1181. Inside, in front of the altar, is his sword, buried up to the hilt in a large stone. The cupola is striking, with concentric circles of brick and stone pulling your eyes upwards. A side chapel contains the remains of frescoes by Ambrogio Lorenzetti.

Sleeping

Montepulciano

Villa Poggiano €€€
Via di Poggiano 7, T0578-758292, villapoggiano.com, off SS146 to Pienza.
Closed Nov-Mar.
Elegance abounds at this beautiful 17th-century villa set in tranquil grounds 2 km outside Montepulciano. Rooms and suites have period furnishings and features, and the spotless bathrooms have marble floors. There's an outdoor stone swimming pool surrounded by statues. No children under 12. They also have self-catering apartments near San Biagio Church.

Fattoria Martiena €€
Via di Martiena 8, T0578-716905, martiena.it.
Closed Jan-early Feb.
Country-style bed and breakfast in a former olive oil mill just to the east of Montepulciano. Rooms have quirky shapes and features; there are open fires and a terrace where you can have breakfast on fine days.

Self-catering

La Bruciata
Via del Termine 9, Località Poggiano, T0578-757704, agriturismolabruciata.it,
This farmhouse 2 km from Montepulciano has been converted to house four clean, good-sized apartments with sitting rooms and bathrooms with showers. There's a buffet breakfast in the farmhouse each morning and a swimming pool in the grounds. Rates are €850 (sleeps two) to €1250 (sleeps four) per week.

Lucignanello Bandini
Lucignano d'Asso (5km south east of San Giovanni d'Asso). T0577-803068, borgolucignanello.com or piccolomini.it.
Grand living at these Renaissance-style, self catering apartments furnished with antiques, period fittings and original features such as wooden shutters and fireplaces.
There are 5 apartments and a villa dotted around the hamlet. There's a swimming pool on the hilltop nearby. Prices range from €1500 per week for 4, to €4400 sleeping 7.

Osteria del Borgo
Via Ricci 5, Montepulciano, T0578-716799, osteriadelborgo.it.
There's a 'country house in town' feel to these two lovely apartments beside a restaurant off Montepulciano's main square. They've been recently restored in a rustic Tuscan style. The larger apartment (€250 per night), which has two double bedrooms and one single, has glorious views over the countryside. The smaller one (€220 per night) has two double bedrooms and looks over the town.

Pienza

Hotel San Gregorio €€
Via della Madonnina 4, T0578-748175, hotelsangregorio.com.
Just on the edge of the historic town centre, this former theatre, built in the 1930s, was recently converted into a hotel. Rooms are simply furnished but clean, with tiled floors and private bathrooms. The hotel also has a number of serviced apartments.

Il Chiostro €€
Corso il Rossellino 26, T0578-748400, relaisilchiostrodipienza.com.
The draw here is the building itself – a converted 15th-century convent in central Pienza. It has lots of atmosphere, with quiet cloisters, comfortable rooms – some of which have frescoed ceilings – and its own restaurant. Bathrooms are a bit tired.

Albergo Rutiliano €
Via della Madonnina 18, T0578-749408, albergorutiliano.it.
Closed mid-Dec-last week Feb.
At this B&B just outside the historic centre of Pienza there are 11 rooms, all air-conditioned, with shiny wooden floors and modern, unfussy furnishings. There's a swimming pool and you can breakfast outside on the terrace when it's fine.

Dal Falco €
Piazza Dante Alighieri 3, T0578-748551, ristorantedalfalco.it.
If you want a clean and simple base, then you might want to try one of these rooms above a popular local restaurant: there are six, each with bathroom. It's just on the edge of Pienza.

Self-catering

Podere Torrenieri
Trequanda, Sant'Anna in Camprena, T0578-748112, agriturismotorrenieri.it, 4 km from Pienza.
The upper floor of this attractive farmhouse has been turned into a reasonably priced apartment that sleeps up to six people. Mountains bikes are at your disposal during your stay and there's a garden too. It's a good base for walkers and cyclists. From €70 per night for two to €180 for six. No credit cards.

San Quirico d'Orcia

Il Rigo €€
Località Casabianca, T0577-897291, agriturismoilrigo.com.
Pretty, country-style B&B in converted farm buildings, set in Tuscan landscape 2 km south of San Quirico d'Orcia. There are books, jugs of flowers and no TVs in the rooms – to encourage you to chat with other guests. Half-board is also available.

Palazzo del Capitano €€
Via Poliziano 18, San Quirico d'Orcia, T0577-899028, palazzodelcapitano.com.
Every room is slightly different in this characterful hotel in the centre of the village. There are terracotta floors and good-sized beds – some of which have canopies with floaty curtains and other romantic features. There's also a garden.

Il Giardino Segreto €
Via Dante Alighieri 62, T0577-897665, giardinosegreto.info.
Sadly there's no secret garden at this small B&B. However, it has six pretty rooms with small, but quite contemporary, bathrooms. The breakfast room downstairs is neat and light, with white tables and chairs. There are lots of steep stairs to negotiate.

Self-catering

Agriturismo Belladonna
Villa Malintoppo, T0577-899920/476 8555, tuscantreasures.it.
A variety of reasonably priced self-catering properties in traditional buildings around San Quirico d'Orcia include an unusual tower perched in the centre of the village.

Around San Quirico d'Orcia

La Locanda del Castello €€
Piazza Vittorio Emanuele II 4, San Giovanni d'Asso, T0577-802939, lalocandadelcastello.com.
Closed Jan-Mar.
Seven good-sized rooms and three suites, attractively furnished, in the centre of this quiet, pretty hamlet. Fresh flowers, period features and a good restaurant (which is closed on Tuesday).

La Locanda del Loggiato €€
Piazza del Moretto 30, Bagno Vignoni, T0577-888925, loggiato.it.
Charming bed and breakfast in the heart of the village, with eight clean, traditionally furnished rooms. There's a sitting area with a grand piano, where tea, wine and little pastries are left out for guests. You take breakfast in the bar opposite.

Montalcino

Dei Capitani €€
Via Lapini 6, T0577-847227, deicapitani.it.
Closed early Jan-early Mar.
There are panoramic views over the Val d'Orcia from this simply furnished hotel in a converted medieval building, once used as a refuge by the Sienese fleeing the Florentine army. It has a pool and a terrace, where you have breakfast in summer.

Il Giglio €€
Via Saloni 5, T0577-848167, gigliohotel.com.
There are just 12 pleasant rooms at this long-established central hotel. Try to get one with a terrace (nine of the rooms have them), as the views are lovely. They also have a number of self-catering apartments in a nearby building.

Vecchia Oliviera €€
Angolo via Landi 1, T0577-846028, vecchiaoliviera.com.
Closed early Dec-early Feb.
Down by the Porta Cerbaia, on the edge of the historic centre, this is a converted olive mill with 11 bedrooms furnished in Tuscan style – tiled floors, brick and beam ceilings, newly painted frescoes. There's a well-tended garden and a small swimming pool. Try to get a room with a view (there are just six).

San Galgano

Borgo Santo Pietro €€€€
Borgo Santo Pietro 110, Località Palazzetto, T0577-751222, borgosantopietro.com, off SS441 from San Galgano.
Closed Jan-Mar.
Honeymooners and luxury lovers will find it hard to leave this elegant hotel, set in 5 ha of immaculate gardens (candlelit at night). They can arrange weddings too. It's a former pilgrims' hostel, dating back to the 13th century – you can still see the medieval bread oven in the spa. Rooms and suites are extremely stylish: swishest of them all is the Santo Pietro Suite, which has a large balcony, an enormous bed and a bathroom with a freestanding bath and separate steam room.

Self-catering

Borgo di Barigianino
Località Barigianino, Rosia, T0577-345644, barigianino.com.
There are eight well-kept apartments at this established *agriturismo* around 10 km from Siena (off the SS73 to San Galgano). It's set in pretty grounds, with a pool, and each apartment has a private section of garden. There's a maid service once a week. Apartments cost from €1230 (sleeps 2) to €1960 (sleeps 6) per week.

Eating & drinking

Montepulciano

Borgobuio €€€
Via Borgo Buio 10, T0578-717497, borgobuio.it.
Daily lunch and dinner, check opening times when booking. There's a real sense of theatre when you dine at this atmospheric restaurant inside a series of cellars: candles on the tables, bold colours and pictures of past guests such as Jack Nicholson. They take great pride in sourcing fresh food and offer three tasting menus: fish, meat and vegetarian. Well worth seeking out.

La Grotta €€€
Via di San Biagio, T0578-757479.
Mar-Dec Thu-Tue 1230-1415, 1930-2200.
It looks fairly modest from the outside but this restaurant, beautifully situated on the edge of town opposite San Biagio Church, has a reputation for the best food in town. There's a tasting menu for €48.

Le Logge del Vignola €€€
Via delle Erbe 6, T0578-717290, leloggedelvignola.com.
Wed-Mon 1230-1430, 1930-2230.
Wooden floors, a beamed ceiling and tasty Tuscan dishes attract locals as well as visitors. There are imaginative touches – loin of rabbit might be served with fresh figs and balsamic vinegar – and a good selection of local cheese.

Osteria Acquacheta €€
Via del Teatro 22, T0578-758443.
Wed-Mon 1230-1500, 1930-2230.
This simple but popular little place by the grand Teatro Poliziano offers Tuscan favourites like Sienese *pici*, as well as a tasty plate of pecorino.

Ristorante ai Quattro Venti €€
Piazza Grande, T0578-717231.
Fri-Wed 1230-1430, 1930-2230.
Situated on the main square, this is a family-friendly restaurant serving Tuscan dishes. Go for a grilled steak or *pici* pasta with tomato sauce.

Trattoria di Cagnano €€
Via dell'Opio nel Corso 30, T0578-758757.
Tue-Sun 1230-1430, 1930-2230.
Relaxed trattoria that does very tasty pizzas, made in their wood-fired oven. As well as all the usual favourites, they offer them topped with *lardo di Colonnata* or (when in season) fresh porcini. Also dishes like duck in vin santo.

Cafés & bars

Caffè Poliziano
Via di Voltaia nel Corso 27, T0578-758615.
Daily 0700-2400.
There's a lovely sepia tinge to this historic café, which retains its *stile-Liberty* interior, with parlour palms, a piano, and walls lined with mirrors and prints. On fine days there's a tussle to get the seats on the little terrace, which has glorious views of the Chiana Valley – you can even see Lago Trasimeno in Umbria.

Pienza

Dal Falco €€
Piazza Dante Alighieri 3, T0578-748551.
Sat-Thu 1200-1500, 1900-2200.
Just on the edge of the town, this restaurant serves good homemade pasta, and main dishes such as traditional Florentine steaks. It's unpretentious and good value.

La Buca delle Fate €€

Corso Il Rossellino 38, T0578-748448.
Tue-Sun 1230-1400, 1900-2130.
Among Pienza's many eateries is this large, airy trattoria with an arched ceiling and red-tiled floor. It offers traditional dishes like *pici* and gets busy at weekends.

Latte di Luna €€

Via San Carlo 2/4, T0578-748606.
Wed-Mon 1200-1400, 1915-2100. No credit cards.
It's best to book if you want a table at this extremely popular trattoria – especially if you want to sit outside. The most popular dishes are homemade pasta with a garlicky tomato sauce followed by roasted *maialino* – sucking pig. Top dessert is the *semifreddo*. Food is good but service can be slightly offhand.

Trattoria da Fiorella €€

Via Condotti 11, T0578-749095.
Thu-Tue 1200-1430, 1900-2130.
This small restaurant in the heart of Pienza offers some imaginative dishes – it's worth booking as it's very popular. Vegetarians could go for crêpes with courgettes and pecorino cheese, while meat eaters might like to try wild rabbit stew with black olives.

San Quirico d'Orcia

Trattoria al Vecchio Forno €€€

Via Piazzola 8, T0577-897380.
Thu-Tue 1200-1500, 1900-2200, closed.
Good-value tasty food, with a menu that might feature cannelloni with Gorgonzola and pumpkin, chicken in Brunello or baked ricotta and kale dumplings.

Il Tinaio €€

Via Dante Alighieri 35a, T0577 898347, iltinaio.it.
Fri-Wed 1200-1500, 1900-2200. No credit cards under €26.
In summer you can eat outside at this restaurant, which serves primi like *ribollita* and main courses such as *faraona* (guinea fowl) in vin santo.

Around San Quirico d'Orcia

Ristorante da Mario €€

Via Soccini 60, Buonconvento, T0577-806157.
Sun-Fri 1200-1430, 1900-2200, closed Aug.
There's no menu at this friendly trattoria, which has been owned by three generations of the Pallassini family. They decide what to cook on the day – it might be *ribollita* or chickpea soup, perhaps pasta with rabbit (or truffles in season) and some tiramisu to follow.

Ristorante del Castello €€€

Piazza Vittorio Emanuele II, San Giovanni d'Asso, T0577-802939.
Wed-Mon 1230-1430, 1930-2230.
Close to the truffle museum, this is a popular spot for a bite as it has seats outside, and during the truffle season it's a good place to taste the local delicacy. Dishes might include ravioli with butter, sage and truffles, wild boar with polenta, or beef in red wine. For dessert try the carrot pie with saffron sauce.

La Bottega delle Crete €

Via XX Settembre 22, San Giovanni d'Asso, T0577-803076.
Tue-Sun 1200-1530, 1830-2200.
Shop/osteria where you can find all sorts of local cold cuts, cheeses and white truffles in season.

Eraldo's €

Lucignano d'Asso, T0577-803109.
Tue-Sun 0800-2000.
Ask anyone in this tiny village 5 km southeast of San Giovanni d'Asso and they'll tell you where to find this long-established family-run shop/café/restaurant. Pop in to buy cheeses, wines and fruit for a picnic, and have a quick coffee or sit outside and enjoy a tasting plate of bread, cheeses and salami.

Montalcino

Boccon di Vino €€€€
Località Colombaio Tozzi, T0577-848233, bsur.it.
Wed-Mon 1230-1430, 1930-2300.
You get views over the Val d'Orcia from the terrace of this restaurant on the road to Torrenieri. *Primi* might include ravioli with pecorino, pears and rocket, or gnocchi with cheese and black truffles. Pork *carpaccio* teamed with hot apple jelly is a popular main. Desserts include a crème brûlée with lavender.

Il Grappolo Blu €€
Scale di via Moglio 1, T0577-847150, grappoloblu.com.
Daily 1200-1500, 1900-2200, closed Dec.
Unpretentious trattoria tucked down a side street, where you can get authentic Tuscan dishes. Look out for *pici* with garlic and cherry tomatoes, guinea fowl in lemon sauce or onions in balsamic vinegar. Meats like rabbit are often cooked in Brunello. It's a good idea to reserve a table.

Re di Macchia €€
Via Scale Saloni 21, T0577-846116.
Fri-Wed 1200-1400, 1900-2100, closed 2 weeks in Jan.
Roberta is the chef and husband Antonio front-of-house at this excellent small restaurant. They grow some of their own vegetables and make the pasta themselves. Dishes are Tuscan with a modern twist: beef with Brunello and spinach, pork with a pepper sauce. Desserts include a crème brûlée that arrives at the table still flaming.

Enoteca la Fortezza €
Piazzale Fortezza, T0577-849211, enotecalafortezza.com.
Apr-Oct daily 0900-2000, Nov-Mar Mon-Sat 1000-1800.
Atmospherically situated in Montalcino's old fortress, this is a great place to taste local wines and olive oils, as well as snacking on bruschetta, salami or pecorino. They stock around 130 different types of Brunello, as well as lots of other Italian wine – they'll ship it home for you.

Osteria di Porta al Cassero €
Via della Liberta 9/via Ricasoli 32, T0577-847196,
Thu-Tue 1200-1430, 1900-2200, closed Wed.
Good value Tuscan dishes at this pleasant osteria, with marble tables and old pictures on the walls. There's a glass panel in the floor enabling customers to see a medieval well beneath. Dishes are simple, such as chickpea soup, sausages with beans or tripe with saffron.

Cafés & bars

Fiaschetteria Italiana
Piazza del Popolo 6, T0577-849043, 1888fiaschetteriaitaliana.com.
Summer daily 0730-2400, closed Thu in winter.
Historic café that dates back to 1888 and retains a period atmosphere. It has a striking *stile-Liberty* interior, with large mirrors, velvet sofas and Murano glass chandeliers.

Entertainment

For more festivals see pages 52-55.

Montepulciano

Cantiere Internazionale d'Arte di Montepulciano
T0578-716368/758473, cantiere.toscana.nu.
Plenty of opportunities to hear both classical and contemporary music at this annual festival held in July and August.

Teatro Povero
Monticchiello, T0578-755118, teatropovero.it.
This village between Montepulciano and Pienza stages a 'Theatre of the Poor'. Written and performed by the villagers. It take place outside in the main piazza each night for three weeks in summer.

Pienza

Incontri in Terre in Siena
T0578-69101, itslafoce.org.
This festival mounts classical music concerts, exhibitions and other cultural activities during July and August.

Montalcino

Sagra del Tordo
On the last Sunday in October, the 'Festival of the Thrush' is an archery competition and parade in medieval costume.

Shopping

Montepulciano

Crafts

Bottega del Rame
Via dell'Opio nel Corso 64 (shop), T0578-758753, rameria.com, workshop next to Teatro Poliziano.
Open mornings and from 1330-1930, closed early Feb.
Signor Mazzetti makes all sorts of lovely copper goods in his workshop. The saucepans, lined with tin, are of very high quality.

Maledetti Toscani
Via di Voltaia nel Corso 40, T0578-757130, maledettitoscani.com.
Mon-Sat 1000-1900.
Handmade leatherware, including shoes, bags and leather-bound journals and diaries.

Food & wine

Maria Caterina Dei
Villa Martiena, Via Martiena 35, T0578-716878, cantinedei.com.
By appointment only. This estate, just outside Montepulciano, is a good place to pick up expressions of the Sangiovese grape, often at better prices than Brunello di Montalcino.

Jewellery

Aliseda
Via dell'Opio nel Corso, T0578-758672, aliseda.it.
Tue-Sun summer 0930-2000, winter 1000-1300, 1600-2000.
Handmade Etruscan-inspired jewellery. There's a little workshop on the premises and they'll do specially commissioned pieces.

Pienza

Crafts

La Luna nel Pozzo
Via Condotti 1, T0578-748073, lalunanelpozzo.com.
Summer daily 0930-1300, 1530-1930, closed Sun in winter.
Traditional local crafts including ceramics and intricate lace.

Around San Quirico d'Orcia

La Dolce Vita
Via Soccini 65, Buonconvento, T339-651 5433, pianigianiiacopo.it.
Mon-Sat (Thu-Sat in winter) 0900-1300, 1500-1930.
This is the shop and workshop of Iacopo Pianigiani. He personally chooses the leather, which he then turns into handbags and shoes. He makes items to order – a handmade pair of shoes would cost upward of €200.

Milletrame
Via Romana 23, Torrenieri, T0577-834078, milletrame.it, northwest of San Quirico d'Orcia.
Mon-Fri 0900-1230, 1430-1930, Sat 0900-1230, call before arriving.
Workshop producing lovely clothes, sheets, cushions and towels made from hemp.

Crafts

L'Angolo di Terracotta
Via Mazzini 2, San Quirico d'Orcia, T0577-847082.
Mon-Sat 1000-1900.
Workshop producing handmade ceramics.

Montalcino

Food & wine

Castello Banfi
Sant'Angelo Scalo, T0577-840111, castellobanfi.com.
Enoteca open daily Apr-Oct 1000-1900, Nov-Mar 1000-1800.
Magnificent castle a few kilometres outside Montalcino, with vineyards, an *enoteca* and a shop. A place to stock up on Brunello di Montalcino. Tours by appointment.

Jewellery

Arte Orafa
Piazza del Popolo 4, T0577-847092.
Mon-Sat 0900-1300, 1600-2000.
Distinctive handmade jewellery.

Activities & tours

Train tours

The Nature Train
Val d'Orcia Railway, T0577-207413, ferrovieturistiche.it.
Round trips €16 on diesel services, €27 on steam services, one child under 10 can travel free with each adult.
Vintage diesel and steam trains run on a circular route from Siena and through the Val d'Orcia and Crete Senese to Monte Amiata. The service is seasonal and dates should be checked beforehand.

The Wine Train
T800-650177, winestation.it
Mid Mar-Nov, €89, 6-14s €59, 5 and under free.
The company operates special train services through the Val d'Orcia during which you taste various local wines and have lunch. It's a full day trip, leaving from Siena, and includes a walking tour of Montalcino.

Transport

Train service from Siena to Montepulciano (1 hr) and Buonconvento (30 mins). Buses run from Siena to Montepulciano (1 hr 30 mins), Pienza (1hr 10 mins), San Quirico d'Orcia (55 mins) and Montalcino (1hr 5 mins).

Southern & Western Tuscany

Contents

Introduction

This is the forgotten corner of Tuscany, a richly varied area hardly explored by tourists yet with a fascinating history and some gloriously tranquil countryside. It's Tuscany in the raw. Here you'll find Volterra, once described as 'a city of wind and rock,' and Massa Marittima, an ancient mining town with an exquisite cathedral square. Between them is a rough, wild landscape: thick oak woodlands, craggy hills and a geothermal area with hot springs that spurt and bubble.

Most of this southern corner is known as the Maremma, less sophisticated than touristy regions, yet with the potential to become the 'new Chianti'. It was once marshland, drained by the Etruscans but then neglected and left to become a malaria-infested backwater. The Medici used prisoners to try to re-drain the marshes, but it was not done successfully until Mussolini took on the task. The pine trees you see today were planted as part of this process.

On the coast, there are not only ritzy resorts but a protected swathe of soft dunes and hills, the Uccellina Park, where cowboys still herd cattle and wildlife thrives. Inland you enter a quiet agricultural region, where fine wines and olive oils are produced and medieval hill towns seem to grow out of the rock.

What to see in…

…one day
This area is too spread out to take in everything in one day. You might opt for a full day in **Massa Marittima** – or **Volterra**, if you're keen on Etruscan history. Or, you could spend a relaxing day walking in the **Uccellina Natural Park**, or do a car tour of the tufa towns: **Scansano**, **Pitigliano**, **Sorano** and **Sovano**.

…a weekend or more
If you have a car, you can combine a tufa towns tour with a drive along the coast, perhaps stopping off for some birdwatching on the **Orbetello lagoon** and visiting the fishing village of **Castiglione della Pescaia**.

Volterra

Volterra feels distinctly different from other Tuscan towns. It's more isolated, perched on the edge of a sheer cliff – the Balze – and the landscape's wilder, hillier and more windswept than that of the rest of the region. It's packed with reminders of its Etruscan and Roman past and is a good starting point for walks and drives.

Museo Etrusco Guarnacci

Via Don Minzoni 15, T0588-86347.
Summer 0900-1845, winter 0830-1345, €8 (combined ticket with Pinacoteca and Museo d'Arte Sacra).

Volterra was one of the most important Etruscan cities, and this fine collection of artefacts gives a glimpse of that mysterious civilization (it's worth getting the audio guide). The ground floor shows the increasing sophistication of burial rituals. The museum has around 600 cinerary urns, which held the cremated remains. In the pre-Etruscan era these had been essentially earthenware pots, but in Etruscan times they were ornately carved with scenes of daily life and Greek mythology, while figures on top represented the deceased and gave clues to their occupations. No 136, for instance, shows a man holding a liver, indicating that he was a religious leader skilled in divination, who would have 'read' body organs.

The next floor covers later years and has a mix of Roman and Etruscan artefacts (the Etruscans were the first kings of Rome). The most important pieces are at either end: the *Urna degli Sposi*, the first-century BC funerary urn of an unflatteringly aged married couple, cuddled together on the ground. The man's middle fingers are bent, making a *scongiuro* sign – still used in some countries to ward off the evil eye.

At the other end is the *Ombra della Sera* (Shadow of the Evening), an elongated bronze statuette of a young boy with a slight pot belly. Dating from the third century BC, it was famously used as a poker by the farmer who dug it up, before it was finally recognized as an Etruscan artefact. Other exhibits include examples of *bucchero* – unique ceramic work that's lustrous black inside and out. The top floor contains more cinerary urns and other items such as mirrors made from polished bronze.

Essentials

Getting around The larger centres such as Massa Marittima and Volterra are small enough to explore on foot – and they're mostly pedestrianized anyway To tour the area you really need a car, however.

Train and bus stations The main train station in the Maremma is Grosseto, which has links to Rome and Siena. Trains go from Grosseto to Follonica, where buses run up to Massa Marittima (piazza XXIV Maggio). There is no station at Volterra. Buses run there from Siena.

ATM Piazza dei Priori 18, and Monte dei Paschi di Siena bank, piazza Martiri della Libertà 2, Volterra; Banca Toscana, piazza Garibaldi, near the cathedral in Massa Marittima.

Hospital Borgo San Lazzero, Volterra, T0588-91911; Viale Risorgimento, Massa Marittima, T0566-909111.

Pharmacy Farmacia Cerri, via Matteotti 15, and Farmacia Amidei, via Ricciarelli 2, Volterra; Farmacia Niccolini, via Libertà 19, Massa Marittima.

Post office Piazza dei Priori 14, Volterra; piazzale Mazzini, Massa Marittima.

Tourist information **Volterra:** piazza dei Priori 2, T0588-87257, volterratur.it, daily 1000-1300, 1400-1800. **Massa Marittima:** via Todini 3/5, T0566-904756, Tue-Sat, Apr-Sep 0900-1300, 1600-2000, Oct-Mar 0900-1300, 1600-1800. **Maremma:** via le Monterosa 206, Grosseto, T0564-462611, lamaremma.info, daily Mon-Fri 0830-1300, 1500-1830, Sat 0900-1300.

Very often, the lid and the chest don't seem to belong together at all. It is suggested that the lid was made during the lifetime of the subject, with an attempt at real portraiture: while the chest was bought ready-made, and apart. It may be so.

Perhaps in Etruscan days there were the alabaster workshops as there are to-day, only with rows of ash-chests portraying all the vivid scenes we still can see: and perhaps you chose the one you wished your ashes to lie in. ”

D.H. Lawrence on the Etruscan urns in Volterra's museum, Etruscan Places, 1932.

Pinacoteca e Museo Civico

Via dei Sarti 1, T0588-87580.
Summer 0900-1845, winter 0830-1345, €8 (combined ticket with Museo Etrusco).

Located in a Renaissance palace attributed to Antonio Sangallo the Elder, this is the town's art gallery. Works on the first floor include a gilded polyptych by Taddeo di Bartolo, *Madonna and Child with Saints* (1411), and two wooden sculptures of *The Annunciation* by the Sienese artist Francesco di Domenico Valdambrino. A highlight of the collection is a wood panel of *The Deposition*, signed and dated 1521, by the Tuscan Mannerist painter Rosso Fiorentino. It's an extraordinarily colourful and vivid work, in which you can almost feel the effort involved in taking Christ's body from the Cross and hear the mourners weeping down below. Another important work in the collection is one of Luca Signorelli's masterpieces, an *Annunciation* of 1491 in brilliant, almost psychedelic colours. The second floor has works by Pier de Witte, and the top-floor gallery gives a panoramic view of the Roman theatre.

Teatro Romano

Off viale Francesco Ferrucci, by Porta Fiorentina.
Summer daily 1030-1730, winter Sat-Sun 1100-1600.

Best viewed from via Lungo le Mura al Mandorlo, just outside the centre, this is an impressively preserved Roman theatre (not to be confused with an amphitheatre), the second one to be built in stone. Constructed in 10 BC, it was dedicated to Augustus and seated 2,000 people. It had all mod cons: a goatskin covering to protect spectators from the rain, and excellent acoustics. The seats were ranged in order of status – the glitterati got the best, with the lower orders squeezed in at the top. You can also spot the remains of a third-century bath-house, built partly using stones taken from the theatre. Citizens would have come here for massages and toning rubs of olive oil and sand. The site was rediscovered only in the 1950s.

Detail from a statue in Volterra.

Palazzo Incontri-Viti

Via dei Sarti 41, T0588-84047, palazzoviti.it.
Apr-Oct Wed-Mon 1000-1300, 1430-1800, Tue 1430-1800, by appointment only in winter, €4.

Built in the 16th century by a local nobleman, Attilio Incontri, this grand old palace later became the home of an alabaster merchant, Benedetto Giuseppe Viti, who altered the interior radically. The rooms are lavishly decorated and filled with furniture, porcelain and alabaster.

Duomo

Piazza San Giovanni.
Daily, free.

Consecrated in 1120, the cathedral has a façade of typical Pisan Romanesque style. The interior was much altered in the 16th century and the zebra stripes were added in later years. The pulpit is 12th century, and there's an important painted wooden *Deposition* (1228) by an unknown artist. Unusually for the era, it depicts emotional, active figures – Nicodemus wields a pair of pliers, Joseph of Arimathea balances on a ladder and Christ is a suffering human, rather than triumphantly divine.

The octagonal **Baptistery**, opposite the cathedral, has a striped marble façade and dates from the 13th century. Its baptismal font was created by Andrea Sansovino in 1502.

Walks & drives around Volterra

Drive south of Volterra to explore a rougher, wilder country, and villages such as Pomarance. There's the Devil's Valley, the geothermic area where sulphurous jets of steam shoot from the earth, the town of Larderello, and the *Colline Metallifere* or 'Metal Hills', exploited for centuries for their silver, copper, lead and zinc. You'll find softer countryside to the east in the Val d'Elsa, particularly south of the SR68, where there are medieval villages like Casole d'Elsa.

There are plenty of possibilities for walks, including the woodlands of Berignone and Monterufoli, or the Castelvecchio Nature Reserve to the east. Ask the tourist office for information and get hold of a 1:25,000 map.

You could also try a climb up craggy Monte Voltraio. Start from Villa Palagione (off the SS439 east of Volterra), turn left through the gates and after around 275 m go right at the red and white flash. Wind steeply uphill through the trees, past a sheer lookout point, and continue to the top and the ruins of a fortified castle. Return on the track leading down to the right. It'll bring you to a crumbling tenth-century churchyard – exposed human bones are occasionally found, but there's no sign of their headstones. Continue past a stone building and back to the start.

Arco Etrusco

Via Porta all'Arco.

This is the world's only standing Etruscan arch, flanked by the medieval city walls. A German general in the Second World War ordered his men to blow it up to impede the advance of the Allies, but local people dug up the road during the night, making access impossible.

Palazzo dei Priori

Piazza dei Priori.
Mon-Fri (usually) 1000-1300, 1500-1900, €1.

This 13th-century palace was Italy's first town hall, and it's still used today. The façade is covered with glazed coats of arms as well as the *canna volterrana*, the medieval city's standard measure. The **Sala del Consiglio**, the main hall, contains a large canvas of the *Marriage Feast at Cana*, and the antechamber has a monochrome fresco, now on canvas, attributed to Luca Signorelli.

Churches in Volterra

Churches to visit include **San Francesco** (by Porta San Francesco), which features the Chapel of the Holy Cross, frescoed by Cenni di Francesco (1369-1415), and **Chiesa San Michele**, a 13th-century church built on top of the Roman forum.

On the edge of town, **San Giusto** is 15 minutes' walk along via Ricciarelli, through Porta San Francesco and ahead. It's an unusual 17th-century church built from yellow stone. At midday, on sunny days, a ray of sunlight shines through a hole and falls onto the meridian line on the floor.

Caporciano Mine & Museo delle Miniere

West of Volterra, 1 km from Montecatini Val di Cecina; Museum, Palazzo Pretorio, Piazza Garibaldi, Montecatini, T347-871 8870, comune.montecatini.pi.it.
Easter-Nov, mine tours (45 mins) Wed-Fri between 1500-1800, Sat-Sun 1000, 1200, then 1500-1800 (tour times may vary), €5; museum Wed-Fri 1500-1900, Sat-Sun 1100-1300, 1500-1900, €3 combined ticket for mine tour, €8 museum and tour of village (3 hrs).

Don hard hats for a guided tour of this old copper mine, built on a site once worked by the Etruscans and once the largest copper mine in Europe. It closed in 1907. An inscription above the entrance to the mine asks for God's protection for the workers. The tour follows a short section of tunnel and doesn't go deep down. Also on show are administrative offices, the enormous lift shaft – known as Alfredo – and the wheel that drove the lift. The museum in the village includes displays on salt mining (which brought wealth in the Middle Ages), alabaster and the area's geothermal history.

Maremma coast

The Maremma coast is a fascinating mix of seaside resorts, upmarket marinas and unspoilt nature reserves, with sandy beaches and lagoons rich in birdlife. North of Piombino, where you can get a ferry to the island of Elba, is the area known as the Etruscan Coast – inland of which are the wild Metal Hills. To the south is the exclusive resort of Punta Ala and, beyond, Castiglione della Pescaia, a walled hilltop town above an attractive harbour.

Parco Naturale Regionale della Maremma

Main visitor centre at Alberese, via del Bersagliere 7/9, T0564-407098, parco-maremma.it. Daily late Mar-Sep 0800-1700, Oct-late Mar 0830-1330. Entrance on coast at Talamone, via Nizza 12, T0564-887173, daily Jul-Aug 0800-1200 and 1700-2000, Sep-Jun, 0800-1300.

The Uccellina Park, as this area around the Uccellina Mountains is often called, is a beautiful coastal stretch a short drive south of Castiglione della Pescaia. It's a protected area, covering 9,800 ha of wild sandy beaches, marshlands, maquis and pinewoods. The land provides habitats for a superb variety of wildlife – from wild boar and porcupines to birds such as bee-eaters, buzzards and woodcock. The fragrant plants of the maquis (including myrtle, juniper, rosemary and lavender) mean that you'll also have a good chance of spotting some lovely butterflies.

Wildlife & walking There are several marked trails to follow. Distances vary from around 5 km to nearly 13 km, and have varying degrees of difficulty – so there's something suitable for everyone. Six of the walking itineraries are reached via the Alberese centre, and three from Talamone. Some trails are closed in summer due to the potential fire risk. Make sure you bring water, wear suitable clothing (walking boots and a hat) and don't light any fires.

Trail A2, Le Torri (5.8 km, around 4 hours) takes in the medieval watchtowers that were built to guard against the pirates who raided this coast for centuries. It also takes you on to gorgeous **Collelungo** beach, a wild stretch of sand strewn with driftwood, which feels about as far from the raucous resorts of the northern Tuscan coast as you can get. Trail A1, San Rabano (7.8 km, around 5 hours) is more challenging: it takes you into the Uccellina Mountains to San Rabano Abbey, a ruined Benedictine complex. Other itineraries range from bird watching on the marshes to night-time wildlife tours and excursions on horseback. All must be pre-booked and all are guided – cost around €9.

For nature lovers

Make a short journey inland from Castiglione della Pescaia to **Ximenes Casa Rossa** (on SS322, T348-826 2128, Sep-May Thu-Sun 1300-1900, Jun-Aug Tue-Sun 1600-2200, €5, free under 12). This 'Red House' was built in the 18th century by the Jesuit engineer Leonardo Ximenes, and was essentially a sluice gate with living quarters – part of a grand plan to drain the marshes. The wetlands that surround it are now a wildlife reserve, and the Casa Rossa is connected to hi-tech cameras that allow you to observe the birds without disturbing them. Boat trips are sometimes available (2-hr excursion €12/€5).

Uccellina Park.

Tip...

If you arrive by car you must park in Alberese, which is inland, and take the shuttle bus to Pratini, where the trails start. In summer (mid-Jun-mid-Sep) you can follow most trails only with a guide because of the risk of fire – book in advance. There is a charge to enter the park, and visitors must leave by sunset.

A beach in the Uccellina Park.

Tip...

The sea tends to become a particularly intense blue in September. It's a lovely time to visit the park.

The spits of land that join Monte Argentario to the mainland have created the **Orbetello lagoon**, an extremely rich habitat for birds. The northern part of the lagoon is a WWF reserve (guided tours Sep-Apr), and the birdlife is extraordinarily varied – you may see egrets, stilts, flamingos and even storks. Orbetello itself is a busy resort, once part of a small Spanish state that held this part of the Tuscan coast in the 16th and 17th centuries.

A short drive south is another important bird reserve at **Lago Burano** (T0564-898829, guided walks Sep-Apr). The lake is not far from the village of Capalbio, from where an 8 km drive inland will take you to the rather incongruous sight of the **Giardino dei Tarocchi** (Pescia Fiorentina, località Gravicchio, T0564-895122, nikidesaintphalle.com, Apr-Oct daily 1430-1930, €10.50/€6) a sculpture garden filled with huge, colourful sculptures inspired by Tarot cards. It was created by the late French artist Niki de Saint Phalle.

If you just want to enjoy a day on the beach, head for **Marina di Alberese**, which is a long unspoiled beach with open access (though you do need a ticket). If you want to stay at the edge of the park there are apartments sleeping two, four and five people at the **Villa Fattoria Granducale** (T0564-407100, alberese.com). It's open all year, €1015-1350 per week, €200-310 per weekend in high season.

Monte Argentario & Orbetello

To the south of the Uccellina Park is Monte Argentario, a rocky 'island' joined to the mainland by two narrow spits of land, with an artificial causeway in the middle. It was a real island until the 18th century, when the channel began to silt up, and it retains an air of insularity. It's a ritzy, glitzy place, where rich Italians have villas and yachts. The northern part, around Porto Santo Stefano, is the most developed, with sandy beaches and a marina – it's from here that you can take a ferry to the island of **Giglio**. The southern part is less developed and more attractive, the focus being around Porto Ercole, an old harbour town.

Cowboys of the Maremma

Few people would associate Tuscany with cowboys, yet the Maremma is home to the last remaining *butteri* – the cattle herdsmen of the marshlands. For centuries these Italian cowboys worked in Lazio too, but now only a handful are left, in the area around the Uccellina Park. They wear distinctive clothing: in winter an *incerata* (a waterproof coat), animal-skin 'chaps' and a felt hat; in summer, a waistcoat and a panama. Their boots are laced, they carry a long stick for opening gates and herding the cattle, and use a practical saddle called a *scafarda*. The *butteri* herd the local Maremman cattle – large white animals with long curled horns – and ride Maremmano horses, an ancient breed. If you're a good enough rider it's possible to ride with them for half a day (see page 299).

There's a story that, when Buffalo Bill took his Wild West Show to Italy in 1890, the *butteri* challenged his cowboys in various rodeo events. The prize was to be the night's earnings. It's said that the butteri trounced the Americans – infuriating Buffalo Bill, who ran off with the takings.

Inland Maremma

The largest town in the south of the Maremma is Grosseto, the main transport hub and the provincial centre. However, the most rewarding places to visit are the small villages that dot the landscape, many of them ancient settlements that seem hewn out of tufa. The landscape is a tantalizing mix of woods and fields and vineyards, a rural land that has been settled since Etruscan times yet somehow feels slightly wild.

Massa Marittima is the loveliest large town in the Maremma, and makes the best base for a tour of the northern part of the region. As in the south, the surrounding countryside is largely unexplored by visitors and offers interesting potential for tours. Hill towns may not offer world-beating artworks or attractions, but they have a low-key appeal – where daily life goes on much as it has for centuries.

It's a fact...

The town is very close to the border with Lazio and once had a dialect so distinctive that there was a Pitiglianese dictionary (the local library has some books and documents in dialect). Some words were similar to Roman: they often ended in the letter 'u' or started with a double 'c' – *qualche*, for example, which means 'some' in Italian, becomes *ccarche* in Pitiglianese.

Pitigliano

75 km east of Grosseto.

View Pitigliano first from the parking place by the Church of the Madonna delle Grazie. It looks almost menacing, with the rock face riddled with holes – former Etruscan tombs that now gaze out at you like angry eyes. It's one of Tuscany's most memorable places.

Once inside the town, originally owned by the influential Orsini family, you'll find a mix of Renaissance and medieval buildings, and a huge 16th-century aqueduct that you can see near piazza Garibaldi. There's a great sense of community: walk through the streets in the late afternoon and you'll find elderly locals sitting outside playing cards, knitting and chatting.

One of the most interesting sights is the Jewish Museum (see below). Other places worth visiting include the **Chiesa di San Rocco,** which has frescoes by Zuccarelli, the cathedral and two museums, contained in the **Orsini Palace**. Most of all, however, it's just good to explore the maze of streets, browse in the shops and taste the local wine – a white called Bianco di Pitigliano.

Museo Ebraico

Vicolo Marghera, off via Zuccarelli, Pitigliano, T0564-614230, lapiccolagerusalemme.it.
Sun-Fri 1000-1230, also 1530-1830 Jun-Sep, 1500-1800 Mar-May and Oct-Nov, 1500-1730 Dec-Feb, €3.

From the mid-16th century onwards, Pitigliano became home to a Jewish community, possibly friends and family of Count Nicolo Orsini's personal physician, a Jewish man who had set up home here. It thrived to the extent that the town was nicknamed 'Little Jerusalem'. Sometimes the Jews were confined to a ghetto, at other times they were allowed to live freely and trade. The community reached its peak in the 19th century, after which numbers began to decline. During the Nazi era numbers decreased even more, and today only three people are left. However the museum, by the former synagogue, preserves much of the old ghetto. You can see the ritual bath, the bakery where the inhabitants made unleavened bread, the kosher slaughterhouse and the cellar where kosher wine was made.

Montepescali

16 km north of Grosseto.

From this small hill town you get a great view of the Maremman plain – you can even see Elba on clear days. The town, where local men gather each day on the steps of Sant' Lorenzo Church, is known as the 'balcony of the Maremma'. It boasts an unexpected treasure in the Romanesque **San Niccolò Church**, just below the piazza. There has been a church on the site since at least the 10th century. Inside are frescoes of the Sienese school dating back to 1300, one showing *Mary Magdalene washing the feet of Christ*. There is also an altarpiece of around 1480 by Matteo di Giovanni: *Madonna Enthroned with Angels and Saints*, painted on wood. The presence of the painting means that the church has to be kept locked. At weekends, just knock on the priest's door (marked '*Parroco*') and he'll show you round. During the week, ask locally for Patrizia, who lives nearby, and she'll open up.

Parco Minerario Naturalistico

Località Ex Bagnetti, Gavorrano, T0566-846231, parcominerario.it, 27 km south of Massa Marittima.
Guided tours daily in Aug, check times rest of year, €6.

Mining in the northern Maremma dates back to the third millennium BC – the ground is rich in metals. They used to mine pyrites ('fools' gold'), which was discovered in this area in the 19th century, and mining stopped only in 1981. On an informative tour here you can learn about the life of the workers, see the cage in which they used to go down to the rock face and the equipment they used. You'll also learn how unfortunate mules were sent down the mine – some spending their whole lives in darkness. You can find more information on Tuscan mining towns at parcocollinemetallifere.it.

Quiet hill towns

Sleepy **Montemassi**, which lies southeast of Massa Marittima near Roccastrada, is dominated by its ruined castle. Perched high on a rock it features in one of Tuscany's most famous – and controversial – artworks, the fresco of *Guidoriccio da Fogliano at the Siege of Montemassi* in Siena's Palazzo Pubblico (see page 155), which is generally attributed to Simone Martini. Montemassi, one of the two castles depicted, was seized by the Sienese in 1328.

Also worth visiting in the area (for their laid-back charm if nothing else) are **Roccatederighi**, **Tatti** and **Roccastrada** – they're stops on the wine trail of the DOC red wine, Monteregio di Massa Marittima (T0566-902756, terreditoscana.regione.toscana.it).

Massa Marittima

For thousands of years the Colline Metallifere – the 'Metal Hills' – surrounding the town have been worked for their valuable reserves of copper and other metals. The trade made Massa Marittima extremely wealthy, and it was nicknamed Massa Metallorum in medieval times. In the 14th century it became a Sienese possession.

There are two parts to the town: the lower *Cittavecchia*, or 'old town', and the upper *Cittanuova* or 'new town', which was built outside the city walls in the 13th and 14th centuries. The two are joined by a wonderfully picturesque street, via Moncini, so steep in parts that you'll almost certainly have to stop for a rest on the way up.

Opposite: Pitigliano. Below: Locals gather in Montepescali.

Tip...

Maremman wines have a good reputation. You can follow a wine route, the Strada del Vino Colli di Maremma (terreditoscana.regione.toscana.it), which runs through Scansano, Montemerano and Pitigliano and takes in four DOC wines: Morellino di Scansano, Bianco di Pitigliano, Ansonica and Parrina.

Duomo

Piazza Garibaldi.
Daily 0800-1200, 1500-1900.

This exquisite cathedral, built to house the relics of St Cerbonius, probably has its origins in the 12th century and is a harmonious mix of Pisan Romanesque and Gothic styles. The façade dates from the 12th and 13th centuries and seems to have been worked, in part, by Giovanni Pisano. The architrave above the main door is carved with scenes from the life of St Cerbonius, and there are also carvings of wild animals and the hunched figure of St Peter, who supports the central column. Inside, the creamy white stone makes the cathedral seem light and airy. To the right of the entrance, under a 14th-century triptych of the *Madonna with Child and Saints*, is a fourth-century Roman sarcophagus. To the left of the entrance are fragments of frescoes of the Sienese school, including parts of the *Journey of the Magi* – look for the monkey being carried on a horse. There's also a splendid baptismal font, carved around 1267.

In the chapel to the left of the altar is the *Madonna delle Grazie* (1316), attributed to Duccio di Buoninsegna and his assistants. Behind the altar is the marble tomb or **Arca di San Cerbone**, delicately carved in 1324 by Sienese master Goro di Gregorio. The sacristy houses relics of the saint, including one of his fingers. The altarpiece itself contains a crucifix, carved by Giovanni Pisano.

Torre del Candeliere

By piazza Matteotti.
Tue-Sun 1030-1330, 1600-1900 in summer, 1100-1300, 1430-1630 in winter, €2.50.

You get great views from this 13th-century tower by the old city walls – on clear days you can just see the sea.

Museo di Arte Sacra

Corso Diaz 36, T0566-901954.
Apr-Sep Tue-Sun 1000-1300, 1500-1800, Oct-Mar 1100-1300, 1500-1700, €5/€3.

This museum up in the Cittavecchia contains important artworks from Massa Marittima's churches. One room contains original carvings from the façade of the Duomo (replaced by copies to protect them from the elements). Attributed to Giovanni Pisano, they are a lion, a griffin and a crouching man who supports a column – said to be St Peter. You'll also find important paintings, notably Ambrogio Lorenzetti's *Maestà* (c1335-40). A gilded work, painted on wood, it features a pink angel sitting at the Madonna's feet and holding a pear, as well as St Cerbonius with geese. Upstairs are works by Sassetta and Sano di Pietro.

Tip...

On the SP49 from Gavoranno, 7 km south of Massa Marittima, is Lago dell'Accesa, a quiet lake with some Etruscan ruins nearby. It makes a good picnic spot and there are signposted trails you can follow around the lake, which also offers some great bird-watching.

Fertility tree

On piazzale Mazzini, linked to the main square by via Ximenes, you'll find a loggia with three large arches protecting the ancient public fountains, where people would wash and also collect their water. They were known as the Fonte dell'Abbondanza. Restoration of the loggia in 2000 revealed an extraordinary fresco beneath one arch – a tree from which women are picking fruit. But the fruits aren't apples or peaches, they're erect phalluses. Two women are even depicted fighting over one. Named the *Tree of Fertility*, the fresco has been dated to the 13th century and is extremely unusual. It's currently covered up for restoration but you will see the image all around the town.

Next to the museum, in the former church of San Pietro all'Orto, is the Museo di Organi Meccanici Antichi (€4). As well as rare pipe organs and other musical instruments, you can see fragments of frescoes by Ambrogio Lorenzetti.

Museo Arte e Storia delle Miniere

Palazzetto delle Armi, piazza Matteotti, T0566-902289.
Apr-Oct, Tue-Sun 1500-1730, €1.50/€1.

Devoted to the history of mining, this low-key museum contains exhibits such as old mine maps, photographs, and miners' clothing such as gas masks, boots and hats.

Museo Archeologico

Piazza Garibaldi, T0566-902289.
Tue-Sun, Apr-Oct 1000-1230, 1530-1900, Nov-Mar 1000-1230, 1500-1700, €3.

This museum by the Duomo takes you back to the earliest origins of the city, with Etruscan finds from tombs, flint axes and artefacts discovered around Lago dell'Accesa.

Page opposite: The Duomo at Massa Marittima.
This page: Visitors walk through the town.

Tufa towns tour

The hill town of Scansano, which dates back to the 12th century, makes a good starting point for a tour. It has an attractive medieval centre, though it really grew in importance in the 18th century when it became the area's alternative capital – the administrative offices moved here each summer in order to escape malaria-ridden Grosseto. There's a small museum you can visit in the Palazzo Pretorio (free), which has some finds from nearby Etruscan and Roman sites, as well as information on local wines. The town's famous for production of Morellino di Scansano, a fine red DOC wine made from a minimum of 85% Sangiovese grapes. There are plenty of places to buy it and try it – along with Maremman olive oils.

Leave Scansano by the SS322 to reach **Montemerano**, a charming medieval hill town with pretty streets and squares, some good restaurants and churches well worth investigating. The **Church of San Giorgio** dates back to the 14th century and contains 15th-century frescoes portraying St George and the dragon. There are also works by Vecchietta and Sano di Pietro, as well as the famous 15th-century *Madonna della Gattaiola* by Maestro di Montemerano. Its title means 'Madonna of the Cat Flap': the painting has a hole in the bottom corner, said to date from the time it was used as a loft door by a priest.

Drive south now to Manciano, then take the SS74 east to **Pitigliano** (see page 286). One of Tuscany's most fascinating towns, it's carved out of tufa and seems to glare down at you from its rocky outcrop. Allow a good couple of hours to explore.

You could now take the road to the isolated hilltop town of **Sorano**, also carved from the tufa. Partly deserted in places due to landslides, it has plenty of atmosphere and a museum/visitor centre in the **Fortezza degli Orsini** (Apr-Sep, Tue- Sun). Then go back along the road but turn off to the east to reach **Sovana**. Perched on a ridge, this is a tiny town that preserves its medieval appearance, although it has Etruscan origins. In medieval times it had an importance that quite belies its size, as it was a fortress for the powerful and vastly wealthy Aldobrandeschi clan who once controlled much of this area. Little more than one street, it has more than its share of interesting buildings. In 12th-century **Santa Maria Church** (piazza del Pretorio, free), for example, there are fragments of frescoes and an exquisite marble *ciborium* – a freestanding canopy that covers the altar – made in the eighth century and very rare. At the other end of the town is the surprisingly large **Duomo** (1000-1300, 1430-1900, closes at 1700 in winter). It too dates back to the eighth century, although much of what you see today is from the 12th century. The interior is serene, with elegant arches and carved capitals.

The road now winds to **Saturnia**, through a landscape dotted with Etruscan tombs and sunken Etruscan roads known as *vie cave*, which also surround Pitigliano. Past the village of Saturnia, on the left, you'll come to the thermal springs. Here sulphurous waters bubble up from the soil and form steaming pools, the **Cascate del Gorello**, where people frequently come to bathe in the therapeutic waters, just as the Etruscans did before them. Access is free. The nearby **Terme di Saturnia** complex offers a range of spa treatments and accommodation.

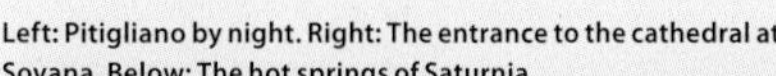

Left: Pitigliano by night. Right: The entrance to the cathedral at Sovana. Below: The hot springs of Saturnia.

Sleeping

Volterra

Park Hotel Le Fonti €€€
Via di Fontecorrenti, T0588-85219, parkhotellefonti.com.
About 10 minutes' walk from the city centre, this large, modern, four-star hotel is a good option for families. There are two swimming pools, a spa and a terrace with good views. Rooms are comfortable and well equipped – the swishest is the suite in an old tower.

Villa Rioddi €
Strada Provinciale Monte Volterrano, Località Rioddi, T0588-88053, hotelvillarioddi.it.
About 3 km southwest of Volterra, this 15th-century country villa has been turned into a lovely small hotel with rustic-style interiors. It's very comfortable, with expansive views and a delightfully situated swimming pool. There's also a self-catering apartment.

Camping

Camping Le Balze
Via di Mandringa 15, T0588-87880, campinglebalze.com.
This wooded site is just 2 km from Volterra, outside the town walls on the northern outskirts. There are pitches for tents, caravans and campervans, and there's a swimming pool.

Self-catering

Podere San Lorenzo
Via Allori 80, Località Strada, T0588-39080, agriturismo-volterra.it.
Set among olive groves 3 km outside Volterra, this is a farm-based *agriturismo* round a 12th-century monastery, now converted into apartments (from €630 per week to sleep two), and some B&B rooms (€). Breakfast and dinner are available and there's a natural swimming pool – it's chemical free so it gets a bit green, but the frogs love it.

Maremma coast

L'Andana €€€€
Tenuta la Badiola, Località Badiola, near Castiglione della Pescaia, T0564-944800, andana.it.
A former ducal hunting lodge set inland in its own grounds, this small hotel has 33 rooms decorated in understated Tuscan style – those in the main house have the best views. The Alain Ducasse restaurant has a Michelin star, and there's a good ESPA spa and a cookery school.

La Parrina €€€-€€
Località Parrina, Albinia, off the via Aurelia, T0564-862626, parrina.it.
This inland estate (in the vicinity of Monte Argentario) belongs to an aristocratic family and is run as an *agriturismo*, with a large farm shop. The family's ancient villa has 12 B&B rooms, with features such as tiled floors and antique furniture – you'll have a private bathroom but no TV or phone. There are also 4 self-catering apartments.

Podere Le Mezzelune €€
Via Mezzelune 126, Bibbona, T0586-670266, lemezzelune.it.
Minimum stay 2 nights. Situated in the northern Maremma, about 5 km from the coast, this stylish farmhouse-style B&B is on the Etruscan coast wine route and you could easily make a day trip from here to

Volterra or the Metal Hills. There are also two small self-catering cottages (€195 per night).

Camping

There are plenty of campsites along the coast, especially between Punta Ala and Castiglione del Pescaia. Ones to try include **Rochette** (via della Rocchette 22, T0564-941123, rocchette.com), which has bungalows as well as tents; **Baia Azzurra** (via delle Rochette, T0564-941092, baiaazzurra.it), which has tents, pitches, bungalows and caravans; and **Etruria** (T0564-933483, campeggioetruria.net), just beyond Castiglione del Pescaia.

Argentario Camping Village
Albinia, T0564-870302, argentariocampingvillage.com.
This camping village has bungalows and cottages (from €830 per week) as well as camping pitches. There are restaurants, a swimming pool and activities – you can go diving, for instance, or join a boat trip to the islands. It's situated on the spit of land that links Monte Argentario to the coast.

Self-catering

Baglioni Residence Alleluja
Via del Porto, Punta Ala, T0564-922050, baglionihotels.com.
There are 32 serviced apartments here, just five minutes' walk from the sea. They're furnished in contemporary style and have kitchens equipped with coffee machines and fridges. Some have private gardens. Stay for one night, or book for a week (from about €2500). Dinner can be booked at the Cala del Porto hotel – there's a shuttle bus.

Inland Maremma

Castello di Vicarello €€€€
Near Poggi del Sasso, Cinigiano, T0564-990718, vicarello.it.
Exclusive isolation at this medieval castle deep in the Maremma countryside, with its own gardens. There are six suites, all furnished with antiques. There's no restaurant, but guests can dine together in the castle, which also has a spa and a pool.

Sovana Hotel & Resort €€
Via del Duomo 66, Sovana, T0564-617030, sovana.eu.
This hotel was created from a house in the tufa. The rooms have beamed ceilings and tiled floors. Public rooms have comfy chairs, while the garden offers views of the countryside.

Tenuta del Fontino €€
Località Accesa, near Lake Accesa, south of Massa Marittima, T0566-919232, tenutafontino.it.
Open Mar-Nov.
You can stay on a B&B basis in the lovely 19th-century villa that sits at the heart of this *agriturismo*. You could go for one of their self-catering apartments. They're in a separate building with a swimming pool and garden, and sleep between 2-6 people (€950 -€1600 per week).

Macchia Piana €
Località Salaiolo 252, Scansano, T0564-507340, macchiapiana.it.
Clean and friendly *agriturismo* with five B&B rooms with private bathrooms and a small outdoor swimming pool. It's surrounded by quiet countryside.

Self-catering

Antico Casale di Scansano
Località Castagneta, Scansano, T0564-507219, anticocasalediscansano.com.
This resort has 14 self-catering apartments. You can take breakfast and dinner in the hotel, and you get free use of the pool. The estate offers cookery courses and also has a spa and stables. From €895 per week (sleeps two).

Pieve di Caminino
Strada Provinciale 89, Roccastrada, T0564-569736, caminino.com.
This ancient property, on a 200-ha estate near Montemassi, has stone buildings that have been converted into double suites (from €650 per week) and apartments sleeping four (from €900). All have terraces or balconies with views, and there's a pool. The estate produces wine and olive oil.

Eating & drinking

La Fenice Park Hotel €€
Corso Diaz 63, T0566-903941, lafeniceparkhotel.it.
Closed Nov-Apr.
Very comfortable hotel in the upper part of Massa Marittima, opposite the Museo d'Arte Sacra. The rooms have traditional Tuscan features and some have a balcony – try to get one overlooking the garden, where you can have have breakfast in summer. There's also a swimming pool.

> “The Maremma is full of secret places. It's perfect for lovers.”
>
> *Cecilia, resident of the Maremma*

Volterra

Albana €€€
Mazzolla village, T0588-39001, trattoriaalbana.com, 4 km east of Volterra.
Wed-Mon 1230-1400, 1900-2130.
Locals and visitors flock to this restaurant in sleepy Mazzolla, housed in a converted stable, so it's wise to book. Come for seasonal antipasti and homemade pasta, such as barley-stuffed ravioli with a butter and balsamic vinegar sauce, or pumpkin tortellini stuffed with ricotta and pinenuts. Lots of game for mains, desserts and good house wine.

Da Bado €€€
Borgo San Lazzero 9, T0588-86477, trattoriadabado.com.
Thu-Tue 1230-1400, 1900-2130, bar 0700-2200.
One of the few places serving traditional Volterran dishes. *Primi* might include *pappa al pomodoro* (a tomato and bread stew), *zuppa alla volterrana* (bread, bean and vegetable stew), or homemade pasta alla chitarra (square spaghetti) with anchovy and shallot sauce. Main courses include pigeon, Volterran-style tripe stewed in a tomato and herb sauce, or salt cod stewed with onions. Reservations recommended.

Enoteca del Duca €€€-€€
Via di Castello 2, T0588-81510, enoteca-delduca-ristorante.it.
Open lunch and dinner Wed-Mon, closed Tue.
Very popular restaurant in a lovely old building in the old part of town. The chef might bring out dishes for you to try, there's a great wine selection and a pretty little garden. Pasta is homemade and dishes might include pigeon with rosemary and olives.

Etruria €€
Piazza dei Priori 6-8, T0588-86064.
Thu-Tue 1200-1500, 1900-2200.
Ornately decorated walls and ceilings make this one of the prettiest restaurants in town. Dishes on the menu might include pappardelle with hare sauce or spinach pasta with a Gorgonzola sauce.

Ristorante La Grotta 56 €€
Via Turazza 13, T0588-85336, ristorantegrotta56.com.
Thu-Tue 1230-1500, 1930-2200.
Friendly little restaurant with tables outside in summer. Start with a chicken liver terrine, then try imaginative dishes such as ravioli with mushrooms and Taleggio cheese, chickpea crêpes with porcini mushrooms, or calf's cheek with a pea purée. For dessert try a hot chocolate and pepper soufflé with rosemary.

Sacco Fiorentino €€
Piazza XX Settembre, T0588-88537.
Thu-Tue 1200-1445, 1900-2145.
Part trattoria, part wine bar, this relaxed eatery offers some refined, innovative dishes based on seasonal ingredients – look out for meats such as hare and pigeon. Desserts are good too and there's a comprehensive wine list.

Maremma coast

Flavia €€€€
Piazza IV Novembre 1, Talamone, T0564-887091.
Wed-Mon 1230-1430, 1930-2230, closed for lunch Jul-Aug.
Pricey but highly rated seafood restaurant in this attractive fishing village. Come for dishes such as the spaghetti with mussels, prawns in white wine and roast cuttlefish.

La Fontanina di San Pietro €€€€
Località San Pietro, Monte Argentario, T0564-825261, lafontanina.com.
Daily 1230-1430, 1930-2200, closed Wed in winter.
Situated on a road with panoramic views, this restaurant specializes in fish. The chef, Umberto, might prepare dishes using eels from the Orbetello lagoon, use seaweed as a flavouring, and you may also see *bottarga* (mullet roe) on the menu. There's an outdoor terrace, which is very pleasant on hot evenings.

Inland Maremma

Antica Aurora €€€€
Via Chiasso Lavagnini 12, Magliano in Toscana, T0564-592030/592774.
Closed Wed.
Try traditional Maremman cuisine at this elegant restaurant in a pretty village 20 km southwest of Scansano. Dishes might include tortelli pasta with duck cooked in Morellino. There's a garden for summer dining and an extensive wine list. Booking is recommended.

Da Caino €€€€
Via Canonica 3, Montemerano, T0564-602817, dacaino.it.
Thu-Tue 1230-1400, 1930-2100, closed Wed.
Set in the well-preserved medieval town of Montemerano, near Manciano, this highly rated restaurant is the place to come for a treat. You dine by candlelight and the menu features dishes such as fillet of local smoked beef with red onions and ricotta. The wine list features wines from all over Italy. If you want to stay over, there are three rooms upstairs.

Il Falco della Maremma €€€-€€
Via Garibaldi, Montepescali T0564-329690, ilfalcodellamaremma.it.
Closed Wed, phone for hours.
Hidden away, this restaurant is full of character. The menu changes regularly, with cuisine typical of the Maremma and of Renaissance Tuscany. So you might find dishes like wild boar with chocolate, veal stuffed with apricots or pasta with pheasant.

Il Tufo Allegro €€€
Vicolo della Costituzione 5, Pitigliano, T0564-616192.
Wed-Mon 1230-1430, 1930-2130.
Tucked down a side street, this very popular restaurant has a simple Tuscan-style interior and a menu that features imaginative versions of Maremman dishes. You might find stuffed rabbit, pappardelle with a lamb ragù or a lasagne with cheese, artichokes and rabbit. Good wine list and selection of Tuscan cheeses.

La Cantina €€€
Via della Botte 1/1A, Scansano, T0564-507605.
Tue-Sat 1230-1430, 1930-2130, Sun 1230-1430, closed Jan-mid-Mar.
Lovely restaurant/*enoteca*/shop where you can taste local food, olive oils and wines. Tables are set under vaulted brick ceilings and the menu features Maremman favourites such as *acquacotta* and pasta dishes. Try the risotto made with Morellino and prosciutto from Monte Amiata.

Ristorante Taverna Etrusca €€€
Piazza del Pretorio 16, Sovana, T0564-616183, sovanahotel.it.
Thu-Tue 1230-1430, 1930-2130.
Lovely rustic-Tuscan restaurant with stone archways and beamed ceilings. It's in the centre of Sovana and has a terrace for summer dining. The menu features fresh pasta and Maremman and Tuscan dishes – look out for wild boar with balsamic vinegar or a meaty stew with olive oil, and for dessert, *crema cotta* with cardamom.

Hostaria del Ceccottino €€
Piazza San Gregorio VII 64, Pitigliano, T0564-614273, ceccottino.com.
Fri-Wed 1230-1500, 1930-2130.
In the centre of Pitigliano, this restaurant has a rustic interior and some tables outside . The menu features soups such as *acquacotta*, and filling pasta dishes. They also serve dishes that date back to the village's days as a Jewish settlement – such as lamb in a tomato and garlic sauce with rosemary.

Gli Attortellati €€
Strada Provinciale della Trappola 39, Grosseto, T0564-400059.
Open for lunch and dinner: pre-booking essential.
This is real home cooking and excellent value. Pretty much everything is home grown and there's no menu – they'll tell you what they've cooked that day. You might find antipasti like fig jam and cheese, then fresh soup with mushrooms and beans, or large tortelloni with a wild boar sauce, or a rabbit dish. The portions are large and the price is set at €26 per person.

La Vecchia Hosteria €€
Via Marconi 249, Gavorrano, T0566-844980.
Fri-Wed 1200-1500, 1930-2200.
Just a short drive from the Parco Minerario Naturalistico, this relaxed osteria offers a good choice of homemade pasta dishes, and main courses like wild boar, fried rabbit or a beef fillet with Chianti. Try some Montecucco wine with it.

Passaparola €€
Via delle Mura 21, Montemerano, T0564-602835, ristorantepassaparola.it.
Fri-Wed 1230-1400, 2000-2130.
Rustic style dining – vaulted ceilings, wooden tables and a large olive press outside. There

are lots of traditional Maremman dishes on the menu, such as *acquacotta*, taglioni pasta with duck ragù and local saffron, and even tripe prepared 'Montemerano style'.

Massa Marittima

Taverna del Vecchio Borgo €€€
Via Norma Parenti 12, T0566-903950.
Tue-Sun 1930-2200, also Sun 1230-1430 in winter.
Brick walls, vaulted ceilings and lots of meat dishes at this good-value trattoria. The menu includes pasta with Cinta Senese and fillet of beef with truffles. For dessert try the *fior di latte* with pine nuts and hot chocolate – it's a little like ice cream.

Il Gatto e La Volpe €€
Vicolo Ciambellano 12, T0566-903575, ristoroilgattoelavolpe.it.
Closed Mon.
Down a picturesque side street, this restaurant offers dishes such as tortelli filled with spinach and ricotta with a meat sauce, casseroled partridge, and duck braised in red wine. There are a few seats outside.

Osteria da Tronca €€
Vicolo Porte 5, T0566-901991.
Thu-Tue 1900-2230, closed in winter.
You could easily miss this atmospheric restaurant as it's tucked away down a back street, but it's well worth seeking out. It's split level inside with brick arches and lots of wine bottles lining the walls, and it offers an excellent choice of regional dishes including tripe or traditional tortelli and Maremma-style salt cod.

Cafés & bars

L'Incontro
Via Matteotti 18, Volterra T0588-80500.
Daily till late.
Marble-topped tables and walls lined with wine bottles at this busy café/bar that's also an *enoteca*. Join locals for an aperitif – or a lunchtime bowl of Volterrana soup served on a slice of bread.

La Vena di Vino
Via Don Minzoni 30, Volterra, T0588-81491, lavenadivino.com.
Wed-Mon 1000-0100.
A lovely, cosy little *enoteca* run by Bruno and Lucio, who serve good wine and simple, good quality food like local meats, delicious beans with melted cheese, or pecorino drizzled with delicious honey.

Entertainment

For more festivals see pages 52-55.

Volterra

Teatro Persio Flacco
Via dei Sarti 37-9, T0588-88204, teatropersioflacco.it.
Built in 1819, this is a small but exquisite opera house. Once used for rehearsals of operas to be staged at La Scala, it is now restored and is used for concerts and theatrical performances.

Inland Maremma

Festivals & events

Maremman food festivals
There are many local food festivals celebrating traditional dishes and regional produce. To name just a few, there's the Aquacotta Festival in Magliano in Toscana (Aug), the Cinghiale Festival (wild boar) in Capalbio (Sep), the Fragola Festival (strawberries) in Marsiliana (May) and the Tortello Maremmano Festival in Poggio Ferro (May) and Roselle (Jun). Local tourist boards have details.

Theatre

Teatro Castagnoli,
Via XX Settembre, Scansano, T0564-509411, comune.scansano.gr.it.
The striking 19th-century theatre in the little town of Scansano had been turned into a cinema, but has now been restored and hosts concerts and plays.

Shopping

Volterra

Crafts

Artieri Alabastro
Piazza dei Priori 5, T0588-87590, artierialabastro.it.
A co-operative of local alabaster craftsmen sell their goods from this shop – from lamps and candlesticks to sculptures.

Legatoria Artistica
Via Porta all'Arco 26, T0588-80616, legatoriaartistica.it.
Mon-Fri 1000-1300, 1600-1900, Sat 1000-1300.
Sells handmade books and paper. They do books to order.

Spartaco Montagnani
Via Porta all'Arco 6, T0588-86184,
Mon-Sat 1000-1800.
Bronze Etruscan-style statuettes, handmade in this workshop.

Food & drink

Enoteca Scali
Via Guarnacci 3, T0588-81170, enotecascali.com.
Summer Tue-Sun, winter Tue-Sat 0900-1300, 1600-2000.
A good choice of wines, local cheeses, cold cuts and cakes.

Jewellery

Cercando l'Oro
Via Guarnacci 55, T0588-81500, cercandoloro.it.
Original items of jewellery in gold and silver, using traditional goldsmithing techniques.

Inland Maremma

Crafts

Sempliciemente
Piazza del Pretorio 8, Sovana, T0564-616030.
Thu-Tue 1030-1330, 1500-1930, sometimes closed Sun.
Handmade toys and wooden dolls in this shop/workroom.

Food & drink

Ampeleia
Località Meleta, Roccatederighi, T0564-567155, ampeleia.it.
Mon-Fri 0900-1700.
This estate makes Maremman wines, which you can buy on site.

Enoteca dei Mille
Piazza Garibaldi 2, Scansano, T0564-507252.
Mon-Sat 0900-1300, 1500-2230.
Over 100 types of Morellino alone in this excellent *enoteca*.

Panificio del Ghetto
Via Zuccarelli 167, Pitigliano, T0564-614182.
Thu-Tue 0730-1300, 1600-1900.
Bakery with *sfrato* – a confection made with walnuts, honey, orange and hazelnuts.

Jewellery

Arte Etrusca
Via del Duomo, Sovana, T0564-614346, artetrusca.it.
Thu-Tue 1000-2000, closed Wed in winter.
Handmade Etruscan-style gold jewellery at this shop/workshop.

Activities & tours

Boat trips

Trips to Tuscan Islands
From Piombino port you can get ferries to Portoferraio, the main town of Elba. It's possible to do a day trip (the crossing takes 50 mins-1 hr, foot passengers around €9, cars €30) but it is more rewarding to visit for a couple of nights.

Ferry companies include Moby (moby.it) and Toremar (toremar.it). From Porto Santo Stefano ferries run by Toremar and also Maregiglio (maregiglio.it) go to Giglio. Maregiglio also run ferries (for foot passengers only) to Giannutri from Porto Santo Stefano.

Paolo Fanciulli
Talamone, T333-284 6199, paoloilpescatore.it.
Paolo the fisherman, as his website is named, is an advocate of eco-friendly, sustainable fishing. He runs trips, demonstrating his techniques and talking about the Maremman coast. Eat the fish you've caught – and even have dinner on the boat that night. Around €80-95 for a full day.

Cultural

Villa Palagione
Località Palagione, Volterra, T0588-39014, villa-palagione.org, 4 km off SS439.
This 16th-century villa has been turned into a cultural centre and offers a wide variety of

residential courses. Learn Italian, do a cookery course, learn how to work with alabaster or go riding or walking. Prices vary – a week-long language course costs around €679 including breakfast and dinner, single room supplement €165.

Golf

There are several golf clubs in the Maremma. They include Punta Ala Golf Club (via del Golf, Punta Ala, T0564-922121, puntaala.net, 18 holes, daily green fees €75) and the Golf Club Toscana (Gavorrano, Località Il Pelagone, an 18-hole course with a golf school and accommodation, golfclubtoscana.com.) Argentario Golf Resort (Porto Ercole, Monte Argentario, T0564-810292, argentariogolfresortspa.it) and Terme di Saturnia Spa and Golf Resort (Saturnia, T0564-600111, termedisaturnia.it) are both luxury resorts with 18-hole courses, accommodation and spa facilities.

Horse riding

Ride with the Butteri
Azienda Regional Agricola Alberese, Località Spergolaia, near Alberese, T0564-407100/407077, alberese.com.
Ride with the working butteri of the Maremma. Leave at 0700 and return about 1200, around €50 per person. Also check out Equinus (T0564-24988, cavallomaremmano.it).

Antico Casale di Scansano
Località Castagneto, near Scansano, T0564-507219, anticocasalediscansano.it.
Lessons last from one hour to a full day, for both children and adults. It also offers riding and trekking holidays.

Sailing

Bareboat Sailing Holidays
T+44(0)208-438 1133 (UK), bareboatsailingholidays.com.
You can charter a boat with or without crew and a skipper to sail from the coast and explore the Tuscan islands.

Watersports

Kitesurf University
Talamone, T328-157 0157, kitesurfuniversity.com and wmania.com.
Easter-end Oct.
A favourite with windsurfers and kitesurfers. This beachside outfit will rent out equipment for both activities (kitesurfing €30 per hour, €100 per day) and also offers courses.

Transport

Trains run from Grosseto to Siena (1hr 30 mins), Pisa (1hr 55 mins) and Rome (1 hr 58 mins). They also run to Follonica (25 mins), where you can get a bus to Massa Marittima; and to Orbetello (21 mins), the nearest station to Monte Argentario. Trains run along the coast from Pisa to Saline di Volterra – changing at Cecina. You must then go on to travel the 9 km to Volterra by bus. Buses run from Pitigliano to Grosseto, Sorano and Orbetello.

Practicalities

Contents

Getting there

Air

From UK and Ireland

Pisa is the main gateway to Tuscany, and regular flights depart variously from Bristol, Dublin, Glasgow Prestwick, London Stansted, Leeds and Liverpool, by carriers **easyJet**, **Ryanair**, **British Airways** and **Jet2**. While it may be slightly less convenient to fly to Rome, it is still an option that many choose. Florence is a growing airport, and currently **Meridiana** fly direct from London Gatwick. At the time of writing, Siena's small airport (siena-airport.it) is expanding and the runway is to be extended: there are no dates or flight schedules available and there is strong local opposition. Overland travel via train and coach or car is viable – more so than for southern Italian regions – but will take a leisurely 24 hours (if you're lucky).

From North America

There are no direct flights to Pisa or Florence from North America, but **Continental**, **American Airlines** and **Delta** fly direct from New York to Rome Fiumicino. **Delta** also flies from Toronto via New York. Other airlines that fly from North America to Rome include: **British Airways**, **KLM**, **Lufthansa**, **Swiss**, **United** and **Air France**. It can also be relatively cheap to fly via London – or another European hub such as Frankfurt or Paris – and connect to Pisa or Florence. To search for cheaper flights to Europe from the US, try europebyair.com (T888-387 2479).

From rest of Europe

Pisa is the most accessible airport, with direct flights from most European cities, including Frankfurt, Paris and Amsterdam. There are direct rail links from Paris, Munich, Vienna and Geneva to international Tuscan train stations.

Airport information

Pisa International (T050-849300, pisa-airport.com), 80 km west of Florence, is the main international gateway to Tuscany. From the airport it's only a 40-m stroll along a covered walkway to the train station, where you can get a train to Pisa Centrale (five minutes) where you change for Florence. Alternatively, a **Terravision** (terravision.eu) bus runs from Pisa Airport to Florence every 90 minutes from 0840-0020 (70 minutes, €10). **Train Spa** (trainspa.it) buses run twice a day from Pisa airport to Siena, via Poggibonsi (just under two hours).

From Florence Airport (T055-306 1300, aeroporto.firenze.it) a **Vola in** bus shuttle (every 30 minutes, €4.50) runs to Santa Maria Novella station. International travellers may choose to travel from

Rome. **Rome Fiumicino** (T06-65951, adr.it) is the capital's principal airport. The **Leonardo Express** (trenitalia.com) rail service connects the airport to the central station, Roma Termini, every 30 minutes from around 0630-2330. It takes 35 minutes and costs €11 (free under 12).

Rail

You can travel with **Eurostar** (eurostar.com) from London to Paris, before joining an overnight sleeper from Paris Bercy to Florence's Campo di Marte station, just northeast of the centre. Book tickets at raileurope.com (T0870-584 8848; search for trains that depart after 1900), or contact **European Rail** (T020-7619 1083, europeanrail.com) a specialist rail agency that can also book rail passes that can save you money. They also offer rail holidays in Italy (T020-7619 1080, eRail.co.uk). From Florence there are good connections from the main station, Santa Maria Novella, throughout Tuscany using the Italian train network (T06-6847 5475, trenitalia.com).

Road

The 1,550 km drive from London to Florence, the region's capital, takes 16 hours' driving time. EU nationals taking their own car need an International Insurance Certificate (also known as a Green Card). Those holding a non-EU licence also need to take an International Driving Permit with them. **Autostrade** (T055-420 3200 autostrade.it) provides information on motorways in Italy and **Automobile Club Italiana** (T06-49981, aci.it) offers general driving information, as well as roadside assistance with English-speaking operators on T116.

Bus/coach

Eurolines (T0870-580 8080, nationalexpress.co.uk) operate three services per week from London Victoria to Florence, with a travel time of around 29 hours. Prices start at £95 return. In Florence coaches arrive and depart at piazza Stazione.

Getting around

Rail

Italy has an extensive rail network, and it's the best way to get around the country on a city-based trip – faster than domestic flights: Rome to Florence takes approximately 1 hour 40 minutes, Florence to Venice 2 hours 45 minutes, and Rome to Naples 90 minutes. Milan to Rome takes a little longer, at just over four hours. Much of Tuscany is well covered by the rail network, though not Chianti and the Maremma.

It's worth knowing that there are several different train services running in Italy: air-conditioned and splendid Eurostar Italia, direct and convenient InterCity, and the slower Regional trains. All can be booked online at **Trenitalia** (trenitalia.com), where the type of train is indicated with the initials ES, IC or REG. Amica fares are cheaper advance tickets (if you can find one), flexi fare costs more but is – you guessed it – flexible, and standard fare is just that. You can buy one-country InterRail passes (raileurope.co.uk) for Italy (available for those over 25 these days), which can be used for three, four, six or eight days in one month and range from £93-195 for an adult travelling standard class.

In general, it's more convenient to book online or at ticket machines than it is to queue at a large station in high season. When using a service such as Eurostar Italia or InterCity booking is advised, and a surcharge in addition to a pass will often be required; however, there is no surcharge on the Regional train service. On many Italian trains it's possible to travel 'ticketless', meaning you get on the train and quote your booking reference when the conductor comes round.

If you can't access the internet you can book and buy tickets at train stations, at the counter or via ticket machines. Remember that you must validate tickets at the yellow stamping machines before boarding.

Road

Car

Driving anywhere in Italy is unlikely to be relaxing, as the Italians have their own inimitable approach to the road. Florence and other towns and cities have pedestrianized centres, so cars have to be parked on the outskirts and buses and trains are a far better option. However, a car is certainly the most convenient way of getting around Tuscany – and essential if you want to visit small villages and wineries. The roads in northern mountain regions such as the Garfagnana are generally quiet, but can be extremely winding. Roads in the southern part of Tuscany are generally the quietest, particularly those in the inland Maremma.

Italy has strict laws on drinking and driving: steer clear of alcohol to be safe. The use of mobile telephones while driving is illegal. Other nuances of Italian road law require children under 1.5 m to ride in the back of the car, and the wearing of a reflective jacket if your car breaks down on the carriageway in poor visibility – make sure you've got one. Since July 2007, on-the-spot fines for minor traffic offences have been in operation – typically they range between €150-250. Always get a receipt if you incur a fine.

Tip...

Unleaded petrol is *benzina*, diesel is *gasolio*.

Speed limits are 130 km per hour (motorway), 110 km per hour (dual carriageway) and 50 km per hour (town); limits are 20 km per hour lower on motorways and dual carriageways when the road is wet. *Autostrade* (motorways) are toll roads, so keep some cash in the car as a backup, even though you can use credit cards on the blue 'viacard' gates.

Be aware that there are restrictions on driving in historic city centres, indicated by signs with the letters ZTL (*zona a traffico limitato*) in black on a yellow background. If you pass these signs, your registration number may be caught and a fine will be winging its way to you. If your hotel is in the centre of town, you may be entitled to an official pass – contact your hotel or car hire company. However, this pass is not universal and allows access to the hotel only.

Car hire

You can hire a car at any of Italy's international airports and many domestic airports; there are plenty of rental companies at Pisa airport. You will probably wish to book the car before you arrive in the country, and it's essential to do so for popular destinations and at busy times of year. Check the opening times of the car hire office in advance.

Car hire comparison websites and agents are a good place to start a search for the best deals. Try holidayautos.co.uk, easycar.com, carrentals.co.uk. Several major car hire companies have offices in Florence, including **Avis** (avisautonoleggio.it), **Hertz** (hertz.it) and **Italy by Car** (italybycar.it).

Check what each hire company requires from you. Some companies will ask for an International Driving Licence, alongside your normal driving licence, if the language of your licence is different to that of the country you're renting the car in. Others are content with an EU licence. You'll need to produce a credit card for most companies. If you book ahead, make sure that the named credit card holder is the same as the person renting and driving the car, to avoid any problems. Most companies have a lower age limit of 21 years and require that you've held your licence for at least a year. Many have a young driver surcharge for those under 25. Confirm insurance and any damage waiver charges and keep all your documents with you when you drive.

Bicycles & scooters

Florence is trying to become a cycle-friendly city. Visitors can hire a scooter or moped from **Alinari** (T055-280500, alinarirental.com) or **Florence by Bike** (T055-488992, florencebybike.it). The minimum age for renting a scooter or motorbike is 18. Prices for bike hire are around €2.50 for an hour, €12 for a day and €45 for a week, while scooter hire starts at about €15 for an hour and €53 for a day.

Under the '*mille e una bici*' bicycle rental scheme run by the local council (comune.firenze.it), bikes can be hired at various points in the city centre. Hire times range from an hour to a whole day.

Other Tuscan towns have their own bike/scooter hire companies – ask at the individual tourist offices. Lucca is the most cycle-friendly city in Tuscany.

Bus/coach

The bus system in Tuscany is quite extensive and more convenient than rail when you're trying to reach smaller towns and villages. There are frequent buses between Siena and San Gimignano, Florence and Siena, Pisa and Arezzo, and between Cortona and Arezzo. There is a reasonable service between Massa Marittima and Follonica (the train station on the Maremma coast). If you are relying on public transport, buses provide the best links in the Maremma. Major bus and coach companies are **Cap** (capautolinee.it), **Florentia Bus** (florentiabus.it), **Lazzi** (lazz.it), **SENA** (sena.it), **TRA.IN** (trainspa.it) and **Sita** (sitabus.it).

Directory

Customs & immigration

UK and EU citizens do not need a visa, but will need a valid passport to enter Italy. A standard tourist visa for those outside the EU is valid for up to 90 days.

Disabled travellers

Italy is a bit behind when it comes to catering for disabled travellers, and access is sometimes very difficult or ill thought out. For more details, before you travel contact an agency such as **Accessible Italy** (accessibleitaly.com) or **Society for Accessible Travel & Hospitality** (sath.org).

Florence Tourism (firenzeturismo.it) has a section on its website with information for tourists with special needs. Most of the **ATAF** orange buses in Florence are equipped with a flat car deck and a space for a wheelchair. A door-to-door minibus service is available, but you need to make a reservation two to three days in advance: contact

Mr Formichetti (T055-5650486, formichetti@ataf.fi.it). The Florence taxi company **So.Co.Ta** (T055-410133, socota.it) has a six-seat van with an electronic platform: you must book two days in advance. Free wheelchair rental in Florence is available from **Arciconfraternita della Misericordia** (piazza del Duomo, T055-212222) and **Fratellanza Militare Firenze** (Oltrarno office, via Sant'Agostino 6, T055-26021, fratellanzamilitare.com).

Emergencies

Ambulance T118, **Fire service** T115, **Police** T113 (with English-speaking operators), T112 (*carabinieri*), **Roadside assistance** T116.

Etiquette

Bella figura – projecting a good image – is important to Italians. Take note of public notices about conduct: sitting on steps or eating and drinking in certain historic areas is not allowed. You need to cover your arms and legs to gain admission to many churches – in some cases shorts are not permitted. Punctuality is apparently not mandatory in Italy, so be prepared to wait on occasion.

Families

Whether they're having a traditional beach break or an afternoon in a gelateria, families are well accommodated in Italy. Children are well treated, and there's plenty to do besides endless museum visits. The family is highly regarded and *bambini* are indulged. Note that lone parents, or adults accompanying children of a different surname, may sometimes need to produce evidence of guardianship before taking children in or out of the country. Contact your Italian embassy for current details (Italian embassy in London, T020-7312 2200).

Health

Comprehensive travel and medical insurance is strongly recommended. EU citizens should apply for a free European Health Insurance Card (ehic.org), which has replaced the E111 form and offers reduced-cost medical treatment. Late-night pharmacies are identified by a green cross; T1100 for addresses of the three nearest open pharmacies. The accident and emergency department of a hospital is the *pronto soccorso*. The main hospital in Florence is the Policlinico di Careggi (viale Pieraccini/viale Morgagni 85, T055-794 9644), outside the city centre. Siena's main hospital is Le Scotte (viale Mario Bracci, T0577-585111).

Insurance

Comprehensive travel and medical insurance is strongly recommended for all travel – the EHIC is not a replacement for insurance. You should check any exclusions, and that your policy covers you for all the activities you want to undertake. Keep your insurance documents separately – emailing all the details to yourself is a good way to keep the information safe and accessible. Ensure you have full insurance if hiring a car; you may need an international insurance certificate if you are taking your own car (contact your current insurers).

Money

The Italian currency is the Euro. There are ATMs throughout Italy that accept major credit and debit cards. To change cash or travellers' cheques, look for a *cambio*. Many restaurants, shops, museums and art galleries take major credit cards. Paying directly with debit cards such as Cirrus is less easy in many places, so withdrawing cash from an ATM to pay may be the better option. Keep some cash for toll roads, if you're driving.

Police

There are five different police forces in Italy The *carabinieri* are a branch of the army and wear military-style uniforms with a red stripe on their trousers and white sashes. They handle general crime, drug-related crime and public order offences. The *polizia statale* are the national police force and are dressed in blue with a thin purple stripe on their trousers. They are responsible for security on the railways and at airports. The *polizia stradale* handle crime and traffic offences on the motorways and drive blue cars with a white stripe. The *vigili urbani* are local police who wear dark blue (in summer) or black (in winter) uniforms with white hats; they direct traffic and issue parking fines in the cities. The *guardia di finanza* wear grey uniforms with grey flat hats or green berets (depending on rank). They are charged with combating counterfeiting, tax evasion and fraud. In the case of an emergency requiring police attention, dial 113, approach any member of the police or visit a police station.

Florence: borgo Ognissanti 48, T055-24811 (*carabinieri*); via Pietrapiana 50r, T055 203911, emergency number T055-328 3333.
Arezzo: via Filippo Lippi, T057-54001.
Lucca: piazzale San Donato 12a. T0583-442727.
Pisa: via Mario Lalli 1, T050-583511.
Siena: via del Castoro, T0577-201111.

Post

The Italian postal service has a not entirely undeserved reputation for unreliability, particularly when handling postcards. Overseas post requires *posta prioritaria* (priority mail) and a postcard stamp costs from €0.60. You can buy *francobolli* (stamps) at post offices and *tabacchi* (look for T signs).

Florence post office: via Pellicceria 3, also at the Uffizi and via Pietrapiana 53.
Siena post office: piazza Matteotti.

Safety

Crime rate in Italy is generally low, though petty crime is higher. Female travellers won't experience the same hassles in Tuscany as they do in southern Italy. A good rule of thumb is to avoid stations and dark areas at night – places like SMN station and Cascine Park in Florence, Pisa station and the narrow streets around the market. Take care when travelling: don't flaunt your valuables; take only what money you need and split it up. Beware of scams and con-artists, and don't expect things to go smoothly if you get involved in buying fake goods. Car break-ins are common, so always remove valuables. Take care on public transport, where pick-pockets and bag-cutters operate. Do not make it clear which stop you're getting off at – it gives potential thieves a timeframe to work in.

Telephone

The code for Florence is 055, that for Siena is 0577. You need to use the local codes, even when dialling from within the city or region. The prefix for Italy is +39. You no longer need to drop the initial '0' from area codes when calling from abroad. For directory enquiries T12.

Time difference

Italy uses Central European Time, GMT+1.

Tipping

Only in the more expensive restaurants will staff necessarily expect a tip, although everyone will be grateful for one; 10-15% is the norm, and it's increasingly common for service to be included in your bill on top of the cover charge. When you're ordering at the bar a few spare coins may speed service up. Taxis may add on extra costs for luggage, but an additional tip is always appreciated. Rounding up prices always goes down well, especially if it means not having to give change – not a favourite Italian habit.

Voltage

Italy functions on a 220V mains supply. Plugs are the standard European two-pin variety.

Language

In hotels and bigger restaurants, you'll usually find English is spoken, especially in the cities of Florence, Siena and Pisa and in places that receive a lot of tourists such as San Gimignano and Chianti. The further you go into the countryside, however, the more trouble you may have, unless you have a smattering of Italian.

In medieval times the most influential writers wrote in the Tuscan dialect, thus establishing it as the language of literature and later as the country's official language. The Italian spoken in Tuscany is therefore considered to be the 'best' Italian – the equivalent of English received pronunciation. Foreign students are advised to learn their Italian at one of the many language schools in the region. The town of Pitigliano in the south of Tuscany once had its own dialect, due to its proximity to Lazio. It has essentially died out today, but you can see examples of the dialect written on a wall in the town square.

Vowels

a like 'a' in cat
e like 'e' in vet, or slightly more open, like the 'ai' in air (except after c or g, see consonants below)
i like 'i' in sip (except after c or g, see below)
o like 'o' in fox
u like 'ou' in soup

Consonants

Generally consonants sound the same as in English, though 'e' and 'i' after 'c' or 'g' make them soft (a 'ch' or a 'j' sound) and are silent themselves, whereas 'h' makes them hard (a 'k' or 'g' sound), the opposite to English. So ciao is pronounced 'chaow', but chiesa (church) is pronounced 'kee-ay-sa'.

The combination 'gli' is pronounced like the 'lli' in million, and 'gn' like 'ny' in Tanya.

Basics

thank you *grazie*
hi/goodbye *ciao*
good day (until after lunch/ mid-afternoon) *buongiorno*
good evening (after lunch) *buonasera*
goodnight *buonanotte*
goodbye *arrivederci*
please *per favore*
I'm sorry *mi dispiace*
excuse me *permesso*
yes *si*
no *no*

Numbers

one *uno*
two *due*
three *tre*
four *quattro*
five *cinque*
six *sei*
seven *sette*
eight *otto*
nine *nove*
10 *dieci*
11 *undici*
12 *dodici*
13 *tredici*
14 *quattordici*
15 *quindici*
16 *sedici*
17 *diciassette*
18 *diciotto*
19 *diciannove*
20 *venti*
21 *ventuno*
22 *ventidue*
30 *trenta*
40 *quaranta*
50 *cinquanta*
60 *sessanta*
70 *settanta*
80 *ottanta*
90 *novanta*
100 *cento*
200 *due cento*
1000 *mille*

Gestures

Italians are famously theatrical and animated in dialogue and use a variety of gestures.

Side of left palm on side of right wrist as right wrist is flicked up Go away

Hunched shoulders and arms lifted with palms of hands outwards What am I supposed to do?

Thumb, index and middle finger of hand together, wrist upturned and shaking What are you doing/what's going on?

Both palms together and moved up and down in front of stomach Same as above

All fingers of hand squeezed together To signify a place is packed full of people

Front of side of hand to chin 'Nothing', as in 'I don't understand' or 'I've had enough'

Flicking back of right ear To signify someone is gay

Index finger in cheek To signify good food

Questions

how? *come?*
how much? *quanto?*
when? *quando?*
where? *dove?*
why? *perché?*
what? *che cosa?*

Problems

I don't understand *non capisco*
I don't know *non lo so*
I don't speak Italian *non parlo italiano*
How do you say ... (in Italian)? *come si dice ...* (in italiano)?
Is there anyone who speaks English? *c'è qualcuno che parla inglese?*

Shopping

this one/that one *questo/quello*
less *meno*
more *di più*
How much is it/are they? *quanto costa/costano?*
Can I have ...? *posso avere ...?*

Travelling

one ticket for... *un biglietto per...*
single *solo andate*
return *andate ritorno*
does this go to Mantova? *questo va per Mantova?*
airport *aeroporto*
bus stop *fermata*
train *treno*
car *macchina*
taxi *tassi*

Hotels

a double/single room *una camera doppia/singola*
a double bed *un letto matrimoniale*
bathroom *bagno*
Is there a view? *c'è una bella vista?*
Can I see the room? *posso vedere la camera?*
When is breakfast? *a che ora è la colazione?*
Can I have the key? *posso avere la chiave?*

Time

morning *mattina*
afternoon *pomeriggio*
evening *sera*
night *notte*
soon *presto/fra poco*
later *più tardi*
What time is it? *Che ore sono?*
today/tomorrow/yesterday *oggi/domani/ieri*

Days

Monday *lunedi*
Tuesday *martedi*
Wednesday *mercoledi*
Thursday *giovedi*
Friday *venerdi*
Saturday *sabato*
Sunday *domenica*

Conversation

alright *va bene*
right then *allora*
who knows! *bo! / chi sa*
good luck! *in bocca al lupo!* (literally, 'in the mouth of the wolf')
one moment *un attimo*
hello (when answering a phone) *pronto* (literally, 'ready')
let's go! *andiamo!*
enough/stop *basta!*
give up! *dai!*
I like ... *mi piace ...*
how's it going? (well, thanks) *come va?* (bene, grazie)
how are you? *come sta/stai?* (polite/informal)

Index

D

E

F

G

H

M

N

O

P